Mapping Leisure

Mapping Leisure

Studies from Australia, Asia and Africa

Edited by

Ishwar Modi and Teus J. Kamphorst

RAWAT PUBLICATIONS
Jaipur • New Delhi • Bangalore • Guwahati • Kolkata

ISBN 978-81-316-0793-0

Published by
Prem Rawat for **Rawat Publications**
Satyam Apts, Sector 3, Jawahar Nagar, Jaipur 302 004 (India)
Phone: 0141 265 1748 / 7006 Fax: 0141 265 1748
E-mail: info@rawatbooks.com
Website: www.rawatbooks.com

New Delhi Office
4858/24, Ansari Road, Daryaganj, New Delhi 110 002
Phone: 011 2326 3290

Also at *Bangalore, Guwahati* and *Kolkata*

Typeset by Rawat Computers, Jaipur
Printed and bound in India

Contents

Preface

The first attempt to publish a comparative study on the spending of time in a number of countries dates back to 1972. In that year publishing house Mouton (The Hague/Paris), published the book edited by Alexandre Szalai and others: *The Use of Time: Daily Activities of Urban and Suburban Populations in Twelve Countries.*[1] The book provides information based on time-budget studies, on time spent on quite a list of activities by the inhabitants of 12 countries, 10 of which European. The time spent on specifically leisure activities is an important issue in the book.

In the years after a number of comparative, more descriptive publications appeared on specific leisure activities in a number of countries. As such can be mentioned participation in Arts and Culture in 8 countries from North America and Europe[2], participation in sports in 15 countries from all over the world[3], and a study on cultural differences in dealing with leisure in 8 countries from diverse continents.[4]

Also given the global developments that took place during the past decennia, among them globalization itself – as part of which can be considered the worldwide spreading of mass communication amenities and their growing reach in terms of coverage as well as applications – but also booming worldwide tourism, the scientific leisure sociology community, gathering in Göteburg, Sweden in 2010, at the occasion of the 17th World Congress of Sociology of the International Sociological Association (ISA), took the initiative to try to produce a new book on developments in leisure from a worldwide perspective.

As title for the endeavour was chosen: 'Mapping Leisure and Life through the Ages'. At the Congress itself, in a special session, nine leisure specialists had presented a paper about the subject in their country. After the Congress quite a number of authors from a great variety of other countries were asked for their cooperation; this stepwise process altogether lead to 45 contributions.

The authors were asked to, indeed, as the part of the title '... *through the Ages*' indicates, not to provide mainly on statistics from time-budget studies based '2010 state of the art' articles on leisure, but to address the way leisure had developed from past to present 'over the Ages'. For some this meant going back for centuries, even, as is the case with, for example, China and India, to a couple of thousands of years before Christ. Others' contributions went back to historically important changes in their respective countries, such as the intrusion of colonialism in African countries. For only one or two cases the authors concluded that there was too little reliable information available on past leisure traditions, norms and values and practices and the way they developed over the years, to extensively address historical features.

Also, as the title 'Leisure and Life ...' indicates again, the authors were asked to approach leisure in the context of the broader, holistic framework of life. What to write about leisure in a country such as Japan, where, until about the year 2000, there was no word for it? By addressing the norms and value system and living conditions and circumstances that shaped through the ages daily life of the Japanese, Scott North in his contribution on Japan succeeds to explain the absence of the word leisure in that specific setting and culture. And what about Mozambique, where, as in all countries and societies, there always was leisure, but where, surely during (a) the colonial period and also (b) after the takeover by the Marxist movement Frelimo, and again (c) after that by the International Monetary Fund enforced shift to liberal capitalism, the social conditions changed so fast and dramatically that the concept of leisure never could flourish and brought to the forefront. This even to a degree where until today, in Mozambique there exists no leisure studies, not to speak about leisure sociology.

Except for meeting a number of criteria, such as preferred length and scientific rules regarding citations, we did not firmly instruct the authors about their approach. To them a free hand was given to write from their perspective about things that they felt to be important for understanding the 'way leisure went' through the ages in the lives of the inhabitants of their country. Also as far as formal requirements are concerned, such as providing an abstract or a paragraph 'conclusions' much of the initiative was left with the authors. This because we expected the strength of the publication to be the provision of insights into specifically the differences in the development of 'Leisure and Life through the Ages' in the respective countries; differences for which there is no place in abstracts or concluding chapters. Knowing that in many countries only few statistical data based on empirical research were available, neither the authors were asked to take those as a starting point for their contribution. As a result in some of them are to be found quite a lot of statistics and tables, in others there are hardly any or none at all.

As a result this book reads nearly like a fiction book. Every chapter has something specific to tell, insights to open, things to teach. There is hardly any repetition or it must be about influences, such as from colonialism, that hit a number of them, but, surprisingly, as leisure is concerned, not always in the same way. Or it must be about the endurance and resistance to fading of rituals and traditions, not seldom based in religion, but then too, the outcome is not everywhere the same. Or it must be globalization and the intrusion of new mass communication technologies during the last three, four decades. But again, globalization did not influence leisure everywhere in the same way, neither did booming tourism.

With every contribution the book grew, not only in terms of coverage of interesting scientific information, but also in size. Taken altogether we ended up to more than 700 pages of text. Therefore, in close cooperation with the publisher Rawat Publications, India, it was decided to divide the content over three books, the first of which is now in front of you. This one deals with 16 countries spread over Australia, Asia and Africa. The second book will address the development of leisure through history in 19 countries of Europe, and the third book will have contributions from the North and Latin American countries. The editors wish you a lot of leisurely reading pleasure.

Notes

1. Szalai, A. and others, (eds): *The Use of Time: Daily Activities of Urban and Suburban Populations in Twelve Countries*. Mouton, The Hague/France, 1972.
2. Hantrais, L. and Kamphorst, T.J., (eds): *Trends in the Arts: A Multinational Perspective*, Giordano Bruno, The Netherlands, 1987.
3. Kamphorst, T.J. and Roberts, K., (eds): Trends in Sports; A Multinational Perspective; Giordano Bruno, The Netherlands, 1989.
4. Blair, K., (ed.): *Arts of Leisure: Multi-cultural Perspectives*; Giordano Bruno, The Netherlands, 1994.

Introduction

There is an inherited capacity of mankind to have and get involved in spare time pass-times. To those practices in different countries are allotted different names and concepts. In the western world, as of the beginning of the industrialization, those practices usually are labeled 'free time' or 'leisure'. At that time the terms referred to non-obligatory time; this means time in which a person was free from household and/or industrial salaried work performances, duties and practices. As the connotation indicates, those duties were experienced as 'not free', this means as obligatory and compulsory. The 19th and a greater part of the 20th century the household and work conditions, though at that time being considered as 'normal', from the perspective of the 21st century we are inclined to label them as rather 'inhuman'. Workday of 12 hours or more during 6 or even 7 days per week the whole year through were no exception. The salaries were low and the work conditions generally very bad.

Regarding the terminology: the term 'free time' is used to underline the aspects of 'being free from household duties and industrial work' and of 'time'. When emphasis is placed on the activities performed during free time, the name 'leisure' is being used. Reading the contributions to this volume, it is exactly with these concepts and terminology, that the discussion starts.

What About is Leisure?

Some of the authors of the 16 contributions that are included in this volume state that not only in many societies the words 'free time' and 'leisure' do not exist, but also that, for example in pre-historic times, life just went the way it went without a sharp distinction between obligatory and non-obligatory activities. It is within this framework that in some articles the 'surplus energy' theory is mentioned: mankind can enter into and take part in spare time pass-times only when able to meet the needs for survival in a time-span that is shorter than the total of time that is available. So, in that case, when a person is not too tired and falls asleep, there is energy and time left for non-primarily-survival-directed behaviour that one could name 'free time'. This surplus energy approach, which actually resembles very much the western industrial concept of leisure as being free from obligations to earn a living and getting daily life organized, falls into the category of spare time pass-times in terms of time '... being free from ...' obligations/duties.

Other authors write that in their cultures this distinction between obligatory and non-obligatory time spending is not applicable. For example, in former days China, the several concepts that relate to what in the west is called leisure, have connotations referring to the Greek concept of scolè. Following the great Chinese philosophers such as Confucius and Dao, it refers to formal or informal education or time spending aiming at personal or societal improvement. This includes being educated by others as well as self-improvement. The final goal of this process is to establish/experience harmony within and between the soul, the mind and the body as well as with the natural and humane environment(s). So, in the case of China, the English language concept of leisure does not refer to '... being free from ...' (obligations/duties), but to '... spending time on/being busy with/being involved in ...' a (self) developmental process.

Again in other contributions to this volume is argued that life as such, including free time and leisure should be subordinated to a higher goal, for non-secular Muslim people being worshipping the Almighty at any time and any place. Secular leisure activities are suspect and might easily turn into sinful behaviour. In the article on Indonesia, the country with the highest Muslim population in the world, an interviewee tells that he practises swimming. His motivation is that the Almighty gave him a body for which he is grateful and for which gift of the Almighty he should take care. Swimming is considered to maintain and/or improve health, which makes it fall into the category of allowed, even recommended religious leisure activities. Moreover, the interviewee goes for swimming in the local swimming facility very early in the morning, preventing him from having to swim with women and/or being tempted to have a glance at some of their body parts.

Reading the contributions on this subject of the different concepts of leisure, the articles reflect more or less the critics that the pre-dominant western, English language term 'leisure' and its connotation faced since its inception. The term simply does not fit all cultures. But not only non-western cultures sometimes have difficulties with the term leisure.

Of course, any definition about whatever phenomenon has exemptions which it should include but does not. The point, however, is: how important are those exemptions? In the west the point is reached that work conditions have improved to a level where going to work is no longer primarily experienced as a duty or obligation. Furthermore, in the west nowadays less than half of the population is actively involved in the salaried labour force. Does being free from paid work as one of the main criteria for leisure, mean that the spare time pass-times of children and pensioners shouldn't be called 'leisure'? To 'solve' this problem, under the influence of leisure psychologist, leisure scientists developed a parallel concept of leisure, namely, that one also can speak about leisure when a person does not experience outside or inside pressure or constraints when doing what he/she does. In short, the distinctive criteria is not that a person objectively is free from obligations, but that he/she feels free.

The criticism of many of the contributors to this volume on Australia, Asia and Africa not only entails the aspect of '... being free from ...' or 'being free to

...', or of '... feeling free ...', but also leisure's fundaments and aims and practices. To start with the fundaments: the aspect of relative factual freedom or a relative experience of freedom which, as stated, in the west are regarded as distinctive criteria for speaking about leisure or not, for a number of the contributors are in reality non-existing human inventions; virtual products of the brain. And, to turn to leisure's aims and practices, some of them, seriously criticizing the western fusion of the concepts of leisure and freedom refer to the Frankfurther Schule, who preach that a person at leisure who, in his/her own experience is/feels relatively free, is not free at all because he/she is just a blind consumer, addicted to gathering material wealth and just following the slogans of and being manipulated by the leisure industry and entrepreneurs who make them believe that buying their products is an act of freedom and/or sets them free.

So, taking into account all those critics and the comments/remarks to find in quite a number of the articles in this volume about the leisure concept and its connotation as, first not fitting historical situation and second as being too and above that old-fashioned western, the question arises: what about is leisure from a global perspective? Or should we conclude that, even if we exclude from the concept the disputable aspect of experienced freedom, exactly due to the 19th and early 20th century contextual character of the term, it is impossible to formulate and unite on a definition that is acceptable for all leisure scientists and practitioners all over the world? The articles in this volume of Australia, Asia and Africa reveal that the differences in approach are very substantial and difficult to bring under one common denominator. That's not a disaster as long as we, leisure experts, when meeting each other start to make clear and decide for what purpose and definition we go in what context. However, there might be another reason to thoroughly re-think the present leisure concept, more specifically this element of freedom that sets it apart from other spheres of life.

Traditions, Rituals and Leisure: The Persistence of Culture

All the authors of chapters who took the phrase '... through the Ages' literally write, sometimes very extensively about the history of leisure in their country, address at a certain point the importance of traditions and rituals and related forms of leisure sort of time-spending. Listing all the examples mentioned would take about half a page, so, for those interested in their naming we refer to the respective articles.

According to de Grazia and supported by many authors of chapters in this volume on Australia, Asia and Africa in his standard work *Of Time, Work and Leisure*, in the times before the industrial revolution, there were each year hundreds of traditional and ritual festivities. Those had, to speak with Stebbins 'a serious (leisure) aspect', such as a religious holy day where the clergy expected the believers to attend the service, but also, what we would call nowadays, a leisure aspect. Meeting, chatting, dancing, playing games, engaging in sport competitions like horse riding, drinking; they all were practised at traditional festivals and rituals. We are tempted to believe – and again the idea is widely supported by writers of the successive articles in this volume that, as far as religious holy days, festivals and rituals are concerned, many of them fully focused on coming to terms with the supra-natural powers (Gods, ancestors, ghosts, evil forces). Sometimes asking those for protection, for forgiveness of bad behaviour or sins or fulfilling a specific wish: in short, more or less in line with what currently happens in many religions. The question is: should those religion driven activities as attending a service be regarded as leisure? Some authors say 'yes', for example because they were practised in spare time not devoted to mere survival; others label them as a separate category.

Whatever the categorization, from the example that the ancestors of the German, the 'Germanen' during Roman Empire times, were said to offer their wives as trophy to the winner of gambling games, it becomes clear that life was not limited to work, war, sleep, and religious duties. However, what makes those traditions and rituals so interesting is their obvious persistence and resistance to vanishing or, to formulate it in a more positive way, their endurance. Even in circumstances where the rationale for practising traditional customs and rituals faded away already for a long time, they continued and continue to play a role in spare time pass-times. Holy days became holidays, the custom of having at least one day off per week (Friday, Sunday) is widespread, celebrating the start of the seasons or of the full moon or the longest day, going for a trip only on astrological prosperous periods, the new year rituals, including staying up through 24 o'clock in the night, wishing each other one minute after the best for the year that just has begun – by the way, not in all countries New Year starts on the same calendar day, nor do we live everywhere in the current year 2016 – and having loud fireworks to frighten the evil spirits; they all stem from past times, even long forgotten periods.

To go one step further, as many authors reveal, their culture intruding new forms of time spending are modified to make them fit into in their country's existing traditions and rituals. The articles provide many examples of, for example as an effect of globalization during the past decennia newly brought forms of spare time spending into an existing culture, which new forms are adapted to existing traditions and rituals. To take the example of the Philippines: in earlier times on free days and in the evenings upper class people used to move around in their carriages in the central park of Manila to see people pass by, occasionally socialize, while listening to music of all kind. In present times they continue to do this in the same park with modern vehicles and listening to the same, but also to different, modern types of music performed. Or, to draw from the article on 'Evolution of Leisure Patterns in Morocco: From Traditional Spiritual Pilgrimers to Contemporary Mall Wanderers', the inhabitants of Morocco used to take a walk during their festive days and meet family or acquaintances in the streets or in the old Medina (market places). Now they go for a walk too, however, choose as destination, as far as facilities are concerned, the highly sophisticated shopping malls, not to buy anything, but to meet others and enjoy the environment.

This endurance of traditions also is obvious in religious practices themselves. Christianity, by western societies is introduced to many countries all over the world. Yet, as the articles in this volume show, in many cases, the way of practising has not become western at all. As the author on Africa, Veena Sharma from India, does in her observations in this volume about Australia, Asia and Africa, you can talk of 'typical African Christianity', thereby indicating that this new religion mixed with former religious traditions and rituals to fit the Africans. As typical African is considered by Veena Sharma for the holistic approach and involvement of Africans in the rituals and services. And to end with an example from South-Africa that we, sort of automatically tend to label to be negative: from the article on South-Africa can be drawn that despite more than 25 years of de-segregation, in South-Africa the ethnic groups still do not mix during their free time. Would the careful reader of this discussion chapter agree with the statement that, from the viewpoint of leisure as it is defined and understood today, this continuing separation is to be considered to be negative only when it is felt as a constraint, this means: is experienced as blocking potentially life enriching activities and experiences? Or are we facing here a more ideological issue? Is the emotion at stake more of the kind of: even if in practice I will never mingle with the other race, I wish to have that option?

Hostility of Clergy and Upper Classes Towards Leisure

Going through all the articles of this volume of Australia, Asia and Africa, remarkable too is the fact that many authors of chapters refer to the basically hostile attitudes and practices of upper and leading classes of countries towards spare time pass-times of the respective populations. Given their mental framework of those times, this is understandable for colonialists that, in most cases without any feelings of guild, occupied, sometimes ruined, but in any case tried to profit as much as possible, even to a degree of robbing-out their colonies. Understandable, because spare time in the definition of the colonial leading classes – following, as Weber writes in his in the Netherlands just newly re-published essay on 'The Protestant Ethic and the Idea (in German 'Geist') of Capitalism' – was idle, non-productive time.

So in Mozambique the Portuguese colonists put in place all sorts of work-laws, forcing the locals to spent a considerable part of their time to labour for the benefit of their colonists without any salary being paid. Not meeting the requirements led to imprisoning and physical punishment, very often leading to death. Were the Mozambicans better off under the reign of the Marxist Frelimo that came to power in 1985 after the colonial period had ended? The answer is 'yes' and 'no'. 'Yes' because the Frelimo leaders did not come from another country but were their countrymen. However, as far as leisure is concerned, the Frelimo leaders were of the same opinion as the colonialists, namely, that free time was idle time and that free time prevented the population from becoming a so-called 'New Man', which is a for his/her country hard working, decent, responsible, honest, ethical behaving, not bribable and whatever other positive characteristics they could think of Mozambican.

May be with the exception of China during a specific historical period and then more or less limited to the Chinese philosophers, the articles reveal that during history all kings, sultans, higher positioned civil servants, leaders and representatives of in fact all the religions all over the world, they all had a critical attitude towards leisure. One of the reasons, such as in Japan, was that leisure simply did not fit in their culture of what we, from a distance, would consider to be a form of collective workaholism. In the case of Japan, the culture requires total subordination to the authorities, public as well as private and far reaching sensibility to the judgments about behaviour of the social groups to which people define themselves as belonging to. Leisure, for which in Japan in the 1990 a new word was invented, came into the picture in Japan in a period of strong economic crisis, due to a decrease in export figures. In that period leisure was regarded as offering a way-out of the economic crisis. Establishing an economy for leisure products could provide work for the unemployed. However, as Scott North describes so lively in his contribution to this volume, speaking about the persistence of traditions: following the Japanese approach, it was collectively organized and took the form of the realization of state controlled holiday resorts all over Japan, not seldom at the price of destruction of the natural environment.

What was and is behind this, sometimes overtly hostile attitude of the leading groups and classes toward spare time pass-times of the population? Would it go too far to state that the main reason for the hostile attitude of the upper and/or leading classes towards leisure was and is, that leisure conflicted with the expectation that the 'vulgus in populo' should not enjoy free time themselves, but devote their lives to facilitating the authorities' possibilities to live, as Veblen describes in his book *The Theory of the Leisure Class*, a true, in all aspects privileged leisure life, to which, by the way, the lower classes, occasionally and exceptionally, were allowed to have access, very often not as participant but as spectator? Would it go too far to state that the fact that it is so difficult for our field to have the clergy and the leading groups and higher classes that form the political elites everywhere in the world, pay attention to leisure and culture other than when it generates income, such as in tourism, is to be explained by the fact that they live on the pocket and wallet of the lower classes, in short, from tax or gift money generated through work efforts of the lower classes? And does this also mean that our fight for attention of our leaders for leisure per definition will fail, unless the leisure area is further commodified and commercialized? Reading the articles in this volume on Australia, Asia and Africa, the most likely answer is 'yes'. For our field the question is: by going in the by the elite preferred direction, what do we win and what do we lose?

May be the answer to that question can be found, among others, by analysing what happened through the ages to toys for children and/or to tourism. In both cases there was a development from self- and homemade 'products' to ready-to-use ones offered by these two branches of the leisure industry. As some authors write, in both cases there was an increase in easy consumerism. Buying ready-for-use products has the advantage that it creates time for entering into other spare time pass-times. However, in the case of toys, it diminishes the learning experience of making toys yourself or seeing them made by your parents. And in the case of tourism, going for an all-inclusive arrangement means that you choose to lay your future tourism experience in the hopefully capable hand of the professionals in the sector.

But what does that do to leisure satisfaction? Sport inquiries reveal that more satisfaction results from winning from a strong opponent than from a weak one. It gives greater satisfaction to master a more difficult Chopin Nocturne or game on your play-station than an easier one. So, coming back to the question: what do we gain and what do we lose when our leaders and authorities, driven by economic motives start to meddle in the leisure area? As is shown in this volume in the articles on Japan and North Korea, the answer might be: more bureaucracy, more consumerism, more professionalism, more ready-to-use made leisure supplies, all leading to a decrease in leisure satisfaction and challenges to face and master. Is that what we want?

Globalization

All authors of articles in this volume on Australia, Asia and Africa, from a chronological viewpoint logically at the end of their articles, mention globalization, and more specifically the relatively recent worldwide spreading of mass media, as a factor deeply influencing leisure. Mentioned are film, radio, television and means of interactive electronic communication such as through phones and later mobile phones. Some authors, such as Modi from India, speak about 'the ICT generation', indicating that youngsters spent a relatively substantial part of their free time on using Information and Communication Technology (ICT) equipment.

Despite the attempts of some governments, such as, be it for different reasons, in China and Indonesia, to control the information coming in through those modern devices from abroad, globalization in terms of opening the world to and for others proved to be a phenomenon that, yes, could be temporized, but not stopped. All the contributors to this volume write that through the mass media, for better or worse, all sort of new information reaches respective audiences in their countries. This also holds for information about other forms of leisure practiced in other cultures. As we wrote above, some of those fit the receiving country and were taken over, very seldom just the way they were, but usually in a to and for the existing culture adapted form. This holds, for example, for films in India and Nigeria. The film technology having been brought to those countries in the beginning of the 20th century, through present times in these countries there are cinemas that show western film productions, but there are also cinemas that exclusively show products of the country, such as in India the well-known Bollywood films.

In Nigeria and other colonized countries the introduction and distribution of film usually went stepwise and was controlled by the colonists. It started with the bringing over of one film equipment to the villages. Shown were mainly educational programmes, such as on foresting, or on using fertilizers in agriculture, but also were shown to the on the main village place gathered audiences, films on hygiene and other subjects that would lead to changes in behaviour benefitting not only the inhabitants of the villages, but also the colonists in terms of preventing indigenous people from falling ill and thereby keeping them fit to work for the colonists. As was to be expected, after the colonial period everywhere film became less patronized.

Adapted to local culture also were baseball and basketball in the Philippines, introduced in the country by the Americans during the period of USA colonization. Regarding basketball; since the Philippines in general do not have the length for properly dunk a ball in the net (dunking is reaching with your hand and the ball over the net and throwing it downwards), they trained on alternative and for the spectator very elegant ways of scoring.

The introduction of television went stepwise too. Beginning with one screen in a village, later on economic developments and improvement of the medium itself made it possible for people to buy and install their own equipment in their home. All authors of articles in this volume on Australia, Asia and Africa of the trilogy write, that this process of privatization of television resulted in a rather substantial change in spare time spending. According to the authors, not only the time spent at home increased, but also leisure became more individualized.

In this discussion on the influence of globalization on leisure we cannot ignore the worldwide indignation about New Zealand being visited by a, due to the apartheid regime, totally white South-African rugby-team. That New Zealand, faced with the pressure from outside did not cancel that visit was due also to the countries' as Toohey, Cushman and Gidlow write 'rather conservative character', brought into the country named 'God's paradise' by the – contraire to Australia to which continent in the beginning mainly British criminals and outlaws were deported accompanied by boatloads of supervising staff – in general higher classed and more well to do immigrants. It is noteworthy that in the process of mobilization of this global indignation towards New Zealand, at that time already nearly everywhere available mass media played an important role.

By the authors considered influential also is the introduction of the computer with web-connection and the mobile phone. Regarding the latter, the introduction of the mobile phone did not only skip in many countries the necessity to lay-out a costly infrastructural wire-system to which to connect fixed phones, but the introduction also created the option to communicate to anybody from whatever place on earth where there were put in place wireless communication transmitting stations. By authors cited studies reveal that this option of instant and immediate networking with to a person relevant others, compensates for the increase in individual spare time pass-times that accompanied the introduction of the broadcasting systems of radio and television.

There is one issue that is addressed in only a few articles included in this volume. That is the question if, as motor of this process of globalization through the worldwide spreading of mass communication equipment should be regarded the mass media industry, looking for new markets for their products, or was it a more demand driven development? Very likely we face here one of the rare occasions in history where supply and demand fully go together, which coincidental combination also explains the speed in which the process materialized.

Leisure and Life through the Ages

Having carefully digested the content of all the 16 articles presented in this volume and having addressed a number of the more general developments in the area, it might be time for a wrap-up.

What we see then is that leisure is from all ages and for all ages. Going through history, spare time pass-times are reflected in the pre-historic paintings to be found on Libyan rocks through war-game apps to install and play on the personal computer or play-station. Even in societies that are at war and/or controlled by intruders and invaders, as was the case during colonialism, there is leisure in the autochthon/indigenous communities. Unless their parents call them in, in war-zones children continue with their football games on their small playing-fields in the midst of their neighbourhoods while missiles are flying around. During the First World War, at the front in northern France, a cease fire was organized to enable the soldiers to celebrate Christmas. To, occasionally, have spare time pass-times and be at leisure seems to be a fundamental human drive.

Furthermore, spare time pass-times, though according to some scientists 'their goal should be in the performance itself', are not just superficial forms of behaviour that hardly have any further reaching value. As many authors write, their permanency and resistance to change and fading away indicate that this aspect of life both is embedded in and at the same time a constituting aspect of a countries' culture. For Turkey even holds that differences in leisure are a major element of the distinction between the four fractions of middle-class Turks. This partly can be explained by the fact that leisure is strongly based and present in traditions, rituals and customs and in norms and value systems, that, seemingly, are felt worth to be maintained and kept. About this enduring aspect, a physician would say: 'Leisure has a lot of mass'. Like a supertanker sailing in the ocean, its route is difficult to change.

But is does not only have mass, it also is a strong phenomenon. Through the Ages all attempts of whatever clergymen from whatever denomination and upper class leaders to tame and control leisure's obvious manifestations have failed. Whatever measures the holy and powerful put upon their subordinates, people always found ways to 'escape' and get involved in leisurely forms of behaviour, even in prison.

Leisure's strength may be illustrated by another example. To use a concept from biological/ecological sciences, from the viewpoint of the person or group at leisure, it can be said that leisure, including arts and culture, stands at the end of the economic chain. From the money that comes-in in a family, a part is reserved for meeting survival requirements, such as food, clothes, housing, and energy. If any, the remaining sum is saved for worse times or spent on leisure. One would think that this fact of being at the end of the economic chain would make leisure vulnerable to changes in the previous links of the chain. Even in countries with income figures below the poverty level of $ 1.00 per day, even in periods of great misery, people tend to continue to perform their rituals and follow their traditions. And, as some articles reveal, for inhabitants of more wealthy countries is valid that there are a number of free time activities that have such a high position in the value rank order of individuals, communities and societies, that they are relatively independent from a decrease in income. In the western world going on holidays, but also celebrating birthdays or holy days or networking through mass communication means with friends and acquaintances have such a high value rank order status.

Despite its mass, leisure is an open phenomenon. It tends to easily absorb new stimuli, be it often in a process of enculturation in which it adapts to local traditions, rituals, customs and ways of behaviour that are common and accepted in the receiving society. In this regard leisure looks like cane: it bows with the wind but does not break. On the contrary, every blow seems to make it stronger in terms of bigger and more varied. And as such a storm can be regarded the relatively recent process of globalization. New technologies provided options for spare time pass-times that were not practiced before and, as the articles show, were easily incorporated.

Leisure's 21st Century Context

The authors of the 16 articles presented in this volume on Australia, Asia and Africa were asked to 'Map Leisure and Life through the Ages' in their respective countries. Having read all the contributions the conclusion can be that, in general, be it everywhere different, the leisure area did develop fine. It is all around, substantial, persistent, durable, strong, it has mass, and scores high in the value ranking order.

Looking back, it is a pity that we did not ask the authors to also briefly address the future of leisure, which is the main item of this final paragraph. So, none of the authors specifically wrote on this issue. Nevertheless it is an important item, about which, may be, also based on the writings presented in this volume, there is more to say than just nothing. For example: may we assume that the sketched developmental processes of leisure are linear, in short, that leisure activities that are increasing will continue to do so, those that are stable will stay stable and those that are decreasing will slowly fade-away?

That is very much the question. All the articles in this volume address the issue of, in terms of leisure time spending, the rather important changes in leisure resulting from the introduction of the mass media and communication devices. In just a couple of decennia, television watching became the favourite leisure activity of the world population. It influenced leisure, among others, in the sense that, as the authors write, leisure everywhere became more individualistic.

Leisure, being a social, contextual phenomenon, apart from being strong and resistant to change, also inhales and breathes the spirit of the time in which it manifests itself. What, in those terms, is there to say about the future? Nobody can and shall deny that the world and our leisure area are facing a number of splendid opportunities, but also of severe threats. Again some examples. The mass media will continue to ever more intensively inform us, inhabitants of the world, about each other, including about our different ways of leisure spending. Will this lead to a process of further unification – one world one people one behaviour – or of increasing nationalism/regionalism and how will one and/or the other influence leisure? Or will both tendencies – as is indicated by using the construction 'and/or' in the previous sentence – unfold together? That would be very nice for the leisure area because unification may lead to breaking down the borders that keep continents, countries, societies, communities and individuals apart and divided, while regionalization may result in preserving the differences between those entities, differences that make life interesting and provide the stimuli to look over the next hill.

However, apart from unification/regionalization there are so many more development on earth that call for attention from the leisure area because they may influence the leisure field. Guess it is true what some experts say that within 40 years we will run out of crude oil. Has there been invented by that time another source of energy enabling us and/or our children and grandchildren to, among others, visit other countries during holidays? Is not leisure, though, as the respective articles in this volume on Australia, Asia and Africa show being different everywhere, yet an integrated part of life and of the world community and in that quality faces exactly the same threats that all societies are facing nowadays? Just to mention some of those threats. To start with not the least: war; poverty and hunger in certain regions of the world; the running out of energy issue; the dioxin hole in the atmosphere; pollution everywhere and of all kinds; the expected increase of scarcity of raw materials – according to some the fuse that will bring fire to the next, the Third World War; environmental damage of all kinds due to air, earth and water pollution; climate change and as a result of that an increasing number of natural catastrophes such as floods, mega-hurricanes and land-slides; the threat of overpopulation – can the world feed the forecasted 7,000,000,000 mouths in the year 2050? species, plants, animals getting extinct; destruction of eco-systems; increasing inequality between genders and also in wealth; increasing consumerism; the present worldwide economic crisis resulting from greed in and lack of control on certain powerful circles; corruption of all kinds; nuclear power disasters such as relatively recently in Japan; illiteracy and lack of proper education; increasing shortage of clean water; insufficient and inefficient sewage systems causing illnesses; the weakening of social structures and bonds in many parts of the world due to increasing individualism, ego-centrism and egoism; and last but not least, nationalism preventing people to have a worldview and become world citizen.

Leisure, spare time pass-times are part of life on earth and, whether we like it or not, our areas will be confronted with the phenomenon listed above and influenced by their followings. How do we deal with all this? How are we going to position our field in these processes? Among others we may address the question: is it time to go for a new leisure paradigm?

Australia

1

Australian Leisure

From Antiquity to Modernity

FRANCIS LOBO

The chapter traces the development of leisure in Australia from antiquity to modernity. It deals with the topic by discussing leisure through slices of time as: prehistoric living; colonization; post-1945; and contemporary Australia. The paper shows how the earliest people lived. After colonization, the importation of leisure activities occurred as indigenous leisure developed in parallel. The development of modern leisure passed through stages of nationhood, wars, natural disasters to better times when the country's economy developed and people were more affluent to enjoy improving lifestyles. The development of Australians was affected by social conditions and so was their leisure.

Pre-historic Living

The lifestyle of indigenous Australians was illustrated by the images in a board game devised by Jessie Mackintosh (circa, 1940). The game had 26 stations before arriving at the corroboree, a gathering of Aboriginal people. Each image, illustrated in thumbnail form (*italicized* in text following) depicted human activity and Australian fauna. It started with *hunters setting out for the corroboree*. In sequence they *dug for honey ants, met storks, threw boomerangs*, discovered *a dry water hole*, passed an *emu*, *made a fire* and stopped at *mya mya* (home) with the family. They then proceeded past a *lyrebird*, *cut a spear*, *decorate the spear* while a *kookaburra laughed*. *Pointing a spear* as *koalas* looked on a *bush fire burned* and a *tribal war broke out*. *Spears were thrown*, *spearheads* were made and *axe heads* were ground as the party went past a *platypus*. *Preparing for the corroboree*, the *hunter took his prey*, a *canoe was cut* to cross the river, a lost *culunga* (cradle) was found, *bullroarers* were sounded as the *party danced* to the *corroboree* where rituals, dances and singing were performed. The images on the board game illustrated how indigenous Australians lived 40,000 years ago.

Activities were categorized into three domains. *Homo Faber* (Frisch, 1974), Man the Worker; *Homo Ludens* (Huizinga, 1971) Man the Player; and *Homo Famillon*, (latin for Family Man). *Homo Faber* took precedence over *Homo Ludens*. Tool making was essential for men as hunters and women as gatherers.

The domain of *Homo Ludens* included artistic activities, games, story-telling and amusements. Intellectual and artistic activities represented in arts, dancing and music, provide evidence of a complex, sophisticated civilisation developed over the course of 40,000 or more. These imaginative endeavours, especially in the nature and function of art, music, and dance in Aboriginal culture provide continuity of creativity in the longest unbroken history known to humankind. Games were part of traditional culture. After the evening meal adults and children sat around the fire, enjoying a cheerful community atmosphere. Children joined in singing and clapping or sat and listened as old men told them stories from the great Dreamtime. Girls played with dolls and copied the art of 'mothering' from their own mothers. So while at play, they were unwittingly preparing themselves for the future. With boys, ball games were popular. Dancing was a common pastime (Ellis, 1994).

The families in Aboriginal households were egalitarian and extended. Each member gave support of every kind to other members. Families shared food and supported kindred groups. The principal function of men was hunting. Women were the gatherers. Parenting the children was their function as was the care of the aged. Older children were often asked to help with food gathering and helped in care of the younger siblings (Ellis and Ellis, 1982).

The dwelling place was known as the 'mya mya'. It was the place where families slept and stored belongings. Families were neither idle nor rich. Consequently, Thorstein Veblen (1970) would find it difficult to develop a theory of the leisure class. Membership of the leisure class is an exemption from industrial toil and the mark of success is 'conspicuous consumption'. It was a term used by Veblen for spending for the sake of prestige. In Aboriginal society there was no time for ladylike uselessness. Women had to work. They were the gatherers. They looked after the children, narrated stories of the dreamtime and prepared meals for the family. Play was instinctive with the children. The boys competed against each other and the girls played imaginative games.

Evidence from photographs in the 1930s taken of communities in remote parts of Australia, untouched by outside civilization reveal how Aboriginals have lived from the earliest times. The photographs reveal children at play, girls at play and children with pets.

Images show music for dancing being provided by beating the ground with sticks (Cockatoo Creek, Central Australia, 1931). Children sing *Mamu tjitji* song as they make a chain with their hands and boys practise spearing by aiming at bark discs (Warapuju Tr. Warburton Range, W.A., 1935). Images of girls at play show them playing fathers and mothers (Ilaura Tribe, Macdonald Downs, Central Australia, 1930). The children first built a windbreak made of stone and they then used pieces of stick and bark to represent people in the camp. Another girl leaped along a line of stones that have been arranged by children (Wiluwiluru Waterhole, Mann Range, 1933). Australian aborigines did not usually tame or domesticate animals. Young emus were occasionally brought back to camp. Emu chicks, their stripes conspicuous against the background of earth, made a happy picture in the camp in far north-eastern Arnhem Land. Two broods were represented among the five chicks shown in a photograph, four showing the brighter more clearly defined stripes being much younger than the fifth taller bird (Caledoy Bay, 1935). Children befriended young dingo pups (Warapuju Tr. Warburton Range, W.A., 1933). A young boy showed his skills in clutching two pampidi lizards around the neck so that they did not bite or escape him (Nyadamarda Tr., Mandora Station, N.W. Australia, 1953).

The foregoing examples show that play among children is universal from the earliest of humans. According to Lynch and Veal (2006) Aboriginals in early times did not have a concept of leisure and work as in Western society. They stated that traditional Aboriginal societies lived culturally and environmentally integrated lifestyles. They referred to the lifestyles of hunter-gatherer societies as *eco-leisure*. In hunter-gatherer societies, while playful and pleasurable activities were engaged in for their own sake, such playfulness and pleasure could be features of any aspect of life. There was no clear demarcation between work and non-work and no separate category of *leisure*.

The definition of leisure and quality of life that has dominated 'Western' thinking has three perspectives: 'adopted a measure of time' (*time*); 'as a container of activity' (*activity*); 'and in terms of meaning' (*experience*) (Jackson, 2006: 3). Although Aborigines did not have a concept of leisure as Western society understands it, their behaviour points to four dimensions. The first and fundamental dimension of Aboriginal leisure is *setting*. Aboriginals consider *setting,* (a derivative of place) as the essence of living. According to Burnum (1988):

> The land had been under (our) control and guidance going back to the Dreamtime; every hill, valley, river, animal and plant had been placed in the landscape for the use of the people ... . In Europe as people developed their civilization from the caves to the cathedrals, they left clear evidence of their achievement for future generations to admire. In Australia, the land itself is the cathedral and worship is not confined to any four walls. Each step is a prayer and every form in the landscape – and everything that moves in it – were put there specifically for people to use and manage. (p. 8)

The landscape board game (Mackintosh, circa, 1940) depicted the place where Aboriginals lived and it incorporated the activities of birds, animals and humans. The icons were the settings in which 'work', 'leisure' and other family activities were integrated into living. Consequently, setting was fundamental to all human activity. It was Goffman who pointed out the importance of setting for human activity:

> First there is 'setting', involving furniture, décor, physical layout, and other background items that supply the scenery and stage props for the spate of human action played before, within, or upon it. (pp. 32–33)

If human action occurs in a setting, why should leisure activity be exempted? It is the position of the author that *setting* be regarded as the fourth dimension of leisure.

Colonization

Australia was colonized in 1788. According to Hamilton-Smith and Robertson (1977), the first fleet society brought over to Australia was differentiated with 19 officers, 190 other ranks, 30 wives, 12 children and about 729 convicts. In the first two decades of settlement authorities paid little attention to leisure and recreation except to curb drunkenness and other 'immoral' behaviour of the convicts. Major holidays in England were celebrated. Sports and pastimes were transplanted from Britain. Daly (1972) reported that cricket was recorded in 1804. The convicts brought with them popular pastimes such as cockfighting and bull baiting (Hamilton-Smith and Robertson, 1977). Government recognition of recreation was limited. As part of active policy Hyde Park in Sydney was established. Otherwise citizens were advised to use their free time to uplift themselves and further their education (Hamilton-Smith and Robertson, 1977).

Transplantation of most British sports and pastimes had exceptions. Australian Football was an innovation of team sport. Surfing and surf-life saving were characteristically Australian innovations. The relatively favourable climate over much of Australia encouraged many to participate in outdoor activities. Uniquely Australian activities such as sheaf tossing, log chopping, chasing the greasy pig, and (today) tractor ballet took place at country and agricultural shows (Hamilton-Smith and Robertson, 1977).

In colonial times, Australia was a man's world both in numbers and tradition. Women were committed to domestic life and were outside public view. A few bucked the trend. On 17 October 1836 Eliza Fraser swept to the *Herald* office in Sydney to 'tell a terrible tale of shipwreck, death and white slavery at the hands of Aborigines' (p. 34) (Personal communication, Eliza visits the Herald, 17 October 1836). Lady Henrietta Macquarie, wife of Governor Macquarie is commemorated in more colonial landmarks than any other woman before or since. Her letter to the *Herald* in 1825 described how husband Lachlan Macquarie was forced to spend the last years of life trying to clear his name 'being too accepting of reformed convicts, too dismissive of landed gentry and erecting buildings too extravagant for a penal colony' (p. 25) (Letter to the *Herald*, The death of Governor Lachlan Macquarie, 3 November 1825). Caroline Chisholm assisted thousands of female immigrants to secure work on many farms. Sickened by exploitation of boatloads of immigrant girls she talked her way to see the governor of the colony and proprietors of the *Herald* to win support in what was to become her life's work (Female Immigrants, 1841).

Males dominated Australian leisure and recreation. In the mid 1920s there were reports that traditions were trampled upon by young females as youth were seen by them to be paramount. This type of a young woman was described as 'the flapper'. However, reports of an individual 'Australian lassie' was described as:

> A clean-limbed, wholesome, sports-loving girl, who can play a game of tennis, golf, or hockey with anyone, who can run a boat, or run car all day if need be, and dance half the night … . (Lifestyle Chasers, 1926: 26)

Literary arts at the turn of the twentieth century were in infancy. When asked to compare literature in the United States and Australia, Miles Franklin (1945) said:

> I used to say that Australia was a little girl with pigtails and America a grand young lady with her hair up, and out in society in one of those décolleté gowns, with the squeezed waist and long train, which was the ambition of the normal little girls in that day. (p. 78)

In 1901, Miles Franklin wrote her first novel, the classic *My Brilliant Career*. The Miles Franklin Literary Award, established in 1954 with the bequest from the author, is the most prestigious literary award in Australia. She was keen to see Australian literature flourish and understood the struggles authors faced. The annual Award celebrates Australian character and creativity. It nurtures the continuing life of literature about Australia.

Radio broadcasts were introduced to Australia in 1923. Radio changed the Australian way of life by its accessibility to individuals in their homes. Family members performed daily routines with the radio on in the background. It was a constant companion of the housewife as she worked on her daily chores (Johnson, 1981). With electricity, urbanization and available leisure time, the cinema started to flourish at the turn of the century. Movies were the mainstay of entertainment for the common people and they continued to flourish till the advent of television in the 1950s (Clark, 1987). During the 1920s the car opened the vast outdoors to urbanites. They were able to bushwalk, camp and picnic in rural areas. As visitor numbers increased to wilderness areas, it was necessary to protect them. One such area was the Blue Mountains National Park in New South Wales (Powell, 1980). The Parks and Playground Movement, established in the 1920s was in response to social problems arising out of rapid urban development. Areas were set aside to offer children an opportunity to play and provide adults chances to recreate (Taylor, 1993). As Australian sporting traditions and games unique to the nation took hold, there was a rise in spectators to sporting events and the cinema. As Lynch and Veal (2006) described, 'sport and spectatorism continued to be central to the leisure culture of Australia and in the 1930s were vital to people's psychic survival through the Depression' (p. 77). The onset of the World War II interrupted the customary lifestyles of Australians.

Post 1945 to Contemporary Australia

Scripting the post-World War II period (Lynch and Veal, 2006) stated that Australia had a huge demographic change from 7.4 million in 1945 to 20 million at the start of the 21st century. The popularity of radio grew. The introduction of television in 1956 was a major revolution; music, drama, and national and international shows could be watched in the privacy of the homes. Since the introduction of television, Australians were able to view international events such as the 1956 and 2000 Olympics in Melbourne and Sydney respectively, cricket matches and the running of the Melbourne Cup. Television provided a shift for Australians to be spectators in their leisure. Mercer (1994) labelled the nation as the 'spectator society'.

In 1924 the life expectancy was 61 years. The lifespan was characterized by three groupings – child, adult and old age. In 1968, life expectancy was 71 years and the groupings of child and adult were separated by 'teen'. In 2008, life expectancy was 81 years and several groupings made up the lifespan – child, adolescence, adult, lifestyle (and others) and the elderly (Australian Institute of Health and Welfare, 2004). Australians generally are living longer (See Figure 1).

Figure 1

Phases of the Australian Life Cycle

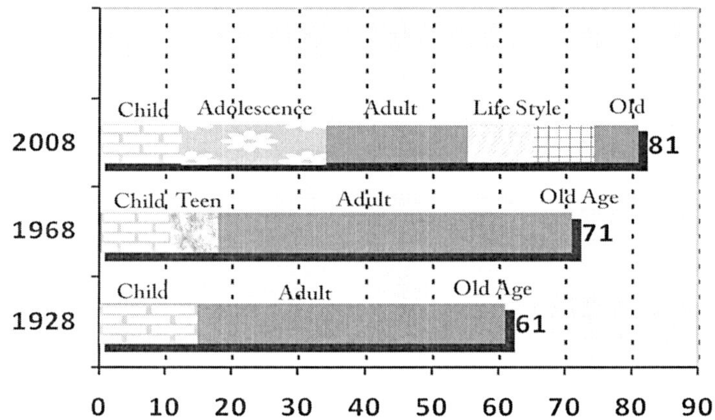

Source: Australian Bureau of Statistics; Australian Institute of Health and Welfare: Australia's Heath 2004
This chart shows that as life expectancy for the average Australian expands so too changes the stages of the life cycle. Baby boomers invented the teenage years as a transition phase to fit between childhood and adulthood. New age segments are still evolving, especially beyond 50.

Source: Salt (2006). p. 104

Figure 2

The Australian Cultural Social System

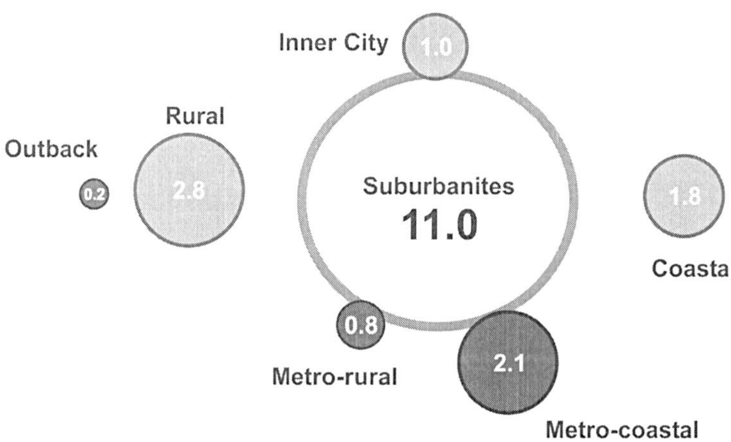

Source : KPMG Property Advisory Services
This Chart shows the main concentrations of the Australian population. Most Australians live in metropolitan suburbia. Other 'metropolitan' orbit the 'burbs: the inner suburbanites; metro-fringe coasters; and metro-fringe rurals. The proportion of Australians living in the Outback is about one per cent of the nation.

Source: Salt (2006). p. 128

Figure 3

Social Mega Wheel: Australia, 2010

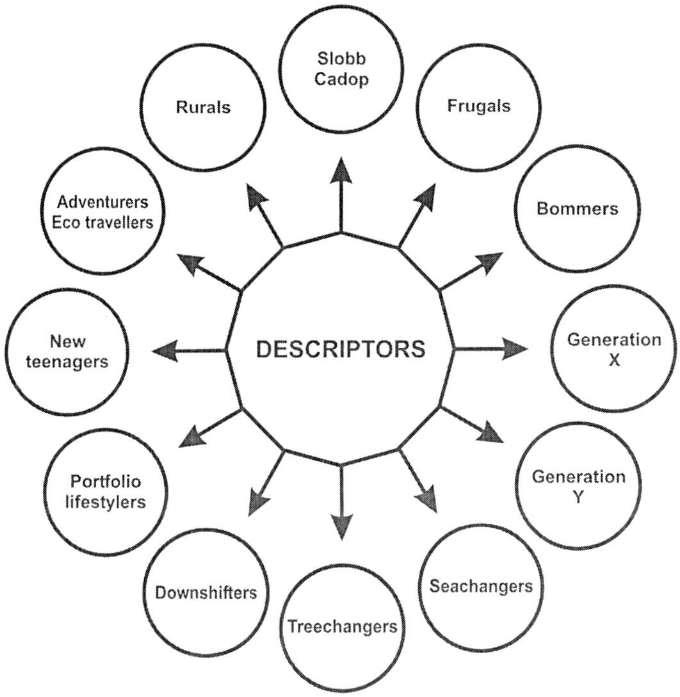

Source: Adapted from Salt (2006) pp. 20–24.

In 2010, Australia's population surpassed 21.5 million. According to Salt, (2006) 15 million Australians fell with the 'orbital influence' of capital cities. The suburbanites were the largest cultural grouping. Approximately 11 million lived in the suburbs. One million lived in the inner suburbs. Coastal metropolitan areas accounted for 2.1 million. The 'coasters' are outside the orbital influence of the big city but live on the coast. Metro-rural areas on the fringe of suburbia accounted for 800,000 people. Well beyond the city, people in rural and regional Australia comprised 2.8 million. 200,000 people occupied the outback. The Australian cultural social system is illustrated in Figure 2.

Salt (2006: 20) used the phrase 'terms of endearment' to capture demographic and lifestyle buzzwords that are incorporated into a social mega-wheel. Descriptors used in the wheel are: SLOBB (Sad Lonely Old Baby Boomers) or CADOP (Clever and Desirable Old People); Frugals; Boomers, Generation X; Generation Y; Seachangers; Treechangers; Downshifters; Portfolio Lifestylers; New teenagers; Adventurers and Ecotravellers; and Rurals. The terms Salt has used are listed in Figure 3. The four core groupings are: Frugals; Boomers; Generation X; and Generation Y.

The topic of generations is a subject of much discussion and humour particularly among cartoonists who portray Generation Y as unique and cannot be copied by their Boomer parents. According to Salt (2006):

Generation Y has not only eschewed boomer culture and fashion, they are celebrating their time in life. Generation Y teenage girls have evolved a fashion that is quintessentially 'young'. The midriff is exposed and jeans are lowered to sit squarely – and precariously – on the widest part of the hips. This look cannot be copied by a 50-year-old baby boomer woman. (p. 86)

Unique fashion is equally applicable to Generation Y males. Hairstyles sporting the Mohawk and Spiky cuts are difficult to copy by a balding 50-year-old male.

In early 2010, the population of Australia surpassed 21 million (See Figure 4). The gender split was more or less even, with males exceeding females by approximately 46,000. Based on Salt's (2006) generational categories, age-band groupings filled in the entire population: Frugals 70+; Baby Boomers 45–69; Generation X 30–44; Generation Y 15–29; and Generation Z 0–14. Figure 5 illustrates the Australian population by generations.

The groupings of generations may be likened to 'social regions', a phrased coined by Goffman (1971). He defined a region 'as any place that is bounded to some degree by barriers of perception' (p. 109). Elaborating on social regions Goffman stated:

> ... when a performance is given it is usually given in a highly bounded region, to which boundaries with respect to time are often added. The impression and understanding fostered by the performance will tend to saturate the region and time span, so that any individual located in this time-space manifold will be in a position to observe the performance and be guided by the definition of the situation which the performance fosters. (p. 109)

Generations qualify as social regions as the performances (behaviours) are configured by the social and economic conditions of their time. Thus, the Frugals who encountered the Great Depression could be configured in

Figure 4

The Australian Population, 2010

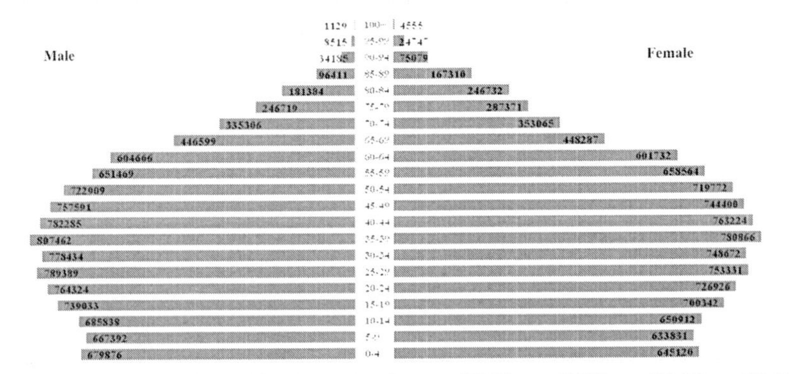

Total population : 21,515,754
Male: 10,780,916
Female: 10,734,838

Source: Cencus Bureau, International Data Base

Figure 5

Australian Population 2010: Generations

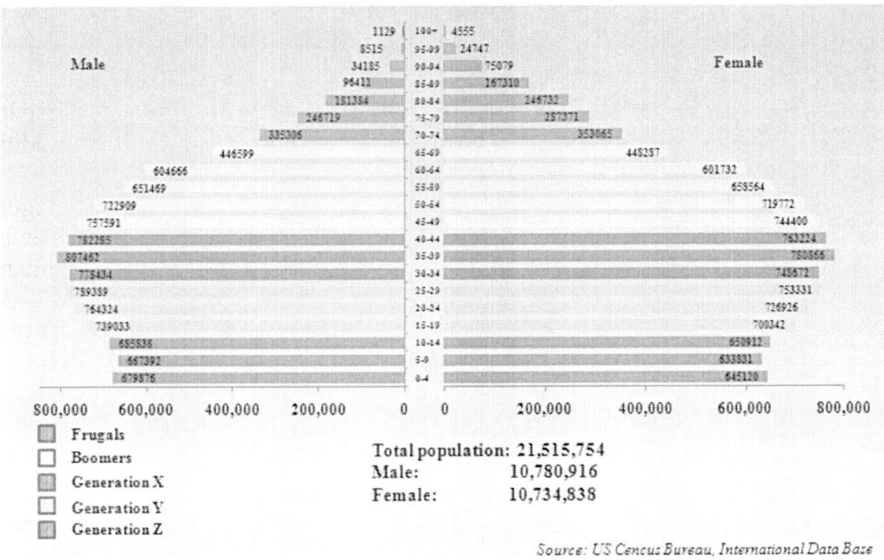

behaviour that featured hard economic times. Consequently, jobs were unstable, as a generation they were debt shy, spent to replace and were ambivalent to fashion. Likewise, the behaviour of the Boomers would tend to saturate the region and the time span. In periods after the Second World War, boomers found themselves in periods of economic growth and full employment. Consequently, they were self-confident, self-centred and self-congratulatory. They acquired high-level jobs and were fashion innovators. Generation X felt 'hard done by', suffered intermittent employment, frequent career change and embraced the city. Generation Y are self-focused, action-driven, earn to spend, peer orientated and asymmetric in fashion. The behaviour configurations of generations are illustrated in Figure 6.

The galloping speed of advancing of technology has had its effects on generations. When the corporate world embraced the use of computers as part of its normal operational process, the Frugals became very anxious and distressed. Many were declared obsolete and lost their jobs. Others were made redundant and some took early retirement. The label of 'Aliens' was given to the Frugals in relation to digital technology. The Boomers had no choice if they wished to advance. Given their self-confidence, they learnt the skills required and the label of 'Transients' was assigned to them. For Generation X, the encounter with digital technology was in the final years of school or when they commenced paid employment. They had to adapt and appropriately, the label 'Adaptives' was assigned. Generation Y grew up with the digital technology from a very young age and was comfortable with it. Consequently, Generation Y members were known as 'Natives'. Digital awareness as it has affected generations is presented in Figure 7.

Figure 6

Social Regions: Generations 2010

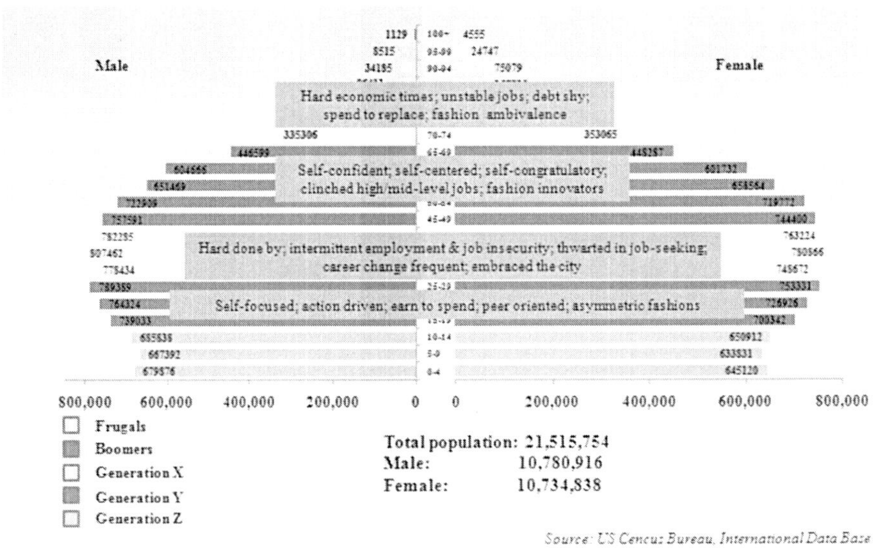

Figure 7

Generations 2010: Digital Awareness

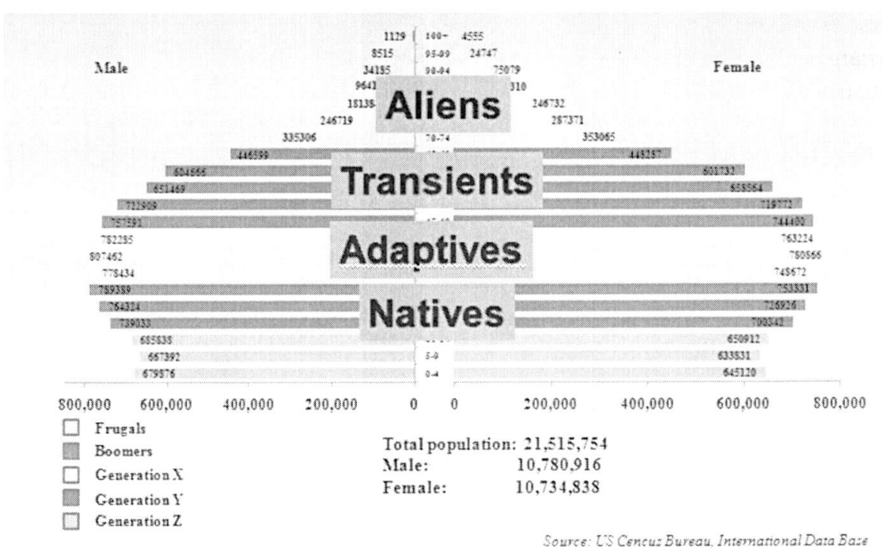

Digital awareness and its relationship to generations is but one example of how social regions adapt to economic conditions and life environment of the time. The illustration may well be applied to education, health, leisure and lifestyle.

Within the leisure domain, sport and physical activity in Australia is used as a standard for emulation by other nations. Sul and Lobo (2010) concluded that Australia is portrayed as land for sports and physical recreation. The sporting image of the nation is projected by international achievements. Sport has been nurtured and embraced by its population. Free time, earned and valued, by many Australians is used for sport and physical recreation. Originally dominated by men, females have made immense headway. Feminine movements have worked effectively to narrow the gap. Participation in sport and recreation is healthy, and gender activity profiles take separate paths. More men participate in exercise programs at high active levels than women. Moderate levels of exercise participation are more equitable between genders as are sedentary levels. Constraints of the lack of time affect both genders, but women are affected more by family responsibilities than men. Attendances at sporting events are well supported by men and women with comparable numbers.

Summary and Conclusion

This chapter has attempted to describe the leisure landscape of Australia from antiquity to the early 21st century. The way of life of Australian Aboriginals was described and interpreted through photographic and hand-drawn images and narratives. Leisure activities during the period of colonization were an importation of British sports and pastimes. Colonial Australia was a patriarchal society, with a few women making their mark in leisure and related activities. Australia entered into modernity with increased life expectancy and varied lifestyles. The diversity has been fostered by the multi-cultural nature of the country. Four waves of migration have played their part in advancing Australia. The dominance of the first Anglo-Celtics was challenged by Eastern-European, Mediterranean and Asian influences. The sum of these influences, according to Salt (2006) moves Australia towards a fluent, transient and mobile 21st century world.

References

Australian Institute of Health and Welfare. (2004). *Australia's Health,* Canberra: Commonwealth of Australia.

Burnum, B. (1988). *Burnum Burnum's Aboriginal Australia.* Cottage Point, NSW: Angus Robertson.

Caledoy Bay, (1935). Wonggo and his son Gamarli (photograph) in Wiseman, J.P. (1996). *Thomson Time: Arnhem Land in the 1930s: A Photographic Essay.* Melbourne, Victoria: Museum of Victoria (p. 10).

Clark, M. (1987). *A History of Australia VI: The Old Dead Tree and the Young Tree Green, 1916–1935.* Sydney: Scholastic.

Cockatoo Creek, Central Australia. (1931). Music for dancing being provided by beating the ground with sticks (photography) in Tinsdale, B.T. and George, B. (1971). *The Australian Aborigines.* Potts Point, NSW: Golden Press Pty. Ltd., (p. 59).

Daly, J.A. (1971). Sport and society – the role of sport and games in the social development of early Australia. *Australian Journal of Physical Education. (55)* 31–37.

Ellis, J.A. (1994). *Australia*'s *Aboriginal Heritage.* North Blackburn, Victoria: Collins Dove.

Ellis, R. and Ellis, J.A. (1982). *Aboriginal Australia: Past and Present.* Netley, SA: Griffin Press.

Female immigrants. (2 December 1841). *Herald*. In *Good Weekend, Sydney Morning Herald Magazine, 22* April 2006 p. 38.

Franklin, M. (21 July 1945). Voices in the Wilderness. *Herald*. In *Good Weekend, Sydney Morning Herald Magazine, 22* April 2006 p. 78.

Fraser, E. (1836). Eliza visits the *Herald*. In *Good Weekend, Sydney Morning Herald Magazine, 22* April 2006 p. 34.

Frisch, M. (1974). *Homo Faber*, Harmondsworth, UK: Penguin.

Goffman, E. (1971). *The Presentation of Self in Everyday Life*. Middlesex, England: Pelican Books. (First published in the USA in 1959).

Hamilton-Smith, E. and Robertson, R. (1977). Recreation and government in Australia. In D. Mercer (ed.) *Leisure and Recreation in Australia*. Malvern, Victoria: Sorrett Publishing.

Huizinga, J. (1971). *Homo Ludens*. London: Granada Publishing. (First published in 1949 by Routledge and Kegan Paul)

Ilaura Tribe, Macdonald Downs, Central Australia. (1930). Little girls playing mothers and fathers (photograph) in Tinsdale, B.T. and George, B. (1971). *The Australian Aborigines*. Potts Point, NSW: Golden Press Pty. Ltd., (p. 33).

Jackson, E.L. (ed.) (2006). *Leisure and the Quality of Life: Impacts of Social, Cconomic and Cultural Economic Development, Hangzhou Consenus*. Hangzhou, China: Zhejiang University Press.

Johnson, L. (1981). Radio and everyday life: the early years of broadcasting in Australia 1922–1945. *Media, Culture and Society*, 3(2), 167–78.

Lifestyle Chasers. (21 August 1926). *Herald*. In *Good Weekend, Sydney Morning Herald Magazine, 22* April 2006 p. 58.

Lynch, R. and Veal, A.J. (2006). *Australian Leisure*. (3rd Ed.), Frenchs Forest, NSW: Pearson Education Australia.

Mackintosh, J. (circa, 1940). Corroboree Game. Folding board game based on aboriginal activities, implements and Australian fauna. National Library of Australia: nla.pic-am23162625-v

Macquarie, H. (1825). The death of Governor Macquarie. Letter to the *Herald*. In *Good Weekend, Sydney Morning Herald Magazine, 22* April 2006 p. 35.

Mercer, D. (1994). Monitoring the spectator activity: an overview of research and policy issues. In Mercer, D. (ed.) *New Viewpoints in Australian Outdoor Recreation Research*. Hepper Marriott, Williamstown, Vic.

Nyadamarda Tr., Mandora Station, N.W. Australia. (1953). A young boy clutching pampidi lizards round the neck so that they are unable to bite him or escape (photograph) in Tinsdale, B.T. and George, B. (1971). *The Australian Aborigines*. Potts Point, NSW: Golden Press Pty. Ltd., (p. 33).

Powell, J.M. (1980). The philistines and the populace: leisure and recreation before 194 5. In Mercer, D. and Hamilton-Smith, E. (eds). *Recreation Planning and Social Change in Urban Australia*. Malvern, Vic: Sorrett. (pp. 26–37).

Salt, B. (2006). *The Big Picture*. Hardie Grant Books: Prahran, Victoria: Australia.

Sul, S. and Lobo, F. (2010). Australian and Korean sport and exercise activities. In Dong, E. and Yi-Kook, J. (eds) *Korean Leisure: From Tradition to Modernity*. Jaipur: Rawat Publications, (pp. 273–276)

Taylor, T. (1193). Sydney's supervised playgrounds: 1932–1975. In Veal, A.J., Cushman, G. and Jonson, P. (eds) *Leisure and Tourism: Social and Environmental Change*. Centre for Leisure and Tourism Studies, University of Technology and World Leisure and Recreation, Sydney. (500–508).

Veblen, T. (1970). *The Theory of the Leisure Class.* London: Allen and Unwin. (First published in 1925).

Warapuju Tr. Warburton Range, W.A. (1933). A Pitandjara girl holding a tame dingo pup (photograph) in Tinsdale, B.T. and George, B. (1971). *The Australian Aborigines.* Potts Point, NSW: Golden Press Pty. Ltd., (p. 36).

Warapuju Tr. Warburton Range, W.A. (1935). Children sing the *Mamu tjitji* song as they make a chain with their hands (photograph) in Tinsdale, B.T. and George, B. (1971). *The Australian Aborigines.* Potts Point, NSW: Golden Press Pty. Ltd., (p. 34).

Warapuju Tr. Warburton Range, W.A. (1935). Boys practising by aiming at bark discs (photograph) in Tinsdale, B.T. and George, B. (1971). *The Australian Aborigines.* Potts Point, NSW: Golden Press Pty. Ltd., (p. 32).

Wiluwiluru Waterhole, Mann Range. (1933). A girl leaping along a line of stones which has been arranged by children (photograph) in Tinsdale, B.T. and George, B. (1971). *The Australian Aborigines.* Potts Point, NSW: Golden Press Pty. Ltd., (p. 34).

2

Mapping Leisure and Life through the Ages in New Zealand

MICHAEL TOOHEY, GRANT CUSHMAN AND BOB GIDLOW

Glossary of Maori Terms

New Zealand's three official languages are English, Maori and New Zealand Sign Language. The following list offers short definitions of Maori words used within this chapter.

- Haka – dance
- Pakeha – a person of predominantly European descent
- Poi – literally a ball. Commonly, a ball anchored to a string or cord used in action games and performances
- Waiata – song
- Waka Ama – outrigger or double-hull canoe

Introduction

This chapter offers an introductory map of leisure in the South Pacific state of New Zealand, taking special interest in the tightening and loosening of social and legislative control on leisure and its effect on 'national identity'. An Arcadian exoticism has inhabited European understanding of New Zealand. It is detectable in such concepts as 'God's own country' (laconically and sometimes ironically abbreviated to 'Godzone'), made fashionable in the early twentieth century by populist New Zealand Premier Richard Seddon (1845–1906), and still detectable in the long-running tourism campaign '100 per cent Pure New Zealand'. Consistent with this image is the construction of New Zealand as a Better Britain in the south; a place where a 'superior strain' of Anglo-Celts was able to flourish in favourable social, political and physical conditions. The image of a country of tough, pioneering, outdoorsy and egalitarian (if slightly rustic) men and women persisted throughout much of the twentieth century and beyond. It is reflected both in a tradition of innovative outdoor recreation, exemplified by such activities as commercial bungy jumping and adventure multi-sport, and in a fondness for masculine 'literary yarns', characterized by

Barry Crump's hugely successful *Good Keen Man* (1960) and other novels and short stories in the same vein.

The availability and type of leisure enjoyed by New Zealanders has been a key component of this image. New Zealanders have been portrayed as 'keen on sport', a notion supported by relative success in international competition (Laidler and Cushman, 1993). In contrast, a streak of democratic anti-intellectualism (sometimes defined as 'tall poppy syndrome') combined with physical distance from the 'cultural capitals' of the northern hemisphere, has contributed to an image of a people more inclined to outdoor than indoor leisure, although the accuracy of this has long been debated, given that New Zealand was well on the way to becoming an urbanized society within 60 years of settler-colonization in the mid-nineteenth century (Fairweather and Mulet Marquis, 2008: 6).

In this chapter it is argued that social and legislative control played a role in structuring the leisure choices made by New Zealanders, and that as New Zealand society transformed from settler to settled, control over leisure tightened in the face of broadening commercial leisure choices. Thus, as New Zealanders enthusiastically embraced such new innovations in active and passive leisure as roller skates, bicycles, swimming baths and cinema to radio, television, jogging, aerobics and disco, governments, churches and interest groups worked assiduously to control and channel access to leisure in a manner which reinforced the image of a healthy, modern, rational and progressive, if somewhat puritanical, nation.

As it charts the tightening and loosening of governmental hands on the reigns of leisure, this chapter will concentrate on the years between 1815 and 2000. By 1815, New Zealand's indigenous Maori population had been joined by a handful of whalers, sealers and missionaries.

Adaptation and Control: Maori and Pakeha Leisure, 1800–1939

Arguably, Maori, and specifically Maori women, formed the core of New Zealand's first leisure industry. Maori involvement in commercial leisure began with the arrival of explorers, whalers, sealers and sailors from the late-eighteenth to early-nineteenth centuries. New Zealand's first Pakeha town – Kororareka, in the far north of the North Island – was blessed with a good harbour, timber, fresh water and a sub-tropical climate, enabling it to cater to the material needs of whaling ships and the recreational needs of their crews. Maori formed an integral component of the provisioning industry, providing timber for the ships and pork, potatoes and sex, for their crews. 'Short-term marriages' between crewmen and Maori women were negotiated sometimes by the women themselves, and sometimes by Maori men, chiefly for the purpose of obtaining muskets (Belich, 2002).

Predictably, Kororareka was dubbed the 'hellhole of the Pacific' by Wesleyan and Calvinist missionaries who began operating in Northland from 1815, but missionary disapproval ran deeper than straightforward opposition to commercialized sex. The entrepreneurial drive which inhabited evangelical Protestantism disapproved of any activity which was not industrious or worshipful of God. To the chagrin of Anglo-Celtic settlers, who began arriving in New Zealand in increasing numbers from 1840, missionary teachings displayed a similarly pious distaste for 'British' leisure, including reading novels (Belich, 2002) and playing sports. In 1841, when colonists attempted to organise a regatta for Maori canoeists on Wellington harbour, Maori refused to take part, apparently due to their observation of missionary strictures against sport. Newspaper reaction to the refusal was typically Eurocentric and patronising towards the 'poor savages', yet it also contained a kernel of insight into the problem of a people whose 'little knowledge' of the new arrivals' culture was affected by the restrictive lens of Protestant missionaries (1841: 3).

The second peopling of New Zealand took place in the last half of the nineteenth century when successive waves of migrants were attracted by 'assisted' (subsidized) sea-born passages and the lure of a better life. The vast majority came from England, Wales, Ireland and Scotland, and they immediately set out on the important business of recreating a modified British society in the South Pacific. The society and economy which emerged in New Zealand was driven by the production of such raw materials as cereals, wool and protein (meat and milk products). The 1861 discovery of a 'payable' goldfield in Otago added mining to the list of primary industries which exported to Britain via steam-powered ships. In return, the latest consumer goods were shipped back along the same trade routes together with capital finance and more migrants to bolster the pioneering workforce. So, while farming was New Zealand's engine room, the economy which it drove was modern, capitalist and industrial. Leisure was thus to be pursued not on a whim, but during clearly appointed and regulated 'spare time'. Such regulation included seasonal markers such as spring and autumn agricultural and pastoral shows which continue to this day as Agricultural and Pastoral (AandP) shows and agricultural field days.

The settlers' stance towards Maori was disturbingly acquisitive, paternalistic, imperialist and dismissive, but attempts at an overt colour bar within New Zealand were largely stillborn. Separate Maori events were a common feature of nineteenth-century sports meetings, but multiple examples exist of Maori competing equally against Pakeha in New Zealand's emerging sports culture. The traffic, however, was mainly one way; most Pakeha showed little interest in Mâori culture other than as a romantic backdrop to their own creation of a Better Britain in the south. Elsdon Best, an autodidactic and energetic ethnographer, did attempt to catalogue 'traditional' (pre-contact) Maori 'games and pastimes', but these indigenous leisure activities were seen by Best and his colleagues as relics of a lost past (Best, 1925). In the conventional mantra of Social Darwinism and a progress-driven British Empire, Maori were a 'dying race', destined to extinction or, at best, absorption within a 'superior' Anglo-Celtic New Zealand identity.

A template for organized public leisure in New Zealand was provided by the Anniversary Fete and Ball, held to celebrate the arrival of the first New Zealand Company ship in Port Nicholson (Wellington). On a fine Monday in January 1841, a rowing regatta, hurdle race (for horses), sailing regatta and rifle match were held, along with a number of 'folk' sports such as a wheelbarrow race, sack race and a climb of a greasy pole. The ludic events were followed by an evening ball which was reportedly 'very numerously attended' (NZG, 1841: 3).

Intriguingly, the Popular Fete had been preceded a few days earlier by a 'select' rowing and sailing regatta. This attempt at social division appears to have been an all but total failure; the 'select' rowing regatta proved a farce, with one of the two competing boats giving up at halfway, while the sailing regatta was abandoned altogether. A more persistent division was that between female and male spheres of leisure. The *New Zealand Gazette* (1841: 3) observed, 'over the room fitted up for the ball, a large white banner, with the words 'Popular Fete,' inscribed, gave token that the amusement of the fairer portion of the creation had not been forgotten'.

The ingredients of the Anniversary celebrations – rowing regattas, horse racing, rifle shooting, folk sports, athletics and an evening ball – were to provide the basis of popular annual events in New Zealand's fledgling towns and villages for the remainder of the nineteenth century. Cricket matches composed of local teams also provided periodic sporting interludes in the pioneering life, as did football matches of various codes. Provincial anniversaries proved popular excuses for a half or full-day off, as did Christmas, New Year, Easter and (English) royal birthdays. None of these holidays were official or universal; individual employers were at liberty to observe them or not. A significant problem was the transposition of Christmas and New Year from the northern hemisphere winter to the southern hemisphere summer. Not only was this disorientating for many migrants, but it also placed Christmas in the middle of the rural harvest season, often preventing farming and rural-worker families from fully enjoying the festivals. Nevertheless, the celebration of Christmas, Easter *and* New Year points towards the establishment of a pan-British or Anglo-Celtic tradition in New Zealand. In contrast, the migrant's home countries usually celebrated one festival (Christmas in England) or another (New Year in Scotland) (Clarke, 2007: 14–15).

The size and frequency of public leisure events grew as New Zealand communities became more established and its settlers transitioned into settled life. Initially, the bureaucratic model of a special committee to organise a specific one-off event such as the Anniversary Fete proved expedient, but this was soon supplemented by sub-committees attached to such voluntary associations as fraternal lodges and ethnic associations. Churches, schools and large employers also hosted picnics and fetes, usually timed to coincide with the high-summer holidays of Christmas and New Year's Day. Evenings and Saturday afternoons also provided leisure-time for some, but the idea of uniform working hours was not enshrined by legislation despite the early introduction of the eight-hour movement to New Zealand. The first piece of industrial legislation to limit working hours was the Employment of Females Act (1873). Based on Victoria (Australia)'s Factory Act (1850), the Employment of Females Act (1873):

> Affirmed the principle of the eight hours day as far as women and girls were concerned, allowed no one to employ women or girls at night, gave them a half-holiday on Saturday afternoon in each week, and a whole holiday on Sunday, Christmas Day, New Year's Day, Good Friday, Easter Monday, 'and any other day set apart as a public holiday,' without loss of wages. (Drummond, 1907: 224)

The concept of the eight-hour working day had arrived in Port Nicholson (Wellington) on 7 February 1840 in the person of carpenter Samuel Parnell.

When asked to build a store for a fellow migrant, Parnell made the condition 'that on the job the hours shall be only eight for the day' (Parnell quoted in Roth, 1966). On being told that there were twenty-four hours in a day, Parnell allegedly replied 'eight of these should be for work, eight for sleep, and the remaining eight for recreation and in which for men to do what little things they want to do for themselves' (ibid.).

As the first successful 'strike' for an eight hour day, Parnell's division of 24 hours into work, sleep and recreation time has been celebrated as a success for the labour movement. It might, however, equally be read as the ultimate endorsement of the capitalist alienation of time. Parnell intimately understood that his time could be bought and sold, and was intent on delineating exactly how much time he was willing to sell each day. It is also clear that the eight-hour day was far from universal. Before 1873, it had applied primarily to comparatively secure tradesmen such as Parnell, and had not extended to women and girls, unskilled men and boys or white-collar workers in shops, banks and offices. Moreover, the conditions awarded women and girls in 1873 were eroded by subsequent amendments designed to improve the profitability of Dunedin woollen mills (Drummond, 1907: 225).

New Zealand's Long Depression (1878–1895) brought unemployment, sweated labour and negative population growth as settlers re-migrated to 'still prospering Australia' (Gardner, 1988: 75). The Liberal Party, New Zealand's first fully-formed political party, was voted into office partially on the back of public concern over the evils of Long Depression-era 'sweating'[1] and worsening labour conditions in general, Along with land reforms which broke up large pastoral estates into 'family farms', the First Liberal Government (1890–1912) enacted a number of laws designed to improve working conditions for urban labour. The Liberal Party had 'reinforced an established pattern of state involvement in the economy and regulation of society' which the Labour Party was happy to expand further still (Wilson, 2009). In 1936, the First Labour Government (1935–1949) heralded the 'Kiwi weekend' when everything was closed' by enshrining the 40 hour week in legislation (Phillips, 2009). The shape and limits of the regulated society sought by successive governments is indicated by two groups whose leisure hours were not-so-fully enshrined by the new legislation. Labour's forty hour week did not extend to farm workers, who still found 'it next to impossible to take part in organised sport' (Somerset, 1938: 34). Even the now-traditional half-holiday was not sacrosanct, as 'a farmer would never think of stopping his team (of horses) on a Saturday afternoon because his son or his teamster wished to play football or tennis' (Somerset, 1938: 34). Nevertheless, the popularity of rugby union in rural areas might be partially explained by seasonal timing. If any season allowed a little respite from the demands of farm work, it was winter (Somerset, 1938: 34).

An almost-contradictory indication of New Zealand's modernity was the inclination of urban-dwelling settlers to 'get away from it all' at any given opportunity. Although New Zealand's metropolitan areas were still modest in the 1860s, summer picnics and other excursions had already become popular. In 1861, for example, Wellington's banks, government offices, and merchants closed their doors and, the day being 'delightfully fine', the city's populace decamped via road and sea for nearby rural locations, bays and islands. The ritual of getting out of town was repeated throughout the colony, no matter how small the village. Commercial operators cashed in on this trend with excursion boats to take holidaymakers to secluded bays. Forms of leisure and recreation, and even inter-provincial sport, benefitted from and were shaped by the introduction of mechanized transport very soon after the initial phase of European immigration and settlement. By the 1880s, rail was competing with steam packets as a fast and convenient mode of transport. New Zealand Railways ran 'excursion specials' to sporting venues and popular picnic spots. In Christchurch, as the tram system extended to the seaside suburb of Sumner, excursion trams became a popular method of accessing the beach resort for promenading and bathing (see Figure 1).

Figure 1

An Excursion Tram Departs Christchurch for Sumner in 1901

From the 1890s, widespread bicycle ownership allowed individuals to access the countryside without relying from trams, trains, boats or coaches. Urban men (initially) and women of all classes used the bicycle to make both short and long leisure trips. Some would simply access nearby parks, beaches and farmland, but many cyclists of both sexes regularly made day trips of 50 miles (80 kilometres) or more. The bicycle and, later, the motorcar also facilitated longer tours of the New Zealand landscape, making it possible for groups and individuals to pursue a range of outdoor activities (see Figure 2).

As annual holidays were extended from half-days and days to weekends, long weekends and, eventually, whole weeks, picnics and day trips were supplemented by more extended breaks from the constraints of urban life. Camping, tramping (hiking), hunting, fishing and beach activities generally, became 'quintessentially Kiwi' leisure institutions. 'Quintessentially Kiwi' has been defined as 'the image Kiwis have of themselves – capable, unphased, ready to

Figure 2

Young Men Camping in the Tararua Ranges, Circa 1901

give things a go (including crazy adventurous stuff), roots in the country and the great outdoors' ('Kiwiana – Christchurch City Libraries,' n.d.).

For an increasingly urban population, regular escapes to the bush or the beach maintained the image of 'country roots'. In a country where patriotism was regularly expressed in terms of (British) imperialism rather than of nationalism, overt enjoyment of the outdoors was an implicit way of expressing a national identity, a sense of 'Kiwi-ness' within the wider identity as citizens of the Empire. Certain leisure sites became identified with a 'Kiwi way of life' – summer Christmas, beachside motor camps (caravan parks), club or publicly owned mountain huts (cabins) and small, ad-hoc holiday cottages known as 'baches' or 'cribs' – all became symbolic sites of ritualized New Zealand leisure. The uniqueness of any of these sites can be questioned. Summer Christmas is a feature of an entire hemisphere, not one country; beach culture is equally entrenched in Australia; camping and sacrosanct summer holidays have long been a part of France's leisure landscape and many North Americans enjoy vacations in family-owned holiday cabins. Nevertheless, the self-image of New Zealanders as a people who instinctively sought active and outdoor leisure remained powerfully and genuinely felt to the extent that even those who do not participate in such types of leisure have often been ready to uphold and defend 'wilderness' values against encroachment on that estate by commercial interests.

If regular 'escapes' from the constraints of city living were deemed a necessary component of New Zealand life, 'going bush' was ultimately as powerful an expression of modernity as travelling on an ocean liner or listening to a phonograph. A succession of modern vehicles – steam trains, bicycles, motorcars and buses – facilitated affordable and convenient access to previously remote locations, and despite regular homilies on the advantages of the simple life by those who had escaped to its charming embrace, such escapes were ultimately excursions rather than migrations. Trampers, campers, bathers and hunters were not actively rejecting an urban life which many claimed to despise; their trips countryside, beach and bush were instead muscular rest-cures, an antidote to modernity rather than an alternative to it.

Perhaps an equally important motivation for visiting the bush and the beach for recreation was to escape the conventionalism of urban life in New Zealand. Somewhat at odds with the image of the capable but 'laid back', egalitarian and essentially rural, New Zealander is the knowledge that New Zealand society was conservative and intolerant of 'improper' behaviour. Children's playgrounds, for example, came comparatively late to public parks, and were customarily locked on Sundays. In 1952, the Wairarapa Cricket Association felt compelled to ask permission before scheduling a match on a Sunday (Winter, 2008: 182). Similarly, in 1957, the Masterton swimming pool was open on Sunday afternoons, but Sunday morning opening was a bridge too far for the town's Borough Council (Winter, 2008: 182). Perhaps the most telling part of the debate was the Christian Ministers' Association's desire to guard not just the Christian Sabbath, but also 'the status of the Masterton Park as an aesthetic centre' versus a Councillor's rational recreation argument that it would 'be better for young men to be in the park watching cricket than strolling up and down the town' (Winter, 2008: 182).

'Strolling up and down the town' was one of the few urban leisure activities offered by New Zealand town and city centres on a Sunday. From 1917 to 1967, New Zealand's public bars closed at 6:00 pm during the week and all-day Sunday. Shops were closed at weekends, and restaurants were unable to serve wine with meals. Sundays were ostensibly for religious observance, quiet indoor leisure and visiting family and acquaintances for high tea. In an environment with such strong social and legislative control, the unfettered freedom of the 'great outdoors' held appeal. But once there, many continued to observe self-imposed codes of conduct. Rule books were a feature of club life even when the activity overseen was not formally competitive. In the late-1890s, women's cycling clubs stressed proper behaviour and graceful deportment while riding. Three decades later, chaperones were still a prominent feature of tramping club trips into the mountains and bush. The introduction of such delicate social mores into active leisure stemmed, at least in part, from a sense of caution amongst club committees who sought to downplay the more radical aspects of their activities. Cycling represented hitherto unparalleled freedom of mobility for young, middle-class women, while weekend tramping trips quietly broke with traditional religious strictures against active leisure on Sundays. Regular instruction on propriety (and overt supervision to ensure that the instructions were observed) were part of the negotiation process between aficionados of 'new' leisure activities and the perceivably conservative society in which they existed. In the case of urban active leisure, the negotiation of Sunday games remained difficult throughout the middle of the twentieth century because they were highly visible and, for the most part, took place on parks and reserves owned or operated by local bodies.

By the inter-war era, clubs were a dominant feature of New Zealand's leisure landscape, and they had long roots which drove back to the archipelago's earliest colonial days. Clubs and voluntary associations migrated from Britain with the new settlers; the earliest were started aboard ship during the voyage out or in England before the prospective settlers even embarked. Sometimes, it appeared that the migrants' favourite leisure activity was simply forming committees; in the case of the Nelson Literary and Scientific Institution, for example, 'two committees (were) appointed, one on board the Whitby, and the other in London, wholly independent of each other' (The Nelson Scientific and Literary Institution, 1842: 15).

A level of social exclusivity also applied. At a meeting to launch the now-renamed Nelson Literary and Scientific Association, the entrance fee was set at two guineas, with an annual subscription of one guinea (NE&NZC, 1842: 55). Election of members was to be 'by ballot, one black ball in six to exclude' (NE&NZC, 1842: 55).[2] Common in gentleman's club and fraternal lodges, blackballing ensured continuity and reinforced social conservatism, by requiring a unanimous (or near-unanimous) affirmative vote for a membership to be passed. Its proposed use caused 'a warm discussion' at the Nelson meeting, with some arguing for open membership to the new Association (NE&NZC, 1842: 55). Such egalitarian aspirations were initially rejected, but were enacted, in part, by the inevitable Association committee, which reduced the entrance fee to one guinea and made exclusion possible only on a majority of black balls.

The Nelson Literary and Scientific Association was clearly an attempt to guarantee the existence of rational leisure in the Nelson Colony from year one. Its necessity was enunciated by the *Nelson Examiner and New Zealand Chronicle*:

> A place of resort of this description is very useful in a new settlement. If the tastes likely to be encouraged by such institutions were not kept alive in some way, we should become altogether barbarous, unrefined, and with the worst species of unrefinement, that of relapse ('Nelson Chronicle and New Zealand Examiner,' 1842: 118).

Rational recreation was thus deemed necessary to prevent 'civilised' migrants from backsliding into barbarity. 'For the colonists generally, civilisation had become an unchallengeable good ... the project of colonisation was also the project of civilisation' (Olssen, 1995: 227). Literary institutes, fraternal lodges, friendly societies, churches sports clubs and even trades unions and the Workers Education Association (WEA) worked seriously towards this goal. In doing so, they helped create a social structure which, if somewhat flatter than that found in Britain, was nevertheless existent and clearly defined. A conspicuous outcome of the creation and defence of this structure was a division of labour which confined women's economic roles to domestic environments (Olssen, 1995: 227). While the importance of women's broader social and cultural contribution to home and family life should not be underestimated – including across a wide spectrum of activities such as visits, outings and picnics through to musical, religious and dramatic celebrations (Laidler and Cushman, 1993), this division of labour affected not only women's access to employment and equal remuneration, but also their access to organized active leisure. If anything, the division between male and female spheres of leisure strengthened during the middle years of the twentieth century, when 'the cultural hegemony of men's sport reigned supreme' (McDonald, 2009: 288). Thus, while women were amongst the first to be protected by the Liberal Government's labour reforms of the 1890s, they, like farm workers, did not automatically gain more leisure time from the 'universal' forty-hour week.

For those who wished for high-culture and intellectual discourse to assume a central role in New Zealand society, the Colony proved something of a disappointment. The popularity of outdoor leisure allowed the continuing development of the image/myth of the New Zealander as naturally at home in an 'untamed' landscape and somewhat ill-at-ease when faced with too-much comfort or inactive leisure. Visiting observers wrote tales of an anti-intellectual New Zealand youth, ready and able to pursue outdoor activities at the drop of a hat, but unwilling to engage in debate on subjects other than sport (see, for example, B. Webb and S. Webb, 1959). But although New Zealand was and is a geographically isolated archipelago which can only be reached by sea or air, the tyranny of distance, even in the mid-to-late nineteenth century should not be overstated. Consumer goods, news reports and peripatetic entertainers were shipped to New Zealand via increasingly speedy steamers, and local newspapers advertised a cornucopia of goods and entertainments to an eager public. That the public were making 'lifestyle choices' with regards to these goods and services is suggested by a doctor who, when commenting on New Zealand's low birth rate at the dawn of the twentieth century, waggishly quipped 'Pianos and bicycles are less expensive than babies' (B. Webb and S. Webb, 1959: 54).

If a doctor could muse over the falling birth rate of Pakeha New Zealanders, a new generation of Maori doctors, lawyers and politicians set out to improve the health of their own people, whose numbers reached a low of 43,000 in 1896. This new Maori leadership, which coalesced in the Young Maori Party (formed in 1909), accepted the regenerative role attributed to sport in modern British culture and applied it to Maori society. From their foundations in the 1920s and 30s, Kiwi-based sports teams playing tennis, hockey, rugby union, rugby league, netball and golf formed part of a conscious effort to reinvigorate Maori communities by marrying indigenous social organization with the very British innovation of bureaucratized sporting structures.

The adoption and adaptation by Maori of cultural competition as a means of preserving and promoting ethnic identity is an interesting and under-researched leisure movement. By the end of the nineteenth century, Caledonian games had become an entrenched part of New Zealand's leisure culture. They comprised a wide range of athletic competitions and also hosted a number of cultural competitions that showcased contemporary interpretations of Scottish traditions. Hibernian and Cambrian societies pursued similar goals, and at the founding meeting (in 1890) of the New Zealand Cambrian Society, one attendee asked, 'What could better foster their national characteristics than the establishment of prizes amongst their people for literary and musical efforts, choral music, and the music of the harp?'(J.B. Williams, quoted in 'Cambrian Society,' 1890: 4). Similarly, Haka, Poi, Waiata and, most recently, Waka Ama were adapted, fostered, promoted and utilized in a range of cultural competitions which injected Maori cultural tradition into the urban leisure environment using modes of competition and bureaucratic organization borrowed from Pakeha tradition.

Was it All Rugby Racing and Beer? Leisure in Mid-twentieth Century New Zealand

In 1965, Christchurch-based singer Rod Derrett scored a local hit with his satirical song, 'Rugby, Racing and Beer', which included the verse, 'Because of your great parentage/You have a national heritage/Of Rugby, Racing and Beer'. Though clearly a nonsense piece, the song provided a powerful and oft-repeated narrative of New Zealand culture in the middle of the twentieth century (McDonald, 2009: 286). But although rugby and racing were, indeed, hugely popular sports in mid-century New Zealand and beer was the national drink of choice, there clearly were 'other things' going on which did not conform to this stereotypical summation. On the international stage, Edmund Hillary climbed Everest, Yvette Williams won an Olympic gold medal in the long jump and Ronnie Moore dominated British motorcycle speedway. Barrie Briggs and Ivan Mauger carried this speedway success into the 1970s, a decade in which soprano Kiri Te Kanawa became New Zealand's best known cultural export as an opera singer. Unless one accepts the unsatisfying explanation of natural ability thriving in a vacuum, further examination of the circumstances of these successes is required. Most glaringly, the Rugby, Racing and Beer version of national identity almost completely overlooks half the population. While women could watch rugby and horse racing, they were denied participation as jockeys (before, 1978) or players. Furthermore, the consumption of beer or any other alcoholic beverage by women in public bars was an informal but strictly enforced taboo. This reflected a more general spatial and social separation of women's and men's recreational and sporting involvement at the time and which had its roots in the paternalistic attitudes of the temperance movement, which drew a close connection between women's alcohol consumption and the prevalence of female prostitution and loose sexual behaviour (McLauchlan, 1994).

It is telling that a contemporary examination of sport's social role in *An Encyclopaedia of New Zealand* highlighted firstly the mountains and bush as recreation playgrounds before going on to describe horse racing as 'immensely popular' (Burdon, 1966: 674). It also hinted that the international success of New Zealand athletes developed from an extremely bureaucratized and competition-centric recreation landscape:

> Visitors to the country sometimes comment disparagingly upon the high degree to which sport is organised, and point out that, instead of being played for their own sake, games have always to be reduced to the terms of a competition. There may be some value in these objections but it should not be forgotten that efficient organisation enables a very much larger proportion of New Zealanders to take an active part in games and sports than would be possible under less systematic conditions (Burdon, 1966: 674–5).

New Zealand's sporting success were thus seen as a result of the country's modernity and bureaucratic 'system' combined with 'ideal' environmental conditions (high protein diet, good climate, outdoor work) (McDonald, 2009: 287).

The eugenic advantage of New Zealand's living and working conditions dated back to New Zealand Company propaganda which sought to lure prospective migrants to its new colonies. The tradition was heartily endorsed by generations of colonial boosters, who saw evidence of New Zealand's superior socio-economic conditions in sporting success over British teams. Perhaps the most famous of these was the success of the '1905 Originals' All Blacks tour of Britain, France and the United States. When asked by an English newspaper to comment on the 'brilliancy of the New Zealand footballers', New Zealand Premier Richard Seddon highlighted the team's 'scientific' approach to rugby before returning to the familiar theme of a superior New Zealand environment: 'The natural and healthy conditions of colonial life produce stalwart and athletic sons, of whom New Zealand and the Empire are justly proud' ('The Premier And The Footballers,' 1905: 3). By the mid-1930s, when the urbanization of New Zealanders was well advanced, the continuity of these virtues was being questioned. Central government's first foray into legislation over sport and recreation, The Physical Welfare and Recreation Act, 1937, was supported by Parliamentarians on the grounds that levels of health and physical fitness of young men had declined, rendering many of them unfit for military service at a time when Germany was threatening its European neighbours and a military role for the British Empire was in prospect (Gidlow, Cushman and Perkins, 1995).

As the twentieth century progressed, rugby's role as an index of national character grew until the sport reached the status of an unofficial religion, a status which seemed particularly evident in rugby 'clashes' with South Africa, clashes which were identified by both sides as 'war' (Nauright, 1997: 92) The *Encyclopaedia* entry attempted to put rugby in its contextual place as New Zealand's 'national game' by admitting that 'it is open to question whether a disproportionate amount of physical and mental energy is not expended on rugby football', while contending that New Zealanders' love of the game was comparable to the 'devotion of Englishmen to the association game or Americans to baseball' (Burdon, 1966: 675). Missing from this analysis is the pan-class nature of New Zealand rugby (absent from British association football but present in American baseball), but Burdon did attempt to unpack some of Rugby's appeal by noting dryly that in the suburban environment of mid-1960s New Zealand, there was 'still a widespread inner conviction that virtue attaches to pastimes which demand physical endurance and in which one is liable to get hurt' (Burdon, 1966: 675).

The high levels of sports participation and organization observed by Burdon were sustained by government legislation which discouraged or flatly eliminated commercial competition for New Zealanders' discretionary time. This legislation limited the working week to forty hours, penalised overtime with heavy taxation and limited shop trading hours. The Shops and Offices Act (1904) had permitted trading hours of 7.00 am to 6.00 pm four days a week, 8.00 am to 9.00 pm one day a week and until 1.00 pm one day a week, with Sunday reserved for rest and religious observance (Kennedy, 2010: 626). In the 1920s, these restrictions were gradually relaxed, with such retailers as bakers, confectioners, fishmongers, fruiterers and pork butchers receiving exemptions allowing them to trade for extended hours. In the years immediately following

World War Two, the Labour Government tightened the last bolts on the 'Kiwi weekend' by reintroducing near-universal prohibition of weekend trading, though evidence suggests that some degree of overt and covert flouting of an overly complex set of regulations regularly occurred.

As well as contributing to high rates of participation in organized urban and non-urban active leisure, these legal limitations on urban entertainment opportunities contributed to the success of private clubs, horse racing tracks and a DIY culture of gardening and home improvements. In even the smallest towns, rugby clubs hosted weekly after-match functions while workingmen's clubs, golf and bowls clubs, the Returned Servicemen's Association (RSA) and other membership-based venues provided a range of entertainment options. In Littledene, a rural Canterbury community, for example, the Workingmen's Club played 'an important part in the life of the district', and its membership encompassed sixty per cent of the area's adult male population (Somerset, 1938: 44). While 'the chief attraction of the Club' lay 'in its license to sell alcoholic liquors', other draw cards included a lending library of about 3000 books, mostly of 'transient fiction', facilities for billiards, quoits and cards, a radio and copies of five different daily and weekly newspapers (Somerset, 1938: 45). Despite its proletarian title, the Club attracted a broad range of members including, 'business men, farmers, artisans, and labourers' (Somerset, 1938: 44). The fact that half of the Club's 260 members, or about thirty per cent of the area's adult male population, borrowed an average of forty books each from the library, suggests that reading was a popular leisure activity (Somerset, 1938: 45).

The popularity of the Workingmen's Club library provides an indication of an alternative New Zealand leisure culture to that of rugby, racing and beer. Twentieth century New Zealanders were happy consumers of entertainment which was light, amusing and imported from 'abroad'. It is unlikely that the 'transient fiction' read by members of the Workingmen's Club was local; in the year that Somerset's own book was published – 1938 – for example, only three other books were written in or about the Canterbury region, and of these, only one – *Remembering Things*, J.H.E. Schroder's 'volume of essays in lighter vein' – might be described as creative writing (Johnstone, 1956: 115). Similarly, cinemas, which were enthusiastically attended by New Zealanders through the inter- and post-war eras, played films imported from Hollywood and Ealing; between 1940 and 1972, a total of only five feature films were produced locally (Belich, 2001).

The resolute, restrictive, 'low-brow' preferences of New Zealanders in the immediate post-World War II period were explored by Bill Pearson in his first (and only) major novel *Coal Flat* (1963) and in an influential literary piece which followed, entitled *Fretful Sleepers: A Sketch of New Zealand Behaviour and Its Implications for the Artist* (1952). Pearson spent most of the 1950s in London, pursuing a PhD (1952) at King's College and escaping what he saw as its suffocating conformity of New Zealand society, an impression no doubt sharpened by his sexual 'differentness'.

One of the few contemporary writers to examine (and perhaps celebrate) New Zealanders' love affair with imported 'low-brow' entertainment was novelist Ronald Hugh Morrieson. His darkly humorous tales of murder and mayhem in small-town New Zealand portrayed a society in the thrall of Hollywood, where the buttoned-down constraint of government legislation and societal opprobrium was countered by an underground world of incorrigible fantasists and reprobates. Morrieson, himself a determinedly small-town alcoholic who lived in unusual domestic circumstances, taught music and played in dance bands, was criticized for his vernacular voice as he wove Americanized slang into the speech of his Kiwi protagonists. The intrinsic sex and violence within his novels was also out-of-step with the 'high culture' style then in vogue in the nascent New Zealand literary scene. It is significant, nevertheless, that in the 1980s, the youthful New Zealand film industry made three of his four novels into films, with the fourth making the conversion to the big screen in 2009, confirming the posthumous plaudit that 'it is doubtful whether the anti-puritan underside of New Zealand small-town life has ever been so vigorously caught' (Lawrence Jones, quoted by Evans, 1998).

Unfortunately for Morrieson, when mid-century New Zealanders did turn to local books, they tended to prefer those which confirmed rather than exposed the hearty pioneering myth. An embryonic literary tradition had begun to coalesce in a handful of publications and institutions, especially the Caxton Press in Christchurch, the literary magazine *Landfall* (which first published 'Fretful Sleepers) and the *Listener*, a radio and television guide which also carved a liberal high-brow niche for itself on New Zealand's magazine stands. Poets and writers such as Charles Brasch, Denis Glover and Frank Sargison injected a 'New Zealand voice' into works which commonly explored issues of nationality and identity.

Popular literature also tended to emphasise landscape as a marker of national identity. Pioneering memoirs, local histories, stories of high-country stations (ranches), tales from the bush and picture books full of photogenic landscapes provided the staple of the local publishing industry. Barry Crump is the best remembered (and most widely read) of a generation of young male writers who retold their experience as government-paid deer hunters in 'the bush'. For those wishing for a more inclusive, blood-free virtual adventure, there existed a formidable tradition of tramping and climbing books such as John Pascoe's *Unclimbed New Zealand* (1938) and Edmund Hillary's *High Adventure* (Hillary, 1955). Tales of 'high country' stations, both pioneering and contemporary, made a third stream of outdoor-centric literature. While the works of Crump and the achievements of Hillary have provided several lifetimes' worth of research possibilities on the role of masculinity and the mythology of the idealized (male) New Zealander, less has been written on the relationship between New Zealand's considerable canon of outdoor literature and the development of tramping, climbing, pig hunting and deer stalking as popular activities.

Pascoe, for example, was 'a well known tramper, mountaineer and photographer' who wrote extensively and influentially on these outdoor pursuits over a lifetime career (Ross, 2008: 143). He provides a startling and prolific example of the contradictory, twentieth century Pakeha man, being urban and educated, a government bureaucrat, a writer and a photographer, but also inclined to 'go bush' at every opportunity. Pascoe profoundly admired the practicality, strength and stoicism of the musterers and deer cullers who formed the prototype for the idealized New Zealand man, yet his own forays to the mountains were not wholly gendered experiences. Female trampers and climbers accompanied him on extremely rigorous trips, and he was a vocal opponent of purely athletic tramping, preferring to recount the quality of a trip in terms other than distance covered. Pascoe, like Hillary and Crump, was clearly inspired by tales of Imperial adventure, but neither his writing nor his lifelong love affair with the bush can be dismissed as a crudely masculinist escape from feminine-ruled domesticity. It is thus somewhat perplexing that male and female trampers are largely missing from the gendered mythology of the New Zealand outdoors, and equally missing from academic critiques of that mythology. The apotheosis of outdoorism as a 'quintessentially Kiwi' quality may have been reached not with Hillary's 1953 ascent of Everest, but rather with the ascent of another Aucklander, self-confessed climber, skier and tramper Helen Clark, to the post of Prime Minister of New Zealand in 1999.

Membership of tramping clubs bore obvious logistical advantages for those wishing to travel to and through New Zealand's sometimes-inhospitable wilderness landscapes and provided literal truth of the old adage 'safety in numbers'. That clubs in general were an instinctive mode of regulating access and improving perceptions of safety is demonstrated by a decision made in the 1950s by the Masterton Borough Council to ban private boaters from the artificial lake at the centre of its public park (Winter, 2008: 187–8). Instead, the lake remained the province of a boating club and a commercial operation which hired out rowboats and provided the Council with a substantial revenue stream. When a father wrote to the council asking if his son could paddle his home-made canoe on the lake, the Council replied with a suggestion that the town's youths should form a suitable club in order to legitimately use the lake. For such bodies as the Council, the default modes for legitimized leisure were a bureaucratic club structure or a commercial operation.

The introduction of television to New Zealand audiences in 1960 contributed in a significant way to the development of more 'passive', individualized and home-centred leisure and recreational pursuits in the second half of the 20th century. Even before this, however, Somerset observed a decline in the popularity of Littledene's Workingmen's Club after returning in the late 1940s and early 1950s. Increased prosperity and improved communications were facilitating new and more individualized ways for rural New Zealanders, like their urban cousins, to spend their leisure time (Somerset, 1974).

Rugby, Riots and Racism: The 1981 Springbok Tour

Two events are routinely pinpointed as heralding the end of rugby union as New Zealand's 'sporting' 'religion'. Greg McGee's play 'Foreskin's Lament' was an insider's critique of both rugby (McGee was an All-Black Trialist) and New Zealand's cultural and moral drift during the middle years of the twentieth century. McGee's play used rugby as a metaphor to examine the strengths and ultimate failings of New Zealand male culture, and to expose the coming-of-age angst of those who had lost faith in their own cultural myths. As such, it preceded (and perhaps inspired) a range of academic enquiry into the relationship between rugby and New Zealand identity.

The poignancy of 'Foreskin's Lament,' together with its critical and popular success, was heightened by the 1981 Springbok Tour. The Tour broke international sanctions against sporting contact with the Apartheid state of South Africa. The New Zealand Rugby Football Union (NZRFU) had consistently espoused the line that politics should be kept out of sport, a refrain which was taken up by New Zealand's Prime Minister Robert Muldoon. As Prime Minister (1975–84) and Minister of Finance, Muldoon lead his National Party with a mixture of bullying autocracy and sharp political savvy. Although he acknowledged that allowing rugby exchanges between New Zealand and South Africa would cause profound unrest domestically and internationally, Muldoon's innate social conservatism and populist 'ordinary bloke' political style, kept him from vetoing a Springbok visit. Behind the scenes, his Government asked the NZRFU not to go ahead with the Tour, but New Zealand rugby's governing body remained intransigent, secure in the knowledge that rugby was more important than politics, and Muldoon, with electoral advantage in mind, refused to press the point. In the context of British Commonwealth politics, this contravened the Commonwealth's 'Gleneagles Agreement', to which Muldoon's National Government had been a signatory.

The 1981 Springbok Tour was a watershed in New Zealand's political and social histories. Anti-Tour activism coalesced around Halt All Racist Tours (HART), but included a wide range of Maori protesters, feminists, and those from various shades of the political left, for whom the Rugby Union's intransigence was a symptom that racial intolerance extended beyond the shores of South Africa. The diverse commitments of Tour opponents fuelled pro-Tour charges that the protestors were merely a 'rent-a-mob' of habitual malcontents and communist agitators. After protests forced the abandonment of a game in Hamilton, police 'drew a line' in Wellington by halting a protest march outside Parliament with the use of batons. Further protests were marred by violent clashes between protestors, the Police and pro-Tour rugby fans. Television footage and still images of helmeted protesters, doing battle with 'Red Squad' riot police became a potent symbol of the Tour. It split the nation, pitted communities and even family members against each other, in a way not seen in previous protests, even that which most roused public ire in the 1960s – the proposal to raise the level of pristine Lake Manapouri in Fiordland to facilitate downstream aluminium smelting (Warne, 2009).

1981 was the high-tide mark of a generation of protest which bestrode the 1970s. That the most violent and cathartic of these demonstrations should have been prompted by a leisure activity – the ostensibly amateur game of rugby union – may seem ironic, but not accidental. Rugby's success as New Zealand's 'national game' had become its weakness. For young baby-boomers who chaffed at the bonds of conformity and social stability, rugby, authority and orthodoxy had become synonymous. Almost three decades after the violence and social upheaval, reminiscences by Ron Don, the Auckland Rugby Union's Chairman at the time of the Tour, remained unapologetic and representative of mid-century self-righteousness:

> Needless to say, I was very pro-tour. I don't regret anything that was said or done in 1981. After the tour, the anti-tour groups were always referred to by

> the media as peaceful protestors. Now these same protestors did tremendous damage to golf clubs, bowling clubs and even fired a shotgun into my home. But we won. We beat the protestors; we beat the media, and most important of all we beat the Springboks (Ron Don, 2006).

In Don's account, the wider political issues central to the conflict are neatly sidestepped, and protestor violence (misbehaviour) becomes the dominant issue. Moreover, the targets of protestor violence that he cites are symbolic of the idealized suburban life – golf clubs, bowling clubs and a private home. Don almost seems unconscious of the image he draws of conformity versus nonconformity. Extending this impression still further, the 'most important' outcome of the 1981 Tour was, for Don, New Zealand's sporting success over the Springboks, more important even than 'some of the most violent civil unrest the country had ever been through' (Bingham, 2001). Don's affirmation also contrasts sharply with the assessment of a front-line riot policeman that 'no one won, everybody lost' in the 1981 Springbok Tour.

Following the Tour, there was no resumption of the normality of a previous generation. Despite Don's insistence that 'we' won, the 1981 Tour demonstrated that a cross-section of New Zealanders identified themselves as a different 'we' from him. Furthermore, his 'we' appeared for the first time to be unfashionable. The genie had been let out from its bottle and no longer could the conceit be maintained that rugby was the national religion, the game of 'everyman'. The duality of being a liberal, educated rugby player, expressed by McGee in 'Foreskin's Lament', had become crystalline to the point of fragility. Overall, rugby now lost ground against a widening range of leisure choices. The 1982 qualification of the national 'All-Whites' football team in the FIFA Soccer World Cup provided an unexpected, if temporary, fillip for association football in New Zealand, and provided a Tour-weary New Zealand public with a national sports team which could be backed without making an overt political statement.

Politically, the 1981 Springbok tour had provided Muldoon with a one-term reprieve by helping to secure the provincial vote. From 1981 to 1984, the National Party clung to power with a one seat advantage under New Zealand's then First Past the Post voting system. In 1984, however, the desire for social and political change symbolized by the anti-tour protests sent voters in droves to the Labour Party which swept into political office in a landslide.

Paying to Play: Leisure in the Wake of 'Rogernomics'

The Fourth Labour Government is remembered for the swashbuckling verbal largess of its leader, David Lange, its Anti-Nuclear policy and, most lastingly, an aggressive, neo-liberal, free-market economic experiment dubbed 'Rogernomics' after its architect, Labour's Minister of Finance, Roger Douglas. In contrast to the tradition of 'insulationism' pursued by his predecessors, and in keeping with the new 'liberal' orthodoxy driving Treasuries in the US and UK, Douglas 'decided simply to throw overboard the entire policy framework of the preceding half century, allow deregulated markets free reign and see what emerged' (Bertram, 2010: 558). Under Rogernomics, state assets were 'privatized', the control of money-flows in and out of the country was lifted, runaway inflation was reigned in through tight monetary policy and a ballooning fiscal deficit was reduced by floating the New Zealand Dollar. Arguably, this classic neoliberal regimen was dictated by the tattered state in which Muldoon had left the country's books, but this 'selling of the family jewels' by a Labour cabinet was nevertheless disorientating to New Zealanders reared in an environment of state intervention, full employment and paternalistic social policy. Adding to the pain of adjustment to the new, *laissez faire*, reality, was Douglas' belief in the necessity of 'quantum leaps' towards clearly defined objectives in order to avoid getting 'dragged down' by interest groups (Douglas, 1993: 200–201). This view, that interest groups were '... vested interests that should be excluded from policy-making', stood in direct contrast to the tradition of participation policy-making by both ends of New Zealand's political spectrum (Goldfinch, 2000: 199–201).

The Fourth Labour Government's rejection of insulationist tradition extended beyond asset sales, abandonment of trade tariffs and slashing of production subsidies; it also lifted protections on what had previously been identified as the 'Kiwi way of life'. A tension already existed between the amateur, do-it-yourself, club-orientated, outdoorsy leisure of the 'quintessential Kiwi' and the developed, consumerist leisure culture of excursion trips, radios, movie theatres, race tracks and, eventually, radio and television. The reaction of the New Zealand public to Labour's deregulation of leisure showed that previous limits on the range and extent of commercialized leisure opportunities were imposed not by the size of the leisure market itself, but by legislative restriction on public access to alcohol, gambling, shopping and similar urban distractions. Between 1984 and 1990, the strict limitations on weekend trading were lifted, and with tariffs on imported consumer durables steadily falling, shopping malls now competed with playing fields, suburban sections and the great outdoors for New Zealanders' discretionary time (see Table 1). Supermarkets and big box retailers also extended their trading hours, requiring the introduction of shift-work retailing, potentially placing a twenty-first century checkout operator in a similar position *vis-à-vis* leisure opportunities as a nineteenth century shop clerk. The mid-twentieth century world of evening clubs and weekend sports was no longer automatically accessible to working New Zealanders.

Table 1

Use of Leisure Facilities (%) in 1990

Facility	*(%)*
Shopping Centre	56
Beach/river/lake	52
Restaurant	46
Club facility	37
Library	32
Video hire shop	25
Urban park/playground	23
Cinema	18
Sports field	18
Gym	13

Source: Cushman and Laidler (1991)

A still more radical loosening of the protective cocoon occurred when the fifth (Clark) Labour Government passed the Prostitution Reform Act 2003, decriminalizing prostitution (including street prostitution), brothels and escort agencies. This liberalization has not met with universal approval. A poll (2011) which asked 1,000 people if the Act should be amended to ban brothels from residential areas returned a 66 per cent affirmative result (Leask, 2011). Moreover, when respondents were asked if the Act should be amended to ban street prostitution, 50 per cent of respondents replied yes, 33 per cent no and 17 per cent were unsure (Leask, 2011). In lieu of such changes, successive Governments have left it to local territorial authorities (municipal and district councils) to regulate acceptable sites for prostitution.

A similar tension between tolerance and prohibition has continued to be felt in the wake of liberalized access to alcohol. Two particularly thorny issues have been the lowering of the legal purchasing age for alcohol from 20 to 18 years, and the proliferation of 'off license' alcohol retailers (primarily supermarkets and dairies). The number of liquor licences more than doubled from 6,295 to 14,183 in the two decades following deregulation under the Sale of Liquor Act, 1989 (Alcohol law reform, 2010). In 1998, the concentration of liquor outlets in the 'poorer parts' of Auckland – New Zealand's biggest and most culturally diverse city – came to national attention after the murder of a South Auckland liquor store owner in an inept robbery attempted by a loosely organized group of young men. Anger over the death was aimed, for the most part, not at youth violence, but instead at the high number of liquor stores in the area, which were seen to fuel violent crime ('Many blame number of liquor outlets for violent crime in Manukau,' 2008).

A further perennial concern over alcohol was a so-called 'binge drinking culture', something which New Zealand shared with other, developed, countries, including Australia. Historically, binge drinking might be identified as a legacy of a male culture rooted in the episodic work and leisure cycle of ships crews, bush camps and goldfields. Belich, for example, identified a male-centric cycle of privation and binging as 'crew culture' while Phillips (1987) applied to it the 'mateship' tag coined by Russel Ward (1958) in Australia.

Arguably, the strong mid-twentieth century legislative restriction on sites of alcohol consumption fostered rather than stymied the perception of drinking as a discrete leisure activity to be pursued for its own ends. There remains a suspicion, however, that recent trends towards binge drinking are driven as much by affordability, availability and advertising as they are by historical attitudes and legislation ('Alcohol Use in New Zealand: Key Results of the 2007/08 New Zealand Alcohol and Drug Use Survey,' 2009). The equal prevalence of women and men as consumers of large amounts of alcohol also undermines the male-centric stereotype of binge drinkers.

With community concern over the availability of alcohol politicized in the wake of the 2008 liquor store killing, South Auckland city councillors argued that local bodies should have a part in the liquor licensing process. New Zealand's then Prime Minister Helen Clark echoed the concern, and a review by the Law Commission was ordered.

Key policy recommendations made by the Commission included returning the minimum purchase age for alcohol to 20 and strengthening the rights and responsibilities of parents for the supply of alcohol to minors (Publication_154_465_Press Release Alcohol in our Lives R114.pdf, n.d.).

These recommendations represented a return to a more insulationist approach to leisure choices than those favoured by governments of the previous 25 years. It is thus not surprising that the National Government's response fell short of the level of regulation suggested by the Commission. Nevertheless, a number of key restrictions on access to alcohol were adopted in the Alcohol Reform Bill (2010). Many of its proposals specifically concentrated on the perceived problem of youth drinking (Parliamentary Library Law and Government, 2010), while at the same time it also sought to reintroduce restrictions on alcohol availability across the board (Parliamentary Library Law and Government, 2010).

The Alcohol Reform Bill (2010) did propose 'making it an offence to promote alcohol in a way that has special appeal to people under the purchase age', a half-hearted acknowledgment that the relationship between rugby union and liquor promotion was not problem-free. Until television advertising of alcohol was legalized in 1992, sports events provided one of the few means by which advertisers could legitimately display their alcoholic wares on television screens. The sponsorship of the All Blacks in 1986 by brewer Lion Nathan, and the appearance of its lager brand on the players' jerseys was a harbinger of a more comprehensive commercialization of rugby.

Rugby's professionalization in 1995 provided an odd and somewhat complex boost to the concept of rugby as New Zealand's unofficial religion. The forces of commercialization and the know-how of multi-national advertising agencies worked assiduously to centralise the All-Black 'brand' in New Zealand's national consciousness. In doing so, they created slick campaigns which both drew upon and strengthened the everyman image of rugby, reasserting the rugby-as-nation mythology. But as rugby and the All Blacks became 'brands', this reestablishment of rugby fandom as a badge of everyman kiwi identity had as much to do with establishing rugby as an international commodity in a crowded leisure marketplace as it did with defining New Zealand identity.

With the shift of live sport to pay-to-view, following the deregulation of television broadcasting licensing in 1988 and which ushered in multi-channel viewing and private provision, including Sky, some commentators despaired at what they saw as over-commercialization. Such an argument seems oblivious to the short history of televised sport. Although an experimental broadcast of the second half of the Barbarians versus Harlequins match was made from the North island town of Waihi in 1954, six years before television's official introduction to New Zealand (a power cut prevented broadcast of the first half), the NZRFU was, until the early 1970s, generally reluctant to break its own monopoly on live viewing by allowing live television coverage of test matches. In the halcyon era of post-war rugby, New Zealanders expected to pay to sit or stand in a stadium and watch their 'national game'. The fundamental shift has, therefore, not been one of payment, but of venue. Mass, stadium-based sport spectatorship has, along with other passive and active forms of leisure and recreation, faced increased competition from privatized leisure opportunities facilitated by the ubiquity of electronic broadcast media.

Horse racing also faced increased competition in a deregulated leisure marketplace. Between 1987 and 1989, the introduction of a weekly televised lottery (Lotto) and electronic gaming machines ('pokies') in pubs and clubs challenged racing's supremacy as New Zealand's primary avenue for legal gambling. Between 1987 and 2000, racing's share of the gambling dollar dropped from 85 per cent to 18 per cent (Phillips, 2010). Complicit in this shift was a widening of the brief of the Government-run Totalisator Agency Board (TAB). Founded in 1951 to provide legal off-track venues for betting on horse races, the TAB was designed to counter the prevalence of illegal off-track gambling, a task at which it was only partially successful, at best (Austrin, 1998: 173). By the mid-1990s, the TAB's role as a means by which the Government could limit and control gambling opportunities had been abandoned and the Agency worked instead to maintain or increase the Government's share of the gambling market (Austrin, 1998: 175). Innovations such as telephone (and, later, online) betting, international betting, television advertising and, from 1996, sports betting facilitated this goal. The guiding rationale behind the Government's control and expansion of gambling was 'to make better provision for the conduct of games of chance, prize competitions, and lotteries for amusement and for raising funds for certain purposes while continuing to prohibit the conduct of such activities for commercial gain' (Gaming and Lotteries Act, 1977).

The 'take' from these new and existing gambling opportunities – Lotto, pokies and the TAB was drawn almost exclusively from local gamblers. The forth innovation in gambling opportunities introduced in the 1990s targeted both local and international gamblers. Since 1994, six casinos have been granted licenses to operate in New Zealand (one each in Auckland, Hamilton, Christchurch and Dunedin and two in Queenstown). The Casinos were established and controlled under the Casino Control Act (1990), which now 'permitted private gain and regarded casinos as a means to stimulate economic and regional development' (Abbott and Volberg, 1999: 23), often because of its popularity among certain types of inbound tourist.

As indicated above, revenue from state-controlled gambling was directed towards charities and incorporated societies via agencies such as the Lotteries Grant Board and Pub Charity (which controlled gaming machines). While increased access to both public and private forms of commercial leisure profoundly altered New Zealand's leisure landscape, clubs and voluntary associations continued to enjoy widespread popularity and the public sector – notably local authorities – continued to promote recreation-for-all, using a rates-based rather than a pay-per-use funding regime. At the end of the twentieth century, 'approximately one in five adults' belonged to a sports club ('Adults – club membership, coaching and competition,' 2011). Men belonged to sports clubs at a higher rate (27%) than women (16%) indicating that the gendered division in New Zealand leisure had continued into the twenty-first century (ibid.).

New Zealanders also participated in the arts in large numbers. In 2000, 2.37 million adults took part in 'close to four different types of arts activity every month'; the vast majority of these did so for enjoyment and entertainment (Heart of the Nation Strategic Working Group, 2000).

It is an irony of the contemporary situation of sport, leisure and recreation in New Zealand that the loosening up of provision and the regulations and licencing which formerly surrounded them, have been accompanied by ever-tighter regulation of health and safety aspects in their implementation. The 1995 collapse of a public viewing platform in a South Island national park administered by a central government department (the Department of Conservation), a 2008 canyoning disaster in the North Island, as well as a number of jet-boating accidents (1999, 2008, 2009, 2010), have been seen to dent New Zealand's reputation for the provision of adrenaline-pumping yet risk-free outdoor adventure experiences. These health and safety concerns are not, however, limited to adventure recreation; they now apply to most recreation behaviour contexts, including the design of children's playgrounds (Ministry of Education, 2005) and school and university field trips/visits.

Conclusion

It is paradoxical that the public façade of New Zealand leisure seems so shaped by the landscape – bush, beach and sprawling suburbia – when it might equally be argued that it is this landscape which reflects New Zealand's social and political mores, including those which govern leisure. National parks, beaches, suburban gardens, rugby stadiums and playing fields provide very public evidence of popular leisure activities. Other sites, such as the race tracks which inhabit the outskirts of towns and cities, or the lonely public halls which mark geographic locations otherwise identifiable only as names on a map, stand as monuments to past leisure powerhouses: regular race meetings and Saturday night dances. Yet evidence from historic sources and recent surveys suggest that a gap remains between a public persona which is, after-all, an image, and the broader recreation interests of New Zealanders. Magazines and newspapers, radio, cinema and television all fed New Zealanders a steady diet of exotic leisure opportunities somewhat at odds with the restricted world of six o'clock closing, weekend gardening and Sunday drives. The radical social and economic restructuring of the 1980s and 90s, and the development of new electronic broadcast media – pay-to-view television and the Internet – have proved unsettling to cherished beliefs about how New Zealanders like to spend their spare time. While nostalgia for seemingly-lost leisure traditions is often expressed, the enthusiasm with which new opportunities to gamble, eat, drink, shop, watch television and surf the net suggests that legislative restriction played a crucial role in shaping New Zealand's leisure landscape throughout much of the twentieth century.

Notes

1. 'Get maximum of work for minimum of pay out of workers' Fowler, F.G. and Fowler H.W. (eds) *Pocket Oxford Dictionary*, 1970, page 859, Oxford University Press.
2. This referred to a traditional form of secret ballot where members dropped a coloured ball, white for affirmative or black for negative, in a specially constructed box.

References

Abbott, M.W., and Volberg, R.A. (1999). *Gambling and Problem Gambling in the Community: an International Overview and Critique.* (No. One). The New Zealand Gaming Survey. Wellington: Department of Internal Affairs.

Adults – club membership, coaching and competition. (2011). *SPARC - Active N.Z. Survey*. Retrieved 12 June 2011, from http://www.activenzsurvey.org.nz/Results/NZ-Sport-and-Physical-Surveys-9701/SPARC-Facts-97-01/Part-3/Adults–club-membership-coaching-and-competition/

Alcohol law reform: Why is change needed? (22 April 2010). *TVNZ*. Retrieved 1 May 2011, from http://tvnz.co.nz/national-news/alcohol-law-reform-why-change-needed-3485403

Alcohol Use in New Zealand: Key results of the 2007/08 New Zealand Alcohol and Drug Use Survey. (2009). New Zealand Ministry of Health.

Austrin, T. (1998). Retailing Leisure: Local and Global Developments in Gambling. In H. Perkins and G. Cushman (eds), *Time Out? Leisure, Recreation and Tourism in new Zealand and Australia.* Auckland: Addison Wesley Longman New Zealand.

Belich, J. (2001). *Paradise Reforged: A History of the New Zealanders from the 1880s to the year 2000*. Auckland: Allen Lane; The Penguin Press.

Belich, J. (2002). *Making Peoples: A History of the New Zealanders, from Polynesian Settlement to the End of the Nineteenth Century*. University of Hawai'i Press.

Best, E. (1925). *Games and pastimes of the Maori.* Wellington: Whitcombe and Tombs.

Bingham, E. (11 August 2001). The code of silence over a tour's infamous bashing - National - N.Z. Herald News. *nzherald.co.nz*. Retrieved 16 April 2011, from http://www.nzherald.co.nz/nz/news/article.cfm?c_id=1&objectid=206678

Burdon, R.M. (1966). New Zealand Society. In A.H. McLintock (ed.), *An Encyclopaedia of New Zealand* (Vols. 1–3, Vol. 2). Wellington: R.E. Owens, Government Printer.

Douglas, R. (1993). *Unfinished Business*. Auckland: Random House.

Drummond, J. (1907). *The Life and Work of Richard John Seddon (Premier of New Zealand, 1893–1906); With a History of the Liberal Party of New Zealand*. Christchurch: Whitcombe and Tombs, Ltd.

Evans, P. (1998). Morrieson, Ronald Hugh. *New Zealand Book Council Te Kaunihera Pukapuka o Aotearoa*. Retrieved 9 June 2011, from http://www.bookcouncil.org.nz/Writers/Profiles/Morrieson,%20Ronald%20Hugh

Gardner, J.A. (1988). A Colonial Economy. In W.H. Oliver and B.R. Williams (eds), *The Oxford History of New Zealand*. Clarendon press.

Goldfinch, S. (2000). *Remaking New Zealand and Australian Economic Policy: Ideas, Institutions and Policy Communities*. Victoria University Press.

Heart of the Nation Strategic Working Group. (2000). *The Heart of the Nation: A Cultural Strategy for Aotearoa New Zealand.* Wellington: McDemott Miller Ltd.

Hillary, E. (1955). *High Adventure*. BCL Press.

Johnstone, A.H. (1956). *Canterbury Books, 1847–1955: A Bibliography*. Christchurch: Whitcombe and Tombs, Ltd.

Kennedy, A.-M. (2010). The history of New Zealand shop trading hours. *International Journal of Retail & Distribution Management*, 38(8), 625–640. doi:10.1108/09590551011057444

Kiwiana, Christchurch City Libraries. (n.d.). Retrieved 5 April 2011, from http://christchurchcitylibraries.com/Society/Culture/New-Zealand/

Leask, A. (6 April 2011). Keep brothels away from our homes - poll. *New Zealand Herald*. Retrieved from http://www.nzherald.co.nz/nz/news/article.cfm?c_id=1&objectid=10717312

Many blame number of liquor outlets for violent crime in Manukau. (2008). *TVNZ*. Retrieved 11 June 2011, from http://tvnz.co.nz/content/1843666/423466/article.html

McDonald, C. (2009). Ways of Belonging: Sporting Spaces in New Zealand History. In G. Byrnes (ed.), *The New Oxford History of New Zealand* (pp. 269–296). Melbourne: Oxford University Press.

Nauright, J. (1997). *Sport, Cultures, and Identities in South Africa*. Continuum International Publishing Group.

Nelson Chronicle and New Zealand Examiner. (1 October 1842). *Nelson Examiner and New Zealand Chronicle*. Nelson.

Olssen, E. (1995). *Building the New World: Work, Politics, and Society in Caversham, 1880s-1920s*. Auckland University Press.

Parliamentary Library Law and Government. (11 November 2010). Alcohol Reform Bill 2010: Bills Digest 1814. Retrieved 11 June 2011, from http://www.parliament.nz/en-NZ/PB/Legislation/Bills/BillsDigests/b/5/c/49PLLawBD18141-Alcohol-Reform-Bill-2010-Bills-Digest-1814.htm

Phillips, J. (2009). Time and society, 1870s–1930s. *Te Ara - the Encyclopedia of New Zealand*. Web page, Retrieved 6 June 2011, from http://www.teara.govt.nz/en/timekeeping/3

Phillips, J. (2010). Gambling. Web page. Retrieved 21 April 2011, from http://www.teara.govt.nz/en/sports-and-leisure/2

Publication_154_465_Press Release Alcohol in our Lives R114.pdf. (n.d.). Retrieved from http://www.lawcom.govt.nz/sites/default/files/press-releases/2010/04/Publication_154_465_Press%20Release%20Alcohol%20in%20our%20Lives%20R114.pdf

Ross, K. (2008). *Going Bush: New Zealanders and Nature in the Twentieth Century*. Auckland: Auckland University Press.

Somerset, H.C.D. (1938). *Littledene: A New Zealand Rural Community*. Wellington: New Zealand Council for Education Research.

The Nelson Scientific and Literary Institution. (2 April 1842). *Nelson Examiner and New Zealand Chronicle*.

The Premier And The Footballers. (18 October 1905). *Marlborough Express*, 3.

Webb, B., and Webb, S. (1959). *Visit to New Zealand*. Wellington: Price Millburn.

Wilson, J. (2009). Liberal to Labour. *Te Ara The Encyclopedia of New Zealand*. Web page. Retrieved 6 June 2011, from http://www.teara.govt.nz/en/history/5

Winter, G. (2008). *A Very Publick Reserve: The Story of a Community's Parks*. Masterton: Wairarapa Archive/Fraser Books.

Asia

3

The Mapping of Leisure in Chinese Cultural Tradition

MA HUIDI

I

Introduction

Profound principles are underlying and expressed in the people enjoy of leisure in ancient China. It was produced in a special temperament, mood and flow, grounded in literature and philosophy. Because of muscles being in rest, blood circulation regular, breathing smooth, nervous system in rest; all the senses (vision, hearing) contribute to the body being completely calm when people in a state of relaxation. So that the people are in a flow of concentration, the thought being agile, the mind free, and thus we can appreciate, can perceive in an optimum way the goodness of life and the beauty of nature.

There is no doubt that it brings physical and mental health, the establishment of cultural values, and also contributes to building a good way of life, if we use and assign leisure time wisely.

In ancient China, leisure is not only a kind of philosophy, but it often is reflected through prospering in poetry, in ritual, in music and in life practice. It is like an invisible ribbon folded around life and labour and it well-nourished the Chinese intelligence and diligence, ingenuity, morality and a cultural ethos, encompassing thousands of years and manifesting itself through various categories of leisure activities, such as: music, chess, calligraphy and painting, poetry, Classic work, Qigong, Taichi, Zen and other skills. Not only to live with pleasure, but also to raise and nourish in a person the ability to create. The approach to leisure in this paper will be from the perspective of Etymology, Confucianism, Buddhism, Daoism; ancient scholars massing life to explore the path through history of Chinese leisure culture tradition, to pay attention to the value of leisure, and also to reflect the people in contemporary in China, who are now living in confusion and are exhausted because of lack of leisure life and idea.

II

Leisure Conception and Practice in Etymological Perspective

Various meanings of leisure (*xiuxian* 休闲) in China's cultural tradition can be traced far back. Etymology can furnish a basis for our interpretations.

As is well-known, Chinese characters were derived from pictographs. Made up of the characters for *ren* (person 人) and *mu* (tree 木), the character *xiu* 休 in *xiuxian* depicts a scene where man is in harmony with Nature – a person leaning back on a tree. The traditional form of *xian* 闲 is *xian* 閒, which has the character *yue* 月 (the moon) in it, invoking a poetic scene with a person appreciating the moon in a leisurely mood – a moment of purity of heart and healthy life. *xian* 閒 originally meant *xian* 嫺, which means both following the norms and the purity and tranquillity of one's intellectual and spiritual world, thus showing man in harmony with himself and with Nature.

xiuxian thus signifies man blending into Nature, reminding us that man is part of Nature and that it is only natural that he should venerate Nature. In ancient times, the Chinese used *tiandi* 天地 (heavens and the earth) to mean Nature and treated them as divine. The earth receives the seeds of the five grains and cares for the six domestic animals, enabling people to live in abundance, while the heavens bestows sunlight and rain, as well as the four seasons, each in its own way beautiful. The beauty of Nature nourishes and edifies humanity. All that man does in his leisure is an expression of his love for *tiandi* in its divinity and his piety to return in a modest way *tiandi*'s boundless favour.

The rich meanings of *xiuxian* in this cultural tradition all point to the dialectic relationship between work and recreation in our human existence and the grounding of our spiritual as well as material life activities.

Leisure Conception and Practice from Confucian, Daoist and Zhuangzi

This ideal of leisure can also be found in Confucian, Daoist and Zhuangzi thinking. The Confucian tradition emphasizes governing through rites and establishing benevolent rule and advocates 'starting from poetry, laying a sound foundation for society through rites, and reaching the ideal society through music', with great importance being assigned to recreation, which is embodied in the six arts of rites: music, archery, chariot-driving, calligraphy, and arithmetics. For the Confucians, a rich and colourful leisure life is man's aesthetic activity in its most sublime form.

The Daoists stressed 'quiet observation of the mysterious' as a path to the Way (*dao* 道), highlighting the introspective nature of man and his withdrawal from the world and emphasizing the individual's capacity for comprehending. 'The Dao generates it, virtue (*de* 德) preserves it, matter gives it form, and circumstances brings it to fruition. Thus, myriads of things all venerate the Dao and value virtue. The venerability of the Dao and the high value of virtue are not designated by anyone, but come to be naturally.' (*Laozi*, ch., 51) Thus, the Daoists believe that we should 'always follow the Dao', have the Golden Mean (*zhong* 中) as the measure of things and peacefulness (*ping* 平) as our expectation, so as to realize the coordination and harmony between man's inner world and the external environment. The beauty of humanity is thus perceived and constructed.

Through *xinzhai* 心斋 (mental fasting) and *zuowang* 坐忘 (sitting still to let all thoughts and desires diminish to the extent where one forgets the world and even one's self), Zhuangzi aims at the calming down of inner tensions, movement in accord with time, identification with the world, and thus adaption to all kinds of circumstances. 'Those who comprehend the virtue of *tiandi* know that it is the primordial source in harmony with the heavens and that it works to smooth out the differences among things and is in harmony with humanity. What is in harmony with humanity is called 'the music of man', and what is in harmony with heavens is called 'the music of heavens'. [The Tiandao 天道 (heavenly Dao) chapter in *Zhuangzi*] Following this tradition, *xiaoyao you* 逍遥游, meaning free and easy wandering, where one 'wanders beyond the four seas' and 'appreciates the great beauty of heavens and earth' became the ultimate wisdom of the Chinese with regard to leisure.

Leisure Conception and Practice from Literator Estate and Its Works

The poet Tao Qian of the Eastern Jin Period penned the lines 'Picking chrysanthemum at the fence east to my abode, I chanced to see the mountains in the south.' The Song poet Su Shi noted, 'rivers, mountains, wind, and the moon – none of these has a definite master. It is those who know how to enjoy leisure that receive their services.' And the eminent writer Lin Yutang of the modern era wrote in *The Art of Life*, 'I would be greatly satisfied as long as I am allowed to befriend grass and trees and to get close to the land. My soul feels a great joy as it creeps comfortably in soil. When inebriated with the land, one's soul feels so relieved, as if it is in the Heaven.'

These worthies of the past were both practitioners of the wisdom about leisure they had inherited from China's cultural tradition and great masters who contributed greatly to the enrichment of that wisdom.

Sages and worthies of China's past often associated leisure closely with natural philosophy, personal cultivation, aesthetic tastes, art and literature, and the cultivation of longevity. It is this wisdom about leisure that gave rise to great works of literature all the way from *The Book of Odes* to *The Songs of Chu* (*chuci* 楚辞*), the Han Odes (hanfu* 汉赋*), the parallel verses (pianwen* 骈文*)* of the Wei-Jin Periods, the Tang poems, the Song lyrics, the Yuan drama, and two short essays written by the literati of the Qing Period in their leisure, as well as gestated the cultural trait of *hehe* 合和 (union of and harmony among different elements). Among the general populace, there were also produced many forms of cultural and structural settings for leisure activity, such as: Tai Ji, Qi Gong, Chinese Kungfu, temple fairs, hawking, aviculture, fish watching, fishing, guessing games, *yinglian* 楹联 (couplet hung on the columns of a hall), poetry societies, academies (*shuyuan* 书院), kite-flying, shuttlecock-kicking, boxing, tea-sipping, book fairs, gardens, Chinese painting, *quyi* 曲艺 (Chinese folk art forms including ballad singing, story telling, comic dialogues, clapper talks, cross talks, etc.), wind and stringed instruments, drama, calligraphy, metal and stone inscriptions, and so on, that represent the cream of Chinese culture. These cultural creations give expression to the intelligence and wisdom of the Chinese people, their morality and ethics, and their hardworking and kindheartedness.

Leisure Conception and Practice from Crowds and Its' Life

China was/is known to the world as a 'land of propriety and righteousness' that venerates the teacher and emphasizes education. This is because the Chinese benefited from leisure education, being its cultural carreer, with jiaxun, or house codes of behaviour, compiled by different families in different historical periods. In particular, the benevolence-centred education was the basis of not only moral practice of the Chinese, but also constituted their leisure life. The house codes are a product of China's benevolence-centred culture. In past thousands of years, various 'house codes'[1] (or *Jiaxun* ®aEVcodes of behaviour compiled by different families in various historical periods.) have nourished and nurtured the Chinese people, and were the basic means for propagating the methods for self-cultivation, for managing the household, and for interacting with other people. They also represent a basic form of education for children on the part of parents that has been continued for a long period of time. According to textual study by a modern scholar, the earliest extant 'house codes' are found in *Admonitions for Boqin* (*xun boqin*), composed by Duke of Zhou, son of King Wen of Zhou.

The 'house codes' contain some maxims about how to handle complicated social relationships, such as 'he who gets near vermilion will be reddened, and he who gets near ink will be blackened' (quoted from Fu Xuan of the Western Jin Period) (meaning people are apt to be influenced by the moral character of those with whom they associate closely). These 'house codes' also teach that one ought to be careful in interacting with friends, making a distinction between friends who are likely to have bad influence on oneself and those who are likely to have good influence; that one should try to emulate those around who are better than oneself and to learn the strengths of others where one has shortcomings; that one should learn to excuse others of their errors just as one would like to be excused while reprimanding oneself for errors as one would want to reprimand others; that one should not demand perfection in others, nor to break up with old friends just for some minor mistake on their part. One should be able to see the weaknesses of those one loves, and the strengths of those one dislikes. 'Harmony' is the basic principle for relationships with friends; however, this means not that one should follow one's friends even when they undertake to do evil deeds, and that one should be willing to go through hard times with friends, and that friends should try to encourage one another in their pursuit of noble ideals.

The saying 'learn things and then review them from time to time' emphasize more that knowledge should be put to practice so as to help save the masses. The significance of this saying has been expounded from many different perspectives. Some have pointed out that learning helps to change one's temperament and nurture one's sentiments, while others have advocated that learning is for the purpose of being able to put one's knowledge to use to enrich the people and strengthen the country. Still others have tried to turn learning into an art in life. In reading books, one should try to form one's own view and be able to select good books, rather than be fooled by inferior writings. It is necessary to take in the contents of a book with one's mind, rather than just read it aloud with one's mouth. It is good to follow a proper sequence, going from easier readings to more difficult ones, and to be able to grasp things in a simple and direct manner again after acquiring broad knowledge. Furthermore, it is necessary daily to reflect on one's own thoughts and conduct in view of what one reads.

Because they were easy to read, understand, memorize, recite, and put into practice, as well as closely related to the moral practice of ordinary people, the 'house codes' and beginning texts for children such as *Master Zhu's Maxims for Managing the Household*, the *Three-Character Classic*, and the *Thousand-Character Text* had a profound effect on popular ethical beliefs, norms for conduct, and rituals, becoming model texts used to correct family moral standards and raise family reputation that have been passed on from generation to generation.

Leisure Conception and Practice from the Womanly Work

As well as experience for thousands of years, the womanly work (*nügong*) is the crystallization of the wisdom and talent of women in traditional China, and an important component of the cultural heritage of the Chinese people. 'Womanly work' refers to the needlework by women, such as embroidery and sewing. It is an important part emphasized by various *nüxun* texts.

Nügong is focused on needlework such as sewing, weaving, and embroidery, but by no means limited to these. In other words, on the basis of such common needlework, Chinese women have put their aptitudes and talents to work in creating and developing a large number of art forms, such as spinning, dyeing, sewing, embroidery, the making of shoes and hats, weaving, facial decorations, and toys. For thousands of years, generation after generation of Chinese women have, through their crafts and skills, worked to create art objects, cultivate their mind, and instill truth, goodness, and beauty into the womanly virtues, womanly speech, womanly appearance, and womanly work required of them.

On surface, *nügong* is only a system of making things with some unique features, but it is capable of taking in many other artistic elements. Women have broad scope in choosing the theme, in designing the pattern and configuration, and in applying colours, all of which have helped to deepen the cultural substrate for the cultivation of feminine virtues.

Nügong has doubtlessly had profound effect on womanly virtues in China. First, *nügong* can directly or indirectly foster womanly virtues. Second, it helps to create a spiritual world of goodness and beauty for women, which is then outwardly expressed through their speech, body, postures, acting, and teaching. Third, it has played an important role in forming the role model of the mother for generation after generation of women, especially in their role of giving birth to a later generation, bringing up their children, and inheriting and passing on the feminine virtues of tolerance, goodness, kindness, and dignity through their own earnest practice. This is also one of the reasons why the traditions of *nüxun* and *nügong* have continued for thousands of years without going extinct.

Leisure Conception and Practice from *YIJING ZHIDONG*

YIJING ZHIDONG (attaining motion through tranquillity)*: as a unique leisure philosophy of China* originated in the special cultural milieu of ancient China.

With regard to the relationship between motion and tranquillity, this science advocates *guirou zhujing* (giving great importance to gentleness and tranquillity), which stresses tranquillity. Emphasizing tranquillity does not mean inaction, but means '*zhi xuji, shou jingdu*' (attaining the ultimate of the void and maintaining tranquillity in sincerity), thus achieving *yijing zhidong*. Similarly, gentleness does not mean weakness; rather, in the words of Lao Zi, 'the most gentle in the world can control the toughest in the world'.

With *yijing zhidong*, one aims at *cunxin yangxing* (retaining one's true mind and nurturing one's nature), *xiuxin lianxing* (cultivating one's mind and refining one's nature), or actively exercising the body and the mind by adjusting one's thinking, breathing, and posture.

Major outward expressions of *yijing zhidong* include *qigong*, *taijiquan*, introspection, hobbies such as playing Chinese zither or Chinese chess, calligraphy, painting, writing poetry, and Zen practice, activities intended to bring about experiences resembling the 'flow' as described and theorized on by the psychologist Mihalyi Csikszentmihalyi.[2]

No doubt, from a practical perspective, the goal of leisure is to satisfy people's physiological, psychological, and spiritual needs and to mould and elevate the individual's cultural-spiritual character as education is conducted through entertainment, thus promoting the multi-faceted development of the individual and making leisure time a new cultural resource for fostering people's upbringing and interests.

In its essence, leisure is the practice and experience of life's meaning and of joyful living, as well as an important humanistic cultural phenomenon and the locus of man's ontological meaning. It is an important stage on which the drama of man's 'becoming' is played out and a beautiful home for the human spirit. It is a kind of wisdom for human life, and the most effective approach to developing the civilized society.

III

Leisure ideas as a culture tradition are thousands of year with us. It is regrettable therefore that they were abandoned until today for a period of 100 years under several big cultural revolutions. Actually, in contemporary Chinese society, 'popular cheap manufacturing' goes hand in hand with 'spirit anemia'. Surveys show that most of the interviewees know little about the tradition and history of leisure culture and its values, and increasingly link leisure with consumption and sensory pleasures. This is followed by all kinds of forms of consumerism as well by as a rise in the number of people constantly indulging possessive desires.

For understanding leisure value holds that most people only simply equal those with eating, drinking and playing; in short with joy. Some media show there abandonment of leisure value by creating numerous 'fool' programs, tempting of believers 'star (film) worship', 'money worship', 'and overnight famousness'. The social etiquette always is in a state of disorder. As Mr Liu Mengxi said, 'Since the late Qing dynasty, Chinese culture tradition moved into the difficulty of deconstruction and reconstruction, facing a challenge that includes how to eat, how to sleep, how to wear, how to walk and how to decently speak with people; all issues that basically are in a state of disorder'.

According to the World Luxury Association Report on 11 January 2012: 'by the end of December, 2011, Chinese luxury market consumption is already up to $12.6 billion (not including private plane, yacht and luxury car), occupy 28 per cent of global share'. China has become one of the largest luxury consumer countries. Demonstrative conspicuous consumption in the areas of leisure and vacation became the main goal of rich people. And some of the younger generation's desires are infinite consumption. Recently, Xinhua Agency also reported: 'a 17 year old Chinese young guy to have purchased iPhone and iPad for which he sold one of his kidneys, resulting in disability.'

Just look at National legal holidays such as National Day, Spring Festival and other holidays. All were named 'Golden Week' indicating the appearance and increase in their function for economy, without the solemnity and holiness that, in earlier times, characterized those holidays. Travel, shopping became the major holiday 'themes', as did sensuality and a 'false experience of freedom and relaxation', providing the people the possibility to conceal their emotions of anxiety, hurry and pressure in life.

In China, the group of intellectuals is rising, who are disregarding reading as being of interest. The total number of libraries is whole China is less than 3000, but only a few invest in collecting new books each year and a considerable number of them lost many readers. The reading situation of the general public is a point of increased serious concern. Per capita read are only 0.4 copies/year. In recent years, no betterment could be observed; even reported was on the phenomenon of bankruptcy of some bookstores in the cities.

Recently, CCTV issued the Investigation 2011–2012 on economic life and discovered the existence of a 'a disease in leisure spending' for which it asked universal attention. According to expert statistics, of the phenomenon of 'leisure disease' are suffering mainly three kinds of people. One is a category who mixes work and rest, is busy with work during holidays and for a long time and so their bodies are in a nervous and anxious state. The second category suffers under excessive leisure; not only during their free time on workdays, but also in weekends they go shopping, for outdoor play, take part in carnivals and wallow in entertainment; as a result their bodies get even more tired. Third, there is the time erratic – sleeping until noon and eat breakfast at lunch time, then spend time on Internet, watching TV and stay up late; they replace the day by the nights or, so to say, reverse 'black and white'.

It is reported that there are 160 million people in China having too high blood pressure, also around 160 million have high blood fat and 200 million are overweighted or obese. All these are becoming chronic diseases; national health killers.

During the past few years, a lot of young people developed into workaholics, working for a car, a house and a credit card, money for which they not seldom loan (and try refund by earning money through working overtime). Recently, such a 'labour slave' confessed: 'I want more work and work hard for my loan.' We see that even more people are chasing wealth, have become the slaves of wealth, at the price of a loss of collective culture, long term (historical) awareness and depth in thinking; forgetting the ancestors of wisdom.

For over 30 years of reform and opening up, Chinese have risen their achievements, a fact recognized all over the world. However, although in each place in the world you can find 'made in China' products, only few Chinese brands are remembered by people. Furthermore, at China's horizon are appearing a number of overwhelming, confusing problems, such as: food safety, house prices, prices of commodities, corruption, education, by officials forced evictions to make place for new investments, environmental protection, increasing number of accidents. According to the China Environmental Development Report (2011), today a considerable number of lakes and rivers are polluted, wetlands disappearing, rivers drying-out. In more than 400 of the 660 cities there is water supply shortage.

Inappropriate human behaviour caused soil pollution, increased soil and water erosion and desertification leading to severe sand storms and floods in 2010. And in the process of expansion of the cities, the highways, railways and development zones, unnecessarily a lot of cultivated land was occupied and huge engineering pollution effected the environment and brought ecological damage to plant and animal species living in those intruded spaces and places.

It is obvious that today's people know very little about leisure cultural traditions or have wrong ideas about those while going for extravagant lifes and endless consumption.

Along with urbanization, the cities cover the shadow of functioning as 'ant caves, humble abodes, shantytowns'. When searching on the website Baidu for 'city, make life better' what leaped out, is that, in many cases, the city makes life worse; most people felt that they are living at a stake; feeling pointless, helpless and alone.

IV

Conclusion

Throughout the long history of Chinese cultural tradition, leisure always has been and still is like a drizzle, dropping in unspectacular ways, influencing the survival wisdom of the Chinese nation and mounding the Chinese culture temperament. The ancients often are associated with natural philosophy, personality accomplishment, aesthetic temperament and interest in literature and art, all this combined in a life style. Classical books sustained for more than 3000 years, such as: the *Book of Songs*, *I Ching*, the *Book of Rites*, the *Tao Te Ching*, writings of Confucius, the Mencius, as well as more classical works from different dynasties, not only are telling the toiling masses about the ancient times crystallization of wisdom, but also are the carriers of Chinese traditional culture heritage. Actually, leisure's tradition conception and the way it developed forms another book through which one can understand Chinese civilization history.

Leisure is not only one of the oldest human ideals, but it also is the most beautiful, good and virtual vision. You can spend time in contemplation and inspire your best talents when you immerse in leisure time. You can get to understand how to become holy, how to shake off the temptation and to go for a utilitarian way of life, how to implement valuable activity, how to choose moral life and how to steer your intentions.

Fundamentally, leisure is a kind of happy life and life experience, it is a very important social phenomenon, an ontological fundament, of making a person 'becoming' and growing through all the important stage of life, it is a kind of intelligence of the life, it is humanity's beautiful homeland, it is also an effective way to develop a civilized society.

Notes

1. The house codes (*jiaxun*) of a lineage group are admonitions for later generations on how to lay a solid foundation for one's moral life and how to manage the household. They played a very important role in educating the lineage group for cultural pursuits and civility. The way by which *jiaxun* was passed from generation to generation was through personal exemplification as well as instruction in words, and special emphasis was given to early education and character-building for children. The house codes were an important part of the Confucian effort to build a cultural order centered on morality, and components of self-cultivation, household management, governing of the state, and the pacification of all under heaven. The core was the value identity of a lineage group, but it was also in harmony and unity with mainstream values.
2. John R. Kelly, *Freedom To Be: A New Sociology of Leisure,* Macmillan Publishing Company, USA, 1987, p. 32.

4

Mapping Leisure and Life through the Ages in India

ISHWAR MODI

Leisure in India changed with the social structure of Indian society during the different historical periods. Yet its uniqueness has been maintained by tradition, particularly before the beginning of modernization.

The value themes of *hierarchy, holism, continuity* and *transcendence* which constituted the Indian tradition encompassing the entire social system of Indian society prior to the beginning of modernization which were so deeply interlocked with other elements of Indian social structure, influenced greatly the traditional leisure structure of Indian society.

These four attributes of Indian tradition have undoubtedly influenced, determined and governed the nature of traditional leisure of the different segments of Indian society, both urban and rural. The nature and form of traditional leisure which we have characterized here broadly as hierarchical, group-institutionalized and group-participation oriented, normative and rhythmic, more particularly in the case of the rural community, corresponds a significant extent to these major attributes of Indian tradition.

Historical Setting and Leisure in India

The earliest known social history of India dates back to roughly 3000 B.C. with authentic proof of the existence of a flourishing pre-Aryan urban Indus Valley civilization. But, in the absence of cohesive and sufficient information about the nature of the then social classes and their patterns of leisure and recreation[1] we can start with the historical period that is with the tribal-cum-agrarian rural society of the Vedic Aryans before the advent of the monarchies beginning with the reign of Bimbisara (542–490 B.C.).[2]

The Vedic Aryans: The Semi Nomadic Tribal Society

When the Aryans entered India they already had three major social classes: the *warriors or aristocracy*, the *priests*, and the *common people* though they were hardly conscious of caste. From the hymns of the *Rig-Veda* and such remarks as ‘a bard am I, my father is a leech and my mother grinds corn’ it becomes clear that at that time there was little trace of the rigid restrictions typical of caste in its mature form. According to Thapar, 'the three divisions merely facilitated social and economic organization.'[3]

In the circumstances it is believed that there existed very little variation in the leisure and recreational activities of these three classes.

Though the ritualistic sacrificial ceremonies of the Aryans had distinct religious overtones they were, at the same time associated with the pleasures of leisure and recreation.

All such activities of leisure of the Aryans as music, singing, dancing and drinking and even the chariot racing, of which we find mention in the Vedic literature, were essentially a part of these sacrificial ceremonies. Some of the Rig-Vedic hymns incorporated ritual dancing[4] with the accompaniment of various musical instruments – the drum, lute, flute, cymbal and the harp.

A highly developed knowledge of sound, tone, and pitch was used in the system of chanting the *Sama-Veda*. Of the two potent liquors *Soma* and *Sura* to which the Aryans were addicted, *Soma*, a libation of which constituted an essential part of sacrifice, was liberally and convivially drunk after the sacrifice.[5]

Not only singing, dancing and music, and drinking of *Soma* but also chariot-racing formed an important element of sacrifice celebrated in later times as the *Vajapeya*.[6]

Thus it is evident that the leisure and recreational activities of the Vedic Aryans who though had class divisions but only in a functional rather than structural sense, were, by and large, normative, group based[7] and egalitarian in character.

The popularity of gambling or the game of dice among the people of all the classes is yet another clear proof. Such activities as racing, hunting and the war-dance were restricted to the virile classes.[8] Towards the end of the Vedic period, the four fold division of society – *Brahmin, Kshatriya, Vaishya* and *Shudra* – had come to stay and was regarded as divinely fixed.[9] However, below the Shudras existed the 'outcastes' or 'untouchables' for whom certain 'unclean' occupations were reserved.[10]

The Aryan Vaishyas who came as cultivators gradually became traders and land owners while the Shudras moved up the scale to become the cultivators.[11] But, at the same time, the principle of the hereditary base of caste remained inexorable.

The Imperial-Monarchical Society

With the emergence of monarchies by about 600 B.C. distinct changes in the structure of society become apparent. In the monarchies tribal loyalties, which were predominant in republics (which in all probability pre-dated the monarchies), weakened and gave way to caste loyalties. The concept of the divinity of the king, with its corollary of the power of the priests and of Vedic ritual, further reduced the status of the popular assemblies of the early Vedic times.[12] The king emerged as the final authority and kingship became hereditary with a preference for rulers of the Kshatriya caste. But this preference remained theoretical since kings of all four castes are known to have ruled; and 'in practice the aphorism 'whoever bears rule is Kshatriya' was applied.'[13]

However, since divinity could be invested in the king by means of elaborate ritual sacrifice conducted by the good offices of the priests only, they claimed higher status. But 'the Brahmin's claim to supremacy was now and then contested by Kshatriya, and we have declarations to the effect that the Kshatriya had no superior and that the priest was only a follower of the king.'[14]

Such a situation brought about a realization of the mutual interdependence – Priest and King – and that 'the office of the king and the priest were complementary.'[15] Therefore, with the increase in the power of the king increased the power of the chief priest (*purohit*) who by now had begun to assume the functions of the chief minister. Brahmins also occupied important administrative positions; many of them were magistrates and councillors. Though the roots of their power were based on traditionally higher status of priesthood, there was a clear shift in favour of a higher socio-economic status as is evident from the then pay structure of the various types of employees.[16] As these class inequalities, which were based on economic status started operating, the Vaishyas emerged as a genuine bourgeoisie. Depending on the nature of their trade they were associated with one or the other powerful guild[17] and exercised considerable influence on the state in spite of the discrimination accorded to them by the two higher classes. Undoubtedly, great fortunes were made by them in trade as indicated by the references in Buddhist and Jaina literature to millionaires. It should be no surprise, then, that this important section of urban society – the rich merchants – tended to ape the nobles (Kshatriyas) who enjoyed certain privileges and did their best to follow the example of the king.[18] The daily life of the privileged and wealthy, as depicted in the *Kamasutra* by Vatsyayana, leaves no doubt that there existed vast differences between the patterns of leisure of these leisured classes and the common masses. Those who could afford the financial resources and time acquired the ability to play *Vina* (a string instrument), to paint and posses personal art collections, take leisurely care of the body, indulge in games of chance at will, have sessions of teaching new words to their parrots and other talking birds, watch fights between quails, cocks, or rams, entertain guests with literary conversation, music and surfeit of alcoholic drinks, master the arts of love-play and keep company with courtesans who according to Vatsyayana were adept in 'the sixty four arts' of love making. The common people of lower socio-economic status were fully occupied in the struggle for mere existence and had neither the time nor the money for such pursuits. It is evident, therefore, that the then social structure determined, to a large extent, its structure of leisure.

The organization and performance, too, of many leisure and recreational activities highlight the association of the notions of hierarchy and class status in these activities. Theatre is perhaps one of the best examples in this regard. Although dramatic performances provided the main entertainment at public festivals,[19] these performances were essentially based on certain discriminatory factors such as sitting arrangements and languages spoken by the actors.

Similarly, dance and music also were the prerogative of the higher class; 'dance performances and music concerts were held mainly in the homes of the wealthy and the discerning'.[20] Also, hunting, listening to tales of war and archery found special favour with the warrior class.[21] The soldiers of the army, according to Megasthenes[22], 'when they were not in service they spent their time in idleness and drinking bouts, being maintained at the expense of the royal treasury'.[23]

Unlike the more sophisticated and characteristic leisure activities enjoyed by higher castes and classes, there were other leisure and recreational activities which the common people enjoyed along with the aristocracy. The most popular were entertainments provided by wrestlers, conch-players, drummers, acrobats, conjurers, mountebanks of every kind, folk dancers, folk singers, swordswallowers, monkey and mangoose-handlers, snake-charmers, and animal-fights whether between cocks, peacocks, buffaloes, oxen, horses, elephants or rams, etc.[24] Professional entertainers who performed many of these feats travelled long distances, particularly at the time of important festivals, in the hope of making substantial profits and provided welcome diversions for the aristocracy and the common people alike. Sometimes these entertainments were sponsored by the state or by some wealthy patron. Often they were arranged near the palace in the enclosure set aside for games and shows when royalty had a grand stand view. These entertainments were associated either with a religious or a secular festival, usually the former. In fact it is difficult to conceive of any aspect of life in ancient India without associating it with religion. It has been said that 'from the moment that he was conceived, an Indian belonged to a caste corresponding to a religious social structure'.[25] Leisure and recreation could be no exceptions.

The New Year began with the spring equinox and was marked by several festivals. Some of these continued for weeks together as did others held at different periods round the year.[26] They provided opportunities to all the classes of society for gay abandon, erotic license, mass debauchery, singing, dancing and drinking and also to forget caste restrictions at least among the sub-castes.[27]

The life of leisure described here excludes by implication the people belonging to Brahmin caste, considering their emphasis on ritual, inherent restrictions, and comparatively negative attitude to pleasures and comfort.[28] Neither could it have been the life style of a sizeable section of the illiterate and the poor orthodox masses who lived their life according to the ancient precepts, separate from, and to a large extent untouched by the dissolute ways of the others.[29] This was particularly true of the rural population which was bound by the routine of labour, harvesting and seasonal observances, and could not compete with the townsmen. Only the nobility and rich merchants could indulge in such leisure activities.

Thus, in the prevailing socio-economic circumstances it should be no surprise that whatever leisure and recreation was available to the rural folk, or for that matter to the majority of city dwellers, was associated with the festivals marking the rhythm of the seasons which dominated collective life round the year.

On the whole, it may be concluded that during the period of imperial-monarchies when definite castes and classes with highly varying socio-economic statuses had firmly come into existence, a distinct pattern of leisure activities emerged. While the nobility, aristocracy and the wealthy classes had a leisured existence, and pursued at will the leisure and recreational activities of a sophisticated and 'class-characteristic' type. The common masses shared with these higher classes only those leisure and recreational activities in which they were permitted to participate to the extent of their hierarchical status in society, or those which were based on a more universalized religico-normative seasonal character.

The Monarchical-Feudal Society

The next phase of change of some consequence in the otherwise comparatively slow changing traditional agricultural Indian society coincided with the emergence what is generally referred to as feudalism. This new politico-economic structure leads to the crystallization of regional loyalty based on a common culture and history.[30] In contrast to the centralized rule over large territories up to the reign of Harsh (A.D. 590–647), and to some extent till about a century later, there emerged small independent regional kingdoms. This was a result of insubordination by the feudatories of the more powerful kingdoms which fell into decline due to continued wars with each other.[31] 'The tendency from the seventh century onwards of granting land in lieu of cash salaries intensified the feudal process'[32] and remained in vogue continuing through the Turko-Afgan and Mughal period and culminated in its most mature Indian form in the 18th century Rajput kingdoms.

The relationship between the king and his vassals was not contractual as in the West but was governed by arbitrary relationship of power and conquest. Priests and councillors as supplementary elites were associated with each level of this monarchical-feudal structure.[33]

The impact of Islam on the social structure accelerated the process of proliferation of sub-castes and eventually Islam itself succumbed to and accepted caste society in India. As a result, authority and social prestige remained with those castes and groups which were traditionally associated with power both among Hindus as well as Muslims.[34]

With the growing power of feudal chiefs also grew their greed for more and more possessions and wealth to meet the cost of the vast variety of their conspicuous consumptions, tastes which they emulated from their overlords and the king. It not only led to the economic depression of the peasantry but also snatched away a major portion of their leisure which they were now compelled to put to use to meet the heavy burden of taxes.

The ensuing Muslim rule in India, particularly the Turko-Afgan regimes, may, by and large, be considered as an extension of the already existing feudal pattern. Even the Mughals have been considered to be 'semi-feudal but with a strong monarchical centre'.[35] However, leaving aside the regimes of a few powerful monarchs, the Delhi Sultanate at various periods was not homogeneous political entity.[36] It was reduced to the status almost of a provincial kingdom.[37] The very fact that, between the thirteenth and the middle of the fifteenth century, during a period of less than 240 years more than 30 monarchs ruled shows how short was the average duration of each monarch. 'They were primarily military adventurers, bent upon prolonging their rule as long as possible and enjoying every luxury.'[38] The ultimate consequence of 'the luxury and profligacy of the Sultans' was the dissipation of the resources of the land and the greatly reduced staying power of the peasantry.[39] Thus, Indian society may, by and large, be divided in two antipodal classes, i.e. the elite upper class consisting of courtiers,

Khans, Maliks, Amirs, provincial Viceroys, Naib-Sultans, Jagirdars and Mansabdars and such others; and the lower class of commoners consisting of peasants, artisans and such other townspeople as petty traders, etc.[40]

Differences between these two classes were antipodal not only in terms of their standard of living and economic standing but also in terms of their leisure and recreations. While the keynote of life of the upper classes revolved around war and pleasures[41] that of the masses and the lower classes was hard work and unremitting toil.

The patterns of leisure and recreation of the upper classes were dictated, as we have seen, by militaristic exigencies of the time and the then feudal-monarchical structure of society. The foundation of this society was the relative strength of the monarch, his vassals, and their vassals. Fearlessness, pride, tenacity of purpose, keenness, aggressiveness in attack, industry, perseverance, patience, loyalty, and watchfulness learned from various wild and domestic animals were prized qualities. And to inculcate them various forms of amusements and sports were designed; these were virtues of an ideal soldier which the average respectable man of that time was.[42] People did not carry walking sticks but rather swords. Games and sports such as polo, fencing, wrestling, horse-racing, dog-racing, arrow-shooting, fighting of various kinds of tamed animals, and *shikar* (the chase)[43] were popular both with the Hindu as well as Muslim rulers. Though some of the favourite pastimes of the Muslim nobility such as polo, horse-racing and hunting, etc. sometimes offended against the fundamental tenets of Islam but by then the position of the monarch had become so powerful that the Ulema had no alternative but to compromise by finding subtle interpretations of the holy law which would sanction these pastimes.[44] Similarly, orthodox opinion was unanimous in condemning all kinds of gambling including *chess, chaupar,* and *nard* (Persian backgammon) played with stakes, but since both chess and Persian backgammon were considered to be excellent aristocratic recreations the authority of sacred injunctions could not banish them. In the same way such social pleasures as prostitution and drinking flourished.

While such games and sports as those mentioned above represented the militaristic nature of the recreations of the higher classes, their purely sensual and aesthetic leisure and recreations also had great variety. Apart from a large harem and concubines (including slaves) which every ruler (Hindu as well as Muslim) maintained, and which occupied much of their time, every court maintained a large number of poets, musicians, dancers, jesters, tricksters, buffoons and clowns, along with *Nadims* (courtiers) who were boon companions of the monarch and whose principal occupation was to entertain the Sultan in his leisure hours by adding to the liveliness of his gaiety and pleasures.[45]

Holding of *darbars* (courts), whether for secular, social or religious purposes, royal processions, pleasure parties, river picnics, *mina bazaars* and scores of such other social occasions were designed in such a manner that whatever other purpose they might have had, they essentially served to please and entertain the royalty and the nobility. Wine and women, music and dancing, lewdness and sensuality, waste and conspicuous consumption formed an essential part of many of these and other such social occasions all the year round.

Though the leisurely luxuries and recreations were beyond the means and capacity of the masses, it does not mean that they and the lower class of society, in spite of their unending preoccupation with hard work, had no leisure and recreation. They did, but its nature and form was of a different pattern. They also participated in public receptions and official celebrations but this participation may be considered more symbolic than real – they were present as spectators rather than as participants. To their share fell the universal and local religious festivals. It has been noted that the more important religious and social festivals of the Hindus 'usually synchronise with the seasons of comparative leisure for the peasantry and are as a rule enjoyed with dances and popular tunes'.[46] Some of these festivals were also associated with fairs and pilgrimages. Similarly, the Muslims, Jains and other communities had their own festivals. Some of the Muslim festivals, Shab-i-Barat for example, are said to have originated indigenously. In the recreation of the lower classes of society the temple,[47] *Chaupal*[48] and roving professional entertainers and folk singers, etc. were important but their leisure and recreations were predominantly linked with their religions which determined both the periodicity and the nature and form of their leisure and recreations. This in no way denies the primary defining function of the social structure. The emergence of the Tantric and Krishna cults is a case in point. The former originated in deliberate opposition to the orthodox Hindu ritual and the *brahmanical* ordering of society and the later came into prominence because its erotic aspects corroborated the character of that society in particular that of the higher classes. The rise of these two cults clearly shows how the structural elements of a society can give rise to a formidable range of religious expression.[49] Whether reformative in nature or reflecting the social conditions prevalent, they certainly provided recreative outlets to the masses which otherwise were beyond their reach. Initiation in a Tantric sect necessitated partaking in the five Ms – *madya* (wine), *matsya* (fish), *mamsa* (flesh), *mudra* (grain), and *maithuna* (coition) and was open to all classes of people irrespective of caste or sex. In the Krishna cult also sensual and erotic pleasures were encouraged, specially singing and dancing in which everyone could partake without being ostracized or suffering in status.[50]

Social Change from Colonialism to Independence and After

Though vestiges of monarchical-feudal social structure remained until Independence, and to some extent even later, the intervening period of British rule brought many changes in the traditional cultural patterns and social structure of India. The impact of Western tradition (its own structure having undergone radical internal metamorphoses by now),[51] posed a serious challenge to the two main attributes of Indian tradition – *hierarchy* and *holism*. According to Yogendra Singh, 'The form of legal rationalism on which the Western tradition was based (by the time it came into contact with the Indian tradition), recognized a contractual-individualistic relationship between man and society. In matters of legal justice and civil rights, it encouraged the values of equality, equity and universalism and not those of status and hierarchy. In contrast with the communal and feministic status allocation system of India, the Western tradition through various bureaucratic structures – administrative, legal and military – and through educational and cultural innovations, introduced new criteria for social stratification which were based on achievement and not ascription, and allocated status only on individual performance and not on charismatic qualities.'[52]

The period of British rule was a period of transition. Its impact was not the same in every part of the country. The pace of change, however, was rapid. The changes that took place in the structure of society in the post-Independence period may be treated as a sequel to the change taking place before Independence and may be summarized as follows:

1. Emergence of the new elite of political-populistic orientation from rural, agricultural and lower middle caste or class background.
2. Increasing differentiation in the elite structure.
3. Slight breakdown in the exclusiveness of upper castes to the elite position and its consequent democratization.
4. Introduction of adult suffrage and a federal parliamentary form of political structure.
5. Conscious legal reforms in Hindu marriage and inheritance law affecting the foundation of traditional Hindu family structure.
6. Introduction of land reforms (e.g. abolition of *jagirdari* and *zamindari*, etc.) and elective village *panchayats*.
7. Increasing industrialization and urbanization, and acceptance of science and technology as factors of human welfare.
8. Breaking isolation of the rural from urban community and increasing communication and interaction between the two.
9. Reinforcing of traditional institutions and widespread modernization without serious breakdown in the social structure but a situation of ambivalence between tradition and modernity.[53]

The overall impact of these changes has been to transform society from 'a static, acquired-status-ridden, tradition-bound, primary-group-oriented, fatalistic society into one that is rapidly changing, achieved-status-dominated, progressive, secondary-group-oriented, universalistic and aspiring.'[54] However, this process of change is not yet over, nor has it yet reached a stage of stabilization. We are still passing through a period of transition.

With the changing socio-political structure the nature and patterns of leisure also became instable, and the work-leisure relationship hanged in a state of imbalance. In the urban areas 'the pressures of urban life', as Srinivas says, made people adopt new schedules of work and personal habits and motivated them to use modern modes of transport, communication and leisure.[55] Urbanization (which is usually coupled with industrialization) added a new dimension to the whole situation. It led not only to the growth of commercialism, monetization of economic relationships, factory and workshop employment for many, but also to the popularization of mass media for leisure and entertainment.[56] Communication studies had revealed that within a structural framework of ranking and distance from the cities, cultural values and information flowed steadily from the cities to the villages.[57] Those urbanities who returned to villages brought with them many elements of modern ways of life and habits from the cities.[58] Increasingly, themes from urban life, contemporary politics and social economic issues were borrowed by the cultural media of the folk tradition.[59]

A comprehensive comparison of the patterns of leisure and recreations in the rural and the urban communities showed many marked similarities as well as distinctive characteristics in the nature and form of these activities until the mid-seventies (Modi, 1985).

Besides the influence of tradition on the leisure structure, the nature and character of economic relations (which are a product of existing socio-political structure) between the feudal and the peasant segments of the village community also determined and influenced the nature of leisure during this period. It has been observed that while economic disparities tend to segregate the groups, religion or to be more precise, the festival cycle offers numerous opportunities for integrated participation.

During periods of transition, when socio-political structures change, the nature and pattern of leisure also becomes instable and the work-leisure relationship also undergoes a state of imbalance. The changes which took place during the pre-and post-independence period did not have the same impact on all segments of society. The pattern of leisure and recreation of the urban and rural segments show sharp differences. Changes in the structure of rural leisure occurred within the framework of the already existing traditional leisure structure rather than in the acceptance of new and modern means of leisure. The dominance of the feudal segment on rural leisure patterns diminished to the point of vanishing altogether. The feudal segment which, to a great extent, was based on its privileged socio-political and economic position, crumbled with the withdrawal of the basis of its power and prestige. As a result such traditional castes, communities and groups which in the old days enjoyed the patronage of the feudal segment and contributed to the leisure and recreational activities of their feudal masters under *jajmani* or otherwise, lost their traditional source of patronage without finding any other. They then either switched to other occupations or are trying to find new support in the wider community. When they do succeed in finding patronage, the character of their relationship with the new clientele is not what is was under *jajmani*. It now has commercial overtones and it is very difficult to say who are the beneficiaries. However, it can be said for the changed socio-political structure and the changed economic relationships between the different segments of the rural community that it has brought certain benefits to the lower sections of the community including more leisure and freedom particularly to all those who once served *beggar* (unpaid or bonded labour) under a rigid feudal system. And because of these changes, the extent of segregation between the people of different castes, particularly among males, has decreased to a considerable extent and certain leisure time activities such as gossiping, roaming about, playing football, volleyball, kabaddi, etc. are now pursued irrespective of caste considerations. Managerial roles in the organization of such annual events as the *Ramlila* (and the dramas) and village fairs remained no longer confined to the higher castes and any enthusiastic young man willing to support the cause was now welcome. The traditional character of village *melas* (fairs), however, while undergoing significant changes and assuming modernized and commercial dimensions, yet retained many of its traditional attributes.

The urban situation remained much more complex. Forces of both modernity and tradition operated simultaneously in urban society. On the one hand, one observed a decline of many such traditional leisure pursuits which were till a few decades ago patronized and sponsored by the royal nobility in accordance with its own norms and customs and also for the benefit of the public. At the same time, continuity in the religious patterns of leisure and recreation was also observed. There was no trace of decline in the number of activities associated with the annual religious-cycle which occur every month of the year and call for some special celebration. Rather, the tendency was towards increasing the number of such celebrations. Several castes, communities, sects and groups still take out gaudy precessions on the main streets of the city, which were hitherto either unknown or if at all celebrated then quite solemnly. This kind of reinforcement of the traditional mode of celebrations which constitute leisure and provide recreation is not averse to the use of modern technology.

The empirical findings of a study of the urban community of Jaipur (Modi, 1985) confirmed that the traditional patterns of leisure and recreation were broadly organized around the royal, public, religious, non-professional and professional patterns of leisure and recreation. The nature and form of these overall traditional patterns of leisure and recreation can be characterized as hierarchical, group-institutionalized and group-participation oriented, as well as normative-religious and rhythmic. Similarly, the empirical findings of a study of the rural community of Garhi Mamur in Rajasthan (Modi, 1985), bring to fore that the traditional patterns of leisure and recreation presented no contrast to the traditional urban situation. Its major attributes and characteristics were to a large extent similar to that of the traditional patterns of leisure and recreation of the urban community. Similarly, the traditional patterns of leisure and recreation both of the urban and the rural community may be traced to the same kind of feudal rule which governed both these communities.

The castes, communities and groups which traditionally entertained the people started either to change their professions or find a new clientele on commercial lines. The commercialization of recreation created impersonal relational patterns in urban centres and the traditional recreational patterns were commercialized because of emerging economic ethos. In the urban community many leisure and recreational activities which were once pursued by royalty or were sponsored by it for the benefit of the public became defunct. Such non-professional leisure and recreational activities as *khel-tamasha, gaali-baji akhadas,* etc. now have only a symbolic significance. And such professional and commercialized means of leisure and recreation as circus and *nautanki* were losing their importance. However, the religious patterns of leisure and recreation still retained their traditional importance. Some of the festivals had been forgotten, but several new ones are being added every year. The pervasiveness of religions and its diffusive character in all walks of life continued to influence leisure and recreational patterns although they had been transformed by current technology and the contemporary styles of life. Among the rural community the fast, feast and the festival cycle continued and several new additions were introduced; for example, the lower castes constructed their own temples and special fairs were introduced. The overall trend of change in the traditional patterns of leisure and recreation was now marked by such characteristics as mass leisure, democratization, commercialization, and individualism.

The patterns of leisure and recreation in the urban and rural community during the post-independence period (prior to the introduction of TV) showed marked differences. While among the major leisure and recreational activities of the urbanities were included the three aspects of mass media – films, radio and press, as also group-oriented and games and sports activities, among the rural community none of the three mass media found a place – they rather indulged in group-oriented, family-oriented, quietistic activities, games and sports, playing cards, chess and chopar. It can be said that the rural setting had gemeinschaft-familiality and communality characteristics while the urban setting predominated in gesselschaft-impersonal collectivity and class characteristic of leisure.

The extent of participation of the rural people in most leisure activities (other than the mass media) was found higher than in the urban community. It could be explained by the fact that they until the mid-seventies had one hour more of leisure time every day than the urbanites.

The simultaneous existence of modern mass media, and the many other means of leisure and recreation, on the one hand, and the assertion and continuity of the traditional ways of employing leisure, on the other, made it increasingly difficult to understand the process of change during this period and also the many new problems it created. Moreover, new dimensions that emerged due to the processes of liberalization, privatization and globalization during the 90s leading to several social transformations in Indian society have further complicated the whole situation. As such we may now examine some of these important sectors/segments.

Globalization and Social Transformations

The all pervasive phenomenon of globalization has impacted the Indian society also as it has others all over the world. Though the process of globalization had started quite a few decades ago but its impact became more evident during the nineties when Government of India started implementing the policies of liberalization and privatization as part of declared state policy.

Since so much has already been said and written about globalization, I would not like to indulge in its rhetoric but would like to straight away go to its impact on the various important sectors and sections of Indian society particularly with reference to its impact on leisure. However, it need not be overemphasized that globalization has impacted the various sections of Indian society differently.

The Changing Rural Scenario

The rural leisure scenario has completely changed during the last thirty to forty years. They still spend time with their children and family members, and chit chat with them. They still gossip and chit chat and spend time with their friends and colleagues but now no more on the chaupals of the village but on the tea stalls or on the newly emerging mechanic shops. They are still pursuing most of those leisure activities which they were pursuing then, though now to a lesser extent. Now practically every rural household has a radio or transistor, and many of them even TVs. Now more people write and read, including the newspapers and other magazines, and some even novels. Many of them have learned new skills. Now they also more often go to towns and cities and its impact is so visible on them – in their dress, fashion and fads. Popular heros and heroines of the all pervasive Indian cinema as well as that of cricket are no more strangers to them. They now know about them and can easily talk about them for hours. So is true about politics. What is most striking is that now many of them possess not only mobiles but also motor-cycles. They are no more strangers to the city nor is the city stranger to them. Easy and more frequent visits to cities due to fast spreading infrastructural and transportation facilities have brought the cities in their easy ambit. However, what is still lacking is the availability of water for their farms and hence continued dependence on monsoon forcing them to commute or ultimately to migrate to the cities. While many of them are unemployed, others who have learned some skills have become sought after entities in the cities having its repercussions on their leisure lives. While some have abundance of forced leisure, others are feeling the pinch of its non-availability. It ranges from 1 to 10 hours. However, on an average approximately 4 hours of leisure or to be precise 3 hours and 53 minutes of leisure was available to the rural people predominated by the farming community, until a few decades ago.

The Migrant Service-providers

The overall general scenario has drastically changed as a consequence of industrialization and urbanization. Large scale migration from rural areas to the cities has added new dimensions both to the rural as well as urban life. While a significantly large section of the migrant groups have become part of the industrial set up, an equally large section of the migrants are providing services of various kinds – skilled, semi-skilled and unskilled. However, in spite of all their efforts, to integrate themselves in the urban life their links with their roots in the villages are still very strong. Even when they have settled in the cities, they very often go back to their villages. Interaction between them and their left behind colleagues in the villages is working as change-agent and transforming the rural scene in many ways. Not only new ideas but also new leisure practices are making in roads into the life of the rural people. Similarly, the lives of the rural migrants in the cities are undergoing new transformations. They now more often go to see movies or else watch more movies on the TV at home. When alone, they are at freedom to roam around the city on their newly acquired two wheelers made possible by easy loan facilities by the banks. They spend hours on the *paan* (betel) shops or on the tea-stalls gossiping with each other, or on passing comments on the passing by young women. They are also contributing to growing alcoholism and other intoxicants. However, they are also learning new skills in their leisure time in the hope of getting better jobs in order to improve the quality of their lives.

The Industrial or the Blue-Collar Workers

While in many developed countries the number of industrial workers is shrinking, it is so far not the case in India, and may be in other developing countries as well. In fact the number of industrial workers is swelling in the face of competing state governments which are vying with each other to attract as many industries as possible by providing new and unprecedented incentives. Their hours of work are not unlimited like that of the farmers or of the domestic servants. Under legal protection the industrial management is not in a position to force them to work more then the assigned work hours. It has resulted in the availability of many more hours of leisure to these erstwhile farmers. Though there are innumerable possibilities of engaging this increased leisure in any urban setting but for want of resources and other structural constraints their choices become limited. And yet they try to make full use of it in new and innovative leisure activities. It was difficult for them to take along their wives and children outside the four walls of their houses in the villages for reasons of traditional taboos and public ridicule. The anonymity of city and the consequent freedom allows them to move wherever they wish to including the cinema halls and the restaurants without any fear. Shopping and of course window-shopping together with members of family and at times with friends is both a pleasure and leisure for them. The crunch of resources either demands them to confine either to home based leisure activities be it passing time with family or the TV or the radio, or choose such outside-home activities which could be undertaken without much financial burden such as going to temples of various Gods, Goddesses and deities. Specific days of the week are considered auspicious and more beneficial to visiting the temples of specific deities. Of late, one can witness a tremendous rise in the number of visitors to the temples. These visits are not only to propitiate and to seek blessings of the concerned deities in these times of financial and other hardships but also to visit a destination where hundreds and thousands 'others like us' will also be there to convert the religious ambiance of the place into that of a *mela* (fair) like atmosphere where you can also eat '*chat-pakoris*' (ethnic fast food) with family and can also buy cheap goods and toys for the children. They cannot think of a less expensive leisure activity than this.

The biggest gain of these farmers converted into the so called blue-collar workers or the industrial workers over the years has been their bargaining power through their unions. Even if they had not succeeded in getting their hours of work reduced from 48 hours per week spread over six days, they had also not allowed the management to extract more hours of work from them. They have no fear of being panelized by the management since it has nothing much to offer them in return in the absence of well defined reward systems or the capacity of handing over 'pink-slips'. As such, though the industrial workers in India are still putting much more hours to work as compared to their counterparts in the west, and yet they now have much more free time at their command then before when they were farm workers back home. In fact, at times they are at a loss to understand as to what use they can put their leisure to. As compared to an average of 3 hours of leisure available to the urban people as a whole, the leisure hours available to the industrial workers are the highest (more than 4 hours) as compared to such other classes of people as merchants, service class and the elites, who by and large are the largest sections of the urban population along with the industrial workers. However, it may not be as true in case of the elites when it comes to numbers. As a consequence of technological advancements and general development in society including the financial betterment particularly of the ever enlarging middle class the sphere of available leisure activities has widened multifold and yet the industrial workers can make use of very limited leisure options that are available.

The White-Collar Workers

As compared to these blue-collar workers, the white collar workers, whose size has tremendously grown over the years, have benefited the most. Their unions are as strong as that of the industrial workers, rather getting stronger every day. During the last Assembly elections in a state the party in power lost the elections due to anti tirade of the *babus* (lower level white-collar bureaucracy). It is again under the pressure of these *babus,* that this particular state government which came to power because of their support, decided, just before the next assembly elections, to appease them, to implement the policy of 5 day work week instead of 6. Since employees of the central government already had a 5 day work week and now that the state governments are also implementing this scheme, the character of leisure at the weekends will undergo major transformation. Only one day weekend had major limitations and constraints. But now that many government employees will have a two days weekend they will definitely like to make use of this newly achieved leisure time by extending the scope of their leisure activities. What will be the shape of these activities is yet to be ascertained. As in the West particularly in America the emergence of the concept of 'long weekends, and the furry associated with it is around the corner in India also. Weekend tourism in all probability is going to get a good boost now since possessing a car, even though a small one, has already taken the shape of a phenomenon. According to a most recent survey of the Marketing Research Division of the Ministry of Tourism, Government of India an increase of 15.5 per cent domestic tourists was registered whereby 650 million people in the country went out for tourism during the year 2009 in spite of recession. As such it is evident that domestic tourism has already become a mass phenomenon and Indian tourism is not dependent on inbound international tourists. It is also noteworthy that the number of outbound tourist is also increasing at a fast pace and now more people (7 million) go out of India then India receives from outside (5 million). Such a situation is likely to have repercussions both for leisure and social transformation.

Emergence of a New Class: The IT Workers and Other Professional

The most important phenomenon of the 21st century that is taking place in a globalizing India is the emergence of an altogether new class – the class of IT (Information and Technology) workers. They are all highly skilled and computer savvy. They have provided a new identity to the genius of India the world over. They are in heavy demand everywhere, both at home and elsewhere in the world. Their competence, efficiency and hard work is phenomenal. They have endeared everyone around. They have transformed the entire socio-economic scenario of the country. Their pay-packets are fairly high and ever increasing. Their demand is so heavy that changing jobs has become like change of clothes. Now within few years of their careers they can afford to buy a car and can also have their own houses since they can now repay back their loans without much strain which was hardly possible for the previous generations. However, the dilemma is that now they have more money but less leisure. They can afford to go anywhere; can buy expensive gadgets both for themselves as well as for other members of the family. This class can now also afford to dine out at regular intervals and can also afford to buy expensive tickets not only for cinema but also for other modern and contemporary stage shows of various kinds. But the main constraint is when to enjoy all these activities. Sunday alone is not sufficient to indulge in all this. As compared to the blue-collar industrial workers or the white-collar service class which has enough leisure but limited resources, this young class of IT professionals and other technically skilled personnel, many of them having management degrees and such other qualifications is constantly under pressure of work. There is always a challenge to prove themselves. They have to prove their sincerity by not leaving the office before others meaning by working even after the prescribed office hours and sometimes until the late hours. It is because of the performance of these young people that India is heading towards becoming a knowledge society. Impressed by the performance of the very small, small and the medium sized industrial sector which provides jobs to 40 million people in the country, the Prime Minister of India, Manmohan Singh has recently announced that in order to have educational and skill developments, new institutions will be established right at the school level to create 500 million trained technicians by the year 2020. Right now India already has a 200 million strong middle class and with the addition of this trained man-power, this middle class will further swell to many more millions. This will not only strengthen both the service sector and the IT sector but will also have far reaching consequences both on leisure and the quality of life of the people which is already undergoing tremendous transformation both social and economic (*Dainik Bhaskar*, 31 August 2008).

Leisure, Youth and Social Transformation

The way social transformation has influenced and altered the leisure practices of the contemporary urbanites cannot be completed without taking into cognizance the changes that have taken place into the leisure lives of the young people in India. Nearly half of the large Indian population is now that of the young. India may as well be considered the youngest country in the world. They are the main targets of whatever is produced and marketed in the country. While on the one hand the market trends try their best to determine their choice, on the other it is they who influence what has to be produced for their consumption. It is in order to cater to the requirements of this large section that practically all urban centres – big, small or middle sized are witnessing the boom of multipurpose complexes. These malls provide almost everything these young people like to look for. Many of these malls do not only have movie halls but also good quality restaurants as well as fast food joints. All sorts of items including the international brands are now easily available in these malls. What is most interesting is that movies or no movies, shopping or no shopping, eating or no eating, these malls have turned out to be hanging places for one and all, particularly the young people. No sooner the evening sets in, hoards of these young people start flocking to these malls. You can see them here, there, everywhere. They are just happy being there in the company of their friends and colleagues. The gender barriers, which were stringent until the last decade of the twentieth century, are crumbling fast. Spending a few hours of leisure there is no big deal. As anybody can read on their faces and from their smiles these hours are not only their leisure hours but also 'happy hours' when they seem to have forgotten all the stresses and strains of the work place, may be also of the family. The emergence of the 'mall culture' has drastically transformed leisure and the lifestyle of young people in urban India. It has also transformed the patterns of interactions.

All through the eighties and the nineties it was a major concern of a very large number of 'sane' and 'sensible' people in the country as to what will happen to person to person and family to family interaction due to the fall out of heavy viewing of TV. People became so glued to TV in the early decades of its arrival that a large section of fast growing TV owners minimized visiting and meeting each other which used to be the second most popular leisure activity of more than one third urbanites. It was second only to such intellectual activities of leisure as reading all sorts of books, journals, magazines and newspapers and other literary activities pursued by more than half (52.5%) of the urban population (Modi, 1985: 121). But now it is no more the case, nor a cause of worry. The new emerging malls have restored meeting each other and that too in a big way.

When these young people cannot make it to the mall, or they don't want to be, would very often like to go on long drives, sometimes one-to-one and at others in mixed groups in different combinations on the pillion. It also provides them privacy. In most cases, this is also an expression of their freedom, freedom from the taboos of segregation. Technological transformations in the form of ready availability of scooters, motorcycles and cars, which were until the last two decades had to be booked much in advance or could be availed through the recommendation of a politician (more so in case of scooters until the end of seventies) are now easily available and can be seen everywhere. A real transportation revolution has taken place. Until the beginning of the twenty first century nobody could imagine, even in dreams, that within the next few years urban India is going to face a traffic jam on its roads both within the cities as well as outside. Motorcycles have almost completely replaced the age long bicycles not only in the cities but to a great extent even in rural areas. The milkman no more comes on bicycle. So also is the case with most service providers including the menial ones. It saves them both time and energy and also gives them a chance to ride far and wide with whomsoever they want to.

The impact of technological transformation on leisure is also visible in the form of cell phones. When you are not together, either at the mall or at the motorcycle, there has to be something to have the feeling of togetherness and being connected. The sharp marketing strategists have devised and offered such schemes where by a group of friends can always remain connected to each other in the form of cell-phone conferencing. What a nice idea, to chit-chat for hours. No problem of boredom, wherever you may be. And at home, when even the whispering conversation may draw the attention of other family members or else may disturb them the internet comes handy to them. You can chat with anybody, anywhere, at any time. And when there is no body around to chat the computer and the internet is there to help you out with your remaining leisure.

With all the above mentioned new developments – the emergence of the 'mall-culture', 'transportation revolution', 'wide spread penetration of the cell and the internet' threatened the all pervasive television and its viewing TRPs (television rating points) started getting dwindled, the TV magnets had to device something to bring back its viewers. They adopted a strong multi-directional strategy. Whatever was missing was brought in a big way in the form of reality programmes, challenge and competition programmes related to music, dance and even laughter. All these programmes will not only have national celebrities from the respective fields as judges but also invoked participation of the masses in the form of their votes in favour of their favourite contestants. Piqued by heavy postal response to these programmes the department of Posts and Telegraphs had to increase the rate of the post card and introduced a system of penalty on ordinary postcards used for the purpose of voting for TV programmes. Introduction of new system of voting through SMS and phone lines for these TV programmes at time chocks the lines at the cost of genuine users. However, these new and ever changing TV programmes in ever new and exotic formats have once again increased the TRPs of the concerned channels. Exclusive movie channels which used to screen good and popular new movies after a long gap now show these movies on short intervals, thus attracting large audiences.

Sports on TV and that too on many channels and that too for longer hours, besides the exclusively devoted TV channels to sports have added a new dimension to TV viewing. TV and sports are now marching, much more than before, hand in hand. A large number of international sports events such as Olympic Games, FIFA World Cup, Commonwealth Games, various tennis and table tennis tournaments taking place in various parts of the world with regular frequency, and of course the cricket tournaments of various dimensions have added several new chapters in TV viewing more so among the youth. Even the housewives who seldom viewed or talked of sports are now also glued to TV for sports whenever it is convenient for them.

On the other hand, screening of latest movies on the TV hardly seems to have done any revenue damage to the cinema halls. The number of movies produced in the country both in the Bollywood as well as in the regional language studios is so large that the cinema halls are happy in exhibiting ever new movies every week/two weeks. Even the worst of movies make the money spent on them and even earn profit since a certain section of the large population is always there to help them out. As such the cinema halls too, which had to face crisis due to the onslaught of TV in the form of reduced visitors, are once again becoming popular centres of entertainment and leisure.

Similarly, radio which had almost gone into oblivion during the last decades has once again emerged as a popular pastime and leisure. The excessive use of mobiles has also helped in the resurrection of radio.

Like TV and radio, the print media has also of late gained substantial ground. Until a few decades ago there used to be only a few magazines of popular interest at the stands, but now the scenario is completely changed. A large number of magazines on a large number of thematic interests are now easily available in the market. Likewise, the number of newspaper readership has also increased tremendously. However, the same may not be said about the reading of books. Reading of books by commuting populations is hardly to be seen. Yet a large number of books both fiction and non-fiction are now being printed in the country and a sizable section of the middle, upper-middle and higher classes are patronizing these publications.

Having said all this, one thing that is most apparent in the contemporary leisure scenario in India is the new emerging tussle between work and leisure. While on the one hand, a large number of Indian population belonging to almost all sections of society is under heavy pressure of work in order to attain and maintain high standards and a certain quality of life, on the other, they are equally conscious of improving the quality of their lives through wholesome leisure which demands not only leisure but also concomitant financial resources. The fast growing Indian economy which is second only to China in spite of the worldwide recession has not impacted the Indian people as adversely as elsewhere in the world. It is not only the economy of India which is on a substantial growth path but also the economies of the countries labelled as BRICSA (Brazil, Russia, India, China and South Africa).

However, economic recession cannot continue for ever. The trends are different in different countries. If I take India as an example, the rise in the salaries in practically all the sectors, particularly in the IT or say among the employees of the knowledge sector has been unprecedented during the last few years. Even the salaries of the public sector employees have recently been increased a good deal. Not only that, their work week has also been reduced to five and as such now these employee will have a weekend of two days instead of one. It is hoped that as soon as inflation goes down and recession recedes everybody can look forward to better days with better earnings and more leisure. May be, the social transformations taking place in spite of all the hurdles, both economic and social and also at times political, will enthuse people to demand not only for better working conditions but also more leisure and better economic rewards leading ultimately towards the realization of a 'leisure society', if not today, may be in near future.

Notes

1. However, information regarding the division of the Indus valley cities into the citadel area, where the essential instructions of religious and civic life, including the Great Bath, were located and the residential area where the urban population lived support conjectures that while the ruling warrior and the priestly classes lived in citadel area the masses of artisans and other classes lived elsewhere in the city. The Great Bath mush essentially have been a centre for the leisure and pleasure of the elites living in the citadel area, though, of course, on occasions of festival and ritual ceremonies it should hae served the masses as well. For details and discussion on this topic see D.D. Kosambi, *The Culture and Civilization of Ancient India in Historical Outline*, Vikas Publishing House, 1970, pp. 66 68.
2. The use of dynastic chronologies in our discussion is only in order to seek help in providing a framework in time, otherwise the emphasis in making periodization is on such factors which account for changes in the socio-economic structure of society. For further discussion on the problem of periodization in history see Romila Thapar, *A History of India* Volume One, Penguin Books, 1966, pp. 20–23. See also K.C. Panchanadikar and J. Panchanadikar, *Determinants of social Structure and Social Changes in India*, Popular Prakashan, 1970, pp. 71–97.
3. Thapar, Romila, op. cit., p. 37.

4. Thapar, Romila, op. cit., p. 42.
5. Thapar, Romila, op. cit., p. 44. According to her also 'The sacrifice was certainly a solemn institution, but it also served the purpose of releasing energies and inhibitions through the general conviviality which followed at the end of the sacrifice and particularly after the liberal drinking of *Soma.*'
6. R.C. Majumdar, H.C. Raychaudhuri and Kalikinkar Dutta, *An Advanced History of India, Macmillian, London, 1967, p. 31.* However, according to Thapar, 'Chariot-racing was a prestige sport and was included as part of the ritual at certain royal ceremonies.'
7. See Thapar, op. cit., p. 42, Yajurvedic *Sogdhi* and *Spiti,* i.e. eating and drinking in common for which the eighth century Aryans prayed are also a pointer in this direction. See also Kosambi, op. cit., p. 174
8. Majumdar, et al., op. cit., p. 31.
9. Michael Edwardes, Everyday Life in Early India, 1969, pp. 5, 24. Divinely fixed division of society is traced to a late Hymn of the *rig-Veda* according to which 'when they divided the primeval being (Purusa) the Brahamana was his mouth, the Rajanya became his arms, the Vaishya was his thighs, and from his feet sprang the Sudras'.
10. Jeannie Auboyer, *Daily Life in Ancient India,* Asia Publishing House, Bombay, 1965, pp. 30–31,
11. Thapar, op. cit., pp. 38–39.
12. Thapar, op. cit., pp. 50–51.
13. A.L. Basham, *The Wonder that was India,* Grove Press, New York, 1954, p. 91.
14. Majumdar, et al., op. cit., p. 44.
15. Yogendra Singh, *Modernization of Indian Tradition*, Thomson Press, Delhi, 1973, p. 132. In his opinion 'The office of the king and the priest were complementary; the priest was the source of moral norms (dharma) which the king was obliged to enforce. Theoretically, therefore, the office of the priest was superior to that of the king. In practice, however, conformity to this ideal was never fully achieved but its ruthless violation was also rare. King always respected the moral and religious prerogatives of the priests.'
16. While the prime minister, the royal chaplain (*purohit*), the king's spiritual master (*acharya*) and the army commander received 48,000 *panas,* the treasurer and the chief collector *24,000 panas,* the accountants and clerks received 500 *panas,* whereas the councellors and the ministers were paid 12,000 *panas*; and artisans received 120 panas. Though the value of the *pana* is not indicated nor the interval (perhaps monthly?) at which salaries were paid, but the ratio of the clerk's salary to that of the most senior official works out at 1:96, and the ratio of the artisans to that of the minister at 1:100. See Thapar, op. cit., pp. 82–83; also auboyer, op. cit., pp. 111–113.
17. Edwardes, op. cit., p. 26. As to the importance of the guilds, the author writes that 'There are references to guilds processing their own force of armed mercenaries, private armies probably used to guard carvans and trading posts but which were sometimes loaned to the king in times of war. Guilds were often extremely wealthy and their chiefs occasionally became the councellors of kings.' (pp. 89–90). See also Jawaharlal Nehru, *The Discovery of India,* Asia Publishing House, 1973, p. 113, where he quotes from Professor E. Washburn Hopkins, *Cambridge History of India,* Vol, I., p. 269 that it is said, that, 'the merchants guilds were of such authority that the king was not allowed to establish any laws repugnant to these trade unions. The heads of guilds are mentioned next after priests as objects of a king's anxious concern.'

18. Edwards, op. cit., p. 95; See also Auboyer, op. cit., p. 233.
19. Auboyer, op. cit., p. 251.
20. Thapar, op. cit., p. 152.
21. Majumdar, et al., op. cit., p. 73; See also Edwardes, op. cit., p. 108.
22. Greek ambassador of Seleucus Nikator who came to reside at the court of Candragupta Maurya in 303 BC. Megasthenes composed a detailed account of contemporary life in India which has not survived, although fragments are quoted in classical Western sources.
23. Quoted from Thapar, op. cit., p. 79.
24. Auboyer, op. cit., pp. 251–253; Also Edwards, op. cit., pp. 106–108.
25. Auboyer, op. cit., p. 143.
26. For detail discussion on the annual cycle of various kinds of rites and festivals and the nature of celebrations and activities attached to them see Auboyer, op. cit., pp. 144–148; and Edwardes, op. cit., pp. 65–69.
27. Thapar, op. cit., p. 153.
28. Ibid., p. 233.
29. Edwardes, op. cit., p. 102.
30. Ibid., p. 241.
31. Ibid., p. 224.
32. Ibid.
33. Yogendra Singh, op. cit., p. 181.
34. Ibid., p. 320.
35. Nehru, Jawaharlal, op. cit., p. 264.
36. Quoted by Majumdar, et al., op. cit., p. 287 from Cambridge History, Vol. III, p. 87.
37. Thapar, op. cit., p. 267; see also Ashraf, op. cit., p. 3.
38. Thapar, op. cit., p. 291.
39. Ibid., p. 150.
40. Ashraf, op. cit., pp. 154–157, 194–195. See also Majumdar, et al., op. cit., p. 392.
41. Ashraf, op. cit., pp. 103, 222.
42. Ibid., p. 222.
43. For detailed discussion and examples, see Ashraf, op. cit., pp. 222–229; See also G.N. Sharma, *Social Life in Mediaeval Rajasthan,* Lakshmi Narayan Agarwal Educational Publishers, 1968, pp. 135–137.
44. Thapar, op. cit., p. 301.
45. Ashraf, op. cit., pp. 60–61.
46. Ashraf, op. cit., p. 237.
47. Thapar, Romila, op. cit., p. 279.
48. Ashraf, K.M., op. cit., pp. 114–115.
49. Thapar, Romila op. cit., pp. 256–262.
50. Sharma, G.N., op. cit., p. 139; and Ashraf, K.M., op. cit., pp. 246–247.
51. See Yogendra Singh, op. cit., p. 85.
52. Ibid., p. 86.
53. Ibid.
54. Richard D. Lambert, *Workers, Factories and Social Change in India,* Princeton University Press, 1953, p. 17.

55. Srinivas as quoted by Yogendra Singh, op. cit., p. 119.
56. Yogendra Singh, op. cit., p. 110.
57. Y.B. Damle, *Communication of Modern Ideas and Knowledge of Indian Villages,* Massachusetts Institute of Technology, Cambridge Mass. 1955.
58. Lambert, op. cit., p. 137
59. Yogendra Singh, op. cit., p. 120. He observes that 'Folk songs now often use metaphors, idioms and tunes of popular cinema songs; many of them refer caustically to contemporary feuds and tensions among various castes and groups; election propaganda is often made through the media of folk dramas, songs and devotional meetings.'

5

The Meaning and Practice of Leisure and Recreation

An Analysis of Three Indonesian Muslim Professionals

IWAN GARDONO SUDJATMIKO, IRSYAD ZAMJANI AND ADRIANUS JEBATU

All social institutions and social actions are influenced either strongly or weakly by the dominant cultural system such as religion or custom. In this regard, leisure in different societies shows different patterns and meanings and even modernization cannot avoid its influence. In the following discussion we will present how some professional Moslems conceptualize and practice leisure under the *sacred canopy* (See Berger, 1966). The influence of Islam is very clear and seems to colour the social transformation such as urbanization and workplace. This analysis will enrich our understanding of leisure which is only seen in a dichotomy of work and leisure but primarily a process where Islamic belief is continuously reaffirmed in the social space of leisure.

Prior to discussing the belief and practice in Islam, we will first discuss the conception of leisure in general. The concept of leisure is considered as a dichotomy of work and leisure though there are criticisms that this perspective is rather simplistic. An analysis states that the continuum is collapsed and one of its causes is postmodernism where the work and leisure can infiltrate each other. In this regard work and leisure becomes 'weisure' as stated by Dalton Conley and an illustration of this proposition is shown as follows (Patterson, 2009):

> 'Weisure' is the blurring of work and play – both what we do and where we do it Weisure is changing modern society, says NYU sociologist Dalton Conley
>
> 'We lose our private sphere,' he says. 'There's less time to be our backstage selves'
>
> Why? Technology, longer workweek and more workers enjoying their jobs.

The concept of leisure has different and more complex reality if it is perceived from the Islamic perspective. In Islam the basic perspective is based on faith that covers all ummat in all their worldly activities and after life. In short, if

Paper contributed to the 17th ISA World Congress of Sociology, RC13/RC09, 'Social Transformations and Changing Leisure Patterns,' Gothenburg, Sweden, 15 July 2010.

we use Geertz's concept of force and scope in religion (1971), Islam has a strong force or norms and rituals that are obligatory ('wajib') and one who does not obey will be sinned in the afterlife and reprimanded with social sanctions from their community. Moreover, the scope of Islam is very broad and Islam should be implemented in all aspect of life such as education, business, politics and interpersonal relation.

The consequences of this strong force and broad scope of Islamic values can be seen within the social interaction and relation where exclusiveness are higher to practicing Moslems compared to nominal or 'secular' ones. For the latter, there seems to be no significant social barrier for them in the interaction with non-Moslems in work, leisure and even marriage. These secular Moslems are relatively more inclusive compared to the practicing Moslems. At the micro level, the scope and force of religion have different impacts. Therefore, we have different Moslems, from practicing Moslems to Statistical or ID Moslems. The most visible activities are the five daily prayers (sunrise, midday, after midday, before dawn and evening) which are obligatory for all Moslems. A 2008 poll shows that 80 per cent of Indonesian Moslems conducted this daily prayer compared to 59 per cent in Egypt; 46 per cent in Pakistan and 34 per cent in Turkey (Honorine, 2010: 35). In Indonesia 52 of the 470 districts/municipalities apply so-called Syariah regional bylaws (Perda Syariat) that authorize some Islamic nuanced rules such as the obligatory to wear Moslem clothing; the obligatory to be able to read Quran for student and for candidates of heads of districts; and the obligatory to pay alms or *zakat* (Bush, 2008: 176).

Most essentially, all Islamic teachings would refer to the five pillars of Islam, i.e. the Admission of Allah and Mohammad; the five daily prayers; the giving of alms; the one month fasting in the holy month of *Ramadhan*; and the pilgrimage to Mecca. Moreover, there is also the six pillars of faith, i.e. the belief in God/Allah; the belief in angels; the belief in books (Torah, Bible, Quran); the belief in prophets; the belief in destiny (*taqdir*); and the belief in the final day.

This paper discusses various interpretations on the meaning of leisure in Islamic teaching and the development of its practices in traditional and contemporary Moslem societies. The Indonesia case study will show how religious meaning and practice of leisure inexorably intersect with political and economic impetus. In this regard, some Islamic interpretations of leisure provide religious legitimacy for Islamist political agenda as well as stimulate critical ways for religious commodification. Regarding the latter issue, as this paper will show, such interpretation has legitimated the proliferation of religious leisure industries in Indonesia. However, the degree to which certain meaning and practice of leisure adopted in the individual level would depend on the scope of Islam each Moslem adheres to. It is that differs practicing Moslems from their more secular fellows.

Leisure in Islamic Teaching

The norms of Islam cover not only religious worship but also all aspects life such as work and leisure. In work the influence of *ibadah* (worship) is also seen such as the pronouncement of the word 'Bismillah' when one begins working or 'Alhamdullilah' after one finishing any activities. Consequently, the five daily prayers should be practiced during the working activities and a similar pattern also occurs in non work activity such as leisure. The relation of *ibadah* in work and *ibadah* in Islam can be seen in the following matrix:

IBADAH (Religious Worship)	
Work (Secular and Islamic)	Leisure (Secular and Islamic)

The matrix shows that Islam influences all adherents with certain norms and activities. On the other hand, there are different degrees between practicing and non practicing or secular Moslems. The practicing Moslems al least practice the Five Islamic Pillars and the Six Islamic Faiths ('Rukun Iman') and the implementation of Syariah (Islamic laws) in social life. On the other hand, non practicing Moslems or Nominal Moslem or Moslem I.D., at least believe and admit in Allah as the only God and Mohammad as God's Prophet. Based on the above matrix we can construct three clusters of Moslems with primary works in the religious sector such as Ulama (religious scholars) and *ustadz* (religious teachers). The second clusters are those who work in secular sectors such as banking despite that there is also Islamic banking (Syariah Banking). A similar pattern also takes place in the leisure sector either in secular ones (tourism) or the religious ones (Religious Tourism/Pilgrimage). The matrix illustrates that all Moslems in their worship, work and leisure must perform obligatory prayers and other rituals where their meaning and practice of leisure have unique features that are different from non Moslem societies.

In Islam, leisure is often related to the concepts of *mata'* and *faragh*, two concepts that are both considered negative in the Islamic view. *Mata'* means momentary pleasure. Al Qur'an often uses this term to indicate the fondness of human to earthly pleasure whilst ignoring the eternal afterlife. A verse like 'surely life on earth is a temporary pleasure that lulls' (*wa ma-l-hayatu-l-dunya illa mata' al-ghurur*) (Qur'an, 3: 185) has pointed to one perspective about leisure. *Mata'* has always been contrasted with the advice to worship diligently and remember God more in a more frequent manner (*dhikr*). Only through diligent worship, one can reach eternal happiness. *Faragh*, on the other hand, means leisure time. This concept is often opposed to the suggestion to work hard (*'amal*). Thus, leisure means laziness and the wasting of free time. Both Qur'an as well as Hadith of the Prophet has repeatedly explained this issue. In Qur'an (94: 7–8), for example, there is a suggestion that reads: *fa idza faraghta fa-n-shab wa ila rabbika fa-r-ghab* (and if you are through with one task, seek another, and to your God, ask). The prophet himself has warned about the dangers of free time in a Hadith that reads: *inna-l-syababa wa-l-faragha wa-l-jidata mafsadatun li-l-mar'i ayya mafsadatin* (surely youth with free time and wealth will destroy a person with the ultimate damage).

Work and worship are two of the matters loved by God, while *mata'* and *faragh* are two matters He loathed. Hard work is always linked with the quality of one's faith. There are many verses in scripture that combines between an individual with faith (*alladzina amanu*) and an individual who works correctly and beneficially (*wa 'amilu al-shalihat*). One Hadith of the Prophet also cites the importance of balance between work and worship; *i'mal li dunyaka ka'annaka ta'isyu abadan, wa'mal li akhiratika ka'annaka tamutu ghadan* (work for your world as if you will live forever, and work for your afterlife as if you will die tomorrow). If work and worship were set in a separate category, then just like Catholicism, Islam emphasizes on the balance between *vita activa* and *vita contemplativa*. However, this separation seems less contextual, as it is related to work organization in the monastery. Islam does not recognize the monkshood or the monastic system. Aside from being a Prophet, Muhammad is also illustrated as a soldier, political leader, trader, and head of household. The Islamic ethics on working seem to be more similar to Protestantism. This matter, for example, is shown in a study by Turner (1998). Turner stated that, to Weber, 'it was the patrimonial nature of Muslim political institutions which precluded the emergence of capitalist preconditions, namely rational law, a free labor market, autonomous cities, a money economy, and a bourgeois class' (1998: 2).

Despite the fact that *mata'* and *faragh* are loathed by God, not all matters related to pleasure is loathed by Him. This is because earthly pleasures are basically God's gift to mankind. In a verse, for example, God says: 'Men are accessorized with the instinct for lust in the form of women, children, properties such as gold and silver, domestic horses, cattles, and vegetation. All those are the pleasures of life (*mata'*) on earth.' (Qur'an, 3: 14). In another verse, God also says (Qur'an, 40: 39): 'The worldly life is nothing more than pleasure,' (*inna ma hadzihi al-hayah al-dunya mata'*). The Prophet also emphasizes on the importance of consoling the heart in his Hadith 'console your heart from time to time, because the tired heart is a blind heart.'

Another well known Hadith is the prophet's suggestion of sports, specifically stating the branches: 'and teach your children swimming, horse riding, and archery' (*wa'allimu awladakum al-sibahah wa rukub al-khayl wa-l-rimayah*). Muslims are encouraged to perform sports in order to maintain physical health. The prophet himself also says that 'health is like a crown worn on the head of healthy people; no one can see it except the ill' (*al-shihhah taj 'ala ru'us al-ashihha' la yaraha illa-l-mardha*). Aside from these three activities, the prophet also suggested running (a Hadith narrated by Abu Daud stated that he once competed in running with his wife Aisyah), hunting, fishing, owning pets, perform arts, and scenery viewing as sports (Ibrahim, 1991).

Leisure in the Traditional Islamic Community

The tradition and history of Islam cannot be separated from Arab's tradition and history. In the beginning of Islam's emergence in the Arabian soil, the Arabs are well recognized as avid poets and singers. Each year, there is the Ukaz festival in Mecca where poets compete in writing and poetry reading. Winners in this festival will acquire some prizes and a high social status. The prophet himself never prohibited the existence of this festival. However, during his era and also the era of the first generation of the four caliphs, the Ukaz tradition did not continue. This is mainly due to the fact that the festival is closely related to booze and women, two matters regarded as forbidden by the Prophet. Until the reign of the Umayyah dynasty around the year 750, which is based in Damascus, the poetry tradition was revived. On this, Hitti (1970: 227) tells the story:

> The Evenings of the Caliphs were set apart for entertainment and social intercourse. Muawiyah (the first Umayyid caliph) was particularly fond of listening to historical narratives and anecdotes, preferably Southern Arabian and poetical recitation. To satisfy this desire, he imported from Al Yaman, a story teller.

The caliphs of the Ummayyid dynasty, according to Hitti, were also well known for conducting horse racing, swimming in grape pools, and hunting with the Saluk dog. A more 'absurd' habit came from the caliphs of the Abbasid dynasty, who reigned after the fall of Umayyid. This Baghdad based dynasty succeeded in building a replica of heaven on earth as described by the Qur'an. They built lush green garden with trees, complete with pavilions, swimming pool, and water fountains. This park played an important role in the daily lives of the wealthy people, where they spent their time to relax, find entertainment, and playing chess. During the reign of Caliph Harun al-Rashid, Baghdad became the central galaxy of music stars. The high rated musicians accompanied by singers from among the slave complement the stories that were immortalized in the classic story of *The Arabian Nights.* Prominent Muslim scholar, Ibn Khaldun, also include stories and traditions of the Muslim community leisure in his legendary work, *Muqaddimah*.

In Islamic tradition itself, the tradition of leisure has been institutionalized in the form of symbolic time's existence. Similar to the Christian and Jewish tradition, Islam also has Friday as the day of *sabbath.* On Fridays, Muslims are only required to perform the Friday prayers for no more than an hour. The rest is a holiday. In addition, Islam also has the holy month Ramadhan, where all Muslims are obliged to fast during the month. Ramadhan created another lifestyle for the Muslim community. They usually sleep longer during the day, and the time after fast breaking is the real leisure time. Life in the evening is usually longer. Muslim communities in some places have a different way to fill it (Ibrahim, 1991: 211). There are social gathering events packed with activities such as fast breaking together, or by enlivening fasting nights by singing religious songs, some stay awake with their peers waiting for sahur time, and many more. In Indonesia, the month of Ramadhan becomes a moment for colossal celebration. Most entertainment shows in television are transformed into Islamic nuances. Singers also compete in releasing their latest religious songs. Fashion houses are also flooded with requests for Muslim attires with a variety of models. The dais collaborated with celebrities in conveying 'serious' Islamic teachings in a banal pop culture package.

After Ramadhan, the people will celebrate Idul Fitri. In a shorter duration of day, the celebration is far livelier. Idul Fitri becomes a holiday moment to gather with family as well as stay in touch with relatives and friends. In Indonesia, this tradition presents the annual tradition called 'mudik'. Several days before the holiday, workplaces begin to dismiss their employees and provide special benefits. Airports, train and bus stations are packed and crowded with passengers. Highways as the main route for inter-city transportation are jammed. Tariffs for transportation mode services are increased twice or even more. On the other hand, following the philosophy of Idul Fitri (purification/cleansed from past sins), each person is somehow demanded to leave the old image behind, replacing it with a new one. The result is a colossal show of consumerism, as everyone is concerned to acquire new clothes, jewelry, vehicle and various properties. The community invades shopping centres where they compete by giving out massive discounts during that moment.

Apart from Ramadhan and Idul Fitri, Muslims have other symbolic times to celebrate. For instance, 12 *Dzulhijjah* in the *Qomariah* calendar is dated as Idul Adha, an occasion where people are required to offer sacrifice by slaughtering sheep, cow, or camel. This annual ritual is performed to have people from all social strata share in consuming the meat. On that day, millions of Muslims around the world gathered in Mecca to carry out a pilgrimage ritual called Hajj, which is very expensive. Moreover, there is also the commemoration of the Prophet's birthday every 12 Rabi 'al-Awal in the Qomariah calendar where people celebrate with various events; from Qur'an study, Islamic activities competition (such as adzan, qiraat Quran, Islamic songs), to performances of religious entertainment. It is worth noting that in many countries where the majority of population is Muslims, the government sets these days as official holidays. In general, the community also draws on these days for vacation interests.

Clash of Ideas about Leisure

Essentially, there are no problems related to the principle of whether leisure is justified in Islam or not. In general, leisure has a good precedent both in the Islamic teaching and tradition. However, the development of modern world presents various forms of a holiday tradition. It could even be said that as a consequence of the modern work organization compartmentalization, leisure has become a part of the work industry itself. This can be seen in the emergence of companies that specializes in tourism services, music, film, sports, culinary, etc. This has led to a specific debate among the Islamic scholars. It especially involves two matters; the form of leisure activity itself and the growing inclusivity of public spaces that make segregation between the sexes nonexistent. In Muslim countries that implement strict Islamic law such as Saudi Arabia, the government draws quite a hard line on entertainment activities. A study conducted in 1988 on the Saudi youth behaviour indicates that most of the Saudi youth take advantage of their vacation time in their house by watching television. They will strictly go out of the house for soccer practice or playing. The latter is the favourite past time activity (Ibrahim, 1991: 214). For women, the Saudi government implements a strict policy for activities performed outside the home.

However, in secular Muslim countries, where the government does not intervene much in the private affairs of its citizens, the growth of entertainment and leisure industry grows rapidly. This issue often triggers disputes. Halal and haram labeling invites a louder debate. A scholar once said that an Islamic recreation must meet the nine elements: God as the intention, no elements contradict with creed such as syirik, kufur and nifaq; things that are not against Islamic law, which are legally forbidden (haram) and syubhat; to cover the *aurat* (forbidden parts of body particularly thigh and breast); to always maintain social manners; no elements of gambling; not containing elements of wastefulness; not containing elements of 'divide and conquer' or hostility, and not containing any elements of harm.

In Indonesia, for example, places of night entertainment are often the attack targets of Islamic fundamentalist groups. They accused entertainment venues as the nest of disobedience. Furthermore, the sending of delegates in international beauty contests reaps pros and cons from the Muslim community of Indonesia. Scholars under the wing of organizations such as Majelis Ulama Indonesia (MUI) and Nahdlatul Ulama (NU) have issued several *fatwas* (religious edicts) concerning these entertainment activities. MUI, for example, has prohibited beauty pageants, playboy magazine, and the art of yogic breathing; while NU has issued prohibition of infotainment show. The reasons for prohibition of beauty pageants and playboy magazine are due to the exploitation of women's body in public, while the prohibition of yoga is associated with the elements of Paganism where yoga is considered as part of the Hindu tradition.

On the other hand, MUI, and later, the Ministry of Religious Affairs often conduct awarding events for entertainment activities which are regarded as 'commendable' and 'enlivening the Syiar of Ramadhan.' In 2005, for example, MUI granted MUI Awards to the soap opera 'Kiamat Sudah Dekat' and singer Opick, Bimbo, and Gigi for their religious songs. Meanwhile, SCTV gained title as commendable television for its high number of religious shows.[1] Since the release of best-selling novel *Ayat-Ayat Cinta* which was then filmed in late 2007, religious leaders from various Islamic organizations have collaborated to provide support. One of the most prominent figures is Din Syamsuddin, Head of P.P. Muhammadiyah. He was even involved in the promotion of 'Ayat-Ayat Cinta' ('Verses of Love') sequel, entitled *Ketika Cinta Bertasbih* ('When Love Chants') which was filmed in early 2009. Another phenomenon of Islamic recreational activity is the emergence of young preachers (*da'i*) who appeared just like celebrities. Some of them come with their distinctive brands such as 'manajemen qolbu' (heart management) and 'wisata hati' (heart excursion). The first is identified with the figure named Ustadz Abdullah Gymnastiar (Aa' Gym) and the latter with the figure of Ustadz Yusuf Mansur. They built religious counseling business, organization of *umrah*, spiritual gathering, religious SMS service, mission television stations, recording studios for Islamic songs, and create virtual pages where their followers can communicate online with the *ustadz*. The customers are mainly from the middle-class Muslim community.

The *fatwas* of the scholars or the pros and cons opinion do not have much impact on the growth of the entertainment industry, particularly in a secular country. Society is not excessively attached to the opinion of scholars. Some people even consider that events such as beauty pageants are beneficial to the promotion of Indonesian tourism. Actions by a group of people who raided entertainment spots also caused resistance from the majority of citizens. Eventually, it all depends on the market. 'Secular' or 'Islamic' recreation is both competing in the entertainment industry markets. As consumers, people are free to choose. However, it must be admitted that the Islamic recreation industry has experienced growth with a precedent that has never existed before in history. Indeed, this is due to the skill of the industry's workers in programme cultivating and packaging, with rather less connection to the *fatwas* of the scholars.

The Cases of Three Moslem Professionals

In the following discussion we will identify how work and leisure are practiced by three professionals who are practicing Moslems (Mr Akhmad: Manager, Mr Bakhrul: Entrepreneur and Mr Chairul: Lawyer). Despite the fact that the three professionals have different patterns of implementing Islamic norms, they still have a similarity that Islam should colour their work and leisure.

(i) The Manager

Mr Akhmad (42) is a figure who represents the mainstream of middle class urban Muslim which began to grow in Indonesia since the late 1990s. A group of obedient students yet was not raised from traditional Islamic institutions such as boarding school (*pesantren*). He is the product of a leading secular educational institution in East Java.

From Rihlah to Watching Action Movies

Recreation *(rihlah),* reading Islamic books, swimming, watching movies, and visiting the home of relatives are activities that fill Akhmad's free time. From these activities, he has stressed the importance of recreation. *Rihlah,* as Akhmad calls it. Lexically, *rihlah* is an Arabic term which means to travel or go on vacation. This term is indeed popular among urban students. *Rihlah* is outbound activities to tourist spots for the purpose of recreation and *nature tadabbur.*[1] *Rihlah* is always religious. In *rihlah,* as stated by Akhmad, besides seeking a relaxed atmosphere to ease tensions from work, there is also *nature tadabbur* as the religious activity. This activity is very common among Muslim activists. *Rihlah* provides Islamic imagination from leisure activities.

Akhmad often visits his favourite *rihlah* spot in the tourist area called Trawas, a mountainous area located in Mojokerto regency, East Java, approximately 40 kilometres southwest of Surabaya city. This activity is usually carried out as often as two to three times a year, and most frequently with the members of Al-Ikhlas and Masjidillah congregational study. Within this community, *rihlah* can be performed twice a year, in the middle and end of each year. The ritual would be held once at the end of the year with Akhmad's company, where *Rihlah* activities are typically performed in two days and one night. Participants usually rent a bus and travel together. They ranged from 10 to 20 people. If their family and children come along, usually a villa will be rented for a night. However, if the participants only consist of adult males, they simply set up a tent and stay overnight in the middle of the forest.

Most of *rihlah*'s activities are for relaxing. The activities include, among others; sports, camping, cooking, organizing several races, and, last but not least, a religious reflection called *nature tadabbur.* The latter activity usually takes about one to two hours, while the remaining time is utilized for recreational activities in general. However, it is the *nature tadabbur* activity that gave a special meaning to the participants. *Tadabbur* is usually delivered by a religious teacher or someone among the participants who is regarded as more senior with a broad knowledge of religion. *Nature tadabbur* can be simply interpreted as a reflection about nature as God's creation. In this activity, the speaker will lure the participants to contemplate the signs of nature that has been observed and how to connect them to the greatness of God. The religious teacher will also invite the participants to reflect on God's ample blessings to them, whether in the form of fortune, health, as well as skills, and encouraging them to share with the unfortunates. In addition, this forum is sometimes used to recite the Qur'an together.

Next to the religiously nuanced *rihlah,* Akhmad often visits public entertainment spots with his family for holiday. Among the favourites are Taman Safari II in Prigen and Jatim Park in Lamongan. Akhmad also swims routinely in his favourite public pools, usually every Sunday or on public holidays with his only son as company. To avoid crowds, he always arrives early in the morning at 6 and leave at 8. This timing is conducted for religious purposes as well. He does so to keep his eyes from the possibility of seeing a woman's *'aurat'* (forbidden body parts such as breast and thigh) when the place is about to be filled with men and women swimming in the same pool under the pool premises.

Besides recreation and sports, reading is another leisure time activity for Akhmad. His hobby is reading Islamic books such as popular religious novels like *Ketika Cinta Bertasbih* and *Ayat-Ayat Cinta,* as well as books about Islamic political in the salafi scholars circle like Ibn Taymiyyah, popular knowledge books on Shari'a banking, the life of prophets, *Manajemen Rasulullah* by Dr Syafii Antonio, and many others. He also enjoys Islamic magazines such as *Sabili* and An-Nida, which are sold in his favourite bookstores. A spares his time to read, especially when relaxing after work or even in the vehicle on the way to the office.

Like other middle class urban, Akhmad also enjoys watching movies or listening to music as hobbies. Basically, he is a fan of action genre films. It has been a favourite since childhood. He is not too fond of romantic or drama movies. Up until now he never quits this hobby. These films taught people about how to become a hero and to care for one another. He likes movies starring Hong Kong actors Jackie Chan and Jet Li, as well as Hollywood actors like Sylvester Stallone, Bruce Willis, Al Pacino, and Arnold Schwarzenegger. Recently, since the appearance of religious movies or soap operas he also began to appreciate them. According to him, religious movies have been able to perform as an alternative to popular films that mostly exploit passion. Popular films such as *Ayat-Ayat Cinta* and *Ketika Cinta Bertasbih* are never missed by him. Moreover, he also encourages his family to enjoy religious movies and soap operas.

Religious Meaning of Leisure

According to Akhmad, leisure is an activity to fill his spare time. Basically, any activity will have no problems as long as it aligns with *shari'a* (religious rules) and does not bring *ma'shiat* (sin making). Activities such as recreation, sports, or reading in certain limits are parts of the mediums that fulfill the needs of human life. They have fulfilled the basic needs of human being from three dimensions; physical, mind, and mentally. Sports fulfill the physical needs to be healthy. With regular exercise, one will be physically fit and worshipping will be more optimal. Reading fulfills the need of human mind for knowledge and insights. With lots of reading, one will be smarter and learn many things. Recreation, gatherings, watching movies, or listening to music also fulfills the mental needs of human beings for leisure and relaxation. Just like walking, there is always a time and place to stop in order to exhale and prepare for the next trip. He quotes a Hadith narrated by Abdullah bin Amr bin Ash: 'Verily upon you the right to God and on you the right to your body, and on you the right for your family. So give the rights to each of its owners (*inna 'alaika lillahi haqq wa inna 'alaika lijismika haqq wa inna 'alaika liahlika haqq. Fa'ti kulla dzi haqq haqqahu*). According to him, recreation and sport activities are means for a Muslim in claiming their rights from their body.

Akhmad also states that it does not mean that the matters above do not have its' precedent in Islam. Moreover, he adds that both God and His Messenger have taught humans on how to manage time as efficiently as possible. In one chapter of the Qur'an, since time is so important, God himself has sworn 'by time' *(wa-l-'ashri)* (Qur'an, 103: 1). In this chapter, it is mentioned that people who are not good in using time are those who lose *(inna-l-insana la fi khusrin)* (Qur'an, 103: 2). Therefore, leisure time should be utilized as much as possible to improve the quality of man himself. In *rihlah,* people will be lured to contemplate on God's creation as God's own appeal submitted within the verses of scripture was, 'do you not think?' (*a fa la tatafakkarun*).

In his opinion, recreation does not necessarily mean sightseeing trips to the forest or mountains, but it can also be done through staying in touch with friends and relatives, visiting the hospital, or 'takziah' at someone's funeral. By visiting the hospital or doing takziah, one will learn to empathize with others and feel grateful for God's blessing. By gathering with relatives or friends, one can also share experience, joy, and sadness. This way, one will be released from work related stress and spirits are renewed. In one *Hadith*, according to Akhmad, the Prophet himself often invited his friends for walks to visit other friends. They chatted, joked, and slaughtered sheep or camels to be devoured together. While regarding sports itself, he has also suggested to his followers to do so. According to Akhmad, in one *Hadith*, the Prophet called on Muslims to learn swimming, archery, and horseback riding. One of the reasons he favoured swimming is to carry out the Prophet's teaching.

Islam forbids the use of free time for things that do not bring any benefits. He highlighted infotainment shows on television that contain rumours if not slander. Gossip, called *ghibah,* is talking about someone without the person knowing that he/she is being talked about, regardless that the information contained truth. In the case where such information is untrue, then it is called slander. In Islam, both are forbidden. According to him, many *infotainment* shows contain *ghibah* and a number of Islamic scholars in Indonesia have once forbid this kind of show. Leisure activities that contain such things, is indeed classified as non Islamic leisure category. Other activities such as clubbing, watching films that invites lust, and trips to places of sin are included in that category. He stated that a Muslim should take advantage of their time for activities that support productivity. If so, then recreation, reading, exercising, and watching movies will be a part of one's worship to God:

> One can give the spirit of worship into every leisure activity because God basically created time as an opportunity that can be exploited by human being to worship Him. *Wa ma khalaqtu-l-jinna wa-l-insa illa liya'buduni* (Qur'an, 51: 56)

Aside from worship, Islamic *leisure* can also contain *da'wah* (religious mission). Movies, music, tourism activities or religious pilgrimage can be an effective medium of preach. In Akhmad's opinion, Islamic teachings are very effective if disseminated through the media of arts and entertainment rather than through a more serious media such as recitation of the Qur'an. The image of Islam can also be built through a well-packaged cultural *da'wah*. He mentions that the emergence of religious teachers (*ustadz*) who appear like celebrities is one of the new strategies of Islamic preaching. Muslims, in his opinion, should appreciate them as they don't rely solely on appearance. The concepts that they offer such as 'dhikr' (God remembering) a la Arifin Ilham, '*wisata hati*' (heart excursion) a la Yusuf Mansur, or '*manajemen qalbu*' (heart management) a la Aa' Gym proved to be very well accepted by the community.

In spite of it all, he argues that in this modern time there are currently a lot of options for holiday destinations and entertainment. He predicts that Muslims in the future will opt for more Islamic holiday destinations. He mentioned that the rise of tourism in the Middle East has been marked by the phenomenal presence of Qatar. This country has transformed itself into one of the new exotic centre of the world. Not too long ago, they built the beautiful tower of al-Burj, successfully organized the XV Asian Games in 2006 with a grand opening and closing ceremonies, as well as establishing stages of arts which combined Arabian and Western artworks.

According to Akhmad, the rise of Islamic civilization is also marked generally by the development of *Shari'a* economic system in the world. This system has become an alternative to the system of modern capitalism which was considered as a failure. Akhmad often invites his colleagues to become customers of Shari'a banks. He also adds that the Islamic banking system proved to be more resilient and it can be justified religiously. He himself has accounts in conventional banks and Islamic banks as well. The main reason for choosing conventional banks is due to the fact that they have more branch offices and ATMs, making it easier for business. The interesting part is the way he deals with the conventional banking system which is identical with *riba* (bank interest), something he calls 'forbidden in Islam.' According to him, Muslim activists like himself with accounts in conventional banks treat interest rates as *rishwah* (bribery). The interest will not be used for their personal purpose, but it will be returned to society through donations to social foundations.

(ii) The Entrepreneur

Mr Bakhrul (43) is a travel entrepreneur. He is also committed to his duties as a lecturer and leader of a *dhikr* assembly, an activity where *dhikr* teacher and his followers meet to recite holy verses as uttered by the teacher. Initially, he was just a university lecturer and Islamic preacher. His activities as a teacher of Qur'an recitation brought him to the position of a reputable religious teacher. In the end of year 2005, he created a routine study community which is categorized in the preaching world as *dhikr* assembly. Since the late 1990s, along with the growth of religious passion in the Indonesian Muslim society, the format of religious activism is indeed more diverse. In addition to the conventional missionary activity that contains verbal rhetoric, the format of religious activity takes a new form through dhikr/remembrance assembly. In the 'business' ethics of this dhikr, an assembly leader usually claims to have a diploma issued by a senior cleric whose name legitimizes competence. Bakhrul claimed that he obtained his diploma from a senior cleric in South Kalimantan.

In 2007, Bakhrul established a travel company that focuses in religious tourism services, both domestic and overseas. For domestic destinations, the sites visited are religious sites, especially the tombs of Walisongo in Java. While for overseas destination, umrah and hajj travel packages as well as tours to historic sites in the Middle East are offered. Since the government applied portion system for the pilgrimage policy in 2004, restrictions are stricter for the ritual. Those who have been on Hajj pilgrimages are only allowed to repeat the ritual after five years. As a result of this policy, many people who have been on pilgrimage and wish to return again to the holy land selected umrah as an alternative. This policy, in fact, makes the business of religious tourism even more intense. Companies providing religious tourism service compete in offering 'umrah plus' packages, where in addition to performing worship in *umrah,* the pilgrims earn pilgrimage bonus tours to other places in the Saudi Arabian territory as well as in other countries such as Egypt and Turkey.

According to Bakhrul, the most important asset in setting up a religious tour service company is not the money but the jamaah/followers instead. Hundred of his dhikr assembly followers were his first clients as well as marketing agents who invited more potential clients. Therefore, in this business, the role of reputable scholars is very central. Major travel companies like Maktour always embrace important clerics figure in each region. These scholars are the ones who encourage their followers to go on religious holidays as well as directing them to choose the related company. As compensation, the company will reward these influential scholars with certain facilities. The business of religious tour grew very rapidly, beating other tourist industries that offer trips to 'secular' sites. Secular tourism business tends to be more exclusive since it is usually enjoyed only by the wealthy people; those who viewed holidays as mere leisure, a self release from work stress and energy revitalization for the upcoming work. While religious tourism belongs to all economic circles; either weak or strong. Fans of religious tourism view leisure as a spiritual journey that must be separated from their jobs. Some have even worked hard to gather the funds in order to embark in this spiritual journey.

The Meaning of Work and Leisure

Bakhrul stated that Islam is a religion that highly appreciates time. In Islamic teachings, taking time for granted or using it for unproductive matters is strictly prohibited. In this case, he argues, a productive time is time used for work in order to earn a living. Work is very central in Islam. Several Qur'an verse or *Hadith* of the Prophet has mentioned the importance of work. He cites a verse which reads: 'and if the prayer has been accomplished, spread on the face of earth to find Allah's fortune (*fa idza qudhiyat al-shalat fa-n-tasyiru fi al-ardh wa-b-taghu min fadhl Allah*)' (Qur'an, 62: 10). According to Bakhrul, the Prophet also teaches the importance of working through some of his sayings like: 'start early in making a living;' 'those who die while making a living are a martyr.' He also mentions a *Hadith* that the Prophet once kissed the hand of a friend that was very rough due to hard working. Like most Muslims, he is among the people who believe that all the actions of a Muslim could mean worship. In this case, work has a special place as worship.

Although God encourages work, He also creates special times for humans to free themselves from the pressures of work. According to Bakhrul, work is part of the non-formal worship *(ghair mahdlah).* Islam encourages balance between *ghair mahdlah* worship (work) and *mahdlah* worship (includes rituals such as prayer, fasting, alms and pilgrimage). People who spend their day only for work will lose the meaning of work itself. Moreover, he also said that the obligation of five daily prayers is a mechanism created by God to control balance between work and worship. Five daily prayers were created to follow the rhythm of human work. The five obligatory prayers are only done during a human's active times; from dawn until sunset. God does not oblige His followers to perform activities between sunsets until dawn. It is a time created entirely by God so humans can fulfill their body's right of rest. In relation to this, Bakhrul quotes a Qur'an verse which reads: 'And He created night as a blanket and noon as a time to make a living (*wa ja'alna al-laila libasa wa al-nahar ma'asya*)' (Qur'an, 78: 10–11).

Based on the above explanation, Bakhrul believes that there is no leisure tradition in Islamic teachings. If leisure is interpreted as idle time *(faragh),* then it is something strongly opposed by Islam. Leisure will then be associated with laziness *(kasal),* wasting *(tabdzir),* momentary pleasure *(mata '),* and games *(la'ib wa lahw)* which can lead people toward forbidden deeds *(ma'shiyah).* Islam basically has no holiday. In regards to this, Bakhrul explains:

> 'In the Qur'an, God forbids his people to work on Fridays. However, this is only valid at the time Friday prayers are performed. After the (Friday) prayers, God explicitly commanded his people to get back to work. Therefore, identifying Friday as a Muslim holiday is completely unjustified. '

For Bakhrul, leisure is an ideological concept. To him, leisure is developed in the materialistic Western secular tradition. The Westerners did not take work as worship and, therefore, does not have what he calls a 'five-time management' which allows people to perform the five daily prayers and are not enslaved by work throughout the day. This is the underlying reason for Westerners to create a leisure tradition, where they set up a special time to escape from the pressures of work. It often develops into forms of negative activities. Unfortunately, Bakhrul stated that modern society takes this distinction between work and leisure according to the Western-style standards. Practices of modern leisure such as vacation and entertainment became common in any society. One of the most phenomenal modern leisure practices is tourism, i.e. traveling to a place as holiday destination. In Indonesia, it is commonly known as excursion or recreation.

In Bakhrul's opinion, the development of leisure traditions brought by the Western civilization which was embraced by the world community, including Muslims, could basically be transformed into positive activities in accordance to Islamic teachings. He suggested a more neutral terminology instead of leisure. Islam, in his opinion, only recognizes transfer of work, as described in one of Qur'anic verses (94: 7); 'and if you are idle, look for another job' (*fa idza faraghta fa-n-shab*). In this regard, Bakhrul took the tourism industry as an example. Islam, indeed, does not recognize tourism. However, according to Bakhrul, Islam is a tradition that grew from trips *(safar)* and adventures *(rihlah).* Islam teaches pilgrimage; i.e. travel to certain places in order to stay in touch, spread the symbols (*shi'ar*) of Islam, or to simply pray. One of the pillars of Islam, hajj, lexically means pilgrimage also. Therefore, for Bakhrul, in its development, tourism can be Islamized as religious pilgrimage travel. Visits to holy places, charismatic clerics, or historic sites are beneficial in adding knowledge and insights of faith. Besides tourism, other activities such as sports or arts can also be developed into positive activities.

Spiritual Practice, Material Motive

Bakhrul is a theology lecturer, religious preacher, as well as a businessman of religious tourism services. As a lecturer, he capitalizes his knowledge into religious materials for his lectures. As a preacher with hundreds of followers, he capitalized his followers as an asset for the early development of his religious tourism business. In brief, he is a scholar who works in the religious leisure industry. These activities of religious tourism are not only part of his job, but also the main leisure practices that he does. As a religious teacher, aside from organizing the trips of his followers who are now his customers, he also accompanies them as a spiritual guide. He and his family often take part in various travel activities managed by the company, both domestic and overseas destination. Even so, he also does other leisure activities routinely such as exercising or listening to Islamic music.

As a businessman and religious mentor, Bakhrul has undergone religious travel dozens of times. Due to its' repetitive routine, he interprets the activities more as work than leisure. Nonetheless, the interesting aspect is his confession about the impression he has on his customers. He admitted that the motivation for religious tourism is not necessarily religious, yet it is also driven by desires that are 'secular', such as seeking entertainment, wasting of money, or to increase social prestige. According to him, the public interest in choosing the *umrah* (pilgrimage to Kabah in Mecca that can be undertaken at any time of the year) packages offered by the company is mostly due to the bonus of excursions given. In addition to historic sites trips in Saudi Arabia alone, the company often offers additional trips to a number of 'secular' recreation destinations such as Malaysia, Thailand and even Singapore. While domestically, religious tours to the tombs of Walisongo are usually paired with additional travels to other tourist attractions such as beaches, wholesale markets, or children playgrounds. 'If most of the followers/jamaah are ladies, then trips to shopping centres must be added as a bonus,' says Bakhrul. For some other followers (*jama'a*h), according to Bakhrul, religious tours also act as a mean to increase social prestige. This applies especially among the middle class circle who lately becomes devoted to religion or the rural communities who have been saving for years in order to fulfill their ambitions of visiting the holy land.

As a scholar, Bakhrul feels uncomfortable with the facts. However, as a businessman, he just perceives it as a business opportunity. Religious tourism, although built on religious foundation, is managed with the framework of secular business. He must also compete with other players who implement various strategies. In this business, the role of scholars is essential. Up to this year, he already has eight branches in several cities across Indonesia, including in Asahan, North Sumatra and Sorong, Papua. To further sustain this business on running, he must regularly build relationships with scholars in these areas. They can effectively deliver promotion to the people. Moreover, according to Bakhrul the market share of religious tourism business would be far greater than general tourism. He realized the growth of Indonesian Muslim society who is becoming increasingly fanatic about Islamic activities. This fact generates the presence of individuals or institutions that serve this specific need are more sought after day after day.

Apart from religious tourism activities, Bakhrul also enjoys reading activities. His favourite topics are ranging from general knowledges to fictions. This should be done because of his profession as a lecturer. He also likes listening to music and watching movies with family on his spare time. According to him, creating an entertaining atmosphere is crucial in enhancing one's imagination ability and sensitivity. He argues that the art of music and performing arts has long been growing in classical Muslim civilization. As long as they contain no negative impacts, then these activities are in fact highly recommended. He witnessed that despite the increasing religious activities of the Indonesian people, the invasion of Western culture that contradicts with Islamic values are also as strong. This is manifested in the abundance of the moral destroying entertainment industry and technology products. Religious tourism industry, he argues, might become an antithesis to counter the global tendency of secularization in the society.

(iii) The Lawyer

Mr Chairul (37) is a lawyer and founder of a law firm and has a skyrocket career as an advocate. Prior to becoming an advocate in Jakarta, he was a law school lecturer at one of the local universities in Sumatera. In 2005 he moved to Jakarta.

The Meaning of Work and Leisure

Despite his background as an activist of Islamic organization and political party who fights for Islamic law, Chairul does not place himself ideologically. Through reading, he knows very well the history of Islam political struggle in Indonesia. Unlike the two other professionals, he is not too fluent in connecting his arguments to doctrines of Islam. This might occur due to the possibility of not undergoing any specific lesson or course on religion. He is the type of Muslim who viewed the world in a pragmatic way. Work, he says, is the nature of human. Only through work a human being will be able to survive. The harder he worked, the higher his quality of life. On the contrary, the lazier he is, the less meaningful his life will be. Moreover, by working, one does not only earn a living for himself, but gives life to others as well. He believes that in Islam, work is part of worship and even commanded by God. 'Especially to those who are already married,' he said.

If work are human nature and religious order, then how about leisure? Chairul also believes that leisure is human nature and, within certain limits, is also a religious order. Humans basically have the tendency to escape from pressure. Every hardworking person must have experienced psychological pressure as a result of his work. If the pressure cannot be managed, one can experience stress. Leisure, in his opinion, is a mechanism to manage the pressure of work. Therefore, he argues, leisure does not stand alone. It is the partner of the work itself. Leisure exists to support work. If leisure stands alone, it is a symbol of laziness as well as a waste of time, money, and energy. Due to its existence to support work, then the law of leisure is automatically attached to the law of work. It can function as worship as well as *ma'shiat* (sin making). It greatly depends on the purpose and form of the activity.

Chairul does not distinguish between secular and religious leisure. It all depends on the perception built by each individual. As an Indonesian Muslim, everyone can measure the activities which are relevant and which violate the norms. He stated that people often create new laws that even the religion itself never arranged for. *Haram* and *halal* are already obvious in religion. Activities such as adultery or drinking alcohol are undoubtedly forbidden. However, just chatting with friends in cafes, watching movies, dancing, or listening to music are of course not included in the category of *haram*. Globalization, modernization, and technological development present many alternative leisure activities for the community. Every person is entitled to choose according to their own measures of needs and values that existed in their society.

Leisure Practices

The practice of leisure in the circle of lawyers, according to Chairul, is very unique. It is not uncommon for several lawyers, including Chairul himself, to meet clients outside the office and outside office hours. In performing their duties, some lawyers usually do not refer to the conventional working hours, allowing them to work and enjoy leisure at the same time. Chairul often discusses a legal case while relaxing and enjoying music in cafes until late at night. He and his colleagues also do case lobbying frequently in some karaoke spots. In this kind of leisure activity there is usually not much of a serious discussion, but it is effective enough to generate large projects. As a Muslim, he admitted of limiting himself in a number of leisure activities, such as declining alcohol consumption.

Aside of leisure activities in order to support work directly, Chairul often takes advantage of his free time as well, spending it with his family during the holidays. He takes his wife to watch movies or go for a trip to Puncak. He admitted of not being too fond of religious activities such as going to *majelis taklim*[2] or following a pilgrimage to the places of the *habaib*,[3] rituals that his neighbours often performed. The religious events that he attends are always associated with the activities of his party. At certain times, such as on Islamic holidays, his party held religious events such as lecture or mass *dhikr*. However, these activities are not too frequently held. Although not very religious in appearance, he claims that he routinely performs religious rituals such as prayer and fasting. During his time at home, he sometimes invites his wife to perform prayers together. His wife is a veiled woman who, he says, has a more religious view. For matters regarding religious obligation, he says, it is the wife who reminded him more.

Essentially, Chairul wanted to engage in religious activities held by the residents in his village. However, his workload hinders him in doing so. Moreover, he assumes that the religious activities are not much of a help in reducing the stress of work pressure. Nevertheless, at certain times he likes to enjoy religious lectures which are shown frequently every weekend on television. Following religious lectures on television, he said, is more relaxed. Unlike, for example, when followed directly in a forum. There are too many people, noise, and no freedom to choose. 'Of course we cannot interrupt the religious teacher or simply leave the room if we feel that the lecture material is not interesting,' he said.

Concluding Remarks

The previous illustrations of three professionals who are practicing Moslems show that the concept and practice of leisure have powerful Islamic values. Though the three have different professions they still have similar pattern that consider leisure in the context of Islam. The case of the manager shows that even though he works in a secular profession he always manages to apply Islamic norms in his workplace and leisure. The strong influence of Islam is clearly shown in the case of the entrepreneur in travel business who is also a preacher. He Islamized his work in leisure industry by providing religious tourism and pilgrimage. The practice of Islam in work is also shown by the lawyer who is less religious compared to the manager and entrepreneur. His busy work schedule left less time for leisure, and yet he still practices five daily obligatory prayers and fasting in the Ramadan month. The three cases illustrate how religious force is powerful and social changes such as urbanization and economic development do not reduce their compliance to religious worships. Moreover, the development of technology such as transportation, communication (TV and film) is accepted in the context of Islam. In one case, the manager also has a bank account in a non Syariah/Islamic banking where the interest is actually forbidden in Islam and he donates it to social foundations instead. A similar pattern also occurs in television and books where they avoid unIslamic programs (such as pornography) but they can still enjoy other non religious programs. In short, the new forms of social transformations in any social institutions (politics or economics) are always 'Islamized' and 'coloured' by Islamic values.

We can come up with the following prepositions in relation to the three cases above:

> *First, the case of Akhmad (lecturer) illustrates that he practices two types of leisure: a 'secular' one such as sport and an 'Islamic' one such as Tadabbur (religious reflection).* He is able to distinguish and balance both types and provide Islamic meanings to both of them.
>
> *Second, the case of Bakhrul (entrepreneur) who works as an entrepreneur of religious tourism considers his work as a part of non-formal worship (ghair mahdlah).* It seems that the internal boundary between work, leisure and worship has collapsed, due to the fact that it is integrated by religious meaning. It is different from 'weisure' where the diffusion of work and leisure occurs in the secular context.
>
> *Third, the case or Chairul (lawyer) considers leisure as more of a secular activity that supports his secular work.* He distinguishes work and leisure despite that the two activities have always been 'tagged along' by religious rituals in the likes of five daily obligatory prayers.

From the previous discussion we can identify the uniqueness of leisure conducted by practising Moslems who strictly comply to Islamic beliefs *(Qur'an and Hadith)*. We can construct several propositions:

> *First, in Islam work and leisure are social spaces that must implement and reaffirm and reproduce the Islamic beliefs (Qur'an and Hadith).* In other religions, leisure is a space that is mostly detached and distanced itself from religious norms. It is different from an analysis (Dumazedier quoted in Pronovost, 2000) that considers leisure 'as an autonomous sphere of production of new social values.'

Second, the social action of practicing Moslems in leisure must be viewed in the perspective of Weber's value rational action, not just rational action. Leisure is an example of Weber's value rational actions where the Moslems have an obligation to realize and perform Islamic values in social space other than the space of religious worship and work. Of course there are also non religious motives and functions of leisure for the Moslem.

Third, leisure – like work and religious worship – can increase cultural as well as religious capital for this world or legitimacy of Islam and for the afterlife as an investment to attain a place in heaven. It is different from an analysis which states that a person needs much free time to increase cultural capital (see Bourdieu, 1986).

Fourth, leisure – like work – is an institution that might possess dysfunctional effects for social relation since it might exclude Moslems from non-Moslem. In several cases, there are even separation between men and women in leisure activities such as swimming.

Fifth, social transformation such as urbanization, industrialization and technology may not change or disturb leisure, work, and the religious worship, they are even become an opportunity to implement and develop Islamic values. The obligatory five daily prayers and fasting, and even Shari'a must be implemented in all those social spaces that have been changed or affected by social transformation.

The above propositions enable us to enhance our understanding of the meaning of leisure in Islam. Moreover, we also witness different meaning of leisure in Islamic teachings as accepted by the Moslems in Indonesia. This is an example of an alternative explanation of leisure in Islam and an effort 'to take critical distance from Western-centred concepts of leisure, too frequently presented as universal' (Pronovost, 2000). This description as well as explanation on leisure will increase our understanding the holistic and unique picture of leisure in Islam in an era of multiple modernities (Roberts, 2010: 9).

Notes

1. 'SCTV, Televisi Terpuji,' *Suara Merdeka*, 21 December 2003.
2. From Arabic words *majlis ta'lim*, etymologically means instructional meeting place. In Indonesia, it usually refers to a religious informal gathering where an Islamic teacher (ustadz) or preacher (da'i) or ulema (kiai) delivers general (not academic) religious teachings or knowledge towards the congregation.
3. A plural form of an Arabic word *habib*, etymologically means both the lover or the beloved. The word is traditionally used to name Hadramy-Arab descent religious teachers who are believed as the descendants of the Prophet Muhammad.

References

Berger, P. (1966) *The Sacred Canopy: Elements of a Sociological Theory of Religion*. New York: Anchor Books.

Bourdieu, P. (1986) *Distinction: A Social Critique of the Judgment of Taste*. London: Routledge.

Bush, R. (2008) 'Regional Sharia Regulations in Indonesia: Anomaly or Symptom' in Greg Fealy and Sally White (eds) *Expressing Islam: Religious Life and Politics in Indonesia*. Singapore: Institute of Southeast Asian Studies.

Dumazedier, J. (1988) *Sociologie empirique du loisir,* Paris, Seuil, 269 p. (Engl. Transl., Sociology of Leisure, New York, Amsterdam, Elsevier, 1974, 231 p.) in Pronovost, G. (2000) 'The Collapse of the Leisure Society? New Challenges for the Sociology of Leisure', in Quah, Stella and Sales, Arnaud (eds). *International Handbook of Sociology,* London, Sage.

Geertz, C. (1971) *Islam Observed: Religious Development in Morocco and Indonesia*. Chicago: University of Chicago Press.

Hitti, P.K. (1970) *History of the Arabs*. New York: St. Martin's Press.

Honorine, S. (2010) 'Pious but Moderate' in *Newsweek*, 12 March.

Ibrahim, H. (1991) 'Leisure and Islam' in Gerald S. Fain (ed.) *Leisure and Ethics: Reflections on the Philosophy of Leisure.* Reston, VA: American Alliance for Health, Physical Education, Recreation and Dance.

Patterson, T. (2009) *Welcome to the 'weisure' lifestyle*, CNN.com, 11 May 2009.

Pronovost, G. (2000) 'The Collapse of the Leisure Society? New Challenges for the Sociology of Leisure', in Quah, Stella and Sales, Arnaud (eds). *International Handbook of Sociology,* London: Sage.

Roberts, K. (2010). 'Sociology of Leisure.' *Sociopedia.isa.*

Suara Merdeka (2003) 'SCTV, Televisi Terpuji.'

The Koran. (1994) (Translated from the Arabic by J.M. Rodwell). London: Phoenix.

Turner, B.S. (1998) *Weber and Islam*. London and New York: Routledge.

Weber, Max. (1993) *The Sociology of Religion* (translated by Ephraim Fischoff). Boston, Massachusetts: Beacon Press.

6

Mapping Leisure and Life through the Ages in Iran

GHOLAMREZA GHAFFARY

There is historical evidence that nowadays human beings do not spend all of their time and efforts on attempts to improve their subsistence level. New achievements in the material and technical fields led to enhancement of their welfare. As a result, after completion of economic activities (work), there remains time for leisure. In Persia the word 'recreation' is more common and it means time for fun and refreshing. Leisure as a more or less to recreation related phenomena is a noteworthy concept for many experts, especially sociologists and social scientists. Sociologists think that 'leisure' is a new reality that emerged from the industrial revolution and furthered during the socio-economic development of the current world. By characterizing leisure as a cradle of meaning and as a significant realm of social engagement and participation, it is important to view it as more than a simply activity or as time left over from other obligations. Early analysts often spoke of leisure as a residual category: time that remained after work, a period of recuperation (from work), or time to be filled after work was done. No doubt such a perspective is valid, in part, but leisure is also an independent domain and subject to many of the same forces that shape the rest of the life course. If changes in the way work is performed come by and patterns of lifelong employment built on explicit career ladders become less prevalent, then the delineation of socially defined passages previously provided by work will also diminish. If so, alternative sources of meaning may emerge, based on what they can contribute to normative definitions of age, structuring of the life course, and personal identity (Han and Moen, 1999). Dumazedier (1967) asserts that leisure is activity apart from the obligations of work, family and society, to which the individual turns at will, for either relaxation, diversion, or broadening his knowledge and his spontaneous social participation, the free expression of his creative capacity' (Dumazedier, 1967: 16–17). The author, referring to the correlation and coherence of three functions of leisure, has defined it as follows: 'The total activities that a person desires and is willing to deals with after release from the occupational, family and social obligations and tasks. The aim of this leisure is rest, recreation, the development of knowledge, perfection the personality, enhancement of creativity and finally expansion of freely participation in the community'. Clocke denotes three principal axes along which definitions of leisure have been developed: time, activities and attitude of mind (Clocke, 2000: 443). As a result, leisure times is multifunctional for the individual and society and more important: leisure is a developmental opportunity and an imperative. Larson argues that adolescence, including leisure time during this period, should be defined and understood as a time of preparation for family life, employment, good citizenship, lifelong learning and personal fulfillment. It also provides an opportunity for the development of communities and societies (World Youth Report, 2003: 222). How the people of a community spend their leisure time could to a large extent show the cultural characteristics and lifestyle of the community.

The most important examples of the lifestyle emerging from urban development and modernity, concern the style of spending of leisure time. Leisure time is the product of increasing urbanization and mechanization. Putting things in perspective: leisure time is the product of industrial society, whereas ongoing urbanization and industrialization have caused significant changes in the job activities, such as, decrease in the number of working hours and more leisure time. Before the industrial revolution, leisure time was not separable from working hours. In this period, people worked permanently, following nature's schedules. After the industrial revolution, with fixed work schedules in industrial settings, work was separated from the family. Consequently, leisure time was separated from the working hours and new leisure activities, such as a variety of forms of recreation and games could be developed. Thus work became a separate part of life, and leisure, while not entailing the whole of non-work time, in modern societies became the 'own time', time for people to enjoy relative freedom to determine their own activities and to do things for pure enjoyment. The important role that young people play in sustaining their families, communities and countries suggests that their discretionary time may represent a potentially powerful force for renewal and change. Around the world, young people are proving that leisure represents a prime opportunity not only for individual development, but also for contributing to family, community and society, as well as for change. In many regions, rates of voluntary participation in community building and community development have increased dramatically among youth. Young people have demonstrated the desire and capacity to use their own time to make an impact on their communities and societies (World Youth Report, 2003: 224).

Moreover, the formation of cultural industries like cinema and television was followed by technology enhancement. The new features of these developments in leisure are:

1. Spreading of leisure over all social classes. In the past time, only the privileged classes had access to some aspects of leisure. However, nowadays the time and opportunity to benefit from it is wide-spread and includes all social classes.
2. Reduction of physical activity. While in the past time leisure activities are often associated with physical activity, nowadays watching performances have increased.

3. Domination of the media in leisure activities. Nowadays using television, radio and other mass media are the main leisure activities.
4. Modern leisure goes beyond the leisure activities tied to the family. In the past, leisure time was spent in the home and with family, but nowadays a significant portion of leisure activities are experienced outside the family.
5. Nowadays multiple agencies are involved in and responsible for operating and filling leisure time (commodification).

Social Developments and Changes in the Leisure Time

In ancient Iran the leisure time was only for the wealthy and elite class. But gradually, it was spread over lower and middle classes too. Nowadays, horse riding, polo, hunting and shooting, which were the important forms of entertainment especially for the superior classes of Iranian society, are practiced by numerous Iran people. Animal games such as shooting pigeons and throwing the rooster, ram and bull-fighting have been abandoned (Behnam and Rasekh, 1969: 352). After the advent of Islam, practicing sport and recreation in accordance with religious orders and advices was encouraged. The scientific, technical, artistic and literary advances of Muslims emerged from the correct and appropriate use of their leisure time. Religious teachings have emphasized the division of time into the three parts: work, worship and recreation. The Prophet of Islam has said: do have fun, because I do not like the violence in your religion. In the past, leisure time, especially in lower and middle classes of society was spent in the home and with family. It was largely informal and to be spent with companions and in dialog with relatives, friends and neighbours. But gradually, when official working time got regulated, particularly for medium to high social classes who were employed in the administrative system, working time was set apart from leisure time. Leisure time got ever more valued and was officially protected by law in the form of regulations of paid work and official leave. Separation of work and leisure time, the increase of the use of vehicles that have increased the mobility of the population, and the mass media such as the press, the radio, the cinema and television in particular have added to the conviction that leisure time was to be regarded as an important category and aspect of life.

During the transition period the Iranian society went through from agriculture to the modern era, the Iran population got gradually acquainted and familiar with the leisure phenomenon and its features. Annual statistics show an increase in the family budget on the spending on leisure activities. In Iranian society before the industrial and administrative development, the spending of time was regulated by social norms and customs. For weddings, for example, it was not unusual to take seven days and nights. The same holds for mourning. Leisure time often was spent in ways that are characteristic for the Republic of Iran and social purposes have ever been more important than individual goals and aims.

Dialogue as the most common form of spending leisure time, has been intensively practiced, not only at homes but also in mosques, coffee houses, on the streets and in many other places. So, 'looking-up and visit people' was one of the most stable traditions and habits of Iranians in the past. This leisure activity still is prevalent. One of the most important parameters of the particular interest of Iranians for the new audio-visual equipment such as radio and TV is the degree to which they use those as item or instrument to talk with others, specifically also in times of loneliness (Behnam and Rasekh, 1969: 327–328).

Many of the researchers speak of individualism and totalitarianism in Iran and state that the propagation of popular sports such as wrestling and weightlifting instead of team games such as football, volleyball and basketball, are a clear indication of those. Perhaps superiority in those sports that do not require the ability of team work, provides evidence for the proposition that Iranian society is emphasizing individual power over group work. But it is unawareness about group games which, especially in rural areas has led and leads to focusing on individual sports. In this process feudalism played an important role because it reduced the practices requiring cooperative efforts (Behnam and Rasekh, 1969: 354–356).

Beside the days and weeks during the year in which people concentrate on work to earn a living, there are days of celebration in which people, free from rules and restrictions, experience leisure in terms of pass-times. In Iran celebrations can be divided into several categories, which include:

1. Ancient myths and seasonal celebrations and rituals
2. Religious celebrations and rituals
3. National, patriotic and governmental celebrations and rituals
4. Family celebrations and rituals
5. Regional celebrations and rituals (Rouholamini, 1997: 15).

Though possibilities to travel still were rather limited, Norooz visitation was considered to be a duty in cities and communities. They were reserved for family visits and for face to face relationships. Among others urban developments, the increase of the population, fragmentation of traditional families and restrictions on employment were factors that reduced Norooz visitation. Also, Iranians are very interested in nature, large proportions of each social class during holidays went to the mountains, plains and gardens. 'Living in apartments is the main reason of the increased desire to depart from home and spend leisure time in green spaces (Abdi and Goudarzi, 1999: 39)'. In recent years, the creation of green space is one of the most important issues in urban planning and it is predictable that the use of green space will grow rapidly.

Age Groups and Spending the Leisure Time

Since regular statistical surveys about leisure and leisure activities in general have not been done in Iran, it is not possible to provide results of longitudinal studies and comprehensive data about leisure and life through the Ages. This also holds for inquiries among different age groups; they too have not been done through history. Available are some data from relatively recent studies, carried out during the last two decades on leisure practices among different Iranian age groups. So, on the coming pages, we will present some of the results of those.

All people do not enjoy the same amount of leisure time and there are lots of styles for spending leisure time, which styles emerged under the influences of lots of limitations on the one hand and opportunities on the other. Findings of the RCIRIB[1] (1986) with a sample size of 1,601 persons older than 15 years, shows that watching television is the most common form of spending leisure time. As many as 79 per cent of the respondents watch television. Other important leisure activities are sitting together in family context, relaxing, listening to the radio and visiting people.

Age has a significant effect on the level of individual participation in leisure activities, but this effect varies depending on the individual characteristics and the type of activity. Having the opportunity to participate in recreation activities is one of the most important findings; seemingly people have enough time to participate in these activities. The survey of youth attitudes and values further shows (Table 1) that there is a significant different between the average hours of leisure time that is available during the week for different age groups of young people.

Table 1

Average Available Leisure Time per Week for Different Age Groups of Young People

Sig.	*Average in hours per week*	*Age*
0.000	64.28	15 to 19
	46.30	20 to 24
	30.27	25 to 29

Source: Survey of youth attitudes and values (2005).

One of the most important issues in the discussion about leisure concerns the situation and the entourages in which leisure time is spent (Table 2). With whom young people spend their leisure can change over the years. Some studies have shown that nowadays young people spend less time with their family than they used to do in former times, however for girls the time spent with their family remained stable and even increased. Nevertheless, going for family leisure is still the main source of the different leisure attitudes to be found among Iran's youngsters. Despite the growth of commercial leisure and the competition of effective factors for drawing attention during leisure time, there are still many forms of recreation which families enjoy with all family members. Yet, spending leisure time with family is more common among women.

Table 2

Company During Leisure Time for Different Age Groups

Age: 25 to 29	*Age: 20 to 24*	*Age: 15 to 19*	*Entourage*
%	%	%	
68	56	54	Family
6	5	8	Relatives
14	25	27	Friends
1	1	0	Others
9	11	8	Alone
100	100	100	Total
Sig: 0.000		Chi-square: 312/403	
Sig: 0.000		V-Kramer: 0.101	

Source: Survey of youth attitudes and values (2005).

Outcomes of inquiries (Table 2) reveal that most people (apart from belonging to a particular age group) spend their leisure time within the family; higher age groups somewhat more than average (68% vs. 54%). However, this age group, compared to the average figure, spend significantly less leisure time with friends (14% vs. 27%). The Chi-square statistic has shown in this field significant difference between different age groups.

The leisure activities include a wide range of forms and characteristics. Some are passive activities, others non-passive activities and there are mix forms too. On this issue, the survey (1996), 'Evaluation of the Social and Cultural Attitudes and Behaviors in Iran', resulted in the following data (Table 3). The categories of very high and high and also the categories of never and rarely were added. Finally, the ratio of high to never has been calculated for each of these activities. The figures in the table should be read as follows: the lower the ratio of high to never (colon 1), the smaller the difference in scores on very high + high and rarely + never on the activities listed. The score 01.0 for 'go to cafes and coffee houses' (last line) means that there is a nearly equal distributions over the 2 answer options on the question: how often do you go to cafes and coffee houses.

Table 3

Leisure Activities According to the Ratio of High to Never

Ratio of high to never	*Activity*
4.22	Watching TV
1.6	Associating with family and relatives
3.5	Resting at home
0.1	Study
65.0	Go to the mosque
63.0	Walking
63.0	listening to the radio
41.0	Go to the park
29.0	Exercise
16.0	Do crafts
05.0	Go to museums and exhibitions
04.0	Go to the cinema
03.0	participating in forums and groups
01.0	Go to cafes and coffee houses

Source: Mohseni, M. (1996)

In the following Table 4, the relationship between the age groups and leisure activities is shown. Measured in percentages of leisure time available per age group, there is a significant difference between the leisure activities in different age groups. For example for watching television is valid that the older the person the more he/she watches television.

Table 5 gives the results of the survey of measuring Iranian values and attitudes (2003). The main leisure activities are respectively studying, the use of media (audio, video and electronics) and resting.

Table 4

Age Groups and Leisure Activities

Watching TV	*Socializing*	*Resting*	*Study*	*Go to mosque*	*Walking*	*Listen to radio*	*Go to park*	*Exercise*	*Do crafts*	*Go to museums*	*Go to cinema*	*Participating in forums*	*Age groups*
1.37	9.6	2.4	9.3	3.0	6.0	7.0	4.0	1.1	21.0	09.0	06.0	03.0	16 to 24
5.47	9.11	4.4	2	4.0	6.0	5.0	6.0	3.0	21.0	05.0	05.0	04.0	25 to 34
8.41	5.5	5	1	6.0	5.0	6.0	4.0	2.0	18.0	03.0	03.0	03.0	35 to 44
7.21	7.5	9.4	6.0	1.1	6.0	9.0	3.0	2.0	13.0	05.0	02.0	03.0	45 to 54
8	9.3	4.9	4.0	5.1	8.0	9.0	3.0	1.0	11.0	02.0	01.0	01.0	> 54
4.68	7.34	4.67	3.79	2.18	6.27	1.60	7.10	8.34	9.74	1.36	3.28	3.0	$^2\chi$
000.0	000.0	000.0	000.0	000.0	000.0	000.0	000.0	000.0	000.0	000.0	000.0	002.0	Sig

Source: Mohseni, M. (1996).

Table 5

Leisure Time Spending on Different Leisure Activities

Per cent	*Total*	*Activity*
23	946	Study
17	738	Resting
6	249	Exercise
19	845	Use of media
9	390	Recreation
9	411	Personal activities
6	251	Art works
4	180	Religious affairs
6	277	Associating with family and relatives
1	63	Other
100	4,350	Total

Source: Office of National Plans (2003).

The following Table 6, shows with whom the respondents spend their leisure time and by far the highest score is with family.

Table 6

Style of Spending the Leisure Time

Per cent	*Total*	*Style of spending the leisure time*
68	3,091	With family
7	333	With relatives
16	739	With friends
1	43	With colleagues
2	90	With neighbours
4	191	Solitary
1	41	Other
100	4,528	Total

Source: Office of National Plans (2003).

Table 7

Leisure Activities in Percentages per Age Group

50 years and older	*30 to 49 years*	*15 to 29 years*	*Activity*
19	21	22	Study
20	1	15	Exercise
1	3	8	Resting
13	16	23	Use of the media
6	7	11	Recreation
15	12	5	Personal activities
1	6	6	Art works
12	5	1	Religious affairs
8	9	3	Socializing with family and relatives
2	1	1	Other
$\chi^2 = 713/430$	Valid Response = 4,352		Sig = 0.000

Source: Office of National Plans (2003).

The survey data also shows a significant difference between the activities for the different age groups (Table 7). In the age group of 15 to 29 years the use of the media has the highest portion and religious affairs the lowest portion. While in the age group of 30 to 49 years study has the highest portion and exercise has the lowest portion and for the age group of 50 years and older, the portions are highest for exercise and lowest for resting.

Moreover (Table 8), with whom the respondents spend their leisure time is different for the age groups. The differences in the factor spending leisure time with friends are striking.

Table 8

Distribution of With Whom Leisure is Spent for Different Age Groups

50 years and older	*30 to 49 years*	*15 to 29 years*	*Mode spending the leisure time*
5	5	7	With relatives
6	4	27	With friends
1	7	1	With colleagues
3	5	5	With neighbours
1	4	2	Solitary
2	6.	8	Other
χ^2 =474/423	Valid Response = 4,528		Sig = 0.000

Source: Office of National Plans (2003).

Travel during leisure time reflects the mobility experience. The following (Table 9) shows that in response to the question about the number of travels for fun and recreation during the past year, 33 per cent of the respondents answer that they have not had any travel for fun and recreation.

Table 9

Number of Travels for Fun or Recreation in the Past Year

Per cent	*Total*	*Frequency of travel for fun*
33	1,519	None
26	1,190	One
19	881	Two
10	462	Three
4	186	Four
2	125	Five
1	47	Six
1	25	Seven
1	28	Eight
0	5	Nine
2	113	Ten and more
100	4,581	Total

Source: Office of National Plans (2003).

Also, in the table is shown the number of travel experience in a year according to the different age groups. The statistics of table show the significant difference between the numbers of trips in different age groups. However, one travel experience in three age groups has the highest percentage, but two and more travel experience for the age group 15 to 29 years is more than the other two age groups. It shows that the young people experience more travel in comparison with the other age groups.

Table 10

Distribution of Travels for Fun for Different Age Groups

50 years and more	*30 to 49 years*	*15 to 29 years*	*Travel*
43	44	34	One
30	25	30	Two
12	14	15	Three
5	5	6	Four
1	3	5	Five
1	1	1	Six
1	1	1	Seven
1	0	1	Eight
1	0	0.	Nine
2	3	4	Ten and more
$\chi^2 = 0.086$	Valid Response = 3,062		Sig = 0.000

Source: Office of National Plans (2003).

Moreover (Table 11), the results of researches conducted at provincial level show the significant difference between the travel destinations of young people and the older demographic groups. The outcomes seem to indicate that the older a person the less he/she travelled for fun during the past year.

Table 11

Distribution of Travel for Fun Destinations per Age Groups

Total	*55 years and older*	*30 to 54 years*	*15 to 29 years*	*Countries*
47	13	15	40	Islamic countries
27	5	8	12	Europe
7	1	1	4	Turkey and the Persian Gulf
12	2	3	7	United States and Canada
4	3	2	2	Other
100	24	29	63	Total
Chi-square: 41/246		V – Kramer: 0.11		Sig: 0.000

Source: Azad Armaky and Ghaffary (2005).

All the foregoing tables dealing with differences in leisure time activities between the generations indicate that there are significant? differences in activities and interests between the different generations. Table 12 shows the significant differences in visits to cities per age group.

Table 12

Visits to Three Categories of Cities per Age Group

Total	*55 years and older*	*30 to 54 years*	*15 to 29 years*	*Cities*
47	65	47	37	Religious
24	20	24	26	Historical
28	14	28	36	Recreational
100	100	100	100	Total
Chi-square: 62/8		V-Kramer: 0.17		Sig: 0.000

Source: Azad Armaky and Ghaffary (2005).

The following (Table 13) shows the scores in percentages of the respective generations on how the weekends are spent. The Chi-square statistic illustrates that there exist significant differences on how the weekends are spent between the various generations. The age group of 15 to 29 years, more than the other age groups, spends its weekends on reading books, exercising and watching exercise as spectator, on excursion and trips, on watching movies and listening to music. While staying at home, participating in religious ceremonies and visiting relatives are the main weekend activities in the old generation.

Table 13

Weekend Spending per Age Group

Total	*55 years and older*	*30 to 54 years*	*15 to 29 years*	*Spending the weekends*
8	6	7	14	Reading books
10	8	8	13	Exercise and watch it
9	16	8	7	To participate in religious ceremonies
26	24	26	28	Excursion and trip?
20	27	22	6	Stay at home
8	5	8	9	Watching movies and listening to music
15	12	17	14	Visit
100	100	100	100	Total
Chi-square: 67/178		V – Kramer: 0.15		Sig: 0.000

Source: Azad Armaky and Ghaffary (2005).

Table 14

Favourite Books per Age Groups

Total	*55 years and older*	*30 to 54 years*	*15 to 29 years*	*Books*
21	4	8	8	Islamic sciences
19	1	4	12	Stories and novels
18	1	4	12	Historical and social
14	4	3	6	Literary and artistic
10	0	4	5	Educational and psychological
15	1	3	10	Technical books
100	15	28	56	Total
Chi-square: 73		V – Kramer: 0.22		Sig: 0.000

Source: Azad Armaky and Ghaffary (2005).

Table 14 shows the relative preferences for books per age group. The preferences differ significantly.

Moreover, as Table 15 shows, in the favourite topics of newspaper, there are significant differences between the various age groups. Those differences are shown in the table below.

Table 15

Favourite Newspaper Topics per Age Groups

Total	*55 years and older*	*30 to 54 years*	*15 to 29 years*	*Age Subject*
15	3	6	5	Political
10	1	4	4	Social
8	0	3	4	Economic
1	0	0	0	Cultural
3	0	1	1	Foreign News
38	3	8	17	Table
8	2	4	2	Events
24	1	4	18	Sport News
100	14	31	54	Total
Chi-square: 125/1		V – Kramer: 0.24		Sig: 0.000

Source: Azad Armaky and Ghaffary (2005).

Finally it seems that the styles of spending leisure time will change in different generations.

The change in the styles of spending leisure time did not occur in Iran's urban population only. This change is also observed in the rural communities which now make-up 40 per cent of the population of Iran.

Leisure in the Rural Community

In this paragraph will be addressed the findings of the survey 'cultural status in the villages of Iran'. In response to the question: 'How the family likes to spend their leisure time', the following results are obtained. Overall 4 per cent of rural families mentioned one activity, 7 per cent mentioned two activities, 5 per cent three forms of leisure time spending, 6 per cent four cases and 2 per cent five. As well 2 per cent of families did not respond to this question.

The following table indicates the favourite leisure activities for family members. The most favourite leisure activities for the rural families are, pilgrimage, tourism and meeting friends and acquaintances in the city for which they have to leave their villages. Next to these trips, the interest focuses on games, exercises, study, art works and going to the cinema and entertainment centres in the city.

Also, 9 per cent of the families don't have the money and time for leisure time activities. They indicate not to be interested in such matters since they are busy with supplying the ingredients for their basic needs of life and prefer to spend their free time and money on those needs.

Observed was too, that in most villages are lacking the necessary facilities for leisure. Concluded can be that the villagers prefer to use their money and free time for pilgrimage, tourism and recreational travels to towns and centres outside of the village. Pilgrimage to holy places such as Mashhad and then Mecca, Karbala and Syria, make up the majority of their leisure aspirations (Iranians cultural behaviours, 211)

Table 16

Favourite Leisure Activities for Family Members in Rural Villages

%	*Number naming this activity*	*Activity*
60	8,750	Pilgrimage
33	4,819	Recreational travel
19	2,802	Pilgrimage and recreational travel
3	473	Visiting travel
8	1,248	Games, sports
2	379	Welfare work
10	1,562	Study, research
0	95	Work
2	366	Shopping
0	5	Rest
0	6	Art works
0	14	Going to town
0	15	Religious activities
1	238	Housework
0	82	Foreign travel
8	1,203	Mecca trip
0	304	Travel to Syria
6	921	Travel to Karbala

Source: Office of National Plans, 2002.

In Table 17 are to found the outcomes of the survey that was conducted in Iran's urban areas (28 provincial capital cities) with a sample size of 13,976 people on the issue of available time for leisure purposes. The average leisure time turned out to be 4 hours and 36 minutes on a weekday and 6 hours and 12 minutes on free days.

Table 17

Mean Leisure Time in Urban Communities per Age Group

Mean leisure time		*Age*
Weekdays	*Free days*	
4	6	15 to 18 years
4	6	16 to 25 years
4	5	26 to 40 years
4	6	41 to 64 years
7	8	65 years and older

Source: Office of National Plans, 2002.

In the following (Table 18) are presented the outcomes of the measurements of the amount of leisure time in rural community during agricultural and non-agricultural seasons. In agricultural seasons, the average leisure time available is 5 hours and 25 minutes; in other seasons 8 hours and 29 minutes.

Table 18

Amount of Leisure Time Available in Rural Communities During Agricultural and Other Seasons per Age Group

Other Seasons			*Agricultural Seasons*			*Age Groups*
More than 9 hours	*5 to 9 hours*	*0 to 4 hours*	*More than 9 hours*	*5 to 9 hours*	*0 to 4 hours*	
31	48	20	9	50	39	15–18 years
25	48	25	11	42	45	19–25 years
20	50	29	5	41	52	26–40 years
21	50	28	7	38	53	41–64 years
35	49	15	24	39	36	65 years and older

Source: Office of National Plans, 2002.

The survey done on the rural community shows that changes in the social and economic conditions of the respondents leads to changes in the favourite leisure activities. So improvement of the rural population's social and economic conditions will increase the tendency to pilgrimage and decrease the preference to go on foreign trips and excursions (Office of National Plans, 2002: 217). The informants of the 1,821 villages were asked about two of the most common styles of spending the leisure time in different age groups. The results show that for seniors the main leisure activities are chatting and sitting in the sun, for adults chatting and coming together in the village square and for young people exercise and playing (Office of National Plans, 2002: 223).

In response to the question which were their main leisure activities and what the main media used, these answers were obtained:

> 77 per cent of rural families said that during the day most of their leisure activity concerns watching TV at home and 12 per cent of them mentioned chatting with friends and neighbors. Also 5 per cent of the rural households mentioned playing sports and the 4 per cent listening to the radio as a main leisure activities. While 2 per cent is allocated to art works, 2 per cent to listening to audio tapes, 2 per cent to reading books, 1 per cent to reading the Koran and prayer, less than 1 per cent is spent on participating in prayer (0, 1%), on reading newspapers and magazines (0, 4%), to going to town for walking through the streets and markets (0, 3%), on participating in religious ceremonies (0, 2%), to welfare work (0, 2%), to using the video (0, 2%), to going to the movies (0, 1%) and to going to the park and amusement park (also 0, 1%).

Certainly the lack of cultural facilities and activities is the main reason for the limitation of the leisure activities in rural villages. The lack of money plays an important role here; in rural areas the funds are missing to build expensive cultural facilities or for bringing over artists and performers to the villages.

Therefore, particularly also for the rural areas it is important that the TV ever more becomes a widespread media and that in the future its reach will further increase through satellite and computer networks.

Conclusion

Nowadays, the amount and importance of leisure time ever more increases, among others due to a in many countries ongoing process of reduction of official working time. Therefore, every person has ever more hours at his/her disposal to be used according to his/her desire and capability. It is obvious that the proper use of leisure time will have a positive impact on a person's life and on society, while the incorrect use of it may cause problems and irreparable damages. This particularly holds for young people to whom is 'the future'.

Leisure time has functions such as rehabilitation of individuals, encouraging creativity and increasing personal and social abilities of people. In fact, a society where people do not have enough and adequate leisure time may have difficulties also in the area of work, because the quality of both work and leisure are interrelated. Lack of desired leisure time leads to lowering creativity in society and increases tension and stress.

Iranian society is a young society and leisure time is one of the major problems the society is facing. In Iran, watching TV is the main activity with which the leisure time is being filled. Although watching television is among the most popular pass-times in all countries, Iran faces the particular circumstance that one of the main motives for watching television is that the urban areas are not suited for spending leisure time of their citizens. During weekend and holidays the cities sort of 'depopulate'; there is a massive influx of people to areas outside the city, which phenomenon reflects the lack of recreational opportunities in the city itself. In fact, the large city Tehran is exclusively important for its citizens because of its economic function and parameters. However, though those who must visit the town for economic reasons are allowed to stay overnight, the majority of the people prefer to commute between their living place and the city, thereby accepting that they have to stand for hours in heavy traffic on the roads.

The lack of recreational and leisure opportunities in the country for various sectors of society including women, older people and adults is evident. It leads to frustration and to reduction of vitality and growth of the communities.

Though it depends also on other factors, the format and content of leisure time spending largely depends on the growth of industrial work and the position of a person in the economic system. The family's social status depends on the father's occupational status. Travel, other than to relatives depends highly on the family income, as does the way the weekends are spent.

Moreover, multiple recreational, scientific, artistic and educational centres have are ever more reducing the role of the family with regard to the style of spending leisure time. Also the introduction and spreading of communication devices such as televisions at home, are further reducing the influences of the family. However, especially in non-industrial areas and societies, families still can play a very important role in guiding youth people towards correct styles of spending leisure time. The family and its economic, social and cultural conditions and status provide the facilities for proper spending of leisure time. The parents are the best advisors for youth in terms of how to improve their leisure time activities and styles because of their comprehensive knowledge and understanding of their children's/youngster's personality traits, talents, desires, strengths and weaknesses. In short, all studies seem to indicate that the most important factor influencing the leisure time and the quality of its spending are personal and family economic conditions.

Note

1. Research Center of Iran Republic Islamic Broadcasting.

References

Abdi, A. and Goudarzi, M. (1999). Tahavlat Farhanghi dar Iran (Cultural Developments in Iran), Tehran, method.

Azad Armaki, T. and Ghaffary, Gh. (2005). Jamehshenasi nasly dar Iran (Sociology of Generational in Iran), Tehran, Jihade Daneshgahi.

Behnam, J. and Rasekh, Sh. (1969). Jamehshenasi Iran (Sociology of Iran), Tehran, Amir Kabir.

Clocke, P. (2000). 'Leisure' in Johnston, R.J., Gregory, D., Pratt, G., and M. Watts, (eds) *Dictionary of Human Geography*. (Fourth edition) Oxford: Blackwell.

Dumazedier, J. (1967). *Toward a Society of Leisure*, New York, Free Press.

Han, S.K., and Moen, P. (1999). 'Clocking Out: Temporal Patterning of Retirement.' *American Journal of Sociology*, 105:191–236.

Mohseni, M. (1996). Barrsi ghraiashha va raftarhaie farhanghi dar Iran (Evaluation of the Social and Cultural Attitudes and Behaviors in Iran), Ministry of Culture and Islamic Guidance.

Office of National Plans (2004) raftarhaie farhanghi Iranian (Iranian Cultural Behaviors), Ministry of Culture and Islamic Guidance.

Office of National Organization Youth (2005)pimaieash arzesh ha va ghraiashhaie Javanan (Survey of Youth Attitudes and Values, Tehran, National Organization Youth.

Office of National Plans (2002) Raftarhaie farhanghi dar roosta (Cultural Behaviors in rurals), Ministry of Culture and Islamic Guidance.

RCIRIB (1985) paimayesh ovghaj fraghat (survey leisure time), Tehran, Research Center of Iran Republic Islamic Broadcasting.

Roholamini, M. (1997). *Ancient Celebrations in Iran*, Tehran, Agah.

World Youth Report (2003). *Rethinking Leisure Time*, United Nations Economic and Social Council.

7

Mapping Leisure and Life through the Ages of Israel

ATARA SIVAN AND ELIE COHEN-GEWERC

While individuals are characterized by unique personal leisure preferences and behaviours, being part of a society, people's leisure behaviours are also shaped by their socio-cultural contexts. Trends and developments which occur in any society brings with along changes to people's leisure perceptions and behaviours. This paper focuses on the Israeli society with the aim to map its leisure and the way it has been shaped by demographic, social and cultural trends during the period prior to its establishment and over its 63 years of existence. Whereas studies focusing on leisure emerged mainly during the 70s, the paper attempts to depict aspects related to leisure starting from the late 20th century when the first wave of immigrants arrived to Israel.

From Late Ninetieth to the Mid-twentieth Centuries: Setting the Scene for Cultural Pluralism

One of the characteristics of the Israeli society is the diversity of its population which comprises people from all over the world. Starting from the late 19th century there were waves of immigration to Israel, consisting of people coming from numerous contexts and representing different cultures. Each wave has been contributing in one way or another to the development of the country while affecting its culture and thus its leisure patterns. The first influx of immigrants into the land of Israel occurred during the years 1882–1903. Motivated by nationalism during these years some 25,000 Jews emigrated from Russia and Rumania. The majority of these immigrants were mainly middle class people who came with their families. They lacked the knowledge of rural life and therefore chose to settle in cities, primarily Jaffa and Jerusalem. Even though only one quarter chose agricultural settlements, they established numerous communities across the country. These communities were mainly agricultural settlements that were based on private farms. Despite their small numbers, these original farmers became the foundation of the later pioneering agricultural settlements. During the first wave of immigration there were also about 2,500 Jews who came from Yemen. The majority settled in the city of

Jerusalem, where many of them encountered economic difficulties as well as a lack of housing, and unfriendly treatment by other residents of the city. As a result, they created separate housing, community, and financial organizations for themselves. To a certain extent such segregation led to the continuation of their hometown lifestyle which was more influenced by the Middle Eastern culture. Even though this wave of immigrants brought with it people from different countries, the revival of the Hebrew language at that time brought about revolutionary changes in education and culture, especially due to the establishment of Hebrew-language schools (Ministry of Immigrant Absorption, 2011a). This set the tone for the development of media and other initiatives which in the years to come affected the leisure consumption of the population with the use of Hebrew as the leading language.

At the beginning of the 20th century, there were two more waves of immigration to Israel which comprised young people with no families who were inspired by the Zionist ideology of building Israel and they were called: 'pioneers' (Ministry of Immigrant Absorption, 2011b and c). These pioneers were determined to bring about changes and improve people's lives and to build a new society which possesses its own language, lifestyle and folklore. They were looking at their existing lifestyles in their places of origin as something which needs to be replaced by a new society in Israel. These pioneers set the foundation for the development of a new culture based on new signs and symbols of their work in Israel and shifted away from their religious-traditional lifestyles at their hometown (Shikma-Avivi, 2006).

The Second wave of immigration to Israel took place during the years 1904–1914. Between these years approximately 35 thousand Jews arrived and they were mainly from Russia and Poland. Similarly to the first influx of immigrants they were motivated by a combination of ideology coupled with anti-Jewish violence and pogroms. Unlike the immigrants of the first influx, the majority of the second wave included single young people, many with a socialist ideology coupled with a belief in the national redemption of the Jewish People in the Land of Israel. Whereas the majority of these immigrants mostly joined as labourers in the agriculture settlements and established several rural establishments, they also founded various institutions and social and political organizations (Ministry of Immigrant Absorption, 2011b). They also continued to strengthen the revived Hebrew language, promoted and improved the education at both primary and secondary levels, and paved the way for the development of tertiary level education, as well as the arts, literature, and journalism.

Inspired by the by the relative successful integration of the immigrants of the second wave of immigrants, and spurred by the hardships of the Jews in their countries of origin, some 35,000 Jews arrived in a third wave of immigration to Israel. The majority of them came from Russia and Poland and a smaller number from Lithuania and Rumania. These immigrants were characterized by nationalist aspirations by the Balfour Declaration which indicated 'the establishment in Palestine of a national home for the Jewish people' and establishment of the British Mandate. Social and political upheavals in Europe also contributed to their motivation. These immigrants continued in establishing new institutions and organizations representing the ideal of 'Hebrew Labor' by constructing and building buildings and roads. They also continued to strengthen the existing agriculture infrastructure and developed among others new forms of settlements which set the basis for the unique lifestyle called: Kibbutz (Ministry of Immigrant Absorption, 2011c). These special forms of living were based on collectivism and characterized by shared work and budget. As years went by the unique characteristics of the Kibbutz, manifested themselves in the communal lifestyles of their inhabitants and were also illustrated in a shared way of undertaking leisure activities within the community. These include among others the collective celebration of holidays and the patterns of spending time with children who were mainly raised in a communal home while sharing most of their time and activities with their peer-groups.

In 1924 another wave of about 67,000 immigrants arrived to Israel. They were also from Eastern Europe and chose to settle in the cities, especially in the city of Tel Aviv. As a result, the cities experienced rapid development during this period. The immigrants established light industry, workshops, small businesses, and construction. At the same time, their contribution could be felt in the agricultural settlements, including the establishment of new settlements as well as new agricultural undertakings, such as citrus cultivation. These new comers contributed greatly to the development of the society during the period of financial crisis beginning in 1926, at which point many people left the country (Ministry of Immigrant Absorption, 2011d).

This wave followed by another wave of immigrants which started five years later in 1929 and lasted for ten years. This wave also included people who ran away from Europe with the rising of Hitler in 1933. These immigrants who were academics and professional settled mainly in the cities and contributed a lot to the urban development of Israel. They also included musicians who founded the Philharmonic Orchestra which were later developed successfully and served as a leisure patterns for people who liked classical music and who regarded this type of activities as 'high culture'. The first Hebrew city of Israel named: Tel Aviv was recognized as the centre of modern Israeli-Hebrew culture (Ministry of Immigrant Absorption, 2011e). This city developed economically and turned into the cultural centre of the immigrants which consisted mainly of those coming from Europe in the above-mentioned forth and fifth waves of immigration to Israel. In addition to the foundation of the first Israeli orchestra, these immigrants further established a museum, published new newspapers and built numerous coffee shops in the city (Shacham, 2011). According to Shor (2008), during the twenties and the thirties, Tel Aviv was well known as a city which consumed popular and hedonistic culture which was different from the simplistic way of living among those settled in the rural settlements. The coffee shops which were further developed as centres for leisure in the city were re-developed with a vintage style as an anti-thesis to the rapid development in information and telecommunication technologies. As such, coffee shops became popular places for leisure which offered warm, intimate and less alienated atmosphere than the one offered by the later developed shopping malls.

Inspired by Marxist ideology of central Europe most of immigrants from Eastern Europe imported the patterns of collectivism and the profound roots of communitarianism. These patterns have been illustrated in people's perceptions, preferences and lifestyles including their leisure behaviours. Most people used to express and to think as part of whole, a whole which replaced the cultures and habits they brought from their countries of origin. Further illustration of this collectivism could be found in certain songs written by the new comers which put more emphasis on the togetherness than on the individual. Thus for example, a popular song had the repeated sentences 'we came to the country to build it and construct ourselves'. Singing and folk dancing in circles by involving all participants and leaving no one alone, were also ways of expressing collectivism. The famous Israeli dance called: 'Hora' was one of the symbols of the Israeli culture since it involved elements of a new culture of togetherness, inclusion, cooperation and simplicity (Shikma-Avivi, 2006).

Beside the kibbutz and the cooperative settlements all over the country, cultural life was very present. Newspapers, literature journals, publishers, theatres, concerts were part of the landscape and the essential expression of leisure activities. Except few comedies, leisure offered mostly opportunities to learn. In the very small and modest apartments, the main thing was the library – sometimes made with simple fruit cases – occupying the centre of the living room. In 1924–25 two universities were founded, the Technion in Haifa for technology and the Hebrew University in Jerusalem for the Humanities. It is also worth mentioning that in 1920, with only about 80,000 inhabitants (83,790 according the first census of 1922 (The Israel Genealogical Society, n.b. and the Central Bureau of Statistics, 2011)) the Jewish population had its elected assembly with a National Committee which was able to coordinate life in all the aspects, including defense, welfare, education and culture which has had its effects on the use of leisure among its population.

From Pluralism to Homogeneity – Portraying the First Two Decades of the State of Israel

The establishment of the state of Israel on 15 May 1948 was celebrated with songs and dances which represent the collective notion of togetherness. Despite these common acts, Israel during its establishment remained an immigration country comprising population of a vast mosaic of origins, languages, cultures and mentalities. The Zionist ideology carried by the national movement for the return of the Jewish people to their homeland and the recommencement of Jewish sovereignty in the Land of Israel undertook efforts to reestablish a sovereign national identity. One of the ways in which this aim worked out was through the renaissance of the Hebrew language which affected people's lifestyles including their leisure behaviour. The need to move from a range of languages spoken in their places of origin to Hebrew as a unified language was clearly manifested through the development of the Hebrew culture and its related signs and symbols. The urge to use Hebrew was further strengthened through the education provided in schools where all activities were held using this language. It is worth noticing that the use of other languages was still a practice which further continued till the seventies. This practice was the results of continuing waves of immigrations to the country from other places. On the whole the state of Israel has been mainly shaped by two parallel processes: wars and mass immigration.

Demographically, during the first few years since its establishment in 1948 and compared with other developed countries, Israel saw a higher rate of population growth. In May 1948 the Jewish population was 6,50,000, at the end of the year, 7,58,700 (8,72,700, including Arabs) and three years later the population had doubled (15,77,800 including 1,73,400 Arabs) (The Central Bureau of Statistics, 2011).

The second important wave of refugees came from Eastern Europe with the end of soviet regime the population grew from four and half million to little more than five and half millions (The Central Bureau of Statistics, 2011). This sudden augmentation of population meant that the government had to supply housing, jobs, medicine and schools on one hand and a great potential of enrichment and improvement in the other.

During the first two decades since its establishment, the new state of Israel had to cope with its neighbours' threats denying its existence as well as with large waves of refugees coming to the country without any means except the motivation to contribute to its development and increase its Jewish population. The forties were dominated with the Holocaust survivors and in the fifties, hundreds of thousands of Jewish refugees flying from Arab countries. All these new comers had the basic needs of food, home and education to survive. Temporary camps with small barracks served as humble shelters, an austerity plan distributed small rations of basic products. Education underpinned by the aim of shaping the new common identity, was provided by women soldiers who went through a fast track training for this purpose.

With the desire for unity, almost all spheres of life were centralized. The state radio and later the introduction of the television in 1968 were under the establishment of the department of the prime minister office conveying the messages of the new ethos of togetherness. The voice of the people was the voice of the government and all activities brought by the immigrants from their places of origin were replaced by collective activities such as group dances and singing in the renewed Hebrew language. Despite this unity, it is worth mentioning that diverse idiosyncrasies still existed among small groups who came to its full expression during family events. Behind the scene of the canonic public expression of the new identity, a cacophonic underground of innumerable languages and idiosyncrasies continued to palpitate.

In addition to demographic changes, Israel had gone through educational trends which affected the leisure of its people. With the above mentioned background during the years after its establishment, education was the main tool to enhance the national identity of the new comers. In a way, compulsory education was the main tool to reshape the different cultures and mentalities owned by the immigrants and carried over from the home countries, into homogeneous one which was underpinned by the socialist notion. As socialization agents, schools were undertaking the role to teach children the Hebrew language and the new ways of life in the new state. Children then became socializing agents of their parents in that they influenced the overtaking of this language over their languages of origin.

In view of the variety of cultures and mentalities and in an attempt to melt all of them into the new culture of Israel, both the school and the army were perceived by the leaders as the melting pots. Schools prepared pupils to serve the state and undertake roles to further develop it. Children coming from many origins and cultures, representing the next generation, were brought together at schools and essentially in the army, and were socialized into the new Israeli society.

As part of the process of building the sovereignty of the new state, an educational law was voted in 1953 which brought an end to schools belonging to political parties. Yet the ideological parties could continue their educational action through youth movements and their leisure activities. The early fifties saw the development of youth movements which were established by the ideological parties as a way to educate young people and activate them to contribute to their society. Youth movements have been developed as major socialization agents for youth in the Israeli society. Youth spent their leisure time participating in a wide range of activities led by these movements such as physical training, community service as well as various expressive activities through which cooperation and related values were nourished. Membership in these movements was perceived as imperative to the development of belonging to the society and was well illustrated in signs and symbols representing collective identities such as uniforms and special ceremonies.

In addition to youth involvement in activities organized by its movements, people of other age groups were also enacting activities which focused on collective aims and led by the socialist notion combined with the prevalence of the Hebrew language and its related practices. Leisure time use was mainly surrounded around collective gatherings in special houses established for collective purposes and titled: The House of the People (which is a translation of: Beit Ha'am' in the Hebrew language). There people would attend theatre performances as well as literature and musical meetings in an attempt to set the foundation for the Israeli collective culture and lifestyle. While unity in leisure pursuits was sought after, it is important to note that those who did not take part in these common efforts but maintained their individual patterns were looked upon to a certain extent as self-indulgent. These were mainly residents of the first big city called Tel-Aviv.

Cultural events were mostly subsidized by governmental or union institutions. Underpinned by the aim to unify the tremendous diversity of cultures and lifestyles into a common way of life, the leaders perceived their role of facilitating people's free-time use as two-fold: providing affordable and reachable entertainment for all as well as supervising people's leisure time in a way that ensures the unity. For example, every worker and employee had the right to take one-week off to go to what was called: 'health house' (in Hebrew is:'beit habra'a') for recreation. These were modest hostels, all-included, and sponsored by enterprises and unions. There, participants were presented with various entertainments and lectures within a recreational and relaxation context. This annual week-off work was the main official leisure event for the middle-class Israelis and it entailed months of early planning prior to its undertaking and long period of reflection and sharing among participants afterwards.

On everyday routine, leisure for most people was filled mainly by listening to the radio, reading the newspapers or readings books which were borrowed from local libraries. On Saturdays which according to the Jewish tradition no work takes place and most entertainment places are closed and there is lack of public transportation, people were mostly resting at their homes. The only type of entertainment which escaped the resting on Saturdays was football matches during which leisure activity took the passive form of spectatorship. The use of leisure had been enacted during Saturdays' evening when people would go out, socialize while picking some snacks offered in the streets and going to cinemas.

While the unity of leisure behaviours was implemented in many places across Israel, during the fifties, the Israeli society experienced some cultural changes. Alongside the adherence to the culture which was based on the Zionist-Hebrew idea and centralization of national-collectivist aims, there was also a certain shift among numerous people to exhibit more openness to the outside world. This was illustrated in the moderate decline of collectivistic values in favour of personal values based on competition, success and pleasure (Bahat-Ratzon, 2004).

The trend towards individualism was strengthened in the Israeli society during the 60s with the younger generation looking for new ways of developing their own identities (Zur, 1969). Unlike their parents who ran away from their hometown cultures and lifestyles for establishing a new Israeli-Hebrew culture, the second generation was looking to adopt different styles from outside Israel. Thus, for example, they listened to imported music from Europe and USA and danced popular dances originated in the West, at which point the Israeli folk dancing lost their uniqueness by becoming one of various leisure activities enacted by people (Shikma-Avivi, 2006). The tendency to adopt music and dance forms from outside Israel became stronger over the 70s but alongside this tendency, there was a growing search among people for cultural signs and symbols which originated in their own upbringing. This was illustrated by the introduction of more traditional-religious types of folklore including religious and ethnic songs which were performed in popular concerts attended by people as part of their leisure activity.

Towards Self-cultivation Within a Collective Context: Trends in Leisure from the Seventies Onward

Whereas leisure has been recognized as a significant domain of life, there were relatively few studies investigating the leisure patterns of Israelis in the first few decades of the state existence. As years went by, more attention was drawn to leisure research in an attempt to identify the characteristics of leisure involvement of Israelis in general as well as to identify patterns of leisure behaviour and preferences among specific groups within the population (Ruskin and Sivan, 2000, 2004 and 2005).

Three national studies on leisure which were conducted during the seventies have identified numerous trends in time-use, leisure participation and attitudes of people. Some important demographic changes between 1970 to 1990 include the growth of the Jewish population from two to four million, the increase of number of people who were born in Israel to about fifty per cent of the population and an overall increase in the education level of the population (Katz, Haas, Weitz, Adoni, Gurevittch, Schiff and Goldberg-Anabi, 1992).

Alongside these demographic changes, there have been some changes in the values held by the Israeli society between the seventies to the nineties (Katz et al., 1992). These include an increase of the importance given to a 'present-orientation', somewhat representing a hedonism perspective. This is illustrated with the increase of percentage of people agreement with the statement: 'life is short and dangerous and one should think primarily about the present'. Another change is related to increase in individualism. An examination of the importance attributed to various needs indicated an increase in emphasis on both cognitive and affective personal needs. More people during the nineties have indicated their desire to study and enrich themselves as well as to be entertained and get involved in expressive activities. At the same time, there has been a moderate decline in the importance placed on collective needs. For example, less people indicated needs to participate public or civic events. However, despite this moderate decline, it is worth noting that the importance attributed to the collective has been high. This has been illustrated in the importance attributed to taking pride in the state of Israel. Alongside these changes, there has been an increase in the importance attributed to leisure time. Thus, for example, in 1990 the majority of respondents attributed equal importance to leisure and work compared with about half indicating this direction in 1970. Another change in value was the tendency towards a more local orientation and decentralization and the weakening of centralized culture. This has been illustrated by the appearance of numerous local newspapers. Furthermore, there was a decrease in the variety, autonomy and privatization of cultural activities. All together, the change of values have affected people use of leisure and created a wide range of leisure offerings and consumptions.

In light of these demographic changes, results of two national studies conducted both in the seventies and the nineties (Katz et al., 1992) indicated that on the whole Israelis spent less time sleeping and resting. There was a decrease in the average amount of time devoted to paid work by those in employment, but a small increase overall, reflecting a possible growth in part-time jobs which could be attributed to more women entering the workforce. There was also sharp decline in time devoted to household and an increase in the leisure time over the weekdays and weekend. One third of leisure time was found to be spent on watching television especially over the weekends. There was also a slight decrease in time spent on reading newspapers and a slight increase in social activities and time spent outside the home on weekends (Katz et al., 1992).

With regard to the leisure participation, there was a decline in arts activities such as going to movies, theatre, museums and classical music concerts. At the same time there was an increase in expressive activities such as social gathering, going out to pubs and restaurant, excursion trips in Israel and abroad, active sports, record playing and video watching. Despite the increase of these types of 'light' activities, there was a decline in participation in listening to popular singers and sports spectating. These changes point to the tendency towards home based and more intimate ways of spending leisure time which could hint to a less collective participation and a general increase in hedonistic values. While watching television remains a popular medium of consumption, there was a search to replace this medium with more interactive activities.

Another study undertaken towards the late nineties (Haas, 1999), indicated a continuing trend of participation in informal and interactive leisure activities. There was a significant increase in both cognitive and expressive activities including going abroad, reading books, engagement in learning and studies and attendance of concerts and entertainment events. At the same time there was a decrease in visiting museums and involvement in hobbies. Some noticeable patterns of leisure behaviour towards the late nineties include participation in new activities such as visiting shopping malls and coffee houses, Internet surfing, engaging in voluntary and public activities and attending operating performance or ethnic music concert. These trends continue to exist. During the decade between 1997 and 2006 many more Israelis are undertaking voluntary activities and the overall rates has increased from 32 to 45 per cents (The Israeli Center for Third-Sector Research, 2007). Surveys further show that half a million of Israelis are involved in volunteering activities which spread over a wide range of areas including providing assistance to new immigrants, elderly, people in need as well as caring for the environment (Veel and Kariv, 2010).

During the early 90s, Israel saw an influential population growth which was the result of a huge influx of immigrants from the former Soviet Union (Ministry of Immigrant Absorption, 2011f). This wave brought with it one million immigrants to the state. Unlike the immigrants that came over prior to the establishment of the state and were infused into the collective demands, these immigrants had the freedom to maintain their patterns. Alongside their successful efforts in learning the Hebrew language, they could create news papers in Russian, specific shops, music ensembles and communitarian activities. Already in 1991 they created a new theatre while using Hebrew with simultaneous translation of their hometown Russian language, a theatre which is regarded now as an inseparable part of Israeli culture.

Public broadcasting and its national agenda lost their monopoly as news and cultural electronic provider. Private media with their commercial aims speak to the people as is, provide programs the public like and not something the people should appreciate. It is interesting to remember that public broadcasting has, by law, the mandate to provide information and entertainment in order to educate and to strength the Israeli canonic values while the private broadcasting aim is to attract and maintain the attention of large audience as possible. An outstanding example is the dominant presence, now, of popular eastern songs which were out of the canonic ethos during the first decades of the state.

Though no large-scale studies were conducted on the leisure consumption and behaviour of the society as a whole, it has been identified that on the whole the society continues with the above time-use and leisure activities participation with an increase in use of information and telecommunication technologies. Since the mid-eighties, Israel was part of the world wide development of the Internet, The penetration and usage of the internet has been growing rapidly and is identified as high in comparison to other developed countries. For example, in 2010, two third of the adult population (64%) age twenty and above used computers and similar percentages (59.4%) used the internet (Central Bureau of Statistics, 2010). The use of internet among youngest aged 13–17 was found to be higher (90%) (Rabin, 2009). Israel was also identified as leading the Middle East Market in social network usage internet penetration and access (Internet World Stats, 2011; Mobile Youth Middle East, 2012). Additional use of technology has been illustrated through the tremendous growth of the mobile phone market in both penetration rate and airtime use. The majority of the population comprises subscribers of mobile phone with a higher rate than other countries such as US, Sweden, Hong Kong and Taiwan. According to Lemish and Cohen (2005), the wide spread use of mobile phone is highly related to several unique cultural characteristics of the Israeli society such as: close familiarity and cohesive social networks and fast dissemination of and infatuation with technological innovations related to communication. The higher use of mobile iphone is also attributed to the political situation calls for special security needs for both civilian and soldiers so people could contact each other in case of event of terrorist attack or military activity.

While one could generalize on the overall patterns of leisure in the Israeli society, it is also important to distinguish between its different subgroups. One division could be made based on the religion. Examination of leisure among religious groups in the society portrays certain patterns which are different than those adopted in by secular people. These patterns have been especially limiting based on the religious demand to engage in religious acts such as reading the bible and in view of the perception that leisure is a waste of time (Paz and Almog, 2009). While these guiding principles have been observed strictly for many years, the development of Israel as a modern nation and the offering of leisure services have brought about changes in the leisure consumption of religious people. One can therefore observes the use of a wide range of recreational leisure activities which cater for self development and fulfillment among this group of the population while adhering to rules set by the religion (Paz and Almog, 2009).

As major consumers of the leisure industry, young people of leisure time in Israel have been demonstrating an increasing Westernization of leisure patterns, with a trend towards use of popular culture. Several studies which were conducted over the past few decades shed some light on ways in which Israeli youth spend their leisure and their attitudes towards leisure activities. Four studies are described below to identify these patterns and attitudes and possible variations over the years.

A study which was conducted in the mid eighties (Sivan, 1984) on leisure behaviour, attitudes and preferences of youth from different educational settings and backgrounds have shown some common leisure patterns as well as some differences. The study examined youth from four main educational frameworks: religious and non-religious in the kibbutz (collective village) and religious and non-religious schools in the city. Results indicated a strong common tendency to prefer and participate in expressive leisure activities such as watching television, meeting with friends, participating in parties and traveling. Most youth participated in these activities between one to three times per week. The frequency of participation in these activities was much higher than the frequency of participation in instrumental activities such as taking study courses or volunteering, which were performed only once or twice a week. In addition to these common patters, significant differences were found between youth from different educational backgrounds with a strong tendency among youngsters from the kibbutz to participate in social activities and for those from religious schools to participate in more religious activities (Sivan, 1986). In addition, it was found that both the kibbutz and the religious environments had influenced the level of participation in voluntary activities. The community life of the kibbutz was found to be an influential factor in the way youth spend their time.

Another study which was carried out in the early nineties (Ministry of Education and Culture, 1993), portrayed the extracurricular activities of high school students in the Hebrew and the Arab Education sectors. Results indicated that in both sectors, watching television remained the most popular leisure activity undertaken at home. Next to this activity was the activity of watching video films which was also popular among the two sectors. In addition to the above activities, about one-third of the students used personal computers at least once a week and the main use was for playing games. The majority of adolescents from both sectors read at least one newspaper a week and at least one book a month. As for activities away from home, going to cinema was found to be the most popular activity among adolescents from the Hebrew sector while attending sports competitions was the most popular among those of the Arab sector. Engagement in sports activities was found to be most popular after-school activities in both sectors. Other activities which were participated by about one-third of the students in both sectors were youth movements, voluntary activities and summer camps. Gender differences were found in this study with males using more information technology by watching television and playing computers and females reading more books and magazines.

A more recent study was undertaken in 2000 among secondary school students (Cohen, 2008). Results indicated the popularity of social (e.g. being with friends and family) and passive leisure activities (e.g. watching TV, talking on the phone). Alongside the popularity of these types of activities, results indicated some participation in community through voluntarism and youth movements. These results highlighted the role that youth movements pay in youth development as being one of the major socialization agents in the Israeli society. An interesting observation in this study was the inconsistency between the preferences of youth for certain activities and their participation in them. Whereas, respondents preferred more active leisure activities such as engagement in sports activities, youth movements and social and political involvement they tended to participate less in these activities compared with passive activities such as listening to music, spending time with friends and watching television. The above studies on youth leisure participation in Israel show that young people like to take part in expressive activities and that this characteristics have been demonstrated over the last few decades. Despite gender differences which were identified in some of the studies, it is important to note that spending time with the family has been one of the leading activity which as noted by (Adler, 2008) illustrate the importance attributed to family among the Israeli young people as part of their identity, a characteristic which was not so dominant in other Western societies. The preference to participate in youth movements and community affairs even though was not practiced to the same extent as passive types of activities could also indicate the social connectivity among young people to their society.

Recent reports on the growing involvement of young people community affairs hint to their growing aspirations in playing a more active role in the society. In addition to the above patterns of leisure use, it is important to note that youth in Israel are also major consumers of media and users of information technologies as reflected in their use of computers and internet. A study among adolescents (Lemish, 2004) have indicted that one third watch television and one forth use the internet about one to two hours per day. The majority of adolescents use instant messaging everyday as a way to communicate with close friends, forty per cent play games and more than one third use the internet to search for information.

Alongside the growing leisure consumption and diversity in leisure behaviours in the Israeli society, it is also interesting to note that the notion of educating for leisure has been rapidly developed during the nineties through policy and practice. Underneath this development was the growing need to provide equal opportunities for the development of leisure knowledge, skills, attitudes and values through educational settings. This was successfully illustrated by the development of internationally well-recognized comprehensive leisure education curricula for schools (Ruskin and Sivan, 2002).

Concluding Remarks

The examination of Israel leisure as portrayed in this paper shed some light on the development of this society and the way in which different social, cultural and technological trends and developments have affected this domain of people's lives. Despite being a young nation, Israel has been undergoing tremendous population growth since its establishment. Its population comprises a mosaic of cultures that people brought with them upon immigrating to Israel. Motivated by the collective need to build a country in which all cultures are blended and a new collective one is created, immigrants called for homogeneity and unity in lifestyles including leisure behaviour. As the nation developed and with its exposure to other modern cultures, the homogeneity turned into diversity in offering and consumption of leisure activities. Change in values and increase in attention to individual-based needs and benefits led to participation in expressive and social activities which are self-cultivating. At the same time, collective needs remain important as illustrated in a growing participation in voluntarism as well as in the significance given to family as a core unit. The recent technological developments have also manifested themselves in the increase in information and communication as a way to be connected and maintain the social context. During its 64 years of existence, the Israeli society has been experiencing waves of mass immigration alongside periodical wars. Changes in leisure patterns have been reflecting the dynamic changes in a wide range of domains of Israelis' lives. Leisure has also developed as a sphere for expressing the tension between individualism and human solidarity, as well as an area where diversity and aspiration for common belonging co-exist.

In his lecture delivered in 1945 in the Hebrew University in Jerusalem, Martin Buber (1984) a well-renowned Jewish philosopher said that the Israeli utopia was 'a trial which did not failed' (p. 145). Building on this statement, it is possible to establish that the numerous waves of Jewish immigrants who came from more than seventy countries, representing innumerous mentalities, habits and beliefs and building a new state with diverse lifestyles including those of leisure, is a trial which did not fail. With its continuing population growth to almost eight millions (7,836.3 million) (Central Bureau of Statistics, 2012), and related developments it could be said that Israel is now a solid and well developed nation where individual aspirations are being sought after within a collective context of togetherness.

References

Adler, H. (2008). Preamble in E.H. Cohen, Jewish identity, values and leisure: Some explorations amongst Israeli general state schools 15–16 years old students (pp. 7–9). Tel Aviv: Tel-Aviv University, Kulman Center, School of Education (In Hebrew).

Bahat-Razon, N. (2004). Performers: Dance-society-culture in the State of Israel. Jerusalem: Carmel, pp. 51–33 (In Hebrew).

Buber, M. (1984). *Paths in Utopia.* Tel-Aviv: Am Oved.

Central Bureau of Statistics (2010). *Persons age 20 and over who used computers or internet by selected characteristics.* CBS, Statistical Abstract of Israel 2010. Retrieved from http://www.cbs.gov.il/reader/shnaton/templ_shnaton.html?num_tab=st09_07&CYear=2010

Central Bureau of Statistics (2011). *Population estimates.* CBS, Statistical Abstract of Israel 2011. Retrieved from: http://www.cbs.gov.il/shnaton62/st02_01.pdf

Central Bureau of Statistics (2012). *Main indicators, the population at the end of December 2011* (In Hebrew). Retrieved from: http://www.cbs.gov.il/reader

Haas, H. (1999). Leisure culture in Israel, 1998. *Panim: A Journal for Culture, Society and Education 10,* 107–139 (In Hebrew).

Internet World Stats (2011). Internet users in the Middle East. Retrieved from www.internetworldstats.com/stats5.htm

Mobile Youth Middle East (2012). Israel leads the Middle East market in social network usage and internet access. Retrieved from http://www.mobileyouthmideast.com/israel-leads-the-middle-east-market-in-social-network-usage-and-internet-access

Katz, E., Haas, H., Weitz, S., Adoni, H. Gurevittch, M., Schiff, M., and Goldberg-Anabi, D. (1992). *The Culture of Leisure in Israel: Changes in Patterns of Cultural Activity, 1970–1990.* Jerusalem: Israel Institute of Applied Social Research

Lemish, D. and Cohen, B.A. (2005). On the gendered nature of mobile phone culture in Israel. *Sex Roles, 52,* 7/8, 511–521.

Lemish, D. and Ribek, R. (n.d.) Israeli children surfing. The Institute for Internet Studies Tel Aviv University (In Hebrew). *Retrieved from* http://www.niis.tau.ac.il/text_item.aspx?tid=215

Ministry of Education and Culture, Division for Social and Youth Education (1993). *Extracurricular activities of 9th-12th grade pupils.* In Hebrew and Arab Education 1990/1. Jerusalem: Special Series no. 946. Central Bureau of Statistics (In Hebrew).

Ministry of Immigrant absorption (2011) The First Aliyah (1882–1903). Retrieved from http://www.moia.gov.il/Moia_en/AboutIsrael/aliya1.htm

Ministry of Immigrant absorption (2011b) The Second Aliyah (1882–1903). Retrieved from http://www.moia.gov.il/Moia_en/AboutIsrael/aliya2.htm

Ministry of Immigrant absorption (2011c) The Third Aliyah (1919–1923). Retrieved http://www.moia.gov.il/Moia_en/AboutIsrael/aliya3.htm

Ministry of Immigrant absorption (2011d).The Fourth Aliyah (1924–1928). Retrieved from http://www.moia.gov.il/Moia_en/AboutIsrael/aliya4.htm

Ministry of Immigrant absorption (2011e) The Fifth Aliyah (1929 1939). Retrieved from http://www.moia.gov.il/Moia_en/AboutIsrael/aliya5.htm

Ministry of Immigrant absorption (2011f). Aliyah from the Former Soviet Union (1990). Retrieved from http://www.moia.gov.il/Moia_en/AboutIsrael/aliyaUssr.htm

Paz, U., and Almog, O. (2009). Recreation and trip culture among the ulra orthodox society in Israel. People Israel – The guide to the Israeli society. Retrieved from http://www.peopleil.org/details.aspx?itemID=7556&searchMode=0&index=1 (In Hebrew)

Rabin, E. (2009). *The Psychology of the Internet- to know the users* (In Hebrew). Retrieved from http://nptech.org.il/blog/?p=213

Ruskin, H., and Sivan, A. (2000). Past, present and future trends of leisure in Israel. *Journal of the International Council for Health, Physical Education, Recreation Sport and Dance, 36*(4), 22–27.

Ruskin, H. and Sivan, A. (2002). *Leisure Education in School Systems*. Jerusalem: Cosell Center for Physical Education, Leisure and Health Promotion, Magness Press, The Hebrew University of Jerusalem (In Hebrew).

Ruskin, H. and Sivan, A. (2004). Leisure behaviour patterns and leisure education in the Israeli society. In Z. Gross and Y. Dror (eds) *Education as a Social Challenge*, (pp. 173–181), Israel, Tel-Aviv: Ramot Publishing (In Hebrew).

Ruskin, H., and Sivan, A., (2005). Israel. In G. Cushman, A.J. Veal and J. Zuzanek (eds), *Free Time and Leisure Participation: International Perspectives* (pp. 141–151). MA: CABI Publishing.

Shacham, O. (2011). *Coffee Shops in Vintage Style in Tel Aviv*. People Israel- The guide to the Israeli society (In Hebrew). Retrieved from http://www.peopleil.org/details.aspx?itemID=30219&searchMode=0&index=3

Shikma-Avivi, T. (2006). The Israeli fork dancing as representatives of culture: From the pioneers till today. Tapuz People Forums. Retrieved from http://www.tapuz.co.il/Forums2008/Articles/Article.aspx?ForumId=293&aId=69515 (In Hebrew)

Shor, N. (2008). *To dance with tears in your eyes – The history of clubs and discotheque culture in Israel*. Tel-Aviv: Resling (In Hebrew).

Sivan, A. (1984). *Leisure of high school youth in the Israeli kibbutz and city*. Remat Gan: Bar Ilan University (In Hebrew).

Sivan, A. (1986). *Influences of beliefs and values on leisure of youth*. Haifa: Multi-purpose instructional Center (In Hebrew).

Sivan, A., and Ruskin, H. (1997). Successful models for leisure education in Israel. *World Leisure and Recreation, 39*(2), 39–40.

The Israel Genealogical Society. (n.d). *Population census from 1922 undertaken by the British mandate* (In Hebrew). Retrieved from: (http://www.isragen.org.il/siteFiles/13/79/5783.asp)

The Israeli Center for Third-Sector Research (2007). *The Israeli Third Sector at a glance. Beer Sheva,* Ben-Gurion University of the Negev.

Sivan, D., Sela-Katz, P., Pe'er, D. (2003). Leisure, work, study and volunteering: Post-retirement trends. *Gerontology, 30,* 1–2, 13–27.

Veel, M. and Kariv, A. (2010). *Volunteering in Israel – Processes towards the year 2010. Volunteering in Israel. The National Council for Volunteering in Israel* (In Hebrew). Retrieved *from* http://www.ivolunteer.org.il/Index.asp?ArticleID=2539&CategoryID=672&Page=1

Zur, M. (1969). Among youngsters- talks together in the Keibbutz movement. A group of members in the Kibbutz movement and Am Oved, p. 279 (In Hebrew).

8

Strategies of Leisure in Japan

SCOTT NORTH

Japan's Leisure Toolkit

Japan's long history makes conceptualizing Japanese 'leisure and life through the ages' daunting. My solution is to limit the inquiry primarily to identifying strategies of leisure in the period that most historians agree coincides with the formation of Japan as a modern nation, that is, from the unification of the country under the Tokugawa military government in 1603 to the present, the period which is best documented and most relevant for understanding the trajectory of contemporary Japanese leisure.

Compared with the literature on work and industry, leisure in Japan has been all but invisible (Linhart, 1998). The contribution of this paper lies in taking a cultural approach that identifies not so much varied leisure forms, but the toolkit of durable cultural principles used to construct strategies of leisure in Japan through the ages. I focus in particular on the evolution of native words that represent concepts of time use.

Leisure Strategies

Cultures are composed of durable strategies and symbols that independently order human social action across time. While action often appears to be motivated by values, in reality, strategies of action produce the values (Swidler, 1986). Within social groups we can identify and classify the repertoires of action in which these basic cultural strategies are manifest. Studying strategies is an approach that permits systematic analysis of complexly interrelated and important areas of human life that resist easy measurement. For example, 'gender strategies' are plans of action that men and women employ to negotiate divisions of labour and power in the household that satisfy individual feelings about appropriate gender identity, even though the resulting order often reproduces burdensome gender inequities (Hochschild and Machung, 1989). Likewise, leisure strategies order the ludic elements of life and give rise to continuities in the practices of leisure even as they vary with age, gender, class, and historical period. Analysis of leisure strategies provides insight into the cultural toolkits of symbols, habits and styles that were used to construct them.

This is, of course, a way of saying that although people make their own leisure history, the freedom to construct leisure practices is often severely limited. Rojek puts it thus:

> You might have free time at your disposal as the end of the working day. But you are not at liberty to dispose of it just as you please ... there are matters of inequality and scarcity to consider. At a basic level, time disposal relies upon income. Your capacity to dispose of non-work time is economically conditioned and culturally coded. It reflects distinctions of class, gender, ethnicity, education and bodily health. Of course, you are free to make choices. But the choices you make are contextualized by how you are situated in relation to scarcity. By scarcity is meant, the unequal distribution of economic, cultural, social and political resources and your position in relation to them. (Rojek, 2010: 5–6)

Regarding Japanese leisure, the time use traditions of the dead generations seem an especially heavy and obdurate nightmare on the leisure strategies of the living. Notions about the ownership of scarce time and constraints on its allocation have particularly important and enduring implications.

In agrarian Japan, time was owned not by individuals but by collectivities, outside which individuals could scarce exist. As a 'late developer,' Japan's trajectory of modernity was so swift that pre-industrial social relations of production lagged economic modernization. The result is the persistence of early-modern obligations and a comparatively weak sense of individual entitlement to leisure.

From this past, nearly devoid of the popular liberation struggles that characterize industrial and political development in Europe or North America, the dominant strategy to emerge in Japan is *omakase*: passively letting others decide. Vertical relations mean that subordinates depend on superiors to determine what is appropriate. Corporate-based leisure was one outcome of this strategy. The most recent manifestation is state-led development of appropriate national leisure strategies (Leheny, 2003).

To assert that *omakase* is the dominant leisure strategy is not to say that individual leisure has not arisen in concert with modernity. But such leisure autonomy as individuals have gained has been shaped by traditional strategies and practices of time use in hierarchical interpersonal relations. Moreover, we need to remember that leisure strategies in modern Japan have been an afterthought; strategies for industrial development, national expansion, and recovery comprise Japan's master narrative.

The following discussion of Japanese leisure strategies is organized around conceptions characteristic of particular eras. I focus on leisure strategies at both the state/political economy levels and the popular level. These categories form a vertical axis for analysis. The horizontal axis is time. As noted, I will stick mostly to the last 400 years, but there are important antecedents in earlier periods.

Shifting Japanese Conceptions of Leisure across the Ages

Native words for leisure show how the concept has evolved. Terminological shifts reflect how Japanese of different ages have used their culture to define and meet the universal human needs for recreation, play, and rest within the contextual constraints of successive historical periods and their associated ethos.

The five periods are: (1) Pre-Edo; (2) Early modern Japan (the Edo period: 1603–1867); (3) The Meiji era to World War II; (4) The postwar leisure booms 1955–1990; (5) Post-bubble leisure (1990). I use the conceptions of leisure in these periods as buoys to which I loosely tether the discussion of strategies of leisure in each era.

The Zen of Pre-Edo Leisure: What is the Leisure of No Leisure?

Classical Japan. The earliest Japanese conceptions of time reflect an absence voluntary leisure. The tripartite division cited by Linhart (1998: 3–4) – *ke*: normal working time; *hare*: sacred time, obligatory rituals; and *kegare*: pollution (menstruation, childbirth, death) – hints at the how the paucity of leisure practices in Japanese life derives from taxonomy. Historical accounts of classical Japanese society (600–1200) show that what leisure there was belonged to the aristocratic elite. Festivals were religious rites aimed at pacifying angry gods (Totman, 1981: 9).

The classical period saw the rise of Japan's famous high culture, such as the 11th century *The Tale of Genji*, possibly the world's first novel, and *gagaku*, court music. Most high culture was concerned with religion, and cultivating 'a vibrant feel for beauty, a keen sensibility, a mordant irony, and an introspective melancholy' (ibid.: 54). It is questionable whether leisure is even an appropriate word to use in connection with pre-modern, pre-market Japanese society.

Medieval Japan (1200–1603). Indeed, scholars dismiss the notion of leisure before the Edo period (1603–1867). David Leheny's study found little hard evidence of leisure consumption prior to the 20th century; he disposes of pre-Edo leisure in two short paragraphs (Lehney, 2003: 44; 50–51). Most see leisure becoming an identifiable category of Japanese life from the last quarter of the Edo period (the first half of the 19th century).

Nonetheless, the Zen aesthetic that infused poetry, such as the famous *Essays in Idleness*, various arts (e.g. *sadô*, the ceremonial way of tea), music, and the theatric storytelling of *Nô* drama of the medieval period, as well martial arts (*budô*), set the stage for early modern, Edo period leisure (Cox, 2002; Totman, 1981: 106–116).

Kô, Yûgei and *Dô*: Moral Uses of Time as Leisure Strategies in Early Modern Japan (1603–1867)

Strategies of Japanese leisure in the Edo period are best understood through study of quotidian practices of leisure, although as a feudal nation with a rigid social hierarchy and strict social codes, there was what might be termed 'state control' of leisure. It is in this period that nascent forms of today's leisure strategies – at both the state and popular levels have their roots.

Pilgrimage, Precursor to Tourism. Pilgrimage is the earliest commonly cited example of Japanese leisure. Roads built to enable Japanese nobles to travel to Edo (Tokyo) to fulfill fealty obligations, paved the way for religious pilgrimage. To defray high travel costs, villages pooled their money. These co-ops, called *kô*, enabled selected villagers to visit shrines and temples to pray on behalf of the whole group. As proof of their visit, the travellers returned with *omiyage*, 'charms issued by the sanctuary.' In this way, Edo era pilgrimage presaged the pattern of later Japanese tourism (Formanek, 1998).

Travellers represented commercial opportunity for holy sites and those who lived along the roads to them. Inns catering to pilgrims' needs provided local specialties, food, and sexual services. The rise of tourism related commerce encouraged government to loosen controls on domestic travel.

Yûgei and the Iemoto-style of Moral Leisure. The markets of Japan's growing cities provided other new opportunities for leisure. *Yûgei* (pleasure activities) were defined through contrast with martial arts, called *bûgei,* and *taishû geinô,* (popular performing arts). *Yûgei* of this period was long neglected as too vulgar for serious study (Nishiyama, 1997). However, in the late 20th century Nishiyama Matsunosuke rehabilitated the distinct culture of Edo (the city), including its forms of leisure.

Nishiyama's study of Edo society noted how late-Edo period residents challenged the rigid, four-class stratification of samurai, farmers, craftspeople, and townspeople/merchants through leisure pursuits. Popular *yûgei* activities included *iemoto*-style arts, like flower arranging, tea ceremony, traditional musical instruments, haiku writing, calligraphy, dance, and gardening (*bonsai*), that remain popular today. Edo residents also enjoyed card games, kabuki theatre, and *rakugo* comic monologues. The last two were, like many of Shakespeare's plays, opportunities for commoners to enjoy a laugh at the expense of their social betters. This mass quality of Edo leisure is another of its notable characteristics (ibid.: 8).

Chaffing at social strictures, townsmen borrowed the *iemoto*-style to create 'cultural communities' within which people took new names (*geimei*) that obscured their social status and made cross-class interaction possible. '... these individuals were creating a new world radically at odds with the feudal ethic that governed daily life ... this world of culture provided a sense of liberation, a sense of freedom, that was sadly lacking in contemporary social reality.' (ibid.: 5)

In her prize-winning study of the same phenomenon, Ikegami (2005) described how *iemoto* 'aesthetic networks' contributed to modernizing Japanese political culture. In these relatively classless civil society gatherings, participants could associate freely. New tastes and ideologies could be developed and spread. Like the culture salons of Czarist Russia, Japanese leisure practices created space for the discovery and articulation of political interests and social identities independent of birth status.

As a market economy expanded, opportunities for leisure and people who could afford them increased. Nightlife becomes evident from this time. Recreational sex, with men or women, was a common leisure practice for townsmen (Früstück, 1998: 62). Businesses catering to eating, drinking, and sexual needs sprung up on unused riverbank land. These were the forerunners of today's entertainment districts.

Throughout the country, the waning fortunes of the military government stimulated local forms of mass leisure. Temples facing declining stipends from the central government in the first half of the 19th century compensated with carnival-like gatherings called *kaichou* and *ennichi*. The former are exhibitions of sacred texts and icons, the latter are frequent festivals in honour of various deities. Both became sources of income. Along with pilgrimage to visit sacred sites, these early strategies for promoting commercially oriented leisure set the tone for later developments (Linhart, 1998).

This picture of growing Edo period leisure should not obscure how little leisure choice was available. Rather than a realm of freedom, the *iemoto* were in fact vertically organized webs of control. *Iemoto* heads had absolute authority over the content of their arts and the standards for achievement of various ranks. *Iemoto* use of 'traditional idioms' bolstered their credibility and helped them survive the transition from feudalism to capitalism (Ikegami, 2005: 165). Even as a strategy of leisure, the *iemoto* were part and parcel of the dominant Japanese pattern of hierarchical social organization. They reinforced the normative framework of expert instruction and validation.

Moral Uses of Time. Edo's serious and highly organized leisure strategies are descended from earlier strategies for allocating scarce temporal resources. Historian Robert Smith argued that, unlike England, where workers rebelled against imposed industrial 'time discipline,' Japan had no such conflicts because pre-industrial Japanese peasants regarded time as 'fleeting and precious, and great moral value was attached to its productive use.' Further, 'Time was not a personal possession, but belonged primarily to families and, through them, to kin, neighbors and villages' (Smith, 1986: 167).

In consequence, industrialization proceeded with relatively little strife because both labour and capital in Japan shared a view of time as collectively held and valued for work rather than belonging to individuals.

Second, it followed that early modern Japanese self-concepts were inseparable from the collectivities to which they belonged. Position in the social division of labour was a powerful formative element in *omakase* consciousness. Combined with family-style ties between masters and underlings, dependency consciousness made underlings docile. Through a 'social multiplier' effect (Alesina, Glaeser, and Sacerdote, 2005) *omakase* passivity in regard to leisure became widely diffused.

This time consciousness and related time use practices can be traced to Edo period farm manuals that stress careful planning to keep households out of poverty and maintain good reputation. Thus, near-constant labour, was the rule for Japanese peasants. With time and land their only resources, they had to provide their own security. Careful husbandry was also the basis of the moral framework for raising and educating children. Leisure activities, such as music, dancing, using slang, drinking alcohol or gambling, in fact any time spent outside the bounds of family and the patriarchal, age-graded hierarchy was prohibited for fear it would bring the family disgrace (Smith, 1986: 175–182).

Similarly, Protestant ethic-style injunctions against sloth and waste and in favour of time thrift and hard work are found in the commercial religions of Edo period merchants (Bellah, 1957), suggesting that other-directed strategies of time use were common throughout Japanese society of the period.

Dô: *Moral 'Ways' of Leisure.* In consequence of the low esteem in which the practice of *yûgei* arts was held, and so that they would not be seen as mere time-wasting entertainment, the *iemoto* rebranded their *yûgei* as philosophies or 'ways' to self-improvement and enlightenment. They drew upon the symbolism and approach to self-transformation through rigorous systematized training and master-student transmission of knowledge known as *dô,* which had first emerged in the medieval period. Appropriating the mantle of *dô*, and standardizing the practices and criteria for making and assessing progress in various arts, the Zen-inspired *iemoto* arts thrived (Cox, 2002). *Iemoto*-style activities came to be regarded as what we might call 'serious leisure' (Stebbins, 1982), moral uses of time that contribute to the collective good rather than *goraku*, amusements of dubious value.

Leisure Strategies from the Meiji Restoration to World War II

The Meiji period (1868–1912) marked Japan's reengagement with the larger world after more than 200 years of minimal contact. After the civil war ended with the victory of the modernizing faction, much of the culture of Edo was repudiated as 'outdated and vulgar' (Nishiyama, 1997: 9). Curiosity about the outside world grew and Japan 'looked West' (*bunmei kaika*), rushing to adopt practices deemed characteristic of 'civilized and enlightened' nations. This meant primarily industrial development, political reform, and colonial aspirations, but leisure pursuits were also part of the picture.

Nevertheless, time conceptions constrained Japanese leisure strategy innovation. All words for work connoted 'obligation to others' and from the Meiji Restoration to the 1930s no satisfactory word for worker could be found that reflected a contractual relationship between autonomous equals (Smith, 1986: 183).

Time consciousness failed to include a realm of 'free time' to contrast with work. Instead, Japan's cultural strategies of time use promoted a preference for 'income over leisure, up to a level near the limits of physical endurance.' (ibid.: 185) Workers only wanted more pay not reduced hours, even when normal hours were 12–14 hours a day or more. Workers never complained about excessive overtime, or the lack of holidays, because doing so would impugn 'the moral basis of the (employee-employer) relationship.' (ibid.: 186) Likewise, insisting on leisure for one's self would be a betrayal of obligations to co-workers.

In any case, leisure was not guaranteed so workers' expectations were not dashed when holidays were cancelled by employer fiat. Similarly, work hours were subject to employer whim. Twenty-four-hour labour days were possible, but workers did not complain. Their peasant sense of time as a collective resource allocated by the leaders of the collectivity was a good fit with what the industrializing state required. Indeed, long work hours and minimal leisure were the common lot of workers in all the industrializing nations (Schor, 1991).

Japanese wives did not object to husbands' long hours and lengthy absences. Men fulfilled social and family roles by working. Wives fulfilled their roles by taking full responsibility for most household affairs and enabling the reproduction of men's labour. Perhaps no society had a better 'fit' between family form, gendered division of labour, and industrial needs (Goode, 1963).

Defining Japanese Leisure by Borrowing from the West. While leisure took a back seat to industrial development, Meiji Japan's opening to the world let the world in. Between 1870 and 1940 foreigners came in ever increasing numbers, bringing new ideas about leisure, travel, and living that were quickly adopted. Japan was anxious to claim the mantle of civilization and so hotel construction, railroad development, and plans for English-style 'garden cities' all flourished. Although originally stimulated by the arrival of foreigners, the building of leisure infrastructure was sustained by increases in domestic travellers. And as they travelled, Japanese needs and standards were transformed: greater choice of foods, beds, and private rooms were preferred over the set menus and shared rooms with futons on the floor found in traditional accommodations (Leheny, 2003: 55–56).

By 1930, the idea that traveling for leisure could serve a moral purpose gained a foothold. The state controlled railroads and its associated travel services company, Japan Tourist Bureau, began to push travel in Japan and her colonies as patriotic duty. In step with Japanese colonization in Korea and China, increasing government promotion of travel was instrumental in defining Japan's national character vis a vis the outside world (ibid.: 43–71). This was just one arrow in the quiver of state-led development strategies that Japan would rely on as the 20th century proceeded.

The Yoka Problem: What to Do with Leftover Time? The etymology of *yoka*, a Meiji era coinage for leisure, shows how ingrained strategies of time use from earlier periods inhibited pre-war era leisure choice. The Japanese characters for *yoka* literally mean 'excess' and 'spare time,' or 'time when one is not occupied with a task.' Even today, when the word is frequently heard, the connotation is not good. It sounds unproductive and makes people wonder why more work is not being done.

The unsavory implications of *yoka* are at the root of 20th century Japanese suspicion of leisure. Linhart (1998: 2) says Japanese suspicion of all forms of leisure is more responsible for our lack of knowledge about leisure than any real absence of leisure in Japanese life. Rather than there being no leisure there is little in the way of leisure studies: *yoka* was not an appropriate subject for foreigners or Japanese to investigate. But that did not mean the people of prewar Japan did not enjoy respite from their labours. Let us see what strategies they employed.

Tanoshimi and Asobi: Prewar Strategies of Leisure. Tanoshimi and *asobi* are ways to think about time use when one has time. Drawing on life history interviews conducted in 1984 and 1985 with Tokyo residents who lived there between the 1890s and 1923 (when the city was largely destroyed by a massive earthquake), Ackermann (1998) discovered that the most common ways of thinking about 'respite from everyday life' were *asobi* (play, pleasure, fun) and *tanoshimi* (enjoyment, delight, things to look forward to).

Ackermann notes that early 20th century craftsmen and factory workers had but two days off a month and apprentices had even less. In these brief windows for *asobi* and *tanoshimi* they enjoyed theatres for performing arts, kabuki, movies, and musical performances. There was also *karyûkai,* the entertainment world of tea houses and restaurants with private rooms for socializing. For those men who could afford it, fun was often provided by *geisha* or other, perhaps less refined, courtesans.

Asobi and *tanoshimi* were segregated by social class. An office worker was not fit to carry the portable shine at the festival ('I was after all not a craftsman.' (Ackermann, 1998: 34)). Horse racing and other gambling imported in imitation of the West were sometimes illegal and those who went to the races were considered of low social class (Nagashima, 1998: 354). A local priest in Ackermann's study did not frequent *karyûkai,* although he did go to the theatre.

Temple and shrine festivals carried on the tradition of leisure that began with the *ennichi* of the Edo period. Ackermann's interviewees recalled that *ennichi* were always enjoyable, but that there had been little other recreation in the pre-Meiji era.

The key distinction is that *asobi* and *tanoshimi* were not 'the opposites of work,' rather they were 'respite from content.' (Ackermann, 1998: 38) For Japanese of this period, *asobi* and *tanoshimi,* meant not having to care about whether others thought what you were doing was 'sensible.' Thinking of spare time in this way was a strategy of leisure that allowed people to sidestep the moral injunction that time should be always full of productive effort. Although *asobi* and *tanoshimi* were passive leisure strategies, they were ways to carve out a realm of relative freedom. Likewise, the concept of *asobi* informs the strategy that makes the individualized electronic and animated leisure of our present age possible.

Activities for Solving the Yoka Problem. Given the emphasis on moral use of time, using *yoka* to become more accomplished was a common leisure strategy. The prewar period saw cooking become a hobby for middle-class women (Cwiertka, 1998). Martial arts took a page from the book of the *iemoto.* Adopting a high moral tone, they rechristened themselves as *budô* (*kendô,* way of the sword), *jûdô, karatedô, kyûdô* (way of archery), making the transformation from ancient warrior military arts to modern sports through invented, traditionalistic notions of Japanese body culture and training (Inoue, 1998). Baseball, both as a government sponsored school sports activity for the promotion of spirituality and as a media sponsored spectator sport, became popular in the early 20th century. Professional teams attracted devoted followers and by the late 1920s there were radio broadcasts of the games (Whiting, 1977). Seasonal leisure activities with family or co-workers, such as cherry blossom viewing, which had been popular since Edo, moon viewing parties, or strolling or picnicking under the autumn leaves, were other ways to fill *yoka* with relaxing yet meaningful content.

The Taisho period saw a government solution to the *yoka* problem as well. Instead of *asobi* or *yûgei,* which were considered insufficiently serious appellations, officially sanctioned state and commercial institutions for arts education began describing their activities as 'culture' (*bunka*) or 'civilization' (*kyôyô) (Cox, 2002: 180), a trend that revived with prosperity in the 1960s.*

By the early 1930s, however, modest leisure expansion stalled under the gloom of the global depression and gathering clouds of war. Japan began to see its situation as an emergency requiring national mobilization. Under state leadership, theatre, the ideal mass entertainment of the wartime period, 'was deployed as a powerful agent in controlling leisure time and in shaping a belief in Japanese cultural superiority.' (Robertson, 1998: 296) Other leisure and luxuries were declared enemies. Citizens were told to use their superior will power to suppress leisure and material desires 'until victory is achieved' (Garon, 1998).

Postwar Leisure: The *Rejyâ* Booms

Militarism and wartime privation further reinforced longstanding Japanese prejudices against leisure and set the stage for institutionalizing state control of daily life. The aftermath of surrender was a struggle to survive. Food was scarce, cites lay in ruins, the economy in tatters. National pride fell to an all-time low. Leisure was the province of the victors, whose well-fed faces and easy-going manner on display throughout occupied Japan were in sharp contrast to the suffering of the native population.

Recycling strategies used to cope with the coming of foreigners in the mid-19th century, Japan sought again to emulate successful Western nations. The state tried to use leisure strategies modeled on the US and Western Europe to stimulate economic growth. The difference was that in those foreign places leisure was comparatively private. In postwar Japan, the state would prescribe lifestyle norms for its citizens, measuring progress toward normalcy by proximity to the standard of 'advanced industrial nations.' However, it would be the 1980s before leisure could become a priority (Leheny, 2003: 1–17; 73–75).

The Persistence of Prewar Strategies of Work and Leisure. Following a brief period of US support for unions as a force for democratizing Japan, the Occupation 'reversed course' from the late 1940s as communist threats in China and Korea made Japan strategically indispensable. American support shifted from labour to the remaining architects of Japan's wartime machine, who were allowed to return to public life to engineer economic recovery in the service of US strategic goals (Johnson, 1982).

Again, workers' lingering pre-industrial time consciousness aided enterprises in deploying temporal resources. After several important strikes were crushed in the late 1950s, walkouts became largely symbolic affairs. There was little evidence of output restriction as a worker response to employer time control. When bosses stayed late, all stayed late. No worker 'would suggest that the obligations of the group are limited to a fixed amount of time sold to the company, after which employees are free of responsibility' (Smith, 1986: 192).

Ethnographic studies of 1960s white-collar workers noted the absence of fixed quitting times, the prevalence of staying late, and work weeks of 62–64 hours, including obligatory socializing (Rohlen, 1974). Factory workers' vacation days went unused and many of those that were used were for sickness, weddings, or funerals. Days off were bad for workers' careers: others would certainly be promoted ahead of those who took time off (Dore, 1973).

With economic growth, jobs paid more and their value to workers, the 'employment rent,' rose (Schor, 1991). Japan's rigid labour market generally gave the stable rewards of 'lifetime employment' to 'regular employees,' hired fresh from graduation from high school or college. Few who succeeded in fierce competition to gain such employment could conceive of risking their careers for the sake of a vacation.

The more workers were paid, the more they became willing to work. Japanese employers were always much more willing to raise salaries than to reduce working hours. Even during the labour strife of the immediate postwar years, employers refused any negotiation of the length of the working day or composition of company welfare benefits. These benefits included recreation, parties, and trips that provided opportunities for building 'human harmony,' but they had the opportunity cost of active leisure planned by individual workers and their families. Japan's enterprise unions acquiesced and fell into line behind the corporate lead on leisure (North, 2005).

Nevertheless, thriving postwar suburbs were full of 'bright new life.' Japan's salaried middle-class workers were considered ideal marriage partners precisely because they had more leisure and more predictable career paths than farmers, merchants, or self-employed professionals (Vogel, 1971). And yet the most common forms of leisure reported for white-collar men are after-hours drinking sessions with workmates and *pachinko* (pinball), semi-legal gambling. Pachinko revenues were estimated to be more than five per cent of Japanese GDP up to the 1990s (Manzenreiter, 1998: 360).

Professional housewives, counterparts of salarymen, had cultivated appropriately cultured leisure from the 1920s. After Japan's Empire collapsed, they were liberated from government demands to bear as many children as possible. As housewives climbed above 10 million in the 1960s, appliances relived some drudgery and gave them more time (Ochiai, 1996). Still the undiminished sway of the injunction to be 'good wives and wise mothers,' their leisure strategies involved finding appropriate, meaningful pursuits for their *yoka*. To fill married Japanese women's unoccupied hours 'culture industries' organized by local and national government agencies and sustained by substantial corporate donations promoted language lessons, tennis, community circles for traditional and modern arts and crafts, and serious hobbies practiced with passion and an eye toward self-transformation as well as 'play.'

By the mid-60s Japan had hosted the Olympics, built the world's first high-speed train line, and doubled citizens' incomes. Even as *The Economist* newspaper dubbed Japan's recovery a 'miracle' in 1962, leisure was returning to Japanese life. The 'search for enjoyment' varied by class, gender, occupation, and region, as well as the historical antecedents that informed appropriate choices of leisure strategies for each social location (Plath, 1964).

The Leisure Boom of the 1960s and 1970s. The spread of television, increased automobile ownership and improvements in public transportation, the lifting of restrictions on international travel, growing awareness of how other nations (and other Japanese) played, and rising incomes fuelled the leisure boom of the 1960s and early 1970s. As used in Japan at this time, the word 'leisure' *(rejyâ)* connoted 'active use' and 'a sense of luxury' rather than the opposite of work (Cox, 1998: 180).

In the 1950s and 1960s policy makers were consumed by national reconstruction rather than recreation. Japanese work hours remained long and leisure was unevenly distributed. Although domestic consumption increased, Japan's economy was still export driven. Leaders in Japan and abroad began to critique the overemphasis on exports and public works-led development and call for 'a more fair and livable society' (Leheny, 2003: 78).

Just before the 1973 oil crisis that brought an end to Japan's period of 'high speed growth,' the newly created 'Leisure Development Industrial Office' of Japan's Ministry of International Trade and Industry made recommendations for improvement of the leisure environment, including reduced working hours, two-day weekends, longer holidays, construction of leisure facilities, restoration of damaged eco-systems, and bureaucratic leisure policy supervision to ensure that leisure development contributes in an orderly way to the national good. The portfolio of this government agency included educating the public about leisure appropriate for 'an advanced industrial country,' as well as the Japanese way to become such a 'normal' nation. A comprehensive overview of leisure in advanced nations was compiled and recommendations for lifestyle changes were made.

A major *rejyâ* recommendation was increased tourism to and from Japan. However, an embarrassing failure involving the promotion of 'nightlife tourism' to Korea's Cheju Island in 1973, forced government promotion of foreign travel to lay dormant for a decade (ibid.: 79–101)

... *And the* Asobi *Backlash.* Synonymous with lifestyle consumption and travel, *rejyâ* struck many Japanese as 'foreign.' The market logic of Western-style *rejyâ* called forth an opposing, humanist intellectual discourse called *asobi-ron*, which emphasized play as a path to 'self-determination or self-actualization.' (Manzenreiter and Ben-Ari, 2004) Advocates of this leisure strategy believed there was moral authority inherent in the ancient word *asobi*, play, which is how the active engagement of children in imaginative activities is described. Still, this naturalist critique of commercialized leisure argued that the state should level the playing field and spread the availability of leisure (ibid.). A large measure of *omakase* passivity remained in this homemade leisure strategy.

The Second Leisure Boom, 1985–90

Following 'slow growth' from 1973–84, Japan's second leisure boom took off on the back of asset inflation and the rocket-like rise in the value of the yen. Japanese reveled in their good fortune and declared that the country's astounding economic power confirmed the superiority of Japanese management and manufacturing prowess.

During this 'bubble economy,' Japanese leisure spending reached surreal heights. Tokyo bars importing glacial ice by air from Norway to use in making drinks. Sales of luxury goods soared. There were $1000 melons and gold plated golf clubs. Japanese bought Pebble Beach and Rockefeller Center. Some of the world's most expensive art was purchased to hang in corporate offices. The orgy of excess made headlines across the globe, obscuring Japan's growing inequality.

Dubbed an 'economic superpower,' Japan simultaneously realized that many of its citizens were not behaving like those in other wealthy countries. Concerned that the fruits of prosperity were not being properly consumed, Japan gave renewed consideration to leisure in the late 1980s.

The 'brutal careerism of the economic miracle' (Field, 2001: xi) came under fire even from Japanese business leaders as Japan's overproduction drew criticism from its trading partners. Sony's Morita Akio, for example, called for shorter hours and improved lives, with emphasis on 'quality of life' over 'quantity of production,' a position echoed in the Economic Planning Agency's 12th Five-Year Plan (McCormack, 2001: 82–83).

Reports issued in 1986 and 1987 by the blue-ribbon Maekawa committee set forth plans to internationalize Japanese markets, assuage trade partner ire, and promote leisure by Japanese workers. The leisure components were reduced work hours, fewer work days, more holidays, and expanded domestic travel and tourism, especially to depopulating rural regions. To revitalize these areas, a Resort Law was passed that opened 20 per cent of Japan's total land area to resort development and subsidized the construction of ski new resorts, hotels, golf courses and other facilities. The goal of sending 10 million Japanese tourists abroad each year by 1992 was achieved by 1990, the first time in history that a government urged such large numbers of citizens to travel abroad (Leheny, 2003).

In the second leisure boom, the state, in cooperation with allies in construction and industry, took the lead in making Japan a 'lifestyle superpower.' Along with 'internationalization,' the word that symbolized this new leisure strategy was *yutori*.

Post-Bubble Leisure: The Failures of *Yutori* and *Kyôsei* in the Lost Decade(s)

Economic growth should have helped more Japanese gain expanded leisure. The problem was whether there was time enough to enjoy the superfluity of goods and leisure opportunities the country produced. Some young people took extended time off between temporary or part-time jobs, but most full-time workers stayed in *omakase* mode, waiting for government to enable leisure.

By the early 1990s, 'affluence and leisure' and 'equal opportunity to realize a multiplicity of values' (McCormack, 2001: 83) were being offered as leisure state antidotes to corporate society. But government attempts to address the needs of the 'almost ascetic' salaried workers whose sacrifices had propelled Japanese success were an incoherent mish-mash that begged the question of whether industrial policy architects had any idea how to do leisure.

Nearly 60 per cent of workers in 1988 said they did not have enough *yutori*, a Japanese word which means, 'time or space to do your own thing.' (ibid.: 85). Despite government leadership on the issue, including the creation of new holidays, after two decades of economic stagnation full-time Japanese workers in 2006 had no leisure increase. An apparent drop in working hours was a statistical illusion, caused by rising numbers of part-time workers. Furthermore, a growing proportion of work time consisted of 'service overtime,' hours worked without compensation (Morioka, 2006). One reliable survey found that full-time employed men aged 20–59 worked an average of 2625 hours a year in 1990, but by 2000 the average increased to 2703 (Mouer and Kawanishi, 2005: 74–75).

Japanese did increase by one hour per week their time spent on media related leisure, but lost an equal amount from active leisure pursuits (Fuess, 2006). No wonder then, that 'stress' was the most recognized foreign loanword in Japan in 2008 (Japan Times, 2008).

Leisure proposals intended to promote freedom in a *yutori no aru shakai* (a society with *yutori*) directly contradicted the cultural strategies that made Japan an economic superpower. The *omakase*, top-down strategy of Japanese leisure led to the creation of new holidays by government fiat. Consequently, nearly everyone in the country took time off simultaneously, resulting in high prices and extreme crowding. There was seldom very little *space to do your own thing* on Japanese holidays. TV and newspapers reported on the 'vacation rush,' with trains running at 150 per cent capacity, all flights full, and expressway backups of 50 kilometres or more. Many people cut holidays short, returning home early to rest up for the return to work.

Leisure and Development: Kyôsei. Business leaders offered the concept *kyôsei*. It means symbiosis, in this case between work, economic growth, and leisure. The term 'leisure business' recognized leisure as 'a specific concept related to new forms of organization of time.' (Ackermann, 1998: 28) It took until late in the 20th century for leisure and work to become oppositional concepts in Japan. The turning point was the establishment of weekends and other consecutive days off. Yet even today less than half of Japanese workers have two-day weekends.

Furthermore, the concept of 'vacation' has not yet taken root, except for among students. Even students get far less of it than they would in the US or Europe. There are 240 plus school days a year, plus weekend club activities. Through the education system students are acculturated for time domination, learning early on that their time is not their own.

Employed Japanese take less than half their allotted paid holidays and the percentage has been declining. Cole (1992) found that high living costs, heavy work loads, concern for reputation among co-workers (who have to cover for absent workers), and 'tacit pressure from management not to take vacations' were reasons for low rates of paid leave usage. Under these circumstances, *kyôsei* means taking vacation all together. That way one avoids sanctions and criticism, but may also fail to find enjoyable leisure.

Contemporary Japan's leisure industry is subsidiary to a larger cultural strategy of economic expansion. 'The potential for a society providing general well-being was hijacked by the mad desire for ever accelerating growth.' (Field, 2001: xi). Studies of contemporary leisure are mostly about work and construction.

Leisure as Development in a Developmental State. The main strategy of post-bubble leisure, the putative silver bullet that boosts growth, pumps money into the countryside, stabilizes population, and provides *yutori*, has been resort construction. But the irony of using leisure as a field of development is the frenzy of work it creates. The 'peace, freedom, and verdant greenery' envisioned by policy makers became, 'a land of chemicalized golf courses, expensive marinas, toll expressways that penetrated the deepest mountains, and resorts that multiplied the ideology and aesthetics of Disneyland, where culture meant consumption.' (McCormack, 2001: 87).

Golf, in particular, represented the confluence of money, deregulation, political power, and hegemonic masculinity that promoted development. Japan went from having 100 courses in 1955 to 2000 courses in 1994, and claimed to have nearly a quarter of the planet's golfers. Demand was apparently so great and money so abundant, that Japanese golf developments expanded into Taiwan, Singapore, and Korea (Ben Ari, 1998), a replay of earlier forms of colonial expansion.

An alternative view is that politicians were promoting a view of leisure appropriate for enhancing the identity of an advanced industrial nation, as well as profit and GDP. The strategy of resort construction as leisure was not a plot, but a happy confluence/coincidence of nationalism, internationalism, and financial shenanigans (Leheny, 2003).

But plot or not, the consequences bear thinking about. Disneyland has become the paradigm of consumption-based leisure in Japan, inspiring a large number of similar attractions (Hamilton-Oehrl, 1998). This 'central cultural symbol of the new Japan' allows 'visitors to consume the prepackaged American symbols of fantasy, love and adventure passively, while depriving them of opportunities for spontaneous festivity and human interaction.' (McCormack, 2001: 100).

And that would seem to be the point we have reached: As a rich nation, Japan determined that it needed strategies of leisure suited to its economic superpower status. Relying on existing cultural strategies, Japan set out to import and then Japanize leisure. But in spite of the emphasis on active *rejya* (such as skiing, hiking, camping, golf and foreign travel), passive leisure (eating out) and domestic travel (*kenbutsu* visiting places to look at things) dominate (Manzenreiter and Ben-Ari, 2004; Graburn, 1998). Hyper-development of leisure facilities outstrips time people have to use them, the space for their construction, or people's real leisure needs. And among the young, the leisure strategy enabled by electronic forms of *asobi*, withdrawing into *manga* comics or animated fantasies in the search for a 'respite from content,' seems certain to increase the passivity of Japanese leisure.

Critics point out that the castle of corporate life has remained untouched by democratic trends making slow inroads in outlying areas of social life such as education and families. But society as a whole is corporate centred and so the corporate clock sets schedules for all. Ironically for a country that strives to be an advanced industrialized nation, slowing down would be admitting that Japan suffers from *Eikokubyô* 'advanced nation's disease.'

Future of Japanese Leisure. That Japan needs more leisure is evident from statistics on worker health and well-being. From male workers rapid rises in hypertension, death from overwork, suicide and the like in the post-World War II period we can see that the ethic of self-sacrifice (*messhi houkô*) remains the corporate membership ideal.

Workers *are* unhappy about their lack of leisure – they say they want to work less, but they currently lack even the leisure to think about the kind of life they have, let alone what they might want.

Japan's 'social multiplier' promotes cultural strategies of leisure in which people may not live to work, but their actions make it look as though they do. Increasing irregular employment may force some people to make a virtue of involuntary leisure. Indeed it is already doing so. But that will simply be yet another example of how, in leaving the allocation of time to the state, the firm, and the village, Japanese through the ages have failed – a failure of the imagination, Leheny says – to find a way to use their cultural toolkit to construct a better leisure model. What they have is an expensive, second-rate imitation of the kinds of leisure they are told they should aspire to.

References

Ackermann, P. (1998). 'Respite from Everyday Life: Kôtô-ku (Tokyo) in Recollections.' In *The Culture of Japan as Seen through Its Leisure.* S. Linhart and S. Frühstück (eds). Albany: SUNY Press. 27–40.

Alesina, A., E. Glaeser, and B. Sacerdote (2005). 'Work and Leisure in the US and Europe: Why So Different?' Harvard Institute of Economic Research, Discussion Paper Number 2068. http://www.economics.harvard.edu/pub/hier/2005/HIER2068.pdf

Bellah, R. (1957). *Tokugawa Religion: The Values of Pre-Industrial Japan.* New York: The Free Press.

Ben-Ari, E. (1998). 'Golf, Organization, and 'Body Projects': Japanese Business Executives in Singapore.' In *The Culture of Japan as Seen through Its Leisure.* S. Linhart and S. Frühstück (eds). Albany: SUNY Press. 139–161.

Cole, R. (1992). 'Work and Leisure in Japan.' *California Management Review*, 34, 3: 52–63.

Cox, R. (2002). 'Is There a Japanese Way of Playing?' In *Japan at Play: The Ludic and the Logic of Power.* J. Hendry and M. Raveri (eds). London: Routledge. 169–185.

Cwiertka, K. (1998). 'How Cooking Became a Hobby: Changes in Attitude Toward Cooking in Early Twentieth-Century Japan.' In *The Culture of Japan as Seen through Its Leisure*. S. Linhart and S. Frühstück (eds). Albany: SUNY Press. 41–58.

Dore, R. (1973). *British Factory – Japanese Factory: The Origins of National Diversity in Industrial Relations.* Berkeley: University of California Press.

Feuss, S. Jr. (2006). 'Leisure Time in Japan: How Much and for Whom?' IZA Discussion Paper No. 2002. Bonn: Institute for the Study of Labor.

Field, N. (2001). 'Forward to the Revised Edition.' In G. McCormack, *The Emptiness of Japanese Affluence* (Revised Edition). Armonk, New York: M.E. Sharpe.

Formanek, S. (1998). 'Pilgrimage in the Edo Period: Forerunner of Modern Domestic Tourism? The Example of the Pilgrimage to Mount Tateyama.' In *The Culture of Japan as Seen through Its Leisure.* S. Linhart and S. Frühstück (eds). Albany: SUNY Press. 165–194.

Frühstück, S. (1998). 'Then Science Took Over: Sex Leisure, and Medicine at the Beginning of the Twentieth Century.' In *The Culture of Japan as Seen through Its Leisure.* S. Linhart and S. Frühstück (eds). Albany: SUNY Press. 59–79.

Garon, S. (1998). *Molding Japanese Minds: The State in Everyday Life.* Princeton: Princeton University Press.

Goode, W. (1963). *World Revolution and Family Patterns.* New York: The Free Press.

Graburn, N. 1998. 'Work and Play in the Japanese Countryside.' In *The Culture of Japan as Seen through Its Leisure.* S. Linhart and S. Frühstück (eds). Albany: SUNY Press. 195–212.

Hamilton-Oehrl, A. (1998). 'Leisure Parks in Japan.' In *The Culture of Japan as Seen through Its Leisure.* S. Linhart and S. Frühstück (eds). Albany: SUNY Press. 237–250.

Hochschild, A. with A. Machung (1989). *The Second Shift: Working Parents and the Stalled Revolution at Home.* New York: Viking.

Inoue, S. (1998). 'Budô: Invented Tradition in the Martial Arts.' In *The Culture of Japan as Seen through Its Leisure.* S. Linhart and S. Frühstück (eds). Albany: SUNY Press. 83–94.

Japan Times (2008). ''Stress' Most Recognized Loan Word Here.' 25 July.

Johnson, C. (1982). *MITI and the Japanese Miracle: the Growth of Industrial Policy.* Stanford, CA: Stanford University Press.

Leheny, D. (2003). *The Rules of Play: National Identity and the Shaping of Japanese Leisure.* Ithaca: Cornell University Press.

Linhart, Sepp (1998). 'Introduction: The Japanese at Play: A Little Known Dimension of Japan.' In *The Culture of Japan as Seen through Its Leisure.* S. Linhart and S. Frühstück (eds). Albany: SUNY Press. 1–21.

Manzenreiter, W. (1998). 'Time, Space, and Money: Cultural Dimensions of the Pachinko Game.' In *The Culture of Japan as Seen through Its Leisure.* S. Linhart and S. Frühstück (eds). Albany: SUNY Press. 359–381.

Manzenreiter, W. and E. Ben-Ari (2004). 'Leisure and Consumer Culture in Postwar Japan.' In *Modern Japanese Society. Handbook of Oriental Studies.* J. Kreiner, U. Möwald and H.D. Ölschleger (eds), Leiden: Brill. 489–524.

Manzenreiter, W. and J. Horne (2006). 'Leisure and Consumer Culture in Japan.' *Leisure Studies*, 25, 3: 451–455.

McCormack, G. (2001). *The Emptiness of Japanese Affluence* (Revised Edition). Armonk, New York: M.E. Sharpe.

Morioka, K. (2006). *Kakusa shakai no kôzô: gurôbaru shihonshugi no dansô.* Tokyo: Sakurai Shoten.

Mouer, R. and H. Kawanishi (2005). *A Sociology of Work in Japan.* London: Cambridge University Press.

Nagashima, N. (1998). 'Gambling and Changing Japanese Attitudes Toward It.' In *The Culture of Japan as Seen through Its Leisure.* S. Linhart and S. Frühstück (eds). Albany: SUNY Press. 345–358.

Nishiyama, M. Translated and edited by G. Groemer (1997). *Edo Culture: Daily Life and Diversions in Urban Japan, 1600–1868.* Honolulu: University of Hawaii Press.

North, S. (2005). ''Welfare for Human Harmony' – Japanese Labor Welfare in Law and Practice, 1947–1985.' *Bulletin of the School of Human Sciences.* Osaka University, 31: 37–60.

Ochiai, E. (1996). *The Japanese Family System in Transition: A Sociological Analysis of Family Change in Postwar Japan.* Tokyo: LBTC International Library Foundation.

Plath, D. (1964). *The After Hours: Modern Japan and the Search for Enjoyment.* Berkeley: University of California Press.

Robertson, J. (1998). 'The Politics and Pursuit of Leisure in Wartime Japan.' In *The Culture of Japan as Seen through Its Leisure.* S. Linhart and S. Frühstück (eds). Albany: SUNY Press. 282–302.

Rohlen, T. (1974). *For Harmony and Strength: Japanese White Collar Organization in Anthropological Perspective.* Berkeley: University of California Press.

Rojek, C. 2010. *The Labor of Leisure: The Culture of Free Time.* London: Sage.

Schor, J. (1991). *The Overworked American: The Unexpected Decline of Leisure.* New York: Basic Books.

Smith, T. (1986). 'Peasant Time and Factory Time in Japan.' *Past and Present,* 111, 1: 165–197.

Stebbins, R. (1982) 'Serious Leisure: A Conceptual Statement.' *Pacific Sociological Review,* 25, 2: 251–272.

Swidler, A. (1986). 'Culture in Action: Symbols and Strategies.' *American Sociological Review,* 52, 2: 273–286.

Totman, C. (1981). *Japan before Perry: A Short History.* Berkeley: University of California Press.

Vogel, E. 1971. *Japan's New Middle Class: The Salary Man and His Family in a Tokyo Suburb,* Second edition. Berkeley: University of California Press.

Whiting, R. 1977. *The Chrysanthemum and the Bat: Baseball Samurai Style.* New York: Dodd, Mead.

9

Mapping Leisure and Life in Korea

ERWEI DONG

Due to Korean peninsula's geographical and historical background, Korean studies have been traditionally oriented towards history, language, religion, and politics which are relatively important to the region. However, the study of leisure and its significance in Korean society have been neglected for decades. Leisure, including tourism, is an important component of both the daily lives of Koreans and the economy of Korea. Therefore, this article provides a comprehensive overview of understanding Korean leisure in relationship with its language, holiday, history, policy, work, economy, politics and constraints.

Leisure and Language

Korea is geographically located between China and Japan. While deeply influenced by Chinese language, Korean language, which is being currently called *Hangul*, was commissioned by Sejong the Great in the 15th century. In East Asian languages including Chinese, Japanese and Korean, there is not a word for direct translation of the English word 'leisure'. Similar to Japanese language, Korean language uses both Chinese characters 餘暇 (餘暇 are Chinese traditional characters) and the phonetic translation 레저 (leisure) to express 'leisure'. In Korean language, 여 is 餘 pronounced as *Yeo and* 가 is 暇 pronounced as Ga. According to the *A White Paper on Leisure* published by Ministry of Culture, Sports and Tourism and Korea Culture and Tourism Institute in 2006, 여가 (Yeoga) is a broad term referring to spare time, specific leisure activities or state of mind. These activities include sports, art appreciation, art creation, domestic and international tourism, hobbies and recreational activities. On the other hand, the meaning of phonetic translation 레저 (leisure) has some commercial connotations limited by being used with terms such as leisure and sports industries (A White Paper on Leisure, 2006).

This paper is written primarily based on *Korean Leisure: from tradition to Modernity* edited by Erwei Dong and Jouyeon Yi-Kook (2010) and Erwei Dong's recent Korean leisure-related publications. The author would like to thank Dr Hyeji Kim's for her contributions.

Table 1

Korean Traditional Festivals and Holidays (Based on Lunar Calendar)

Adopted from Korean leisure from tradition to modernity (Dong and Yi-Kook, 2010)

Festivals and holidays	*Significance*	*Date*	*Major events*	*Traditional foods*
Seollal or Gujeong	Korean New Year	The 1st day of the 1st month	'Charye (ancestor memorial service),' dress up in 'Hanbok (traditional Korean costume),' 'Sebae (deep bows to elders)'; 'Yut-nori', 'Neolttwigi (Korean See-saw)'	'Tteokguk (sliced rice cake in soup)'
Jeoungwol Daeboreum	First Full Moon Festival; Fire Festival	The 15th day of the 1st month	'Geuybul-nori,' 'Juldarigi (Tug of War),' 'Jisinbalgi (treading on the earth god),' 'Dalmaji (moon rise watch)'	'Bureom (cracking nuts)'; 'Ogokbap (rice cooked with red beans, sorghum, and millet),' 'Namul (dry herbs), ' 'Yaksik (rice cake)'
Samjinnal	First day of spring	The 3rd day of the 3rd month	'Hwajeon Nori (flower pancake game)'	'Hwajeon (flower rice pancake)'
Hansik	Cold Food Festival	The 105th days after 'Dongji (winter solstice; 22 December in the solar calendar)	visit ancestor's grave to worship, clean and maintain	'Ssuktteok (mugwort rice cake),' 'Ssukdanja (mugwort dumplings,) 'Ssuktang (mugwort soup)
Sawolchopail	Lantern Festival; Buddha's Birthday	The 8th day of the 4th month	celebrate Seokgamoni's birthday	'Jjintteok,' 'Hwajeon (flower rice pancake),' 'Eochae (sliced fish and vegetables),' 'Eomandu (fish dumplings)'
Dano	Spring Festival	The 15th day of the 5th month	Wash woman's hair with 'Changpo (Sweet Flag)' boiled-water; 'Gu-nae (swing),' 'Ssireum (Korean wrestling)'	'Suritteok (mungwort rice cake),' 'Yaktteok (herb rice cake).
Yudu	First harvest offering	The 15th day of the 6th month	Clean hair and body to get rid of evil spirits	'Samgyetang (ginseng chicken broth),' 'Yudumyeon (five colored noodles),' 'Sudan (rice dumplings)'
Chusok	Harvest Festival; Autumn full moon day	The 15th day of the 8th month	'Charye (ancestor memorial service),' 'Seongmyo (visiting their ancestors' graves),' 'Beolcho (removing weeds around the grave); 'Ssirem (Korean wrestling),' 'Juldarigi (Tug of War),' and 'Ganggangsullae (Korean round dance).'	'Songpyeon (half-moon shaped Korean rice cake)' and food made with fresh harvest
Dongji	Little New Year	22 December (solar calendar)		'Adzuki (red) bean porridge'

Leisure and Festivals/Holidays

As a form of leisure and culture, traditional festivals are being celebrated for many centuries by Korean people. 'Korean traditional holidays are directly linked to the veneration of ancestors, agricultural activities, and religious observances' (Schulz, 2006: 95). Korean people retained many traditional festivals such as Korean New Year, First Full Moon Festival, First day of spring, Cold Food Festival, Lantern Festival, Spring Festival, First harvest offering, Harvest Festival and Little New Year (Table 1).

In fact, the traditional festivals are very similar to Chinese traditional festivals due to influence of Chinese culture. In order to celebrate the harvest and enjoy free time, a variety of games were created by ancient Koreans based on their social strata, gender classification and social gathering (Dong, 2007). Well-known games played or activities participated in during the festivals and holidays are Nelttwigi (seesaw), Kunettwigi (swing), Chajon Nori (Juggernaut Battle) and Yut-nori (four-stick game). Particularly, Nelttwigi (seesaw) and Gu-nae (swing) are traditional girl's games. Two girls play Nelttwigi by jumping at each end of the board put on a rolled-up straw mat. Interestingly, nowadays Kunettwigi is an outdoor game that became a girls' competition game. Normally, one girl or two girls play with one swing to bounce as high as possible to compete with other player(s). Chajon Nori is one of the traditional strength games for celebration of the harvest. Played by two teams composed with only male teammates, the teammates push each other to pull their opponents down to the ground. Yut-nori is a tradition board game involves more than four players and played during the lunar New Year in Korea. Yut indicates four wooden sticks with two sides: flat side and round side. The sticks are tossed in the air, a score is computed based on the landing side of the sticks and a token is moved on the board according to the score achieved. In addition, Korean people play Jianggi (chess) and baduk (Go) during both holidays and non-holidays. Both games are board games played by all age groups and become one of most popular games in Korea.

Table 2

Korean National or Public Holidays (Based on Solar Calendar)

Adopted from Korean leisure from tradition to modernity (Dong andYi-Kook, 2010)

Name of holiday	*Date of holiday*	*Description*	*Significance*
New Year's Day or 'Sinjeong'	1 January	Public holiday	Celebrating New Year
Independence Movement Day	1 March	National holiday	Celebrating the declaration of independence from Japanese colonial rule
Children's Day	5 May	National holiday	A holiday of events and celebrations for children
Memorial Day	6 June	National holiday	Commemorating soldiers and civilians who died for Korea
Constitution Day	17 July	Public holiday	Celebrating the proclamation of Korean constitution

Cont'd...

... Cont'd

Independent Day (Liberation Day)	15 August	National holiday	Celebrating Korea's liberalization from the Japanese colony.
National Foundation Day	3 October	Public holiday	Celebrating the creation of ancient Korean kingdom founded by the legendary founder (Dangun Wanggeom) of the kingdom in the year 2333 BC.
Hangul Day	9 October	National holiday	Commemorating the invention and the proclamation of Hangul (Korean alphabet)
Christmas	25 December	Public holiday	Korea is the only East Asian country to celebrate Christmas as a public holiday.

On the other hand, Korea is a society in transition that moved from a six-day-work-week to a five-day-one (Edginton, 2010). Due to the increased income and urbanization, more and more Koreans pursue a higher quality of life. Therefore, national or public holidays became more important for Koreans and being celebrated by Korean people. During national holidays, except for bank and offices, other services such as departmental stores, restaurants, museums or parks remain open for business. Table 2 below indicates list of Korean national or public holidays based on solar calendar. Interestingly, while Korea is viewed as a Buddhist country, Christmas is a public holiday in Korea which is the only East Asian country to celebrate it as a public holiday.

Leisure and Policy

Since the formation of the Korea government in 1948, Korean leisure policies are being modified over time (Noh, 2010). As early as 1953, Labor Standard Act was enacted to legalize paid holidays for 12 days for all workers. The legalization of the paid holidays can be thought of milestone for Korean people because 'the leisure life of the public was not excited due to the influence of a work-focused philosophy based on the Confucian culture in the traditional agricultural society after Korea's liberation.' (p. 40). However, the national policy was primarily focused on the restoration of the damaged natural environment due to the Second World War and Korean War. With the growth of Korean economy since 1960s, tourism-related policies and sport related policies were summated. After Tourism Promotion and Development Fund Act and Tourism Resort Development Promotion Act were enacted in 1972 and 1975, respectively, Korean government constructed many large scale tourist resorts (e.g. Bomun Complex in Gyeongju in 1974 and Jungmun Complex in Jeju Island in 1978) in the beginning of 1974 to alleviate the unbalanced development of public recreation and leisure facilities that were mainly located in the metropolitan areas to elaborate the sphere of leisure life for the public (Noh, 2010). In 1982, Korean government revised the National Sports Promotion Act to emphasize leisure industry focused on tourism development. In 1900s, Korean government established the Long-term Tourism Promotion Plan (1992–2001) to reestablish awareness of tourism to accelerate international tourism and for national

Table 3

Summary of History of Korean Leisure Policies

Adopted from Korean leisure from tradition to modernity (Dong and Yi-Kook, 2010)

Period	*Social and cultural changes*	*Leisure laws and policies*	*Major events*
Until 1960s	Agriculture society	Labor standard act (1953)	Independence from Japan (1945)
	Confucian culture	Cultural properties act (1960)	Establishment of Korean government (1948)
			Korean war (1950–53)
1960s	Industrialization	Tourism industry promotion act (1961)	April 19th uprising (1960)
	5-year economic development	International tourism corporation act (1962)	May 16th Coup d'etat (1961)
	Gyeongbu Highway	National Land construction plan act (1963)	
	Diversional activity	Master plan for tourism promotion implementation (1968)	
		National museum	
		National park committee (1967) Focus on tourism	
1970s	Superficial political stability	Tourism promotion and development fund act (1972)	Constitution for revitalizing reform (1974)
	Successful economic development	Tourism resort development promotion act (1975)	
	Seamaeul movement	Implementation of natural land development plan (1972–81)	
	Consciousness of leisure activity	Charter for nature (1978)	
	Outdoor activity		
1980s	Political instability	National sports promotion act (1982)	Abolition of curfew (1982)
	Democratization process	Enforcement decree of tourism industry act (1984)	Asian Games (1986), Seoul Olympics (1988)
	Mega sports event	Establishment of Ministry of culture and Ministry of Sports	
	Public awareness of improvement of one's lifestyle	Liberalization of overseas travel (1989)	
		The second national land development plan (1982–91)	

Cont'd …

... Cont'd

1990s	Political democracy	Cultural and Tourism integration plan	Daejeon Expo (1993)
	Globalization of economy	Long term tourism promotion plan (1992–2001)	Economy crisis (1997)
	Cultural globalization and nationalism	Special tourism district zone (1994)	Financial aid from IMF
	Localization and liberalism	Cultivation of conference industry	
2000s	Information society	New national land plan	2002 FIFA world cup (2002)
	Change of population structure	Formed marine leisure sport industry	40 hours workweek system (2003)
	Polarization of income and expenditure	Kumgang tour (2002)	
	Decentralization of government Political and economic cooperation between South and North Korea		

tourism environment. In 2000s, the marine leisure sports industry was added to the New National Land Plan by the Ministry of Construction and Transportation. From 1953 to present, Korean government enacted many leisure and sports-related policies which contribute to leisure and tourism development (Table 3). Noh (2010) summarized characteristics of Korean leisure-related policy as: (1) lack of content related to leisure; (2) subordination to other policies; (3) decentralization of leisure policies; and (4) lack of communications between governmental agencies.

Leisure and Work

Korean people experienced many development stages including Korean War (1950–1953), military dictatorship period (1960s–1980s), compressed economic growth (1960s–2000s), economic crisis (1997) and global economy (%). In the 1960s, development of labour-intensive light industry and infrastructure established economic development foundation. In the 1970s, governmental financial policies including loans, special depreciation allowances, and low tax rate supported heavy and chemical industries. Due to the economic reform, work hours and wages increased from 1960s to1983. However, work hours declined from1985 to 1998 (Table 4). As Table 4 indicates, Korean working class earns more money as work hours are decreased after 1985.

Table 4

Average Monthly Work Hours and Income (in hour.minute/won)

Adopted from Korean leisure from tradition to modernity (Dong, Yi-Kook, 2010)

	Average monthly work hours			*Wages*			
	Total hours worked	*Normal time*	*Overtime*	*Total earnings*	*Regular payment*	*Overtime payment*	*Special payment*
1975	217.0	N/A	N/A	46,019	N/A	N/A	N/A
1980	223.9	195.3	31.2	176,058	129,212	25,772	21,074
1985	225.5	192.7	32.8	324,283	239,486	39,191	45,605
1990	209.5	181.4	28.1	642,309	443,829	70,020	128,460
1995	209.1	183.7	25.4	1,222,097	827,944	111,348	282,804
1997	203.0	179.6	23.4	1,463,300	1,012,352	118,245	333,702
1998	199.2	179.1	20.1	1,426,797	1,050,063	100,480	276,253
1999	208.1	183.3	24.8	1,599,210	1,114,192	130,709	354,308

Source: Ministry of Labor (Korea), December 1975 – December 1999.

Change of work hours also affected leisure time. Table 5 shows the change of average time spent on leisure activities from 1981 to 1999. As the table shows, Korean people spent more time on leisure activities on weekends than weekdays. There are two peaks in total leisure time in 1981 and 1995, respectively.

Annual expenditure on leisure per household is increasing dramatically since 1980 in both urban and rural areas (Table 6). Interestingly, farm household spent 7.7 and 3.9 times than urban household spent in 1980 and 1985, respectively. However, the expenditure of urban household dramatically increased since 1990, in which it was 5.9 times that of farm household, and the 1997 expenditure showed highest with the amount of 777,100 won.

Table 5

The Change of Average Time Spent on Leisure Activities (in hour.minute)

Adopted from Korean leisure from tradition to modernity (Dong, Yi-Kook, 2010)

	Weekday	*Saturday*	*Sunday*	*Total*
1981	0.32	0.42	1.04	2.18
1983	0.25	0.37	1.02	2.04
1985	0.27	0.38	0.53	2.06
1987	0.30	0.39	1.05	2.02
1990	0.29	0.38	0.52	1.59
1995	0.26	0.43	1.06	2.15
1999	0.26	0.31	0.37	1.34

Sources: Korean Broadcasting System (KBS), 1982; 1984; 1986; 1988; 1991; 1996
Korea National Statistical Office, 2000

Table 6

Annual Expenditure on Leisure per Household (in won, %)

Adopted from Korean leisure from tradition to modernity (Dong, Yi-Kook, 2010)

	Urban Household			*Farm Household*		
	Amount	*Percentage*	*Annual rate of increase*	*Amount*	*Percentage*	*Annual rate of increase*
1980	4,650	2.6	9.1	35,755	1.7	
1985	10,539	3.3	4.0	41,222	0.9	
1990	322,000	4.7	10.6	54,515	0.7	
1995	668,000	5.3	14.2	126,689	0.9	
1997	771,000	5.2	1.7	130,947	0.8	
1998	586,000	4.5	–24.0	121,506	0.7	
1999	719,000	4.9	22.6	121,304	0.7	

Sources: Korea National Statistical Office, 1990–2000b. Ministry of Agriculture and Forestry, 2000.

Passive leisure activities (e.g. watching TV, listening to music and reading) are mainly chosen by Korean people (Table 7).

Table 7

Major Leisure Activities Participated by Korean

Adopted from Korean leisure from tradition to modernity (Dong and Yi-Kook, 2010)

Leisure Activity	%	Leisure Activity	%
Watching TV	79.7	Gambling	17.4
Watching Video	43.2	Electronic Amusement	16.8
Singing	39.2	Billiard	15.3
Watching Movie	36.8	Bowling	13.6
Climbing/Fishing	32.3	Swimming	10.2
Reading	31.5	Badminton	8.3
Listening Music	30.4	Golf/Ski	4.5
Driving	28.1		

Source: Korea Consumer Protection Board, 1999.

Watching TV is listed as the top participated activity by Korean people. Interestingly, watching TV time is positively associated with the change of living space over time (Table 8). Average size of living space per household was increased from 41.4 m^2 in 1975 to 58.8 m^2 in 1995 (Table 8). The average time of watching TV was also increased from 6.81 hours in 1985 to 9.09 hours in 1999.

Table 8

The Change of Living Space and Watching TV Time

Adopted from Korean leisure from tradition to modernity (Dong, Yi-Kook, 2010)

Year	*Living space*				*Year*	*Watching TV time (hours)*		
	Size (m^2)		*Number of rooms*					
	per household	*Per people*	*per household*	*number of persons in a room*		*Weekday*	*Saturday*	*Sunday*
1975	41.4	8.2	2.2	2.3	1981	1.49	2.26	3.15
1980	45.8	10.1	2.2	2.1	1985	1.48	2.23	3.10
1985	46.4	11.3	2.2	1.9	1990	2.03	2.45	3.40
1990	51.0	13.8	2.5	1.5	1995	2.23	3.07	4.02
1995	58.6	17.2	3.1	1.1	1999	2.47	3.08	3.54

Sources: Korea National Statistical Office, 1997; 1999 and 2000
Korean Broadcasting System (KBS), 1982; 1984; 1986; 1988; 1991 and 1996
KBS, 1982; 1984; 1986; 1988; 1991; 1996

Leisure and Economy

Since the beginning of the economic development plan in 1960s, 'Miracle of Han River' has brought the rapid economic growth in 1960s and 1970s resulted in greatly influencing Koreans' leisure. Due to the abolition of the curfew in 1982 which was originally imposed by American occupation troops at the end of World War II (UPI, 1982), night-time leisure activities significantly increased, resulting in large amount of liquor consumption, new entertainment establishments and emergence of pleasure-seeking business. In particular, karaoke, night clubs and gambling activities attracted working class because these activities were simple form of pleasures-seeking group activities. Korea Professional Baseball was established in 1982, the Korea Folk Ssireum (Korean wrestling) Federation and Korea Professional Football League were founded in 1983. Later, Korea also hosted Asian Games in 1986 and Seoul Olympics Games in 1988, resulting in the country caught up in the fever of sports of leisure purpose. A new word, *lei-ports*, was formed to represent popularity of leisure and sport in 1980s. Due to booming of sports, sports faculties were built nearby public areas where created more leisure opportunities for Korean people. Popularization of private cars can be thought of as a turning point in modern Korean leisure in the 1980s (Kim, 1993). Because automobiles greatly increase the mobility of Korean people, day trips, outdoor recreation, dinning out and mass tourism became popularized. However, Korean economy underwent disastrous economic crisis in 1997, which significantly influenced Korean people leisure (Kim, 2010). According to the Korea Cultural Policy Institute (KCPI), inactive, inexpensive and indoor leisure activities (e.g. watching TV, reading newspapers, dinning out, family gatherings and surfing internet) increased due to the economic crisis.

In the 2000s, internet-based activities have been rapidly spreading due to the wide use of computers. Various leisure-based social networks (e.g. fan clubs of celebrities) are established through online cafes (e.g. Cyword) and blogs (e.g. Naver and Daum). Outdoor recreation is also gaining more popularity. Korean people love to spend their free time in their national parks as well. Since Jirisan National park became the first national park in 1967 in Korea, a total of 20 national parks have been designated by Korean government. Because of the availability of public transportation and close proximity to most residential and work areas, Korean national parks are relatively easily accessible to the public (Kim, Lee and Klenosky, 2002; Lee and Han, 2002), and more than 38 million visitors have visited Korean national parks in 2009 (Dong, Lee and Lee, 2010).

Leisure and Constraints

As a leading theory in leisure studies, leisure constraints have been studied decades in North America. Hierarchical model of leisure constraints (Crawford, Jackson, and Godbey, 1991) are most used by leisure researchers in leisure constraint studies. Crawford, Jackson, and Godbey (1991) categorized leisure constraints as intrapersonal, interpersonal and structural constraints. Although leisure constraint theory is a major theory in the field, Korean leisure scholars have rarely studied leisure constraints until the late 1990. Fortunately, a few scholars did conduct research on leisure constraints. For example, Kang (1997) conducted a study to explore differences between demographic and social economic status in the perception of leisure constraints among 660 adult residents of Seoul in Korea. He created five items to measure leisure constraints including lack of leisure facilities, lack of leisure resources (time and money), lack of leisure education, the pursuit of monetary gain, and other constraints. Kang found the most respondents considered lack of leisure facilities as the most serious constraint and lack of time and money as the second most serious constraint. Kang addressed that the development of leisure facilities should be focused on improving the level of leisure engagement for the citizens of Seoul. Pyo and Kim (2001) conducted a study to examine how family life cycle influences the perception of leisure constraints among 675 urban housewives in Seoul. Because they adopted Crawford and his colleagues' model: intrapersonal, interpersonal, and structural constraints in their research, Pyo and Kim found that the newly married respondents considered intrapersonal constraints as the most significant constraint whereas the respondents who were preparing for their children's wedding thought of the structural constraint as the most serious one. Meanwhile, the rest of the respondents considered the interpersonal constraint as the most severe constraint. Later, Song and Yeo (2004) investigated the demographic and socio-economic status differences in the perception of leisure constraints among 570 urban workers in the Seoul area. According to the finding of this study, a total of five items including agreement of family members, family obligation, the consent of close friend(s), lack of leisure companion, and consideration of social reputation are grouped as the interpersonal constraints. Lack of time, lack of skill, pressure from job obligation, and feeling uncomfortable are categorized as the intrapersonal constraints. The structural constraints included lack of money, lack of information, uncomfortable transportation, and friends' economic difficulties. Most recently, Dong and Yi-Kook conducted a leisure lifestyle study by using cultural anthropological approaches in Seoul in 2008. Leisure activities and leisure constraints were included in Dong and Yi-Kook's study. Dong and Yi-Kook used freelisting technique to explore various leisure constraints instead of the existing leisure constraints categorized by Crawford, Jackson and Godbey in 1991. Dong and Yi-Kook found social and self-imposed constraints (e.g. study pressure, spouse decision, taking care of children), psychological constraints (e.g. lack of energy, lack of motivation and tiredness) and structural constraints (e.g. time and money) are faced by Korean people. The studies on leisure constraints of Koreans demonstrate that Korean people perceive various types of leisure constraints, which cannot be simply interpreted by the existing leisure constraint theory. In addition, Dong and Yi-Kook's study provides an alternative way to study leisure constraints in a cross-cultural setting.

Conclusion

Korean people had been enjoying their traditional festivals and holidays nearly five thousand years. Due to modernization, urbanization and globalization process in Korea, the traditional leisure has been transformed to a new form of leisure. With rapid growth of income and expenditure since 1980s, Koreans have gained more spending power for leisure industry. Since successfully hosting professional sport and cultural events, Koreans' leisure activities become more diversified. The diversification of leisure activities will continuously contribute to Korean people's well-being and enrich the quality of life.

References

A White Paper on Leisure (2006). Ministry of Culture, Sports and Tourism/Korea Culture and Tourism Institute.

Choe, S., and Cheon H. (2010). Economic crisis and the change of work and leisure in Korea. In E. Dong and J. Yi-Kook (ed.) *Korean Leisure: From Tradition to Modernity* (pp. 128–152). Jaipur, India: Rawat Publications.

Crawford, D., Jackson, E.L., and Godbey, G. (1991). A Hierarchical Model of Leisure Constraints. *Leisure Sciences, 13*, 309–320.

Dong, E. Yi-Kook, J. (2010). *Korean Leisure: From Tradition to Modernity*. Jaipur, India: Rawat Publications.

Dong, E. (2010). Korean traditional festivals and holidays. In E. Dong and J. Yi-Kook (ed.) *Korean Leisure: From Tradition to Modernity* (pp. 3–14). Jaipur: Rawat Publications.

Dong, E., and Yi-Kook, J. (2010). Leisure lifestyles and health in urban Korea. In E. Dong and J. Yi-Kook (ed.) *Korean Leisure: From Tradition to Modernity* (pp. 59–75). Jaipur, India: Rawat Publications.

Dong, E. (2007). Games, hobbies, and toys. In G. Xu and V. Dharwadker (ed.) *The Greenwood Eencyclopedia of World Popular Culture: Asia and Pacific Oceania* (pp. 151–160). Westport, CT: Greenwood publishing group.

Dong, E., Lee, B. and Lee, Y. (2010). Current issues in Japanese, Korean, and Chinese national parks. In Y. Hsu (ed.). Proceedings of the Conference on Visions and Strategies for World's National Parks and Issues Confronting the Management of World's National Parks (I). Zhonghe, Taiwan: Huali publishing.

Edington, C. (2010). Korean leisure: from tradition to modernity; a significant contribution to understating leisure in an evolving society and culture. In E. Dong and J. Yi-Kook (ed.) *Korean Leisure: From Tradition to Modernity* (pp. viii–x). Jaipur: Rawat Publications.

Kang, B. (1997). A study of factors associated with limitations on leisure activities of Koreans in Seoul. *Journal of Korean Society of Leisure and Recreation, 14*, 75–86.

Kim, M. (1993). *Yeoga-ui Sahoehak* (Sociology of Leisure). Seoul: Hanul.

Kim, M. (2010) The leisure transformation in Modern Korea. In E. Dong and J. Yi-Kook (ed.) *Korean Leisure: From Tradition to Modernity.* (pp. 17–33). Jaipur: Rawat Publications.

Kim, S., Lee, C., and Klenosky, D. (2003).The influence of push and pull factors at Korean national parks. *Tourism Management*, 24, 169–180.

Lee, C., and Han, S. (2002). Estimating the use and preservation values of national parks' tourism resources using a contingent valuation method. *Tourism Management*, 23, 531–540.

Noh, Y. (2010). Korean leisure policies. In E. Dong and J. Yi-Kook (ed.) *Korean Leisure: From Ttradition to Modernity* (pp. 34–58). Jaipur, India: Rawat Publications.

Pyo, Y. and Kim, Y. (2001). The relationship between family life cycle and leisure activity and leisure constraints. *Journal of Korean Sociology of Sport, 14(2)*, 457–467.

Song, W. and Yeo, I. (2004). The influence of leisure constraints on leisure satisfaction and life satisfaction of urban workers. *The Korean Journal of Physical Education, 43(4)*, 685–697.

Schulz, C. (2006). Korean terms for calendar and horary signs, holidays, and seasons. In H. Sohn *(ed.). Korean Language in Culture and Society.* (pp. 86–100). Honolulu, HI: University of Hawai'i Press.

UPI (6 January 1982). Around the World; South Korea Lifts Its 36-Year-Old Curfew. New York Times. Retrieved 1 November 2010 from http://www.nytimes.com/1982/01/06/world/around-the-world-south-korea-lifts-its-36-year-old-curfew.html

10

Mapping Leisure in the Philippines

MANUEL ENVERGA

Cultural Globalization and the Philippine Colonial Experience

On 14 July 2011, the cinemas of several large shopping malls in the Philippines stayed open to show the second installment of Harry Potter and the Deathly Hallows, which was being released simultaneously throughout the world. Despite the late hour, people lined up and watched in order to be one of the first people in the world to see the film ahead of everyone else, not just in the country, but, owing to the Philippines' advanced time zone, also throughout the world. Though they may not have consciously thought it at the time, their participation in a midnight screening of a blockbuster movie like the eighth, and final, Harry Potter movie was a form of participation in a leisure activity that would occur at a global scale. In a small way, they were thus participating in globalization, since fans throughout the world would be doing the same. In addition, it is global trade and consumption, and the transportation and information networks that they rely on, that have allowed for the popularity of a cultural product like Harry Potter.

The term globalization is said to have first appeared in academic literature in the 1960s, though the term is over 400 years old (Waters, 2001). It is most prominently driven by the expansion of multinational corporations, operating on the logic of profit maximization, and has implications on politics, economics and society (Korten and Klaus, 1984, Barber, 1996 and Gelinas, 2003). As such, it is possible to discuss globalization in economics, politics and culture. This chapter, which maps leisure patterns in the Philippines, is mainly concerned with cultural globalization, which entails the rapid transfer of media and cultural practices between localities. With regard to the sociology of leisure, it is informed by the works of Parker (1975), Gunter and Gunter (1980) and Wilson (1980) in its recognition of the difficulty involved with defining leisure, and consequently, the enumeration of a list of leisure activities. As such, a broad range of leisure activities are discussed, such as those discussed in Veblen (1953), which include gambling, artistic pursuits, sport and religious celebration. The chapter also refers to technologically mediated leisure practices, such as television and film viewing and internet-related activities, which are discussed in Peterson (1980), de Zengotita (2005) and Miller (2008).

In this chapter, the discussion of leisure practices is connected to cultural globalization. There is recognition that colonialism between the sixteenth and nineteenth centuries set the stage for cultural globalization (Waters, 2001). The development of large sailing vessels that could transport many people at a time allowed people to move around and interact with local populations, thereby leading to the insertion of previously foreign values into local contexts. In the case of the Philippines, there was direct colonization by Spain for over 300 years, but Manila, the capital city, served as an intersection for large-scale trade between Europe, Asia and the Americas through the Manila-Acapulco galleon trade. Fleets of Chinese junks would deliver silks, spices and other exotic materials to the city, which would then be loaded into galleons going to Acapulco, New Spain (Summers, 1997). Spanish colonists, Asian migrants, and other traders that were in the city thus influenced the culture of people living in Manila. They were influenced primarily by what Appadurai (1996) referred to as ethnoscapes, or the set of people who move around and internalize cultural traits of the localities in which they find themselves, but also serve as transporters of their home cultures' practices.

In discussing manifestations of foreign cultural influences on the Philippines, Zialcita (2005) refers to clothing and architectural styles. To the former, he mentioned that the Philippine costume was influenced by Indian and Chinese styles of dress, combined with Spanish and local preferences. In articulating about the latter, he mentioned that early in the Spanish colonial period, attempts were made to build tall palaces of cut stone with vaulted ceilings, as was the trend in Latin America and Spain. These were later abandoned, however, due to the persistence of earthquakes, and replaced with more light and flexible kinds of architecture that would not collapse as easily, but which still possessed vestiges of Spanish architecture styles.

One theme that recurs throughout this chapter has to do with the way that Philippine leisure patterns reflect the cultural preferences of elsewhere. This is not to say, however, that Philippine leisure patterns are only derivative of outside influences. Rather, leisure patterns may be thought of in terms of localization due to what Giddens (1990) refers to as relativization and reflexivity, which implies that people in the Philippines do not take in cultural patterns wholesale. They internalize what they want to borrow from other cultures, and combine them with local patterns. Zialcita (2005) expresses this in terms of various players accepting, rejecting, or modifying foreign elements according to their own perceptions. Thus, leisure patterns in the Philippines should not be thought of as blind imitation, rather it is the localization of foreign influences.

Using the framework of cultural localization, this chapter traces leisure in the Philippines. It is divided into four subsections, which discuss leisure in four periods in the country's history: the Spanish Colonial Period, the American Colonial Period, the Post-World War II Period and the Contemporary Period. Each section discusses the leisure practices of the time, and discusses how they may be thought of as localized versions of foreign cultural practices, if they are indeed so.

Leisure in the Spanish Colonial Period

The Spanish colonization of the Philippines, which lasted for about three hundred years, was the earliest period under which leisure practices developed.

During this period, Philippine society was highly stratified along racial lines. Colonial privilege was marked 'by categories of racial nativity (peninsular versus creole) and *mestizaje* or 'blood' mixture between Spanish, Chinese and *indios*' (Kramer, 1986: 39). The last was the term used to refer to natives of the archipelago. For the most part, wealth was concentrated among the Spanish born in the Iberian Peninsula and those born in the Philippines who profited immensely from the galleon trade. Summers (1998) estimated that their per capita annual income 'was roughly 45,000 *reales*, which made them some of the wealthiest citizens in the Spanish empire. By the 19th century, however, enterprising Chinese and *indios* became comparably wealthy. Robert MacMicking, a British citizen who worked for Ker, Doering and Co. and visited the Philippines in the mid-19th century, remarked on the wealth of Chinese merchants, saying that: 'The amount of business done by some ... Chinamen ... is very considerable, some of them frequently making monthly purchases to the extent of ten or fifteen thousand dollars' (MacMicking, 1967). As such, the social groups discussed above possessed the freedom from industrial production and resources that are requisites for engagement in leisure activities. They would also constitute the Philippine equivalent of what Veblen (1953) referred to as the leisure class.

Leisure activities in the Spanish colonial period generally took place in the city of Manila, the political, economic and educational centre of the colony. It was where the Governor-General's palace was located, and in the city was the port where galleons coming from or going to Mexico were docked. It was also the place where the social groups engaged in leisure lived. Leisure activities of this time could be categorized into two types: fine arts and music, and sport spectatorship.

Fine Arts, Music and Leisure

Artistic pursuits refer to activities in which leisure time is spent practicing music, painting, and the performing arts. Alfred Marche, a French naturalist and ethnographer who was sent to the Philippines in the 1870s described people in the Philippines as having 'very marked artistic tastes; among them one finds designers, some painters, very skilful wood sculptors ... (They) adore music and they play it at every turn, but they abuse and over-abuse the voice' (Marche, 1970). The arts were thus a significant leisure activity.

Music was said to be particularly vibrant in Manila. Summers (1998) discussed that religious music was particularly prominent in a city where Catholicism was widely practiced. Consequently, there were many choirs and orchestras were established to accompany religious services. With regard to leisure practices, however, people from the upper echelons of society either participated in or watched musical performances. MacMicking (1967) observed that Manila's inhabitants have 'a good ear for music, and execute many of the finest operas with spirit and taste'. Joseph Earle Stevens, who worked for the Manila branch of the American firm Henry W. Peabody towards the end of the Spanish colonial period, noted that in Manila:

> Everyone appears to be able to play on something. Such of the native houses are too frail to support pianos, shelter harps and violins, and other stringed

> instruments, while some of the more expensive structures contain the whole selection. Of an evening in the suburbs it is no uncommon thing to hear the strains of a well-played Spanish march issuing from the thatch of a rickety hut, or to find an impromptu concert going on in the little tramcar which is bringing home a handful of native youth with their guitars or mandolins. Every district has a band ... and the nights resound with tunes from all quarters. (Stevens, 1968)

Musical skill is thus described as one that is exhibited throughout the city. Many households in the city have at least one musical instrument for people to play, but some others actually have several. Musical performances may thus be considered a part of the leisure practices of the Philippines during this time. Carl Heinrich Arthur Tannert, a German diplomat stationed in Manila at the end of the Spanish colonial period shares that in Manila, 'everywhere one hears the sound of harp, guitar and violin'. In another passage, he described the sounds coming from a creole, or *mestizo*, household across the street as having:

> Lively and lilting violins and guitars ... (playing) the famous Zaragoza March ... (Later on, there were) trembling mandolins (and) the sound of a strong sonorous baritone ... . A light woman's soprano voice joined in – with thrilling enthusiasm they sang, in the loud fiery, life-burning dance, impressive and meaningful, so that one ... could understand every word: 'Cuando una niña de quinze abriles/Siente en la Habana lo que es amor/Con los suspiros que das u pecho/Despierta a toda la poblacion. (Tannert, 1996)

The observations of such travellers to the Philippines thus indicate how the performance of music was an important aspect of leisure.

Apart from presenting music themselves, people in Manila were also fond of musical performances. John Foreman, who resided in and travelled around the Philippines, and who later published a work on his personal observations described Manila as having four main theatres: the Teatro Filipino, the Teatro de Tondo, the Teatro del Principe and the Teatro Zorilla. Opera spectatorship was a particularly prominent activity in the city. Stevens, commenting on the success of the opera remarked:

> The grand opera company which is here (in Manila) is doing remarkably well, and 'Faust' was given the other evening to a crowded house. The theatre Zorilla is round, like a circus, and in the center of the ring sit the holders of our regular orchestra seats, facing the stage ... . The orchestra is a native one, led by an Italian conductor ... . The musicians, who battle with the difficult score, grind out their music quite as successfully as some of our home performers. (Stevens, 1968)

His observation suggests that he found the Philippine opera, which performed in the Zorilla Theatre, to be quite talented. It was also mentioned that the opera is well-attended, having been crowded in its performance of Faust. In other references to the same opera company, he mentioned that the group had performed: Fra Diavolo, the Barber of Seville, Carmen and the Cavalleria Rusticana. The presentation of such a variety of operas suggests that there was demand for it, which indicates that musical spectatorship was an important facet of Philippine leisure.

Music was also an important part of afternoon strolls and carriage rides in Luneta Park, which was another leisure activity of the time. Its popularity was such that Stevens commented that the Park was a rival to the opera as a venue for socializing and music. He discusses it in terms of the following:

> Luneta, where society takes its airing after the heat of the day is over. Imagine an elliptical plaz, about a thousand feet long … . Running around its edge is a broad roadway … . In the center of the raised ellipse is the band-stand, and on every afternoon, from six to eight, all Manila come here to feel the breeze, hear the music and see their neighbours. Hundreds of carriages line the roadways, and mounted police keep them in proper file … . To take a chair, watch the people walking to and fro, and see the endless stream of smart turn-outs passing in slow procession; to hear a band of fifty pieces render popular and classical music with the spirit of a Sousa or a Reeves … . After the music is over the carriages rush off in every direction. (Stevens, 1967)

Marche also describes Luneta as a gathering place for socializing and listening to music. According to him:

> Military music is heard at the edge of the sea, on the Pase do le Luneta, sanded walk at the foot of which is found a beautiful esplanade which serves as a drill ground … during the time when the music is played, this esplanade is animated by a great number of vehicles. The Victoria, the landau with silver ornaments in which the affluent merchants or the rich *mestizos* in silk garments of vivid colors relax. (Marche, 1970)

Charles Wilkes, who led the American naval scientific expedition to the Philippines in the 1840s, discussed the social gathering, reporting that: 'Most of the better class resort here, for the pleasure of enjoying it … (They) promenade in groups backwards and forwards during the time the music is playing'. Frank Marryat, a serviceman on the HMS Samarang, observed during his visit to Manila, that congregating in the Park was 'considered one of the principal and most favourite recreations at Manila' (Marryat, 1974). Gatherings at the Luneta are thus described as social events in which people would go out at the end of the day to stroll or ride around the park, to the accompaniment of lively music played from a bandstand.

Sport Spectatorship

Sport was a leisure activity commented on by Veblen (1953), and its spectatorship is a significant category of leisure in the Philippines during the Spanish colonial period. Among the most prominent activities of the time were bullfighting and cockfighting.

Bullfighting was discussed by Stevens who described the Manila bull ring a place to rival the opera. In his account of the last fight to occur therein, he described a bull and tiger fight that had just taken place:

> The show opened amid breathless excitement … . Then great shouts of 'El toro! El toro!' arose, as off at the small gate, at one side, appeared the bull, calmly walking forward … . And renewed applause arose, as the small heavy cage containing the R.B. tiger was rolled up to a sliding door of the central structure … . The audience howled, jeered at the tiger, bet on the bull, and criticized the man with the pitchfork as he gave the tiger several hard pokes in the ribs … . To make a long story short, there occurred four or five of these

> mild attacks, always incited by the man with the pitchfork, during which the bull stepped on the tiger, making him howl with pain, and the latter badly bit the former on the legs and nose. (Stevens, 1968)

The bull ring in Manila was a versatile area that could be used for fights not just between man and beast, but among two beasts as well. Foreman (1906) also discussed bullfighting in the city. According to him, 'In the suburb of Paco (in Manila) there was a bull-ring ... as a bull-fight there was simply a burlesque upon the national sport as seen in Spain'. His account on Philippine bullfighting indicated that the sport, as it was performed in the archipelago, was not of the same calibre as that in Spain. Consequently, its audience did not come solely from the elite.

A similar lack of class distinction may be seen in the spectatorship of cockfighting, which is an activity that has been widely-reported by travellers to the Philippines. Fedor Jagor, a German who visited the Philippines in the middle of the 19th century and published a book about his travels, made the following observations:

> The chief amusement of the Indians is cockfighting, which is carried on with a passionate eagerness that must strike every stranger. Nearly every Indian keeps a fighting cock. Many are never seen out of doors without their favourite in their arms ... . The sight is one extremely repulsive to Europeans. The ring around the cockpit is crowded with natives ... . Each bird is armed with a sharp curved spur, three inches long, capable of making deep wounds, and which always causes the death of one or both birds by the serious injuries it influcts ... . Incredible large sums, in proportion to the means of the gamblers, are waged on the result. (Jagor, 1965)

The account above discusses how cockfighting is the main source of amusement in the archipelago. He described how the activity appears repulsive to Europeans, and was thus a leisure activity for the natives, particularly the poorer ones. A report by Ivan Goncharov, a Russian civil servant who had travelled with the frigate Pallada in the 1850s, suggests that 'Chinese and mestizos' were also in attendance in such events. A similar observation is made by Paul Proust de la Gironiére, who spent many years in the Philippines in the 19th century. According to him, the 'half-breeds, Indians and Chinese' have a great passion for cockfighting.

The popularity of cockfighting as a leisure activity is seen in the large number of fighting cocks that are found in the city. Sir John Bowring, a British civil servant and a prolific writer, observed that:

> There is hardly a locality which has not more cocks than human inhabitants. On the Puente Grande of Manila, at between four and five A.M., hundreds and hundreds of 'the shrill clarions' are heard on all sides, and from vast distances; it is a string of signals passed from mouth to mouth, from the port of Bangui in North Ilocos, to Manog, the southernmost point of Albay. There are cocks in every house, at every corner, at the foot of every tree, along the quays and shores on the prows of every coasting ship, and, as if the living were not enough, they are sculptured, they are painted and charcoaled ... on every wall for public admiration.

Bowring's account indicates that fighting cocks are to be found all throughout the city of Manila, such that one cannot help but hear them in the early hours of the morning. Their prevalence is heightened by the images that are painted or sculpted of them, and displayed throughout.

Foreign Influences to Leisure during the Spanish Colonial Period

The preceding sections discussed two of the key categories of leisure activities that have been observed during the Spanish colonial period in the Philippines. In examining music as a Philippine leisure practice during the Spanish colonial period, one finds that the musical practices that were described have aspects rooted in European culture. The accounts, with regard to the musical instruments that were found in households were of European origin, including the piano, harp and violin. In addition, tastes for opera reflected European sensibilities, since performances included such compositions as Carmen, Faust and the Barber of Seville, which were created by European composers. With regard to sport spectatorship, bullfighting was described as a well-attended event, though its origins are also recognized to be Spanish (Foreman, 1906). There were thus many leisure practices that were appropriated into the Philippine context from Europe. Given its location as an intersection for global trade during the Spanish colonial period, it comes as little surprise that Philippine leisure practices have foreign influences.

The case of cockfighting, however, provides a counterpoint to the argument that leisure practices are completely foreign-derived. Jagor (1965), who commented on the prevalence of cockfighting as an activity in Manila, also remarked that the practice is likely to have predated Spanish colonization. He discussed that cockfighting was observed in accounts of Magellan's expedition, which suggests that it was already a leisure practice before the archipelago was encountered by European explorers. This suggests that leisure practices in the Spanish colonial period were a mixture of appropriations from Europe combined with prevailing practices that predated colonization.

Leisure in the American Colonial Period to the EDSA Revolution

The time period being covered in this section of the chapter moves from the start of the 20th century, up to 1986. The period saw a number of political changes in the Philippines. It began with the American colonial period, in which the United States followed Spain as the administrators of the archipelago. It is also during this period that the country participated in the Second World War, and subsequently gained its sovereignty in 1946. The newly established Republic of the Philippines then went through the Marcos dictatorship, which lasted twenty years. In 1986, democracy returned to the archipelago following the bloodless EDSA Revolution, which deposed the Marcos regime. Though the Philippines underwent a number of political transformations during the 20th century, much of its leisure activities were influenced by the American colonial period, and persisted until the 1980s, which suggests that the United States had a strong cultural influence on Philippine leisure practices.

The Americans, who followed the Spanish as colonial administrators of the Philippine archipelago, instituted a number of changes that affected the inhabitants of the area. Manila, however, continued to be the political, economic and cultural capital of the Philippines. As such, the most popular leisure activities of the time were practiced in the urban centre. Frank Carpenter, an American who visited the Philippines twice while it was under American rule, described the changes to Manila in the following way:

> I find her a new city. The ragged, dirty, scrambled municipality of 1899, with its mud roads, moss-grown buildings and multitudinous shacks, has largely disappeared, and in its place has risen a modern metropolis ... . Our American forces found Manila a haphazard place, with the streets wretchedly paved or not paved at all ... . We took over a city without adequate sewage disposal and one of the filthiest of its size in all the Orient. We rolled up our sleeves and did not stop until we had made it one of the cleanest places east of the Suez. To-day the streets are well paved and well lighted, and electric cars whiz by me almost everywhere I go ... . Now there are motor trucks and automobiles everywhere, and we have here one of the best motor-vehicle markets of the Far East. (Carpenter, 1929)

Thus, the Americans modernized the city of Manila. They passage above suggests that transportation and sanitation services were drastically improved during the occupation.

The American colonial period, which officially began in 1898, when Spain ceded control of the archipelago through the Treaty of Paris, entailed transformation on political and economic administration. However, certain cultural practices prevalent during the Spanish colonial period continued. For example, Norman Chivers, an American who visited the Philippines during the time, recounted that concerts took place in Luneta Park, saying that the place 'became thronged in the evening with leisure-bent crowds of people, happy in the opportunity to enjoy the excellent concerts of the Constabulary or Army bands'. Thus, the practice of promenading and listening to music at the Park continued. However, there were changes to leisure practices introduced during the American period, which persist until the present: film viewing and basketball.

Film Viewing

The first motion picture screenings to occur in the Philippines happened in August of 1897, a year after the revolution against Spain had broken out, and a year before the American s officially gained control over the archipelago. Films were introduced by two Swiss businessmen: Leibman and Peritz whose cinema was located on Manila's busiest commercial street named Escolta (Pilar, 1983). The cinema was successful for two months, but by November of the same year, ticket sales dropped, and soon it closed down. The medium was unable to keep up with the diverse choices of shows offered by theatres. Film showings resumed in 1900, during which control of the archipelago had been transferred to the United States. The start of the 20th century saw the construction of several new movie theatres, such as the Cine Walgrah, the Gran Cinematografo Parisien the Cinematografo Rizal and the Cinematografo Filipino, as well as the conversion of theatres that showed dramas and dances, into film theatres.

In 1909, with the increasing popularity of film in the United States and Europe, film distributing agencies were established in Manila, which guaranteed an 'abundant supply of films at cheap introductory prices' (Pilar, 1983). This led to the establishment of even more cinemas to cater to audiences in Manila. At first, many of the films that were first shown in the Philippines were said to come from Europe, particularly France, Italy and Denmark (Martin, 1983). The dominance of European films over American ones has been attributed to the latter sending defective or 'junk films' to the Philippines (Deocampo, 2003), such that one film 'exhibitor complained that 90 per cent of the prints from American exchanges were worn out almost beyond being showable, with splices, torn sprockets, ends and titles missing' (Thompson, 1985). Philippine audiences were thus more inclined to view films coming in from Europe than from the United States.

European dominance of the Philippine film market ended at the start of the First World War, when American films overtook them (Martin, 1983). This pattern coincided with the production of films by Philippine film companies who had the advantage of producing works that aligned with the culture of their audiences. They were not as successful as Hollywood films, which enjoyed greater visibility (Lumbera, 1983). As such, 'Philippine film companies had no choice but to aim their products at ... viewers whose low socio-economic status had impaired their ability to fully comprehend the language and content of Hollywood cinema' (Lumbera, 1983). It is during this time that Philippine movie audiences became segmented. The more prosperous inhabitants of Manila preferred films that came in from Europe and the United States, while local films were attended by the less wealthy. The former thus looked at the latter with condescension, which indicates the cultivation of a sense of distinction in the medium of film.

Basketball

Veblen (1953) discussed athletic sport as a popular activity engaged in by the leisure class. In the Philippines, basketball is arguably the most popular sport, both to play and to watch. The sport's popularity spans age groups and skill levels, with tournaments being played in the primary grades up to the college level. Spectatorship of the game is also a significant leisure activity, with audiences watching college basketball, the Philippine Basketball Association, the country's professional league, and broadcasts of American National Basketball Association (NBA). The sport's prevalence is so great that basketball courts are to be found in almost every municipality throughout the archipelago.

The Americans, who are credited with inventing the sport, introduced basketball to the Philippines. Military academies, which were the first institutions to have organized sport in the United States, are credited with the introduction of sport into mainstream society (Pope, 1995). By 1895, the organized sporting events spread to universities on the east coast, such as Harvard, Yale and Brown. Within two decades, it became a widespread practice among educational institutions. Basketball, along with baseball and tennis were among the sports popularized throughout the United States.

Public education was one of the priorities of the American colonial government. Between 1899 and 1901, many school 'buildings were repaired in towns which were occupied by American soldiers, and the beginnings of a public school system was soon established' (de la Costa, 1965). The Americans transplanted basketball into Philippine culture through the mass education system. By the second decade of the 20th century, James Robertson, a Librarian of the Philippine Library in Manila, noted:

> In all parts of the archipelago, the Filipino boy (and in the schools, the Filipina girl) is taking, as if by magic, to the idea of outdoor sport. Baseball, basketball, volleyball, tennis and all field sports to be witnessed at home in any of the college meets, are now a fully recognized part of child and adolescent life among Filipinos. (Robertson, 1913)

Within fifteen years of administering the Philippines, the United States had introduced sport into the local culture. Robertson's account indicates that the playing of outdoor sports, including basketball, occurred mainly in the context of schools, which indicates that educational institutions played a significant role in making sport a Philippine leisure practice.

Unlike leisure practices in the Spanish colonial period, however, basketball was not confined to the city of Manila. Like film, it is not a leisure activity that is practiced exclusively by the wealthy. Basketball was observed by the anthropologist Stoodley (1957), who observed that in a *barrio*, or small town outside of Manila:

> ... boys play marbles with each other and practice shots on the basketball court on the plaza if they can get hold of a rubber ball they use for the purpose ... . Basketball does not get to be a 'game' until a boy is in his teens. The smaller boys take turns trying to get the ball in the basket, or they try to keep the ball away from each other. Often they forget ttownshe basket and run around the lanes of the barrio with the ball, but this is not seen as a departure from the game. Rules for play are loosely made and often disregarded; the emphasis is on expression and 'fun' and not on winning. (Stoodley, 1957)

In the account cited above, a number of conclusions may be drawn. First, considering that the observations were published in 1957, playing basketball persisted even after the Second World War and the American withdrawal from the archipelago in the 1940s. Second, one finds that young boys living in small towns played the sport, where hoops are set up for the purpose of playing basketball.

Basketball continues to be a relevant leisure activity up to the present. Describing the context for the EDSA Revolution that deposed the Marcos dictatorship in 1986, Sumsky (1992) noted that Araneta Coliseum was a place for Manila's middle class to watch basketball games. Basketball has thus been a leisure practice in the Philippines for nearly a century. Recently, Bartholomew (2010) examined basketball's significance to contemporary Philippine culture. In his work, he recounts his experience playing basketball with some of the locals in Manila:

> ... I watched my teammates sprint, slide and leap in their thong sandals, with nothing between their feet and the ground but a thin rubber pancake, I felt like I was watching people drive blindfolded ... Playing in flip-flops had become such an iconic feature of the Philippine (basketball) game that it had been enshrined in song by the Tagalog rappers Legit Misfitz who recorded 'Air

> *Tsinelas*' (Air Flip-Flops) ... (The game) was my introduction to the Philippine circus layup. In the States these are shots that you toss up when you drive into the heart of the defense, get stuck in the air between taller defenders and have to get rid of the ball before you land ... Well, Filipinos have turned the circus layup into an art form. While many Filipino players are graceful leapers with hang time to spare, when they're five-foot-six, even great hops aren't enough to dunk. So the body-twisting, triple-clutching, no-look seemingly impossible layup has replaced the dunk as the measuring stick of basketball artistry. Even in semipro and professional games, players will execute these tricky moves. (Bartholomew, 2010)

In the passage above, basketball in the Philippines is contrasted with that of the Untied States. One observed difference is the footwear that is used to play the game. Whereas shoes are used in the United States, flip-flops or thong sandals, are used by Philippine basketball players who are unable to purchase more appropriate footwear. Another difference is the 'circus layup' as a demonstration of basketbal artistry. Due to the fact that Filipinos are not tall enough to dunk on ten foot tall basketball hoops, they measure basketball prowess through the ability to do a difficult layup, which requires agility and grace, but does not require that a person hang onto the basketball rim. The passage above is thus an indication that basketball continues to be significant as a Philippine leisure activity up to the present, and that it is one in which intricate meanings have been developed.

Foreign Influences to Leisure between the American Colonial Period and the EDSA Revolution

An examination of two significant leisure practices in the Philippines under American colonial rule further exemplifies the idea that foreign influences shape leisure practices throughout the archipelago. Film is a case in point. As a medium in which content and technology was produced in Europe and the United States, Philippine audiences had no choice but to consume the media products of such countries. The case of basketball is similar in that it was transmitted into Philippine culture through the public education system instituted by colonial administrators.

At the same time, however, cultural practices derived from outside the Philippines were localized. In the case of film, local film products were produced at the start of the 20th century, and were differentiated from Hollywood and European products through their relatively simplistic plots and storylines. Nonetheless, such films exemplify the localization of a formerly foreign medium. Basketball also serves as an example of appropriation of a foreign influence into Philippine culture. From the attire that is used to play the game, to the meanings that are attached to certain basketball moves, clearly the game is played differently from the United States, its country of origin.

Leisure in the Contemporary Period

The contemporary period refers to the past two and a half decades in Philippine history. Globalization is a multifaceted concept, and its consequences on social reality have been discussed and debated upon across academic fields. It has been described as having a number of characteristics, which include the breaking down and overcoming of barriers, particularly those belonging to the nation-state, as well as the formation of a global capitalist system. As such, it is seen as a system of 'total control of the world by powerful supranational economic interests' (Gelinas, 2003). Globalization has also engendered the decline of the traditional nation-state system by eroding the boundaries between the global and the domestic. In the present social milieu, the global penetrates the local. Self-contained indigenous local cultural practices are no longer like those found in the works of early anthropologists. Instead, globalization has led to the adoption of cultural practices that are no longer localized. This erodes the traditional notion of a nation-state as being a politico-legal entity that has a homogeneous and distinct culture within it.

In the contemporary period, the Philippines' culture has been influenced by globalization in that its leisure practices became similar to those seen in other parts of the world. Though there are many aspects of leisure that may be traced to globalization, this chapter focuses on two categories of activities: technologically mediated activities and health and fitness activities.

Health and Fitness Activities

Health and fitness have become increasingly popular over the past two decades. Throughout the world, gyms have proliferated, the market for athletic footwear and apparel has increased, and the number of personal trainers has multiplied. The trend towards health and fitness has also penetrated into the Philippines, with Filipinos engaging in activities and consuming products related to being fit and healthy. This is manifested through participation in street runs and the proliferation of gyms throughout the country.

Street runs have become one of the latest popular trends in the Philippines, with at least one running event occurring each weekend in the city of Manila. According to the event organizer, 16,000 people attended one of the most recent major running events, the Unilab Run United 2. The participation by such a large number of people indicates that running has become a significant leisure practice. In October, the Philippines will be hosting the Southeast Asian championships of the international running event, the Adidas King of the Road. In so doing, the country is contributing to the culture of running at a global level.

Fitness is also seen in the proliferation of gyms, or fitness chains, throughout the Philippines, with the two most popular being international companies based outside of the country. Fitness First, which was started in the United Kingdom, has seventeen clubs throughout the country, while Gold's Gym, which has its roots in the western part of the United States, has six branches. The continued existence of such places indicates that fitness clubs are places for practicing leisure in the Philippines.

Technologically Mediated Activities

Information and communications technologies have been spreading throughout Philippine society, and have made inroads into the leisure practices of Filipinos. Among the most prevalent technologically mediated leisure activities are television watching, the use of mobile phones, and using the Internet.

Television watching is a popular leisure practice in the Philippines at present. The globalization of television has coincided with the growth in satellite technologies in the latter half of the twentieth century, and has allowed for the transmission of media products at an unprecedented scale (Thomas, 2005). It is estimated that in the year 2000, 11 million households owned televisions, thereby making it one of the most widely consumed type of mass media in the country. The growth in cable and satellite television viewership in the Philippines coincided with the EDSA Revolution of 1986, which led to the liberalization of laws on the ownership of satellite dishes (Valdez, 2004). At present, it is estimated that 29 per cent of households with televisions subscribe to either a cable or satellite provider. As such, they have access to transnational programming, including CNN, BBC, ESPN, StarTV, as well as non-English language programming (Thomas, 2005). This provides television audiences with an array of media choices produced throughout the world. It is this same technological infrastructure that allows youth culture to be increasingly exposed to animated programming from the United States and from Japan (de Vera, 2006). Although television programming has penetrated the Philippines, local television channels are also consumed. The two largest broadcasting networks in the country are the ABS-CBN Broadcasting Network and GMA Network, Inc. (Valdez, 2004). Both networks produce television shows that are widely consumed throughout the country. Thus, regardless of the type of programming, television viewership is thus a widely practiced leisure activity in the Philippines.

Mobile phones are products of countries outside the Philippines. Companies that produce mobile phones such as Nokia, Motorola and Apple, are all based outside the country. However the usage of the technology is one of the most prominent activities in the Philippines. Nagasaka (2007) remarked that one third of the Philippine population is a mobile phone subscriber. The technology is not only used by businessmen, but by 'school teachers, taxi and jeepney drivers, and vendors in the public markets'. As such, it is a valid claim that 'cellphones have become a major icon of Philippine life' (Pertierra et al., 2002: 151). The popularity of mobile phones lies in that Filipinos use them to communicate with one another through text messages or SMS, which are low cost ways for sending messages from one unit to another. They are thus a medium for people to socialize with one another. Whereas people would go to Luneta Park to socialize during the Spanish colonial period, they presently make use of mobile phones to keep up with one another. Mobile phone communication is thus a significant form of technology-mediated leisure.

One final leisure practice to be discussed in this chapter is the use of the Internet, particularly the use of social networking sites. Filipinos have been reported as one of the most active users of social media throughout the world. In a 2008 survey on social network site usage by Universal McCann, 83 per cent of Philippine respondents reported that they had an account on a social networking site, giving it the highest percentage out of the 29 countries that were studied. A similar finding was made by the Oxford Business Group, which stated that: 'One in three Filipino Internet users have a blog, and social networking and gaming have been on the rise'. As such, the evidence suggests that social networking sites are an important leisure activity to Filipinos. The prominence of Internet social networking, according to Nadal (2011), may be attributed to its ability to allow Filipinos to stay in touch with one another, regardless of geographic location. In a country where one-tenth of the population is overseas, social media allow families and friends to maintain their social bonds despite being physically apart from one another.

Foreign Influences to Leisure in the Contemporary Period

The examples above suggest that Philippine leisure in the contemporary period is influenced by trends occurring throughout the world. The large-scale purchase of devices such as mobile phones, televisions and internet-ready devices indicates that the Philippines has access to such products, which are available at a global scale. How Filipinos use them, however, suggests that aspects of the local culture also influence the technologies. The use of text messaging instead of calling on mobile phones exemplifies this idea. Also, the existence of local television programming alongside cable and satellite shows indicates the continued importance of local cultural practices, despite the existence of foreign media products. With regard to fitness and health, the popularity of health clubs and street runs indicates that the country has a connection to health and fitness trends throughout the world.

Conclusion

To close this chapter on leisure in the Philippines, it may be worth restating the argument that has recurred throughout the chapter, which is that Philippine leisure practices have been greatly influenced by cultural practices that developed outside the archipelago. During the Spanish period, musical appreciation and bullfighting represented activities that came about in Spain, while in the American period, one finds film and basketball transplanted into the local culture. In the contemporary period, technology-mediated forms of leisure and health and fitness activities indicate that Philippine leisure patterns are susceptible to global trends and practices.

The key caveat discussed in the chapter, however, is that practices are not appropriated into Philippine culture in the exact same way that they are practiced elsewhere. The discussions in the preceding sections of the chapter indicate that foreign practices are changed, or are done alongside already existing leisure practices in the Philippines. Basketball and film, which were introduced during the American colonial period, illustrate the former, in that they were practiced differently by Filipinos than they were elsewhere in the world. Cockfighting is a case in point for the latter, in that it persisted alongside Spanish bullfighting.

Philippine leisure may thus be characterized by its ability to appropriate cultural practices, as well as the pattern to retain aspects of the local culture and combine it with foreign influences.

References

Appadurai, A. (1996). *Modernity at Large: Cultural Dimensions of Globalization*. Minneapolis: University of Minnesota Press.

Barber, B. (1996). *Jihad Versus McWorld*. New York: Times Books.

Bartholomew, R. (2010). *Pacific Rims: Beermen Ballin' in Flip-Flops and the Philippines' Unlikely Love Affair with Basketball*. New York: New American Library.

Bowring, J. (1963). *A Visit to the Philippine Islands*. Manila: Filipiniana Book Guild.

Carpenter, F. (1929).*Through the Philippines and Hawaii*. New York: Doubleday, Doran and Company, Inc.

de la Gironiére, P. (1962). *Twenty Years in the Philippines*. Manila: Filipiniana Book Guild.

Deocampo, N. (2003). *Cine: Spanish Influences on Early Cinema in the Philippines*. Philippines: National Commission for the Culture and the Arts.

De Zengotita, T. (2005). *Mediated*. New York Bloomsbury Publishing

Fitness First Philippines (2011). *About Us*. Available at: http://www.fitnessfirst.com.ph/ph/aboutus/about_us.asp.

Foreman, J. (1985). *The Philippine Islands*. Manila: Cacho Hermanos, Inc.

Gelinas, J. (2003). *Juggernaut Politics. Understanding Predatory Globalization*. London and New York: Zed Books.

Giddens, A. (1990). *The Consequences of Modernity*. Cambridge: Polity Press.

Gold's Gym Philippines (2011). *About Us*. Available at: http://www.goldsgym.com.ph/about.html.

Goncharov, I. (1974). Voyage of the Frigate 'Pallada'. In *Travel Accounts of the Philippines*. Manila: Filipiniana Book Guild.

Gunter, B. and Gunter N. (1980). Leisure Styles: A Conceptual Framework for Modern Leisure. *The Sociological Quarterly* 21(3): 361–374.

Jagor, F. (1965). *Travels in the Philippines*. Manila: Filipiniana Book Guild.

Kolata, G. (2003). *Ultimate Fitness*. New York: Picador.

Korten, D. and Klauss R. (eds) (1984). *People Centered Development: Contributions toward Theory and Planning Frameworks*. Connecticut: Kumarian Press.

Kramer, P. (2006). *The Blood of Government: Race, Empire, the United States and the Philippines*. USA: University of North Carolina Press.

Le Roy, J. (1968). Philippine Life in Town and Country. In *The Philippines Circa 1900*. Manila: Filipiniana Book Guild.

Lumbera, B. (1983). Problems in Philippine Film History. In Guerrero R. (ed.) *Readings in Philippine Cinema*. Quezon City: Experimental Cinema of the Philippines.

MacMicking, R. (1967). Recollections of Manilla and the Philippines. Manila: Filipiniana Book Guild.

Marche, A. (1970). *Luzon and Palawan*. Manila: Filipiniana Book Guild.

Marryat, F. (1974). Borneo and the Archipelago. In *Travel Accounts of the Philippines*. Manila: Filipiniana Book Guild.

Miller, D. (2008). *Stuff*. Cambridge: Polity Press.

Martin, P. (1983). The 'Silent Pictures' Era in the Philippines. In: Guerrero R. (ed.) *Readings in Philippine Cinema*. Quezon City: Experimental Cinema of the Philippines.

Nadal, K. (2011). *Filipino American Psychology: A Handbook of Theory, Research and Clinical Practice*. Hoboken, NJ: John Wiley and Sons, Inc.

Nagasaka, I. (2007). Cellphones in the Rural Philippines. In: Pertierra R. (ed.) *The Social Construction and Usage of Communication Technologies*. Manila: University of the Philippines Press.

Oxford Business Group (2010). *The Report: The Philippines 2010*. Available at: http://www.oxfordbusinessgroup.com/country/Philippines.

Pertierra, R. (2002). *Txt-ing Selves: Cellphones and Philippine Modernity*. Manila: De La Salle University Press.

Pilar, S. (1983). The Early Movies. In: Guerrero R. (ed.) *Readings in Philippine Cinema*. Quezon City: Experimental Cinema of the Philippines.

Parker, S. (1975). The Sociology of Leisure: Progress and Problems. *The British Journal of Sociology* 26(1): 91–101.

Peterson, R. (1981). Measuring Culture, Leisure and Time Use. *Annals of the American Academy of Political and Social Science* 453: 169–179.

Pope, S. (1995). An Army of Athletes: Playing Fields, Battlefields, and the American Military Sporting Experience, 1890–1920. *The Journal of Military History* 59(3): 435–456.

Robertson, J. (1913). Notes from the Philippines. *The Journal of Race Development* 3(4): 467–490.

Runrio. (2011). *Runrio Trilogy Leg 2 Run United Race Results*. Available at: http://runrio.com/2011/08/runrio-trilogy-leg-2-run-united-2-race-results.

Stevens, J. (1968). Yesterdays in the Philippines. In *The Philippines Circa 1900*. Manila: Filipiniana Book Guild.

Stoodley, B. (1957). Some Aspects of Tagalog Family Structure. *American Anthropologist* 59(2): 236–249.

Summers, J. (1998). Listening for Historic Manila: Music and Rejoicing in an International City. *Budhi: A Journal of Ideas and Culture* 2(1): 203–254.

Sumsky, V. (1992). The City as Political Actor: Manila, February 1986. *Alternatives: Global, Local, Political* 17(4): 479–492.

Tannert, C. (1996). *Ultramar*. Vienna: Angelina R. Banke.

Thomas, A. (2005). *Imagin-Nations and Borderless Television: Media, Culture and Politics Across Asia*. London: Sage.

Universal McCann (2008). *Wave 3: Power to the People*. Available at: http://www.archive.org/details/UniversalMccannWave3PowerToThePeople.

Valdez, V. (2004). Philippines. In vom Busch (ed.) *The Asia Media Directory*. Singapore: Konrad Adenauer Foundation.

Veblen, T. (1953). *The Theory of the Leisure Class: An Economic Study of Institutions*. New York: New American Library.

Waters, M. (2001). *Globalization*. New York: Routledge.

Wilkes, C. (1974). Narrative of the US Exploring Expedition. In *Travel Accounts of the Philippines*. Manila: Filipiniana Book Guild.

Wilson, J. (1980). Sociology of Leisure. *Annual Review of Sociology* 6: 21–40.

Zialcita, F. (2005). *Authentic though not Exotic: Essays on Filipino Identity*. Manila: Ateneo de Manila University Press.

11

Leisure as *Distinction* in the Turkish Middle Class

Nursing Babies, Collecting a Trousseau, Meeting at the Malls, or Surfing?

ZERRIN ARSLAN

In this article, the differences between the urban middle classes in Turkey have scrutinized through their life styles, everyday life and leisure habits.[1] Several questions are asked: what the middle classes do in their everyday lives, routines and leisure times; how do they present their differences from the other classes and also social groups; how do they construct their class distinctions? Such questions involve certain judgements on people's routines, attitudes, and consumption patterns, as well as their taste, lifestyle and leisure. Particularly, when a specific distinction, that is a trademark, can be identified to differentiate a certain group of urbanites under scrutiny, the label 'middle class' is easily applied to such groups.

Leisure as the construction of class distinction, referring to Bourdieu's theory on distinction as represented in his book, *Distinction* (1984), is investigated in the context of the contemporary Turkish society in Ankara. In this study, the inner stratification of the Turkish middle class, as well as leisure corresponding to each stratum are defined in social, cultural, and economic terms, thus making it possible to determine the distinction of each stratum. A historical overview of the changes in the Turkish society in the period of transition from the Ottoman Empire to the Turkish Republic is also included.

The first section explains the theoretical and conceptual frameworks, and the methodology employed in the study. In the second section, the Turkish middle class fractions are analytically constructed utilizing the correspondence analyses and demonstrated the association among the habitus, combination and volume of social, cultural, and economic capitals. Thus, the characteristic of each fraction has been displayed in social spaces. In the third section, everyday life, lifestyles and leisure in the Turkish society are described in a historical perspective, starting with the Ottoman Empire and extending to today's Turkey. In the conclusion, the leisure is matched with the corresponding middle class fractions. Thus, the way leisure is involved in the construction and presentation of *class distinction* among the fractions of the Turkish middle class is emphasized.

Theoretical and Conceptual Frameworks and Methodology

This study relies on two theoretical and conceptual bases, one regarding the definition of middle class, and secondly, Bourdieu's theory about class distinction, including the concepts of habitus, social, cultural and economic capitals, and class fractions and positions. Therefore, the literature on the middle classes and Bourdieu's theory are employed in a complementary way.

The Middle Class(es): The class and stratification studies in modern societies have usually been grounded on the theories of either Marx or Weber. Marxian concepts, including exploitation, domination, subordination, ownership or property, and Weberian concepts, such as occupational and social status or prestige, transformations in life and lifestyle, have enabled scholars to study social classes. Marxist authors have analysed classes in the context of the relations of production, exploitation, and the antagonism inherent in the class relationships that provide the fundamental power for social change. Weberian writers have focused on the relations of market and occupational schema. Some others, such as Bourdieu (1984), on the other hand, have developed their own conceptual tools, adopting concepts from both Marx and Weber. Some other authors, moreover, emphasize the significance of consumption and lifestyle including leisure.

A widespread tendency in recent studies is to determine ways of consumption, lifestyle and leisure in order to distinguish a social group from the others. This approach concentrates more on the cultural dimensions, rather than the economic and social ones. The cultural approach to social classes frequently uses class and occupational structure interchangeably, and exploits cultural assets as well as economic and social ones. Bourdieu's study, specifically *Distinction* (1984) on French taste, can be seen as a turning point, with its emphasis on culture.

The occupational schema is the most known and widely used indicator to draw the class boundaries in recent class analysis and stratification studies. Occupation is an 'extremely powerful indicator of an interrelated network of social advantage and disadvantage' in the modern society (Crompton, 1996: 114). Occupational scheme is hierarchically defined referring the employee's or worker's skills like that:

- Professional occupations
- Intermediate occupations
- Skilled non-manual occupations
- Skilled manual occupations
- Partly skilled occupations
- Unskilled occupations (Crompton, 1996: 53).

The concept of middle class generally refers first three groups. In words, middle class refers to the capitalist/bourgeois and the working class/proletariat. Such a broad definition of the middle class covers the petty bourgeoisie or traditional middle class of the Marxists, together with the old and new middle class of the Weberians, and those working in new jobs in public and private sectors, and also in service sector.

In addition to the most known occupational characteristics, each society also has its own social class structures and social groups. Boratav (1995: 7), for instance, defines the Turkish urban class and social groups in nine categories: unemployed, retired, high-qualified, salaried, white collar salaried, unqualified service worker, blue collar worker, crafts/marginals/self-employed professionals, small or medium/large employer.

In the current study, the urban middle class is eclectically defined excluding only the big employers and entrepreneurs, and the manual workers working in factories, mines, etc. Nevertheless, classes cannot be reduced to occupational positions. They include social, cultural, and economic differences as well. In other words, the social, cultural and economic capitals, their compositions and volumes determine the class position of each individual. The distinctive class positions, in Bourdieu's words (1984), reflect on their taste and aesthetical dispositions, as well as their lifestyle and leisure. In the context of this study, the middle class distinction is defined according to leisure.

The occupational schemes indicate a hierarchy emphasized in the literature on stratification. Generally, mid-occupations are accepted as middle class occupations. Put differently, the white-collar employees, public and private officers, and professionals comprise the middle class in industrial and advanced societies (Kalaycıoğlu, 2011). In this study, urban occupational scheme is eclectically constructed utilizing the stratification literature and Boratav's urban social classes in the Turkish society. While such preference excludes only the capitalists and the workers in industry and mine, it covers the urban employment and occupational characteristics in Turkey (Boratav, 1995: 7; Kalaycıoğlu et al., 1998: 134; Kalaycıoğlu et al., 2008). Housewives are added as an independent category in this unitary scheme with nine categories:

Housewives: Women who do not take place in occupational hierarchy or employment status.

Unqualified service workers: Waiters, watchmen, janitors, clerks and drivers.

Retirees: People who receive pensions.

Blue-collar workers: Salaried technical workers in services or workshops.

White-collar workers: Salaried workers, i.e. nurses, teachers, dentists, bank officials, accountants, policemen.

Self-employed: Craftsmen, tradesmen, shopkeepers, workers in marginal or informal jobs; qualified middle-class such as medical doctors, lawyers and accountants who have their own offices, but not employ any staff.

High-qualified professionals: Engineers, lawyers, specialist medical doctors, surgeons who don't have their own offices, but work in elite and qualified jobs.

Small employers: People who employ one or two permanent workers.

Medium/large employers: People who employ six or more permanent workers.

The advantage of such grouping is that, while taking occupation as the basic determinant, it demonstrates the associations between material and non-material sources of various classes, which define class inequalities in a given society (Parkin, 1979: 17–18). In other words, occupation is a fundamental, and an appropriate tool to correlate with social, cultural and economic characteristics, or *capitals* in the context of this study, of the respondents as well as to scrutinize lifestyles and leisure of the middle class fractions.

Theory of Distinction

The employed fundamental concepts in this study are defined below:

Social, Cultural and Economic Capitals, and *Habitus:* The concept of capital is broader than the monetary conception of economics. Monetary and non-monetary connotations have been used in social sciences, emphasizing different dimensions (Bourdieu, 1984, 1985, 1986; Field, 2008: 6–7; Halpern, 2005: 5–7).

Social Capital refers broadly to the networks, or to the resources they offer to individuals. In other words, it is 'the sum of the actual and potential resources that can be mobilized through membership in social networks of actors and organizations' (Anheier, Gerhards and Romo, 1995: 862). Therefore, social capital refers to various relationships from kinship networks to work- and interest-based relationships. In this study, social capital is considered to be established through these types of relationships and networks.

Cultural Capital takes various forms. Bourdieu (1986) defines three forms of cultural capital as objectified, institutionalized and embedded states. It covers formal education, total time spent in school, number of books and other cultural objects possessed, in sum 'long-standing dispositions and habits acquired in the socialization process, the accumulation of valued cultural objects such as paintings, and formal educational qualifications and training' (Anheier, Gerhards and Romo, 1995: 862). While formal education, as its institutionalized form, and number of books and possession of original paintings and sculptures, as its objectified form, are involved in the cultural capital, such activities as going to cinema, theatre, and concerts, visiting museums, and etc. indicate long-standing dispositions and habits, and represent the embedded form of cultural capital. The embedded state also covers leisure activities. Especially, the dichotomy of high and low culture depends on the accumulation of cultural capital, creating distinctions among people and their leisure activities (Arun, 2009; Bennett, 2005, Bourdieu, 1984; DiMaggio and Useem, 1978; Holt, 1995, 1998, 2000, 2002; Katz-Gerro, 2002; Lamont, 1992; Peterson and Kern, 1996). In assessing cultural capital, this study takes formal education, books, original paintings and sculpture as basic elements. Accordingly, in analysing the class distinction, this study considers the former two states as involved in cultural capital, and leisure activities are taken to reflect the third.

Economic Capital refers to monetary income, and other financial resources and assets. Compared to other forms of capital, economic capital is the most liquid and convertible form. Economic capital is only taken into consideration as monthly income in this study.

Habitus and *Lifestyle:* Habitus and lifestyle designate all practices of the agents in their everyday lives (Bourdieu, 1984: 169). *Habitus* defines the set of all kinds of temperaments, skills, behaviours and attitudes, and ways of acting acquired through the socialization process. It includes all acquired aptitudes also referring to habitual activities and experiences of everyday life that are usually taken for granted by individuals. Indeed, habitus mostly implies a system of dispositions acquired from social, and also physical or material milieu.

Lifestyle refers to characteristic sets of behaviours in a given time and place, including social relations, eating, clothing, consumption, entertainment, and also leisure activities. Unlike habitus, lifestyle refers to more or less constructed and stylized ways of life, which are shaped in relation with habitus, and the composition and volume of the capitals. Age, gender, occupation, education, and also habitus determine lifestyle. Each social group or homogenous social grouping has a distinctive lifestyle produced with the interaction of the schema of social practice, the habitus, and the social, cultural and economic capitals (Bourdieu, 1984, 1985).

Taste: For a given social class or group, lifestyle and leisure preferences, and attendance to various cultural events or cultural consumption are associated with the judgement of taste. According to Bourdieu, the capitals and habitus of a person determine her/his everyday practices, routines, choices, and preferences aimed at beautifying the daily life. *Taste*, as a conceptual instrument, carries a sociological meaning, referring mainly to the cultural patterns of everyday choices and preferences of individuals. In this study, taste and aesthetics are basically about popular taste, in line with the sense and usage employed rather than the Kantian understanding of aesthetics (Bourdieu, 1984: 178). Popular taste refers to spontaneous and functional taste in the daily choices of individuals (Auslender, 1996; Bourdieu, 1990: 77–94, 2000; Petersen, 1997a, 1997b; Schapiro, 1953; Warde, Wright, and Gayo-Cal, 2008). In this context, Bourdieu defines three levels to classify and label the tastes of different social classes. 1) Legitimate taste: It refers to the highest educational capital of the dominant class and its fractions. 2) Middle-brow taste: It characterizes the middle class. 3) Popular or Low-brow taste: It is the most common among working classes (Bourdieu, 1984: 194). While taste is also about the human ability to judge what is beautiful, good, and proper (Ruth, 1955: 1–2), it also covers the preference for and attendance to various cultural events, and the practices, experiences and ways for doing something to relax, to take pleasure, and to beautify the life (Bourdieu, 1984, 2000; Peterson, 1997a, 1997b, 2005). Therefore, taste covers leisure of different social groups and class fragments.

Leisure: Occupational changes have led to differentiations in the scope of the 'necessary' counterpart of work. While paid employment and family life may comprise the essential part of the normal 'adult' existence, leisure is also a prerequisite for a 'healthy' and 'balanced' lifestyle. It is an activity to which the individual turns at will for relaxation, diversion or broadening her/his knowledge and her/his spontaneous social participation, the free exercise of his creative capacity apart from the obligations of work, family and society. It is also freedom (Kelly, 1983) and an experience for pleasure and enjoyment (Moorhouse, 1989: 17). In this context, leisure is related with liberty, fulfilment, choice, and growth (Frisby, 1989; Hargreaves, 1989; Katz-Gero and Shahit, 1998; Rojek, 1989a, 1989b, 1999, 2005; Warde, 2006; Wynne, 1998). Leisure has been subject to critical discussion and research on four major statements: (i) Leisure is taken as 'relations', which are regulated by the notions of social 'health' and 'normality'. It refers to the ways people spend their 'free' time; (ii)

Leisure as those 'practices' aimed to discover and improve personality, and to fulfil its requirement for pleasure; (iii) the perception and experience of leisure in modern society; and (iv) leisure in relation to the state, the nature of the state power and the role of the state in regulating everyday life (Rojek, 1989a: 1–8). To summarize, leisure refers to those activities and experiences individuals prefer for relaxation, and pleasure, in contrast with the 'obligatory and necessary' activities, or obligations, of work, family and society. In this sense, leisure includes those activities and 'practices' that individuals perform with the aim of personal discovery and fulfilment, or pleasure and enjoyment. In this context, leisure is related to liberty, fulfilment, choice, growth, and pleasure in everyday life. In other words, leisure as activities, preferences, practices or experiences is also associated with the tastes of social groups and the fragments of a given class. It should be noticed that in the Turkish literature, however, leisure is utilized only recently with the meanings summarized above. Words like enjoyment, entertainment, pleasure, free time activity and hobby have usually been preferred in previous studies instead of leisure and leisure activities.

To sum up, the middle class covers those people working in mid-occupations in the occupational scheme; the capitals indicate both monetary and non-monetary assets; class fraction refers to an inner stratum of a given class, distinguished according to the combinations and volumes of the capitals; habitus is the result of the objectification of social structure, and the socialization process at the level of individual subjectivity; lifestyle is a stylized way of life in a given time and place for a homogeneous social group or a class; taste is the cultural patterns of everyday choices and preferences of individuals; and finally, leisure is a unitary definition employing the aforementioned first, second and fourth points in this study. Thus, each fraction and their leisure are explained in association with the class taste.

Methodology

In this study, distinction among classes is based on a series of related assumptions: (i) People possess different levels of social, cultural and economic capitals; (ii) This difference is caused the different combinations and volumes of capitals; (iii) The difference between combinations and volumes of capitals and habitus leads to the fragmentations in a given class; (iv) Each class, and its fractions have different tastes, lifestyles and leisure. These assumptions were statistically tested with a quantitative field research and the author's observations and small talks with the city dwellers in Ankara.

The inner stratification of the middle class was constructed through the labels of social, cultural, and economic capitals as the categorical data. Following this, a multiple correspondence analyses was constructed with four categories of each capital,[2] and nine categories of occupations with a total of twenty-one categories; and these categories were clustered within four different clouds on the correspondence analysis graph. In this way, the first, second and third assumptions were statistically demonstrated in social space. As a consequence, the fragmentation of the Turkish middle class is analytically constructed, and each fraction's combination and volume of the capitals and occupations are illustrated in the correspondence analysis graph as social space, which can be seen on Figure 1 in the next section.

Analytically Constructed Fractions of the Turkish Middle Class

The fractions of the Turkish middle class are constructed via multiple correspondence analyses, and represented in social space by using four labels of each capital including social, cultural and economic, and nine labels of occupations. The resulting joint plot, Figure 1 below, displays the associations among the labels. The labels are clustered into four distinct clouds, each cloud consisting of one label from each capital, and close-positioned labels of occupations. Each cloud represents a different fraction of the Turkish middle class, named and coloured differently, considering the structural and socio-psychological characteristics of the samples derived from ethnographic data as well as the academic literature, and writings from magazines, newspapers and their supplements. The horseshoe shape of the quadratic bow is directed towards the bottom. The fractions from the lower to the highest are located from the left to the right of the Figure 1. The clouds include: The Lower/Bitter Middle Class, coloured with yellow; the Middle/Resentful Middle Class with blue; the Upper/Contemptuous Middle Class with purple; and the Well-off/Happy Middle Class with pink.

The Lower/Bitter Middle Class: This fraction consists of lower levels of capitals (C1, S1, EC1) and occupations as housewives, blue-collar and unqualified workers. Considering the labels of cultural capital, only a portion of them had finished primary education. Economic capital is located closer to the blue cloud. The reason for this is that the respondents clustered in the yellow cloud

Figure 1

Fractions of the Turkish Middle Class in Social Space

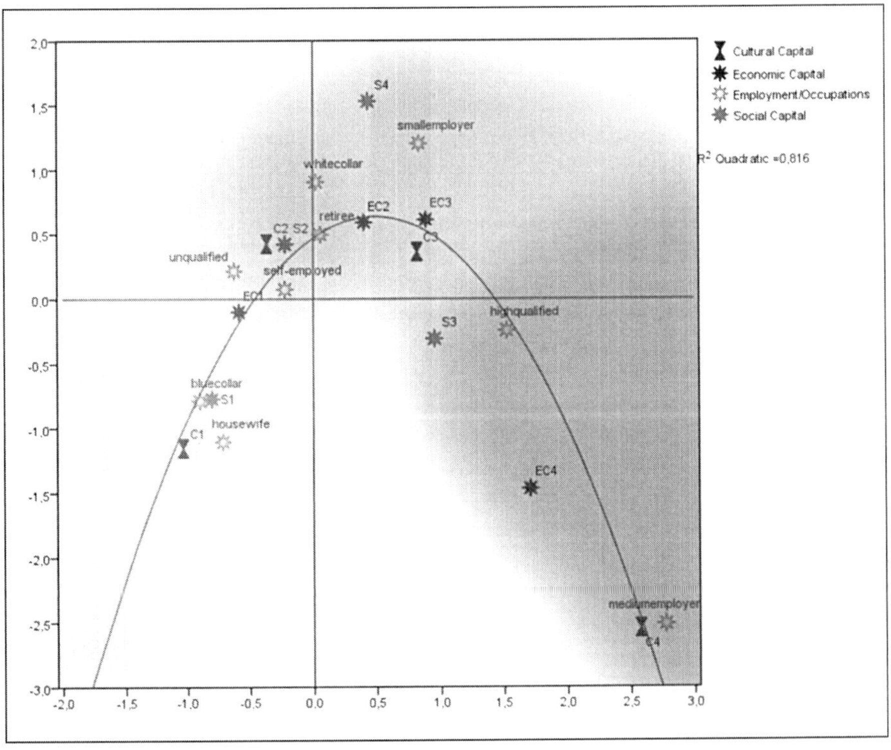

have relatively higher economic capital, while they have lower levels of social and cultural capitals. The lower/bitter middle class is characterized with a socially closed relationship. Although this fraction generally spends time at home with family members, and rarely with its first-step relatives, neighbours coming as drop-in visitors are also usual. Moreover, constantly being in economic hardship is one of the defining characteristics. Their household expenditures are fundamentally for daily required consumption such as food, rent, heating, cloths and transportation, not for cultural consumption or entertainment. Members of this fraction are not mobile within the city; many of them have not yet visited any of the famous sites of Ankara. Housewives are usually less educated, and dependent on a single male breadwinner, and their social activities remain restricted to housework, cooking, and watching television, and contacts with family/kin, and neighbours. Indeed, family and the TV appear to dominate the leisure time of this fraction, hence a family- and TV-struck middle class.

Fractions of the Turkish Middle Class: Social Capital: S1 (Lower), S2 (Middle), S3 (Upper), S4 (Highest); Cultural Capital: C1 (Lower), C2 (Middle), C3 (Upper), C4 (Highest); Economic Capital: EC1 (Lower), EC2 (Middle), EC3 (Upper), EC (Highest); Employment/Occupations: housewife (House Wife), unqualified (Unqualified Service Workers), retiree (Retiree), bluecollar (Blue Collar Workers), whitecollar (White Collar Workers), self-employed (Self-Employed), highqualified (High Qualified Professionals), smallemployer (Small Employer), mediumemployer (Middle-Size Employer).

The Resentful Middle/Middle Class: It is coloured in blue, and is constructed with the second levels of capitals (S2, C2 and EC2). The centre is loosely surrounded with unqualified employees, self-employed, retired and white-collar respondents. While this cloud is distant from the bitter/lower middle class, it is in closer proximity to the Contemptuous/Upper Middle Class. This fraction designates emulative capacity of its members for the eating, clothing, lifestyle, consumption patterns, and entertainment, holiday and leisure habits of higher fractions, since they are familiar with them but lack the economic opportunities of higher fractions. They usually depend on a restricted monthly income, frequently postponing big expenditures, and falling in economic hardship if unexpected expenditures emerge. Still, they demonstrate signs of resentful emotions towards the higher fractions. Veblen's (1992, 2005) comment that people tend to imitate those in higher positions seems to correspond well with this fraction. Lamont (1992), in a study on French and American middle classes, labelled this process as 'moral inclusion and exclusion processes'. Members of this fraction usually have close relatives in the same city, and close friends from school and work, and they meet frequently in the evenings, and at weekends. In short, this fraction can be coined as an 'emulation-centred' middle class.

The Upper/Contemptuous Middle Class: This fraction is represented with the purple cloud. It is flimsier compared to the middle/resentful middle class. Perhaps the most significant feature of the upper/contemptuous middle class is that the cloud has a loose form that is built up around the third levels of cultural and economic capitals (C3, EC3), the fourth level of social capital (S4), and small employers as occupation. Most of its members have undergraduate degrees, and are positioned closer to high-qualified professionals. The looseness of the boundaries of the cloud results from the level of social capital that includes membership in trade unions, interest groups, and charity organizations, and positioned closer to the registration of official employment, such as white-collar and retirees. Although the upper/contemptuous middle class seems to have interconnections with the middle/resentful middle class, there is a visible distance with the lower/bitter middle class. They can be expected to have negative feelings for those in the lower social strata. They usually have close friends, mostly previous classmates, and they usually go out together or meet at home. This fraction has a more comfortable life compared to the previous fractions, and distinguishes itself from the others, and looks at them with contemptuous emotions.

The Well-Off/Happy Middle Class: This fraction is the fourth cloud, painted in pink. The members of this fraction are high-qualified professionals, or medium-size employers with the highest economic and cultural capitals (C4, EC4), and third level of social capital (S3). The most distinguishing feature of this fraction, especially for those with the highest social capital, is the distance to all other fractions. Given that they possess highest levels of cultural and economic capitals, and employ highest two occupational status, this fraction can be considered to enjoy a self-appointed qualification. They do not have any connection with other fragments, especially with the lower/bitter and middle/resentful fractions, with the exception of their employees or the housekeepers they employ as domestic labourers. They interact mostly with highly qualified professionals with higher levels of social capital. The distances and interconnections of the well-off/happy fraction with the others can be explained by the fact that it lives in isolated middle-class neighbourhoods, works in isolated workplaces, and commute to work with their private automobiles. They prefer to avoid daily contacts with the others unless necessary. However, their unconnected lives should not be considered as a disregardful and neglectful behaviour towards other lower fragments and classes. Rather, the types of contact are different from the relationships with family members, kin, friends, and also neighbours who possess more or less equivalent levels of capitals. They are usually informed about the life and working conditions, social and cultural values of all other fractions and also the classes. As expressed by someone during the field study, 'they have the money, they have the chance.'

Everyday Life and Leisure in the Turkish Society

The emergence of consumption and leisure, in a Western sense, can be traced back to the mid-19th century and to the process of modernization in general. Western lifestyles and consumption gradually spread all over the Empire, with the non-Muslims (Greeks, Armenians, and Jews) adopting them first, and the Muslim population following them. Events such as the Crimean War, when thousands of foreign soldiers came to Istanbul, provided further impetus by exposing the Ottoman population to Western lifestyles (Aktüre, 2001; Bali, 2004, 2008; Etöz, 1998, 2006; Faroqhi, 2005, 2006; Karababa and Ger, 2010; Orçan, 2002). The foundation process of the Republic, the early Republican period between 1920s and 1940s, also led to a gradual change in the consumption patterns and habits of the Turkish society. More recently the policies toward opening the Turkish economy, and closer integration with global economy, starting with the 1980s have been a major factor bringing out further drastic changes.

Everyday life, in its broadest sense, could be defined as what a person does, feels or thinks, at a specific time and place (de Certeau, 1984; Lefebvre, 1984 and 1991). As such, everyday life is considered as the interwoven economic, cultural, and religious practices that are developed by a society in conjunction with the variables of time and space, whereby the time element refers to differentiation in the dissolution and integration of these practices in a process, and the space dimension defines the concrete borders for the operationalization of this differentiation (IŞın, 1995: 79). In the case of Turkey, the change and transformation of everyday life and leisure with regard to a specific time and place should be studied in parallel to the historical Turkish modernization. The periodization developed in this study, therefore, follows the modernization process in its broadest sense. In that sense, the distinction in everyday life and leisure, starting with the period of the Ottoman Empire, could be summarized in three historical periods: (i) the Ottoman period[3] (1299–1920); (ii) Through the Modern Turkey, and (iii) the Modern period, starting with the foundation of the Turkish Republic[4] in 1920s. The existence of gender-based differences in everyday life and leisure, in addition to historical differences, should not be forgotten. A further point to be noted relates to the differences between various religious communities (Faroqi, 2005; IŞın, 1995; Mikhail, 2007; Rizk Khoury, 1999; Sadji, 2007).[5]

In the Ottoman Period

A major feature of the studies and discussions on lifestyles and leisure in the Ottoman Empire is their almost complete focus on the court and the elite, emphasizing the everyday life in Istanbul, the imperial centre and, historically, the late Ottoman period. In geographical terms, some provinces of the Empire, such as Damascus, Cairo, Mosul, and the Balkans are also included, mostly due to the availability of documents, and the languages and alphabets used (Faroqhi, 2005; Rizk Khoury, 1999; Sadji, 2007).

The Ottoman society consisted, most basically, of two main social classes – the ruling class (*hassa*), and the ruled (*amme*).[6] The ruling class, apart from the royal family, is composed of the educated elites – such as the highest army officials, bureaucrats and the theologians (the *ulema*). The ruled, or the people, included the Ottoman folk (Rizk Khoury, 1999), which was composed of both Muslims and non-Muslims. An Ottoman *middle class* has also been defined, as a feature specific to Asian societies, and seen as a consequence of the *tımar*[7] system. This middle class included various social groups, from civil servants to soldier families, retired soldiers, intellectuals, businessmen, and merchants. In the Ottoman Empire, the social classes and communities were listed as: the ruling classes; non-Muslim Greek merchants, brokers and land owners in western Anatolia and Istanbul, and their Muslim counterparts in the southeast; soldier-civil intellectuals as representatives of the exploitative class production relations within the *eşraf*[8] and the petty bourgeois (Timur, 2008: 18–20). The eşraf possessed the local authority in the economy and everyday life in small cities and towns (Karpat, 2008: 32–54). It should be noted, however, that despite the existence of various social groups, the Ottoman society was predominantly a rural society throughout the Ottoman period.[9] Religion, furthermore, was a fundamental feature in the organization of urban everyday life, in either Muslim or non-Muslim neighbourhoods that were built around the mosques or the churches (Faroqhi, 2005: 39).

A three-level classification of the Ottoman culture is widely used: *High culture* refers to the written culture produced by the ruling class and the literate and well-educated urban and religious elites. This written culture is dominated by the Ottoman language, the use of which is limited to the elites. *Folk culture* indicates the oral culture of the illiterate and the ruled. The daily Turkish dominates this culture, also implying that the folk cannot read, write nor understand the Ottoman language. *Popular culture* is placed between these two, referring to those excluded from the elite, while these people and their native languages are reflected in a written culture (Faroqhi, 2005: 3–9). Popular culture, in this sense, could also be regarded as a middle class culture. It is interesting to note the similarity between this classification and the aforementioned classification of taste and culture by Pierre Bourdieu. With regard to the four statements of contemporary leisure studies, in consequence, all these statements can be traced and investigated through the Turkish modernization process continuing since the 16th century.

Religion played a predominant role, influencing the social and historical formation of everyday life, practices of entertainment, enjoyment, pleasure, and leisure. In various studies on everyday life in the Ottoman era, the terms preferred have mostly been collective entertainment, enjoyment, or pleasure, rather than leisure. Beside these, some authors (Faroqhi, 2005; Işın, 1995; Karababa and Ger, 2010; Orçan, 2004; Yanıklar, 2006) have examined leisure and leisure activities through the development of consumer culture. The court and the elite started to consume the prominent goods in their everyday life. The prominent goods naturally emphasize the high culture or the written culture, not ordinary people or oral culture (Faroqhi, 2005: 3–9).

The Ottoman Era is further classified into various periods (Faroqi, 2005; Ger and Karababa, 2010; Işın, 1995; Rizk Khoury, 1999), but no such periodization has been preferred in this study. The 'Tulips Period' (1718–173), however, deserves to be noted, as it represents a breaking point between the earlier era when everyday life is organized according to religious codes, and the transition to a Western style as a consequence of increasing interaction with Europe. Until at least the 16th century, the Ottoman everyday life was essentially regulated by the religious and sumptuary laws that required content with what one possessed, and abstinence from promiscuous lifestyles (Faroqhi, 2005; Karababa and Ger, 2010). The accounts of foreign travellers, at the time, reflected the typical orientalist view, as they mentioned 'that the prominent leisure pursuit of a high-ranking Ottoman was to sit in silence and meditate', and regarded the Ottomans as lazy people that 'love sloth more than work', spending whole days playing chess or instruments.[10] Military and cultural expeditions into Europe starting with the 16th century, however, started a gradual change of this simple and plain lifestyle (Erimtan, 2007; Faroqhi, 2005; Sajdi, 2007). The 'Tulips Period' between 1718 and 1730 represented the turning point in this transformation from frugal consumption and lifestyles to conspicuous, ostentatious and prominent consumption (Orçan, 2004; Toprak, 1995; Yanıklar, 2006).

In typical Ottoman neighbourhoods that are traditionally built round the mosque, the everyday life of the ordinary men occurs within the 'house-mosque-bazaar' triangle, while the women spend the day within the house (IŞın, 1995: 82). Neither for the men nor for the women can we speak of leisure in its modern sense with its aforementioned four dimensions. In the cities, men spend the spare time remaining from family and work, idling and chatting in front of their shops, playing games like chess or domino, meeting others at the mosque at prayer times, or gathering at dervish lodges (called *dergah, zaviye,* or *tekke*) for conversations on religion, history, and heroisms of the Ottomans or the Turks. Women, on the other hand, spend all their time at home, going out occasionally for neighbour or family visits, and rarely for shopping. What this description reflects is a circular routinization of everyday life, albeit there are differences for men and women. Hence, we cannot speak of a habitualized leisure in the daily lives of men and women. The activities of entertainment, enjoyment, and pleasure, in contrast to the necessities carried out for the society, family and work, can perhaps be regarded as an element of leisure. Yet these activities are almost solely for men.

In the pre-modern Ottoman times, the leisure gardens offer a 'third place', a space of pleasure away from home and work (Karababa and Ger, 2010: 2). Even if unique to the members of the court and its entourage, these gardens were the only places where men and women could spend time together outside their houses, yet these gardens were restricted to the court members until the 19th century. The annual migration of the court and its entourage, upon the Sultan's decree, to the waterside residences of the Bosporus or to summer palaces in the Anatolian side of Istanbul could also be regarded as some sort of leisure garden activity. The women of the Ottoman palace, who could use closed carriages for transportation, had more opportunities to go to different pleasure places. As recounted by the famous traveller Evliya Çelebi, the leisure gardens around the Golden Horn (also known as *Sadabad*), were popular sites of the time. The *Kağthane* Creek around the Golden Horn, and the *Göksu* Creek on the Asian side of the Bosporus were the most popular leisure places for new enjoyments. As the demand from the ordinary people increased, starting with the late 18th century, the court members ceased to frequent these sites (Erimtan, 2007; IŞın, 1995). Those leisure gardens can be viewed as historical forms of picnic and brunch places, the most common third places for the urbanites of our time.

The intellectual leisure, furthermore, was also for the court and the elites. Most common forms among the Ottoman elites in the pre-modern and early modern times included the reading and writing of the Ottoman language, poetry recitals, conversations on religion or literature, and traditional Islamic arts such as marbling (*ebru*), calligraphy, gravure or miniature. Although Islam prohibits the painting or sculpting of human and animal figures, the Ottoman elites developed interest in fine arts such as painting and sculpture, and later photography, particularly after the 18th century (Faroqhi, 2005). Such leisure activities are mostly regarded as part of the high culture. Proficiency in reading and writing in the Ottoman language was not merely a leisure and pleasure activity for all well-educated Ottoman elites, but also an obligation if they wished an official post, or social prestige and status. Hence, it also provided a distinction for the elite. The distinctive leisure for the bureaucrats was mostly reading and writing the Ottoman history, literature and the Persian language and literature; for the high army officials it was geography, history and rarely religious subjects; for the *ulema* it was the Quran and related writings as well as other subjects.

Being a disciple of an Islamic sect or a dervish lodge – such as a *dergah*, *tekke*, or *zaviye* – and following the doctrines of its sheikhs were very common among the elites. Thus, a disciple could spend his leisure times for reading, citing, or listening to religious or other narrations and stories, together with the sheikh and other disciples in the lodges (Faroqhi, 2005; Rizk Khoury, 1999; Çaksu, 2007; Mikhail, 2007; Sadji, 2007). These occasions also brought the elite and the ordinary people together. Such leisure was not limited to the man, for the women could also attend; the few literate women around the court were concerned with reading, writing, citing or talking on religion. Our knowledge on the daily of the women in the Ottoman Empire is, however, severely limited (Faroqhi, 2005).

Another site for pleasure and leisure since the 16th century was the coffee houses (Akkach, 2011; Çaksu, 2007; Faroqhi, 2005; Karababa and Ger, 2010; Mikhail, 2007; Sadji, 2007). The earliest examples of coffeehouses appeared in Mecca and Cairo in the 1510s. After the Ottoman conquest of Arab lands, they became popular in Istanbul in early 1550s, quickly spreading all over Istanbul, and even to small towns in Anatolia (Faroqhi 1986; Karababa and Ger, 2010). Coffeehouses thus emerged as alternative sites for the Ottoman Muslim men to gather, read, cite, talk, discuss and spend time playing games such as backgammon, dominoes or chess. In other words, coffeehouses replaced the dervish lodges for men, who formerly spent most of their time in prescribed spaces such as work, mosque, dervish lodge, and home. The barbers used those places as shops, while the jannisaries, junkies, devoted disciples and dervishes gradually started to frequent these sites. Traditional performers, the *meddah*[11] and the *köçek*[12], performed their plays in there. As the coffeehouses started to gain a new role by becoming the centres of political opposition, they were frequently prohibited, and sometimes continued to function secretly.[13]

Despite the importance of reading and writing as intellectual leisure among the elites, there was not an established printing press in the Ottoman Empire until the late 19th century.[14] The Quran and other Islamic texts had been written and copied by hand, and possessed by the libraries of the dervish lodges. These texts were shared among the disciples, and read individually or together in the dervish lodges. The print journals and books, on the other hand, were shared in the coffee houses (Çaksu, 2007; Faroqhi, 2005; Işın, 1995; Mikhail, 2007; Rizk Khoury, 1999; Sadji, 2007).

The taverns served as yet another type of entertainment places, definitely more marginalized forms of entertainment for the non-Muslim population of

Istanbul, as wine-drinking was strictly prohibited by Islamic law. This prohibition, however, was not completely effective, for the Muslims from the lower strata, but also often dervishes, janissaries and poets from the *ulema* were frequenters of these taverns. It should be reminded that these places were solely for the male population. Moreover, the Turkish shadow theatre, the *tuluat*[15] theatres, and the *meddah* shows clearly appealed as entertainments to the Muslims, specifically in the Ramadan evenings. Modern western theatre and cinema were also introduced to the cultural life in Istanbul in the 19th century.

The *Turkish hamam*[16] can be added as another form of pleasure and leisure, specific to the Ottomans. The *hamam* is a place for rest and relief for men, but for women it has a dual function. For the Ottoman women, who did not have a life outside the house, going to the bath served as a kind of meeting activity: they prepared for this special occasion with foods, drinks, cloths, and bathing stuff, and went to the bath together with their daughters, sisters, acquaintances, neighbours and housemaids, if they had any. In this context, the *hamams* also serve as a place to 'show off'. More importantly, they functioned as a place for young women that have reached marrying age to present themselves, and for the women relatives of young men to observe them. This custom is still alive in Anatolian towns.

In addition to all these forms of pleasure and leisure, the Sultan and the court usually organized public ceremonies and festivals. Such collective enjoyments and entertainments were usually held for special occasions, such as military successes, or for dynastic events, such as the birth or circumcision ceremony of the crown prince and Sultan's sons, or the weddings of the Sultan's sisters and daughters. These ceremonies and festivities, especially the grandiose ones participated by the whole city population, were very important to serve as a means of legitimizing the Sultan's imperial power. Such events included the guild parades, from the smiths to taxidermists, and performances from fireworks to conjurers, parades, or sports games, Turkish shadow shows, the *meddah* and the *köçek*, or the clowns and acrobats; dinner was served to all, whether rich or poor, elite or ordinary folk, Muslim or non-Muslim (Faroqhi, 2005, 2006; IŞın, 1995). Indeed, the Ottoman ceremonies and festivals suspended all the distinctions of everyday life, and ultimately demonstrated and presented the sultan's established authority. These entertainments were generally continued for several days, sometimes even more than one or two weeks. The most regular festivals were the religious ones, which were organized in the evenings of the Ramadan months, or during the *Eid al Fitr* and *Eid al Adha*. In the words of Evliya Çelebi:

> There have been such amusements and pleasures on these green fields that no words can fully describe. All gentry, noblemen and prodigal sons of the plutocrats of Istanbul adorned the valley with more than 3,000 tents. Every night these tents were illuminated with thousands of candles, oil lamps and lanterns. In the evening the leading groups were entertained by musicians, singers, minstrels and performers ... until sunrise while 100,000 fireworks adorned the sky with lightning, stars, butterflies, etc. and the entire Kağıthane was bathed in this radiant splendor. Guns were fired from dawn to dusk. Besides these tents, scattered along the two banks of the Kağıthane River, were more than 2,000

shops vending not only foods and drinks but also myriad valuables. Every day the clowns, jesters, jongleurs, bear, monkey, donkey and dog trainers, puppet shows, birdmen, and sword eaters, about 360 entertainers performed and made great profit. Four janissary platoons were assigned by the palace to maintain order in this area. Most of these janissaries used to swim in the Kağıthane River.[17]

A final leisure activity, unique to the Ottoman or the Middle East neighbourhoods, could also be included to the list of leisure activities summarized above. This relates to the habit of gathering in front of the doors of houses or shops, or at the street corners. This habit can be observed in the gravures and miniatures or in the accounts of European travellers. This habit has ceased to exist as the traditional neighbourhood structures and relations in cities were broken with the advent of urbanization and modernization.

One final note should be made with regard to women's leisure, for all the leisure activities explained above are predominantly part of the men's everyday life. The scarcity of information about the lives and daily routines of women can be compensated to an extent by reading between the lines of the general studies on everyday life, and social and cultural life. The daily routine of a woman is typically arranged according to when the man of the house leaves and come back to home (Faroqhi, 2005, 2006; Işın, 1995). For a woman of lower-classes, the time when the man is out is occupied by the housework, daily tasks of cleaning, and cooking for the whole family. What would constitute an entertainment in this routine could at most be a visit to the next door to chat with neighbours. For the women of the court, however, it is more plausible to talk about leisure and pleasure (Faroqhi, 2005). For the few literate women of the ruling class, activities of intellectual leisure, such as reading and writing about poetry, and history and literature of the Ottoman Empire and Europe, are possible. What is unique to these women is the needlework or embroidery. Sophisticated and challenging handiworks, such as tambour and lacework, are mentioned as a serious and prominent leisure activity for the women of the court, and higher-classes (Işın, 1995). The delegation of the daily routines and housework to the maids may be assumed to enable these women to engage in such activities. Women in lower-classes, on the other hand, were occupied with such handiwork only with the spread of domestic appliances.

In conclusion, it does not seem plausible to speak of leisure in the Ottoman era, in its current sense, but we should note that the activities mentioned can provide a guide in considering the leisure of the middle class in today's Ankara. In the next section, a general account of leisure in modern Turkey is provided, followed by the presentation of the findings of the field research.

Through the Modern Turkey

The first implications of an evolution towards a western style in social and cultural life in the Ottoman Empire emerged in the first half of the 18th century, but gained prominence particularly in the mid-19th century. The major factor behind this transformation was the influence of capitalism already established in Europe, affecting the patterns of consumption, and everyday life and leisure outside as well as inside Istanbul (Aktüre, 2001; Bali, 2008; Etöz, 1998, 2006;

Faroqhi, 2005, 2005; Karababa and Ger, 2010; Kezer, 1999; Orçan, 2002). A second factor is the weakening of religion and traditions as the major regulators of everyday life, being replaced with the rules of modern life. In this period, Istanbul, Beyoğlu and Pera have become the centres of the transformation in patterns of consumption, entertainment, and leisure. The shop windows along the avenues started to exhibit Western-style commodities and fashion, while the number of theatres offering Western-style plays and operas increased. The shows in the coffeehouses also started to change, influenced by Western-style plays and operas. Furthermore, newspapers and magazines in the Ottoman language were growing, novels and stories were being published.

The differences between men and women, however, remained. For the men, Western-style leisure activities started to replace the gatherings before the shops, religious or historical stories shared in the mosques or lodges, or the hours of joy in the hamams. Wandering along the streets of Pera in Western clothes, watching shop windows, and sending time at newly opened patisseries have become common among upper-class men. Coffeehouses started to present shows that imitated Western plays, and operas. Upper-class and ordinary Muslim started to visit wine-serving taverns more frequently. Picnics in leisure gardens or boat-trips along the Bosporus or the Golden Horn have become more popular. With the spread of printing, intellectual leisure also started to transform, as the reading and discussion of newspapers and stories in coffeehouses replaced the intellectual activities performed in dervish lodges.

The most drastic change and transformation, however, concerns the daily life of women. The Ottoman women started to gradually leave the house in the 19th century, with the women of the court leading. This includes merely the women gaining visibility, however, rather than their participation in the working life. Women in modern clothes, that is, can now be seen in Pera, even if rarely, among those shopping, watching the shop windows, or sitting at the patisseries. Women can be seen outside, inside closed carriages, wandering in leisure gardens, or boat-tripping along the golden Horn. Until the Republican era, the most significant indicator regarding the daily life of women, even for the royal family members, is their visibility in public. Apart from that, the daily routines and habits within the house remained quite the same, for both the court members and the ordinary women. These changes, for men and women, started mostly in Istanbul, spreading gradually to other cities of the Empire in Anatolia and the Balkans.

Arguably, the real transformation in daily life and leisure took place in the Republican era, with certain turning points. The early Republican period, between 1920s and 1940s, was characterized with the adoption of the fundamental elements of the transformation in everyday life and leisure, and efforts towards spreading them throughout the country. The political transformation from a monarchical empire to a modern republic and the constitution of its ideological apparatus were accompanied with the social and cultural reforms by the young state aiming at the social transformation from a traditional agricultural society to a modern one.

A significant change in this process was the replacement of Istanbul as the capital with Ankara, a small central Anatolian city with an economy basically of agriculture and husbandry (Aydın, Emiroğlu, Türkoğlu and Özsoy, 2005: 338–378; Etöz, 1998: 81–91; Etöz, 2006: 11–42; Şenyapılı, 2004; Şenyapılı, 2005). Ankara of the time suffered serious deprivations, due to lack of housing, infrastructure, fresh water in houses, or roads and public transportation (Aydın, Emiroğlu, Türkoğlu and Özsoy, 2005: 378–450; Esendal, 1957; Karaosmanoğlu, 2006a, 2006b; Şenyapılı, 2004: 22). A new city began to be constructed outside the old city, which was protected, but not changed or renovated (Tekeli, 1994; Tekeli, Şenyapılı and Güvenç, 1991: 53–95; Tunçer, 2001: 75). The new city started to develop with the planning and construction of a series of urban structures, such as streets, avenues, squares, public spheres, leisure and recreation parks (Cengizkan, 2002, 2004, 2005a, 2005b, 2006).

After being designated as the new capital city, Ankara has gone through a remarkable transformation in its social and cultural life. Particularly, there was an influx of people with degrees in higher education, who had already internalized the Western norms of social and cultural life. These were called by the native people of Ankara as 'strangers' (Aydın, Emiroğlu, Türkoğlu and Özsoy, 2005; Esendal, 1957; Karaosmanoğlu, 2006a, 2006b; Şenol Cantek, 2003; Şenyapılı, 2004, 2005). The strangers had a crucial role in the reconstruction of Ankara's social and cultural life in line with the westernized Republican ideology, with reflections in the entertainment culture both during the day and at night. The secular Republican ideology and modern westernized social and cultural norms were combined and diffused within the everyday life of old Ankara, reflecting a mental life, as described by Simmel (1950), and a mode of urban daily life, mentioned in Wirth (1938). A by-product of the formation of such a social and cultural life in modern Ankara was a major line of segregation between the natives of the city and the strangers, or the newcomers. The natives were accustomed to the daily life of a typical traditional small town, while the newcomer republican elites constructed, and lived in a modern, westernized, and secular everyday life.

The beginnings of the construction of a Western-style modern everyday life and pleasure had already been observed in the transformation of the Pera district during the late Ottoman period. The provincial life of this small Anatolian town was confronted with the influx of restaurants, patisseries, coffeehouses, taverns, and casinos as well as theatres and cinemas. The newcomers from Istanbul and İzmir were actively engaged in the reconstruction of everyday life (Aydın, Emiroğlu, Türkoğlu and Özsoy, 2005; Bahar, 2003; Esendal, 1957; Karaosmanoğlu, 2006a, 2006b; Şenol Cantek, 2003; Şenyapılı, 2004, 2005). A significant dimension in this process that should not be ignored is the 'regulative role of the state'. In its attempt toward harmonization with European codes, such as the adoption of the metric system, the young Republican administration regulates the lives of both the elite, by constructing practices of pleasure and leisure compatible with the functioning of the public administration, and of the ordinary folk. Men and women are taught the manners required by the modern civilization day and night, at home and in public. Women are given the additional task of the organization and management of the house and leisure time.

Perhaps the most significant change in modern daily life from the Empire to the Republic has been the participation of women in working life. Now pleasure and leisure gained a real meaning for women, and they were introduced to activities like needlework or reading, activities that were once spared for women of the ruling class. Participation in working life also allowed the women to discover new things to do outside the necessities of family, work, and social life.

A second turning point emerges in the wake of the Second World War. By this time, a significant portion of the population had been urbanized, experiencing and adopting the necessities of modern life to a certain extent. The extensive changes in the aftermath of the War, particularly the mechanization of agriculture, led to an influx of hue populations into the cities, where they also started to experience the modern life. The involvement of the state in the modernization and regulation of everyday life has gone through a change. In general, the newcomers attempted to create their leisure habits through their relationships at work or by imitating their neighbours or relatives. Those newcomers that could be employed in the public sector started to live a life similar to the already urbanized population. The men employed in the informal sectors started to frequent coffeehouses in their neighbourhoods as places of leisure and pleasure, while women who were mostly working as day labourers imitated the owners of the houses they were cleaning. These women were mostly engaged in those activities they newly learned in their free time. They included cooking, child care, sewing and needlework for the family and for preparing trousseau for daughters and sons, which were also functional in supporting the budget and maintenance of the household. The newly urbanized population, even if rarely, adopt the prime form of leisure and go for picnics in weekends or on holidays. With the increase in literacy, reading western literature, and listening to music also started to be expressed as free time activities, or hobbies. All these practices constructed in the early republican period were also containing the roots of the leisure habits of the current urban middle class.

The period starting in 1980s was a further turning point, whereby Turkish economy started a closer integration with the world economy, accompanied by the effects of worldwide social, economic, and cultural transformations. What follows is that current changes of leisure are linked with the transformations of social, cultural and economic structures, and thus of work and urban occupational structure. In recent studies, researchers in both academia and media (e.g. Ayata, 2002, 2010; Bali, 2004; Karademir-Hazır, 2008; Şimşek, 2005, 2010) are particularly interested in the social groups employed in new jobs in the service sector – the so-called 'new middle class'.

The recent transformations of urban culture and urban life, in its various dimensions, have been subjected to various studies (Acar and Ayata, 2002; Ayata, 2002, 2010; Ayata and Ayata, 2000; Doğuç, 2006; Durakbaşa and Cindoğlu, 2002; Kandiyoti, 2002; Kandiyoti and Saktanber, 2002; Özyeğin, 2002). In this literature, lifestyle is generally discussed in relation to everyday routines and habits, or 'consumption patterns, cultural consumption, entertainment, meeting and eating out, leisure activities and hobbies'. These discussions carry a parallelism with what Bourdieu conceptualises as 'stylized everyday life'. This 'stylized everyday life' or 'lifestyles' can be defined as the ways disposable income is spent, or as the way time and money are spent for pleasure, entertainment and cultural consumption. In line with this, recent works focus on everyday life practices and daily routines in Turkey – such as leisure activities and hobbies, sports and outdoor activities, habits of eating and drinking out, meeting out with family members and friends, visiting shopping centres and malls not only for shopping but also for dining, socializing, strolling the shop windows, or for entertainment in theatres or concert halls (Akçaoğlu, 2008; Ayata, 2002, 2010; Bali, 2004; Karademir-Hazır, 2009; Öncü, 2002; Şimşek, 2005, 2010; Tutalar, 2008). All these new habits and routines in everyday life construct and display distinctive tastes, lifestyles and leisure.

Leisure in Modern Turkey

While everyday life and leisure in western forms in İstanbul was the result of the integration between the capital city and European economy in the second half of 19th century after this time (Toprak, 1995: 25–28), their spread in Ankara occurred after 1923 when it was announcement as the capital of newly established Republic. In that time, Ankara was typically a small Central Anatolian city with an economy basically of agriculture and husbandry, and a rural social and cultural life (Etöz, 1998: 81–91; Etöz, 2006: 11–42; Şenyapılı, 2004; Aydın, Emiroğlu, Türkoğlu and Özsoy, 2005: 338–378). Ankara of the time suffered serious deprivations, due to lack of housing, infrastructure, fresh water in houses, or roads and public transportation (Aydın, Emiroğlu, Türkoğlu and Özsoy, 2005: 378–450; Esendal, 1957; Karaosmanoğlu, 2006a, 2006b; Şenyapılı, 2004: 22), and a new city began to be constructed outside the old city, which was protected, but not changed or renewed (Tekeli, 1994; Tekeli, Şenyapılı and Güvenç, 1991: 53–95; Tunçer, 2001: 75).

A city cannot be defined merely through population size, and the existence of urban structures, but should be considered as a social entity (Wirth, 1938). Becoming a capital city, in that sense, required not only the establishment of state and public institutions, but also necessitated both educated/skilled and uneducated/unskilled labour to carry out various functions. Thus, Ankara had started to attract many educated or uneducated people from Istanbul, and other big or small cities of rural Anatolia. This also meant the coming of highly educated people, who had internalized Western social and cultural life, and these newcomers had been called by the native people of Ankara as 'strangers' (Aydın, Emiroğlu, Türkoğlu and Özsoy, 2005; Esendal, 1957; Karaosmanoğlu, 2006a, 2006b; Şenol Cantek, 2003; Şenyapılı, 2004, 2005). The strangers have a crucial role in the construction of the Republican and westernized ideology in Ankara's social and cultural life and in the entertainment culture both during the day and at night in urban life. The secular Republican ideology and the modern, westernized social and cultural life combined and diffused within the everyday life of the old Ankara, reflecting the mental life, as Simmel (1950) stated, and the mode of urban daily life, as Wirth (1938) mentioned. An obvious differentiation had emerged between the native people of Ankara, and the strangers: While native people had typical traditional, small town daily routines, the strangers as the elites of the Republic set out to live a modern, westernized, and secular everyday life. In the early Republican period, there were few meeting places, such as taverns, casinos, restaurants, patisseries and café houses. The strangers, especially those coming from İstanbul and İzmir, constantly complained of the poverty of social and cultural life in Ankara. In response, a new way of social and cultural urban life would be constituted and shaped by the new inhabitants and their participation, in such places as restaurants, balls, taverns and casinos during the night, as well as cinemas, theatres, and operas (Aydın, Emiroğlu, Türkoğlu and Özsoy, 2005; Bahar, 2003; Esendal, 1957; Karaosmanoğlu, 2006a, 2006b; Şenol Cantek, 2003; Şenyapılı, 2004, 2005).

Considering the academic literature on Turkey, lifestyle is generally discussed in relation to everyday routines and habits, or 'consumption patterns, cultural consumption, entertainment, meeting and eating out, leisure activities and hobbies'. These discussions carry a parallelism with what Bourdieu conceptualises as 'stylized everyday life'. Therefore, in discussing lifestyles, recent works focus on everyday life practices and daily routines in Turkey – such as leisure activities and hobbies, sports and outdoor activities, habits of eating and drinking out, meeting out with family members and friends, visiting shopping centres and malls not only to shop but also to eat, meet, stroll, window shop and entertain in places such as cinema, theatre, concerts, etc. (Akçaoğlu, 2008; Ayata, 1988, 2002, 2007, 2010a, 2010b, 2010c, 2010d, 2010e; Bali, 2004; Karademir-Hazır, 2009; Öncü, 2002; Şimşek, 2005, 2010a, 2010b, 2010c; Tutalar, 2008). The transformations of urban culture and urban life, in various dimensions, have been subjected to scrutiny (Acar and Ayata, 2002; Ayata, 1988, 2002; Ayata and Ayata, 1996, 2000; Doğuç, 2006; Durakbaşa and Cindoğlu, 2002; Kandiyoti and Saktanber, 2002; Özyeğin, 2002). Actually, 'stylized everyday life' or 'lifestyles' can be defined as the ways disposable income is spent, or how the spending time and money for pleasure, entertainment and cultural consumption, eating, drinking, meeting out with friends and family members, and holiday habits. While they hold an important place in visual media, newspapers, periodicals as well as television programs, the broadcast of private TV channels has been a turning point since the 1990s. All these new habits and routines in everyday life construct and display distinctive tastes, lifestyles and leisure. Actually, tastes cover all preferences from clothing to entertainment, from reading to watching television, etc. in everyday life. Besides these, in the context of the study, tastes refer to different attitudes from cultural consumption, hobbies, entertainment and leisure.

Leisure in the Turkish Middle Class Fractions

This section depicts the leisure habits of each middle class fraction in relation with their positioning in social space according to the composition and volume of their capitals, from the lower to the upper.

The Lower/Bitter Middle Class: The members of this stratum do not go out for picnics, sports activities, circuses, concerts or dining; they do not have hobbies or leisure habits regarding literature, music, photography or any other fine art, nor are they in the habit of reading, or listening to music. One informant, for instance, sufficed to say 'I used to deal with the garden!' The few activities listed, other than watching TV, include housework like cleaning or ironing, taking care of children, grandchildren or the old, playing with children, spending time with the family. This fraction is, moreover, strikingly immobile. They almost never wander in the city; they have never visited the great mosques, the old Castle, or the *Anıtkabir* (the mausoleum of Mustafa Kemal Atatürk, the founder of the Republic).[18] One exception to this is the visits to the hometown every 3–5 years. As one interviewee puts it: 'I never go beyond Dışkapı! But my daughter goes to cinemas or whatever'. The only instance of eating out for another interviewee was when they had to go to the hospital. While the men in this fraction have some mobility due to work, women's daily life is centred on the family, relatives, and TV. In short, the leisure habits of this stratum are 'struck between housework, family and neighbours', and they are 'repressed by the needs, the line between enjoyment and doing what is required becomes blurred'. This, in turn, corresponds with the 'taste of necessities', defining the taste of the lower class.

The Resentful/Middle Middle Class: Thanks to the working experience, the leisure habits in this fraction correspond perfectly with the aforementioned opposition of family, and working life. As employees, the members of this fraction have annual leaves, hence vacation habits. On these vacations, they visit their elders in their hometowns, they have some hobbies or regular sports activities, and they occasionally dine out, or go to brunches in weekends. More significantly, they have various habits and activities that they do solely for enjoyment in their free time – ranging from picnics, to reading, listening to music, watching sports, playing cards, smoking *nargile,* handiworks such as needlework, lacework, embroidery, wood painting, marbling, or growing pigeons.

In describing the tasks related to family and the house, like cooking, cleaning, child care or playing with children, women in this fraction do not offer any expression of fondness or content; on the contrary, they emphasize that they must perform them whether they like it or not. Men and women in this fraction seldom perform, though they are fully informed about how to access if they would want to, various sorts of habits and activities – such as literature, playing musical instruments, painting, sculpture, theatre or other fine arts, chess, crosswords, card games, sports like basketball, volleyball, swimming, scuba diving, or tennis. They are also informed about relatively more sophisticated personal and team sports, such as trekking, skating, camping, climbing, rafting, riding, golf, or taekwondo, though they can neither spare neither money nor time for them. Yet they encourage their children to acquire such habits, deeming them helpful for developing their physical, intellectual, and social skills. This hope is reflected in one interviewee's words: 'We could not go, but I am sending my son to all courses I could. Even to skating courses. After all, he should reap the benefits of living in Ankara. He should play an instrument, meet with different circles.' In the end, the resentful/middle middle class strives to equip their children with 'popular' skills and habits that they themselves envied but could not acquire.

The Upper/Contemptuous Middle Class: The members of this fraction have an extensive list of hobbies and leisure habits – they regularly perform some sports, such as tennis or swimming; they meet with friends at the food courts of luxurious malls, where cuisines of various countries are served; they customarily read, listen to music org o to theatres, and have extensive knowledge on various branches of fine arts, some even practice them. Sparing for those activities they enjoy is always desired, though they seldom have the time. Perhaps as compensation, they encourage their children to engage in activities reflecting a higher level of taste, and more expensive – this may be some sort of elite fine arts, such as playing cello or piano, or some extreme sports like rafting or sailing. They usually employ others to help in housework, yet they may occasionally cook for fun, otherwise neither men nor women in this fraction speak of any home-based habits or activities. In this context, the upper/contemptuous middle class has, if not by themselves, then for their children, leisure habits that correspond to a 'mall- and sports-centred' and 'average but dissident' taste.

The Well-Off/Happy Middle Class: Holiday for this fraction means extreme vacations abroad; gatherings with friends are usually outside, but houses are not completely closed to visits; in parties/receptions/gatherings organized at home, for small or big groups, hosts may cook some exotic dishes they learned abroad or at a cooking class (Karadoğan, 2010), accompanied with foreign drinks; when engaged in sports, it is with skiing, golfing, or sailing. The leisure habits and activities of the well-off/happy middle class, in short, correspond to an 'outward and extreme sports oriented' and 'unique/elite' taste; they construct the distinction of this fraction by freeing them from all necessities, and differentiating them from all other classes and strata.

Conclusion

This study has presented a description of the fractions of the middle class, according to the categories reflecting their levels of capital, the forms of employment and occupations, and their composition and volume. Considering through the development of leisure in the Turkish modernization process, the cloudings-clusterings-groupings formed by the positioning of the categories on the correspondence analysis graph, together with the distances among each other, the middle class living in these districts of Ankara is divided into four levels. What this study reveals, within the limits of its sample, is that the middles class is fragmented, and that each fraction displays different leisure habits.

And what do these four fractions for leisure? The lower/bitter middle class looks after children; the resentful/middle middle class prepares trousseau for the daughters; the contemptuous/upper middle class meets with friends at malls, without being bothered by anyone; and the well-off/happy middle class – they sail to freedom!

Notes

1. This study is based on data collected for the author's PhD. Dissertation, *Urban Middle Class, Lifestyle and Taste In Keçiören and Çankaya, Ankara: Distinction Through Home Furniture, Furnishing And Decoration* in Middle East Technical University (METU), Graduate School of Social Sciences, Department of Sociology, Spring 2012, (Advisor: Professor Dr Sencer Ayata and Co-Advisor: Assoc. Professor Dr Helga Rittersber-Tılıç). An earlier version was presented with the title 'Leisure as *Distinction* in the Turkish Middle Class: A Case of Ankara, Turkey', at the Second ISA Forum of Sociology, 1–4 August 2012, Buenos Aires, Argentina.
2. Social Capital: S1 (Lower), S2 (Middle), S3 (Upper), S4 (Highest); Cultural Capital: C1 (Lower), C2 (Middle), C3 (Upper), C4 (Highest); Economic Capital: EC1 (Lower), EC2 (Middle), EC3 (Upper), EC (Highest)

3. The Ottoman Empire was originally founded by Turkish tribes under Osman Bey, in the north-western Anatolia around 1299. In the 16th and 17th centuries, the Ottoman Empire had stretched its dominance from the southern borders of the Holy Roman Empire to Vienna, Hungary, and the Polish-Lithuanian regions in the north, to Yemen and Eritrea in the south; and from Algeria in the west to Azerbaijan in the east. It controlled much of southeast Europe, Western Asia and North Africa. Following its dissolution in early 20th century, the Republic of Turkey emerged as a modern state in the remaining territory, in 1920s.
4. The transition from the Empire to the Republic, in its various dimensions within modernization process, has been subject to a vast literature, too complex to be summarized in a few paragraphs. Numerous works have studied the social, economic, cultural and political dimensions of the modernization processes and Turkish politics from the Ottoman Empire to modern Turkey. Various approaches employed included 'Enlightenment progress discourse, coalesced in Orientalist scholarship, and acquired further academic rigour in formulations such as the Marxian 'Asiatic mode of production' and 'Oriental despotism', and Weberian-inspired modernizationist and developmentist theories' (Sajdi, 2007: 4). This study will mention only the literature that is directly related to the socio-historical formation of everyday life and leisure during the Turkish modernization process, and will not attempt to provide a summary of this vast area of research.
5. The sample of the field research explained in the study does not include any non-Muslim informant, reflecting the current demographics of Turkey.
6. These terms literally mean the elites, and the folk/people, respectively.
7. *Tımar* is a land granted by the Ottoman Sultans between the fourteenth and sixteenth centuries, with annual tax revenue of less than 20,000 *akçes* (Retrieved from http://en.wikipedia.org/wiki/Timar).
8. The notables in a town or village.
9. Since there were no regular population records or polls during the Ottoman Empire, there are only estimations about the population, which put the numbers around 4–5 million for the 14th century, from 12–13 million to 20–22 million for the 16th century, and 15–16 million before the First World War. In the 19th century, approximately 20 per cent of the Ottoman population were residing in the cities, with the remaining 80 per cent in rural areas (Faroqi, 2005, 2006). As of 2007, in contrast, the people living in cities are almost 80 per cent of the whole population, qualifying Turkey as an urban population.
10. Sariyannis Marinos, 'Recreation and entertainment in Constantinople in the early Modern period', 2008, *Encyclopaedia of the Hellenic World*, Constantinople. url: http://www.ehw.gr/l.aspx?id=11512
11. Storyteller.
12. Young male dancer performing erotic dances in women's dance costumes.
13. For studies on the coffeehouses as political places, and spaces for the development of public sphere, in a Habermasian sense, see Çaksu (2007), Işın (1995, 2000), Karababa and Ger (2010), Kırlı (2001, 2009), Kömeçoğlu (2001), Mikhail (2007).
14. The first print-machine was used in 1719–1720 by *İbrahim Müteferrika*, but it could not function properly, due to the general enmity towards the printing of Quran, and other Islamic texts.
15. Turkish popular or improvisional theatre.
16. The Turkish bath.

17. Niki Gramm, 'Pleasure jaunts in Ottoman times', *Hurriyet Daily News*, 27 October 2012.
18. The free transportation offered by the municipality for more than 15 years, at least on religious and national holidays, does not seem have provided the necessary incentive.

References

Acar, F., and Ayata, A. (2002). Discipline, success and stability: The Reproduction of Gender and Class in Turkish Secondary Education. In D. Kandiyoti and A. Saktanber (eds), *Fragments of Culture: The Everyday of Modern Turkey* (pp. 90–111). New Brunswick, NJ: Rutgers University Press.

Akkach, S. (2010). Leisure Gardens, Secular Habits: The Culture of Recreation in Ottoman Damascus, *METU, JFA*, (2010/1) (pp. 67–80).

Anheier, H.K., Gerhards, J., and Romo, F.P. (1995). Forms of Capital and Social Structure in Cultural Fields: Examining Bourdieu's Social Topography. *AJS (American Journal of Sociology)*, 100(4), 859–903.

Arslan, Z. (2010). *Urban Middle Class, Lifestyle and Taste in Keçiören and Çankaya, Ankara: Distinction Through Home Furniture, Furnishing And Decoration.* (Unpublished Ph.D. Thesis, Middle East Technical University, Ankara, Turkey.

Arslan, Z. (2012). *Leisure as Distinction In Turkish Middle Class: A Case of Ankara, Turkey*, Oral Presentation, The Second ISA Forum of Sociology, 1–4 August 2012, Buenos Aires, Argentina.

Ayata, S. (2002) The New Middle Class and the Joys of Suburbia. In: D. Kandiyoti and A. Saktanber (eds), *Fragments of Culture: The Everyday of Modern Turkey* (pp. 25–42). New Brunswick, NJ: Rutgers University Press.

Ayata, S. (27 May 2010). Finansal Krizden Toplumsal Krize, *Radikal*(downloaded in 27 May 2010 from http://www.radikal.com.tr/Radikal.aspx?aType= RadikalHaber Detay&Date=27.5.2010&ArticleID=999015&CategoryID=104).

Ayata, S., and Ayata, A.G. (2000). Toplumsal tabakalaşma, mekœnsal ayrışma ve kent kültürü. In F. Atacan, F. Ercan, H. Kurtuluş and M. Türkay (eds), *Mübeccel Kıray için yazılar* (pp. 151–173). İstanbul: Bağlam.

Akçaoğlu, A. (2008). *The Mallification of Urban Life in Ankara: A Case of Ankamall.* Unpublished master's thesis, Middle East Technical University, Ankara.

Aktüre, S. (2001). 1830'dan 1930'a Ankara'da Günlük Yaşam. In Y. Yavuz (ed.), *Tarih İçinde Ankara II* (pp. 35–74). Ankara: ODTÜ Mimarlık Fakültesi Yayınları.

Anheier, H.K., Gerhards, J., and Romo, F.P. (1995). Forms of Capital and Social Structure in Cultural Fields: Examining Bourdieu's Social Topography. *AJS (American Journal of Sociology)*, 100(4), 859–903.

Arun, Ö. (2009). Yaşlı bireyin Türkiye serüveni: Turkiye'de yaşlı bireyler arasında kültürel sermaye dağılımı. *Gaziantep Üniversitesi Sosyal Bilimler Dergisi*, 8(1), 77–100. Retrieved from http://sbe.gantep.edu.tr

Auslender, L. (1996). *Taste and Power: Furnishing Modern France*. Berkeley, Calif: University of California Press.

Ayata, A.G., and Ayata, S. (1996). Konut alanları, cemaat ilişkileri ve kent kültüründe kadınlar: Ankara araştırmasının sonuçları In E.M. Komut (ed.), *Diğerlerinin* konut sorunları, (pp. 65–70). Ankara: Chambers of Architects of Turkey.

Aydın, S., Emiroğlu, K., Türkoğlu, Ö., and Özsoy, E.D. (2005) *Küçük Asya'nın bin yüzü: Ankara*. Ankara: Dost.

Bennett, T. (2005). The historical universal: The Role of Cultural Value in the Historical Sociology of Pierre Bourdieu. *British Journal of Sociology*, 54(1), 141–163.

Bahar, B.L. (2003). *Efsaneden tarihe Ankara Yahudileri*. İstanbul: Pan.

Bali, R.N. (2004). *Tarz-ı hayattan life style'a: Yeni seçkinler, yeni mekânlar, yeni yaşamlar*. İstanbul: İletişim.

Bali, R.N. (2008). Mayer Mağazası ve Georg Mayer. In Georg Mayer (ed.), *Türk Çarşısı* (Y. Öztel, Trans.), İstanbul: Kitabevi.

Bennett, T. (2005). The Historical Universal: The Role of Cultural Value in the Historical Sociology of Pierre Bourdieu. *British Journal of Sociology*, 54(1), 141–163.

Boratav, K. (1995). *İstanbul ve Anadolu'dan sınıf profilleri*. İstanbul: Tarih Vakfı Yurt Yayınları.

Bourdieu, P. (1984). *Distinction: A Social Critique of the Judgment of Taste* (R. Nice, Trans.). London: Routledge. (Original work published 1979).

Bourdieu, P. (1985). Social Space and the Genesis of Groups. *Theory and Society*, 14(6), 723–744. Retrieved from http://www.jstor.org/stable/657373.

Bourdieu, P. (1986). The Forms of Capital. In J. Richardson (ed.), *Handbook of Theory and Research for the Sociology of Education* (pp. 241–258). New York: Greenwood Press.

Bourdieu, P. (1990). *Photography: A Middle Brow Art*. Stanford, CA: Stanford University Press.

Bourdieu, P. (2000). The Aesthetic Sense as the Sense of Distinction. In J.B. Schor and D.B. Holt (eds), *The Consumer Society Reader* (pp. 187–205). New York: The New Press.

Çaksu, A. (2007). Janissary Coffee Houses in Late Eighteenth-Century Istanbul, in *Ottoman Tulips, Ottoman Coffee. Leisure and Lifestyle in the Eighteenth Century*. London: I.B.Tauris. (pp. 117–132).

Cengizkan, A. (2002). Bağ Evi'nden Villa'ya: Ankara Keçiören Bağ Evleri ve Kent Konutu Tipolojisinde Dönüşüm. In A. Cengizkan (ed.), *Modernin Saati* (pp. 119–142). Ankara: Mimarlar Dernegi; İstanbul: Boyut Yayın Grubu.

Cengizkan, A. (2004). *Ankara'nın ilk planı*: 1924–25 Lörcher planı, kentsel mekan özellikleri, 1932 Jansen Planı'na ve bugüne katkıları, etki ve kalıntıları. Ankara: Ankara Enstitüsü Vakfı.

Cengizkan, A. (2005a). 1957 Yücel-Uybadın imar planı ve Ankara Şehir mimarisi. In T. Şenyapılı (ed.), *Cumhuriyet'in Ankara'sı* (pp. 24–59). Ankara: ODTÜ Yayıncılık.

Cengizkan, A. (2005b). Producing Ankara through Residential Architecture: Generating and Re-generating the City after 1975. In T. Korkmaz (ed.), *Architecture in Turkey Around 2000: Issues in Discourse and Practice* (pp. 33–62). Ankara: Chamber of Architects of Turkey.

Cengizkan, A. (2006). 1957 Yücel - Uybadın İmar Planı ve Ankara Şehir Mimarisi. In T. Şenyapılı (ed.), *Cumhuriyet'in Ankara'sı* (pp. 24–59). Ankara: ODTÜ Geliştirme Vakfı.

Crompton, R. (1996). *Class and Stratification: An Introduction to Current Debates*. Cambridge, Oxford: Polity Press.

de Certeau, M. (1984). *The Practice of Everyday Life*, Steven Rendall,(tr.), Berkeley:

Dimaggio, P. and Useem, M. (1978). Social Class and Arts Consumption: The Origins and Consequences of Class Differences in Exposure to the Arts in America. *Theory and Society*, 5(2), 141–161.

Doğuç, S. (2006). Yeni Orta Sınıfların Gözünde Zenginlik ve Yoksulluk. *Toplum ve Bilim*, 104, 73–91.

Durakbaşa, A., and Cindoğlu, D. (2002). Encounters at the Counter: Gender and the Shopping. In D. Kandiyoti and A. Saktanber (eds), *Fragments of Culture: The Everyday of Modern Turkey* (pp. 73–89). New Brunswick, NJ: Rutgers University Press.

Erimtan, C. (2007). The Perception of Saadabad: The 'Tulip Age' and Ottoman – Safavid Rivalry, in *Ottoman Tulips, Ottoman Coffee. Leisure and Lifestyle in the Eighteenth Century*. London: I.B.Tauris. (pp. 41–62)

Esendal, M.Ş. (1957). *Ayaşlı* ve Kiracıları. Ankara: Dost Yayınevi.

Etöz, Z. (1998). *19. yüzyıl Ankara'sında sosyal ve kültürel yaşam*. Unpublished doctoral dissertation, Ankara University, Ankara.

Etöz, Z. (2006). 19. yüzyıl Ankara'sında mahalleler ve gündelik yaşam. In F. Şenol Cantek (ed.), *Sanki Viran Ankara,* (pp. 11–43). İstanbul: İletişim.

Faroqhi, S. (2005). *Osmanlı kültürü ve gündelik yaşam: Ortaçağdan yirminci yüzyıla,* İstanbul: Türkiye Ekonomik ve Toplumsal Tarih Vakfı.

Faroqhi, S. (2006). *Osmanlı Şehirleri ve kırsal hayatı*, Emine Sonnur Özcan (Tr.) Ankara: DoğuBatı Yayınları.

Field, J. (2008). *Social Capital*. London, New York: Routledge.

Frisby, D. (1989). Simmel and Leisure. In C. Rojek (ed.), *Leisure for Leisure: Critical Essays* (pp. 75–92). New York: Routledge.

Gramm, N. (2012). Pleasure jaunts in Ottoman times, *Hurriyet Daily News*, 27 October 2012.

Halpern, D. (2005). *Social Capital*. Cambridge, Malden: Polity Press.

Hargreaves, J. (1989). The Promise and Problems of Women's Leisure and Sport. In: C. Rojek (ed.), *Leisure for Leisure: Critical Essays* (s. 130–150). New York: Routledge.

Holt, D.B. (1995). How Consumers Consume: A Typology of Consumption Practices. *The Journal of Consumer Research*, 22(1), 1–16.

Holt, D.B. (1998). Does Cultural Capital Structure American Consumption? *The Journal of Consumer Research*, 25, 1–25.

Holt, D.B. (2000). Does Cultural Capital Structure American Consumption. In J.B. Schor and D.B. Holt (eds), *The Consumer Society Reader* (pp. 187–205). New York: The New Press.

Holt, D.B. (2002). Why do brands cause trouble? A dialectical theory of consumer culture and branding. *The Journal of Consumer Research*, 29(1), 70–89.

Işın, E. (1995). *İstanbul'da Gündelik Hayat,* İstanbul: İletişim.

Kalaycıoğlu, H.S. (2011). Toplumsal yapı: toplumssal kurumlar, gruplar ve toplumsal değişme, In: *Dünden bugüne Türkiye'nin toplumsal yapısı*. Bursa: Dora Yayıncılık. (pp. 3–15).

Kalaycıoğlu, H.S., Kardam, F., Rittersberger-Tılıç, H., Çelik, K., and Türkyılmaz, S. (2008). *Ankara kent merkezinde toplumsal tabaklaşma, hareketlilik ve sosyoekonomik statü araştırması*. TÜBİTAK (Project No: SOBAG 104 K 039). Unpublished Research Report. Ankara, Türkiye.

Kalaycıoğlu, H.S., Kardam, F., Tüzün, S., and Ulusoy, M. (1998). Türkiye için Bir Sosyoekonomik Statü Ölçütü Geliştirme Yönünde Yaklaşım ve Denemeler. *Toplum ve Hekim*, 13(2), 126–137.

Kandiyoti, D. (2002). Pink Card Blues: Trouble and Strife at the Crossroads of Gender. In Deniz Kandiyoti and Ayşe Saktanber (eds), *Fragments of Culture: The Everyday of Modern Turkey* (pp. 277–293). New Brunswick, NJ: Rutgers University Press.

Kandiyoti, D., Saktanber, A. (eds). (2002). *Fragments of Culture: The Everyday of Modern Turkey*. New Brunswick, NJ: Rutgers University Press.

Karababa, E. and Ger, G. (2110). Early Modern Ottoman Coffeehouse Culture and the Formation of the Consumer Subject, *Copyright Journal of Consumer Research 2010*, (from http://www.provost.bilkent.edu.tr/guliz/karababa_ger_preprint.pdf)

Karademir-Hazır, I. (2009). *Different Facets of New Middle Classness: A Case Study in the City of Ankara*. Unpublished master's thesis, Middle East Technical University, Ankara.

Karadoğan, R. (2010). Kitchen aid ve ekmek makinesi: Yeni orta sınıf mutfakta. *Birikim*, 260, 60–65.

Karaosmanoğlu, Y.K. (2006a). *Ankara* (23rd ed.). İstanbul: İletişim.

Karaosmanoğlu, Y.K. (2006b). *Yaban* (53rd ed.). İstanbul: İletişim.

Karpat, K.H. (2003). *Türkiye'de toplumsal dönüşüm*. Ankara: İmge.

Katz-Gerro, T. (2002). Highbrow Cultural Consumption and Class Distinction in Italy, Israel, West Germany, Sweden and United States. *Social Forces*, 81(1), 207–229.

Katz-Gerro, T., and Shavit, Y. (1998). The Stratification of Leisure and Taste: Classes and Lifestyles in Israel. *European Sociological Review*, 14(4), 369–386.

Kelly, J. (1987). *Leisure, Identities and Interactions*, London: George Allen and Unwin.

Kezer, Z. (1999). *The making of a National Capital: Ideology and Socio-Spatial Practices in the Early Republican Ankara*. Unpublished doctoral dissertation, University of California, Berkeley.

Kırlı, C. (2001). *The Struggle Over Space: Coffeehouses of Ottoman Istanbul, 1780–1845*. Binghamton: State University of New York.

Kırlı, C. (2009). Kahvehaneler: Ondokuzuncu Yüzyıl Osmanlı İmparatorluğu'nda Kamuoyu, in *Osmanlı Kahvehaneleri: Mekân Sosyallik ve İktidar içinde*. İstanbul: Kitap Yayınevi (pp. 95–119).

Lamont, M. (1994). *Money, Morals, and Manners: The Culture of the French and American Upper-Middle Class*. Chicago: The University of Chicago Press.

Lefebvre, H. (1991). *Critique of Everyday Life* (Tr. John Moore). London: Verso.

Lefebvre, H. (1984). *Everyday Life in the Modern World* (Tr. Sacha Rabinovitch). New Brunswick, NJ, USA: Transaction Books.

Mikhail, A. (2007) The Heart's Desire: Gender, Urban Space and the Ottoman Coffee House, in *Ottoman Tulips, Ottoman Coffee. Leisure and Lifestyle in the Eighteenth Century*. London: I.B.Tauris. (pp. 133–170).

Moorhouse, H.F. (1989). Models of work, models of leisure, in C. Rojek (ed.), *Leisure for Leisure: Critical Essays* (pp. 15–36). New York: Routledge.

Orçan, M. (2004). *Osmanlı'dan günümüze modern Türk tüketim kültürü*. Ankara: Kadim.

Öncü, A. (2002). Global consumerism, security as public spectacle, and the cultural remapping of Istanbul in the 1990s. In D. Kandiyoti and A. Saktanber (eds), *Fragments of Culture: The Everyday of Modern Turkey* (pp. 171–190). New Brunswick, NJ: Rutgers University Press.

Özyeğin, G. (2002). The doorkeeper, the maid, and the tenant: Troubling encounters in the Turkish urban landscape. In D. Kandiyoti and A. Saktanber (eds), *Fragments of culture: The Everyday of Modern Turkey* (pp. 43–72). New Brunswick, NJ: Rutgers University Press.

Parkin, F. (1979). *Marxism and Class Theory: A Bourgeois Critique*. London: Tavistock.

Peterson, R.A. (1997a). Changing Representations of Status through Taste Displays. *Poetics*, 25, 71–73.

Peterson, R.A. (1997b). The Rise and Fall of Highbrow Snobbery as a Status Marker. *Poetics*, 25, 75–92.

Peterson, R.A. (2005). Problems in Comparative Research: The Example of Omnivorousness. *Poetics*, 33, 257–282.

Peterson, R.A., and Kern, R.M. (1996). Changing Highbrow Taste: From Snob to Omnivore. *American Sociological Review*, 61(5), 900–907.

Rizk Khoury, D. (1999). *Osmanlı İmparatorluğu'nda Devlet ve Taşra Toplumu, Musul,* 1540–1834. İstanbul: Tarih Vakfı Yayınları.

Rojek, C. (1989a). Leisure and 'the ruins of the bourgeoisie world'. In C. Rojek (ed.), *Leisure for Leisure: Critical Essays* (pp. 92–112). London: Macmillan Press Lmd.

Rojek, C. (1989b). Leisure time and leisure space. In C. Rojek (ed.), *Leisure for leisure: Critical Essays* (pp. 191–203). London: Macmillan Press Ltd.

Rojek, C. (1999). *Decentring Leisure: Rethinking Leisure Theory*. London: Sage.

Rojek, C. (2005). *Leisure Theory: Principles and Practices*. New York: Palgrave.

Rutt, A.H. (1955). *Home Furnishing* (2nd ed.). New York: John Wiley and Sons, Inc. and London: Chapman and Hall, Ltd.

Sabev, O. (Orhan Salih). (2007). The First Ottoman Turkish Printing Enterprise: Success or Failure?, in *Ottoman Tulips, Ottoman Coffe: Leisure and Lifestyle in the Eighteenth Century*. London: I.B.Tauris. (pp. 117–132).

Sajdi, (2007). *Ottoman Tulips, Ottoman Coffe: Leisure and Lifestyle in the Eighteenth Century*. London: I.B.Tauris.

Schapiro, M. (1953). Style. In A.L. Kroeber (ed.), *Anthropology Today: An Encyclopaedic Inventory* (pp. 287–311). Chicago: University of Chicago Press.

Şenol Cantek, L.F. (2003). *'Yaban'lar ve yerliler: Başkent olma sürecinde Ankara*. İstanbul: İletişim.

Şenyapılı Ö. (2005). Gençlik yıllarımın (ve öncesinin) Anakarasında eğlenme-dinlenme mekânları. In T. Şenyapılı (ed.), *Cumhuriyet'in Ankara'sı* (pp. 310–356). ODTÜ Yayıncılık: Ankara.

Şenyapılı T. (2004). *'Baraka'dan Gecekonduya: Ankara'da Kentsel Mekânın Dönüşümü:* 1923–1960. İstanbul: İletişim.

Şenyapılı T. (2005). Ankara kenti 'ikili yapısında' dönüşümler. In T. Şenyapılı (ed.), *Cumhuriyet'in Ankara'sı* (pp. 216–245). Ankara: ODTÜ Yayıncılık.

Simmel, G. (1950). The Metropolis and Mental Life. In K.H. Wolff (ed. and Trans.), *The Sociology of Georg Simmel* (pp. 24–31). Glencoe, Ill: Free Press.

Şimşek, A. (2005). *Yeni orta sınıf*. İstanbul: Epokhe.

Şimşek, A. (2010). Rahatı kaçmış, endişeli bir sınıf. Retrieved 6 June 2004, from (http://www.birgun.net/research_index.php?category_code=1275302137&news_code=1275302179&year=2010&month=05&day=31

Tekeli, İ. (1994). Ankara'nın başkentlik kararının ülkesel mekân organizasyonu ve toplumsal yapıya etkileri bakımından genel bir değerlendirilmesi. In E. Batur (ed.), *Ankara Ankara* (pp. 143–169). İstanbul: Yapı Kredi Yayınları.

Tekeli, İ., Şenyapılı, T., and Güvenç, M. (1991). *Ankara'da sanayi üretiminin tarihsel gelişim süreci*. Ankara: Milli Prodüktivite Merkezi Yayınları.

Toprak, Z. (1995). Tüketim Örüntüleri ve Osmanlı Mağazaları. *Cogito*, 5, 25–8.

Tunçer, M. (2001). Ankara'da tarihsel çevrenin korunmasına yönelik politikalar. In Y. Yavuz (ed.), *Tarih içinde Ankara II* (pp. 75–109). Ankara: ODTÜ Yayıncılık.

Tutalar, L. (2008). *Globalization and Shopping Malls in Ankara: Four Cases*. Unpublished master's thesis, Middle East Technical University, Ankara.

Veblen, T. (1992). *The Theory of the Leisure Class: An Economic Study of Institutions*. New Brunswick: Transaction Publishers. (Original work published 1899)

Veblen, T. (2005). *Conspicuous Consumption*. New York: Penguin Books.

Warde, A. (2006). Cultural Capital and the Place of Sport. *Cultural Trends*, 15(2/3), 107–122.

Warde, A., Wright, D., and Gayo-Cal, M. (2008). The Omnivorous Orientation in the UK. *Poetics*, 36, 148–165.

Wirth, L. (1938). Urbanism as a Way of Life. *The American Journal of Sociology*, 44(1), 1–24.

Wynne, D. (1998). *Leisure, Lifestyle, and the New Middle Class: A Case Study*. London, New York: Routledge.

Yanıklar, C. (2006). *Tüketimin sosyolojisi*. İstanbul: Birey.

Africa

12

From Precolonial, Colonial to Postcolonial

A Survey of African Leisure

VEENA SHARMA

This wide ranging title seems to presume that the word 'African' which can be used to define a singular over-arching entity, even though the Continent is made up of fifty four countries, each of which, in turn, consists of a variety of religious, ethnic and linguistic groups. As a consequence it seems to presuppose that there is something that could be called 'African' leisure. So, before going on to discuss leisure in Africa it becomes necessary to clarify as to what is meant by the terms 'leisure', 'Africa' and the phrase 'African leisure'. The essay recognises and asserts that leisure is not a monolithic idea drawn from Anglo-Euro-American models only, that it is a fluid evolving concept that takes varied forms in differing temporal, spatial, historical and cultural contexts. It emphasises that leisure is not a discrete entity occupying a space dissociated from historical experiences and other varied aspects of social and cultural life, and that it is not the monopoly of any one ethnic or racial group. Different peoples in different geographical and cultural situations have understood leisure in their own ways and devised methods for experiencing and actualising it, with or without using the term. In line with Akyeampong and Ambler the essay takes the idea of leisure to be a 'conceptual package,' and not a 'list of recreational activities',[1] that are often labelled as 'leisure activities'. It stresses the fact that leisure is not a 'fixed or natural category[2]' but a 'social and cultural construct', a 'fluid phenomenon' that draws from particular geographic, historical and economic situations. Leisure, as such, would mean different things to different peoples according to their location in space and time and the world views upheld by them. The attempt in this essay is to, again using Akyeampong's words, 'flesh out local perspectives in terms of choices made in particular contexts and the terminology used ... to explain these choices.[3]

The term 'African' (rather than the name of a particular country in Africa) has been used, even by Africans themselves, to express phenomena that arise from the Continent. As such there must be certain elements or characteristics that give credence to the word 'African'. Is it colour or race? Is it the common history of colonization – a 'gift of Europe' as Ali Mazrui called it[4] – that almost the whole continent suffered? Is it culture? Or is it some spiritual or metaphysical beliefs? What is it that connects Africa, particularly Africa south of the Sahara? In fact, the origins of the movement for equality and independence also started with the construction of a Pan-African identity calling for the liberation of 'Africa'. The movement did not make distinctions between countries or nations as geographic entities. It addressed the Continent of Africa and the African people. What then is Africa and Africainity?

Kwame Nkrumah the first President of Ghana, a great promoter of the Pan-African identity wrote that in spite of the great differences between Africans from different parts of the Continent the forces that united them were greater. He wrote, 'In meeting fellow Africans from all parts of the continent I am constantly impressed by how much we have in common. It is not just our colonial past, or the fact that we have aims in common, it is something which goes far deeper. I can best describe it as a sense of one-ness in that we are *Africans*.'[5] Despite his impassioned plea for and a belief in an African identity Nkrumah did not identify what he meant by that 'something ... deeper.'

Mazrui projects that one of the factors that united Africans may have been European cartography that by determining the boundaries of Africa made Africans look upon themselves as one in relation to the Europeans.[6] The shared geography (with all the differences in language and culture) and the shared history of colonization, according to Mazrui, mark an African identity. The European domination and the racism practised by the colonisers made the Africans look upon themselves as one entity.

Notwithstanding the colonial impact – a historical intervention of a few decades only which nevertheless brought changes greater than Africa had undergone in several centuries – there is something deeper that by and large connects Africans. Many reasons are extended for this. The cross-Continental migration due to the 'population explosion' caused by better varieties of food brought in by ships from Indonesia and other Asian seafarers, and due to better tools and weapons after the coming in of the iron-age during the middle of the first millennium B.C., caused an intermingling of peoples across 'western and central Sahara, between North Africa and the regions of the Niger river' and right down to the southern tip of Africa.[7] This movement brought about a 'diversity that is nonetheless rooted in a profound and ancient unity ... . Pan-African unity (as such) is a political ambition of modern times, but its roots go far back into the past'.[8] The political ambition, it may be argued, arose from the perceived fundamental unity of the people of the Continent.

While different migrant groups evolved their different socio-economic patterns and different rituals according to the geographic and climatic situations at hand, there remains, at a fundamental level, a world view that connects Africa. One may then, venture to say that there are similarities in metaphysical conceptions, approach to divinity, to the environment and to social structures and socio-religious practices which connect sub-Saharan Africans. Writing from the perspective of African philosophy Kwame Gyekye writes:

> I believe that in many areas of thought we can discern features of the traditional life and thought of the African peoples sufficiently common to constitute a legitimate and reasonable basis for the construction (or reconstruction) of a

philosophical system that may properly be called African – African not in the sense that every African adheres to it, but in the sense that that philosophical system arises from, and hence is essentially related to, African life and thought. Such a basis would justify a discourse in terms of 'African philosophy' ...'[9]

African Leisure

African leisure can then be looked at from several points of departure. It can be seen from the perspective of the world view and how it embeds into it leisure practices as a way of expressing interconnectedness of humans with each other and with the cosmos, and with the spiritual world. It can be viewed in terms of the metaphysical understanding of the universe and the ultimate goals of life set by Africans. Another way it can be looked at is by examining and analysing the idea of freedom – what it means in the African context and how it relates to leisure and leisure practices, and how the concept itself evolves with changing historical contexts and conditions. These analyses may get particularised due to the differing policies followed by the various colonial rulers. So, that which within the colonial situation may be perceived as leisure by one group, placed in a particular socio-economic-political situation, may be seen to be work by another group that is hierarchically differently situated within the same conditions. Relations of power and alternative understandings of what is 'moral' also tend to 'redraw the boundaries of difference'.[10]

As such, before proceeding it would be useful to cast a glance at the kinds of colonial intervention that different parts of Africa experienced.

Colonial Intervention

The colonial period in Africa can be looked at from the standpoint of the different kinds of policies imposed by the British, French and the Portuguese. The policies had specific implications for the evolution of leisure in these areas and for the Continent as a whole. While some experiences and the resultant responses were similar for the whole Continent, other policy measures led to differing results so far as the leisure experience and practices were concerned. In Anglophone Africa two types of colonies emerged, mainly due to climatic conditions – 'settlement' colonies and those in which small groups of business men, administrators, soldiers and missionaries lived in environments different from that of the 'mother' country.[11] Then there were the mining and the wage labour economies depending on the kind of resources that were to be extracted from the colony. France, on the other hand, 'followed a policy of assimilation aimed at producing an elite class ... introducing a favoured class of Africans to French culture and civilization and raising them to the status of Frenchmen, to avoid the rise of African nationalism in the territories under her rule'.[12] The policy led to the emergence of a small class of African elite, who imitated Western patterns of living and behaviour, while the bulk remained exploited and maltreated.

Portuguese territories, on their part, were the worst so far as the condition of locals was concerned. The 'indescribable misery' of the system of 'forced' labour in Angola was described by one of their own (i.e. by a Portuguese official) who was sent there to give a white-washed report on it, but he was so moved by the condition he witnessed that he wrote in 1947 (for which he was thrown into prison):

> ... the situation is worse than simple slavery. Under slavery ... the native is bought as an animal; his owner prefers him to remain as fit as a horse or an ox. Here the native is not bought, he is hired from the State, although he is called a free man. And his employer cares little if he sickens or dies, once he is working, because when he sickens or dies his employer will simply ask for another.'[13]

While all the regions suffered oppression at the hand of the coloniser the nature of that oppression differed due to the policies followed by the mother country. The difference in policies led to the differences in the role that leisure played in the emergence of socio-cultural-political contexts of the regions concerned.

Traditional Africa: Ritual Performance and Theatre

Many of the traditional African practices which connect the individual to the cosmos, often expressed in theatre or ritual performances, which could be seen both as religious expressions and as forms of entertainment were, and perhaps still are, a highly evolved forms of leisure. There are practices which differ from their Western counterparts in that all concerned ('audience' and performers) participate in them, even as they aim to close the gap between the cosmic and the human. 'Ritual theatre,' as Wole Soyinka writes, 'establishes the spatial medium not merely as a physical area for simulated events but as a manageable contraction of the cosmic envelope within which man ... fearfully exists.' Sense of space in ritual theatre is 'intimately linked with the comprehensive world-view of the society that gave it birth'. It becomes a space which through its management of 'the immensity of ... spatial awareness makes every manifestation ... a paradigm for the cosmic human condition.'[14]

Taking up one of the themes in traditional mask-drama – 'a symbolic struggle with chthonic presences,' Soyinka states that the goal of the conflict is the

> harmonious resolution for plentitude and the well-being of the community ... . The so-called audience is itself an integral part of that arena of conflict; it contributes spiritual strength to the protagonist through its choric reality which must first be conjured up and established, defining and investing the arena through offerings and incantations. The drama would be non-existent except within and against this symbolic representation of earth and cosmos, except within this communal compact whose choric essence supplies the collective energy for the challenger of chthonic realms.[15]

The theatre arena thus becomes a replica of man's efforts to 'master the immensity of the cosmos with his miniscule self ...' an attempt 'to come to terms with the spatial phenomenon of his being'.[16] The goals of connecting to the cosmos and maintaining the solidarity of the group – both are expressed through the performance. Leisure in this case is imbued with highly spiritual overtones.

Drawing out the distinction between the world views (one binary and the other cohesive) that define the Western and African conception of drama, Soyinka writes:

> The serious divergence between the African approach to drama and the European will not be found in lines of opposition between creative individualism and communal creativity, nor in the level of noise from the auditorium ...

> They will be found more accurately in what is a recognisable Western cast of mind, a compartmentalising habit of thought which periodically selects aspects of human emotion, phenomenal observations, metaphysical intuitions and even scientific deductions and turns them into separatist myth (or 'truths') ...[17]

Performance and traditional morality are fused together in ritual. Neither leisure nor art here is seen in terms of time abstracted from other activity. In fact they are integral to the health of the community and some of the things of greatest import to the community happen during this time. They refer to activities in which an individual may find self expression and an expansion of the self beyond the limits of the merely individual.

The mask, an aspect of the ritual theatre, brings up another dimension of the leisure experience. The sculpting of a mask is as spiritual an exercise for the sculptor as it is for the viewer and the participant in the ritual. Edogo in Chinua Achebe's *Arrow of God* is a dedicated carver. Achebe writes that after having carved 'the face and head he had been a little disappointed .... But the owners of the work had not complained; in fact, they had praised it very highly. Edogo knew, however, that he must see the mask in action to know whether it was good or bad. To isolate a mask, to make it static, is to remove it from its context, it has to be seen in movement, possibly above eye level, and perhaps illuminated by the intermittent light of torches.'[18] The function defines the mask. A special philosophy of 'seeing' goes into the mask, that is what imbues it with beauty and significance. The holistic and integrated nature of the performance makes it imperative that the participant know the culture in which it arises to appreciate it fully. It is not just religious or metaphysical ideas alone that are played out by the mask and the ritual. Pure entertainment is also part of the function of the masks. Achebe lets us know that some masks are just for fun and frolic, others may be fault finding masks, and they play rough. 'They whip bystanders who they themselves trick into misbehaving, like laughing at a mask that represents deformity.'[19] Ritual, secular fun and dispensation of justice are all blended into the one act.

Nelson Mandela reiterates this when, as a Xhosa, he writes, '... the traditional religion of the Xhosas is characterised by a cosmic wholeness, so that there is little distinction between the sacred and the secular, between the natural and the supernatural.'[20]

There are other, lighter aspects of leisure. In rural Africa where colonialism had not yet made a deep impact on the daily lives of the people leisure practices for young boys consisted of free play in which they unwittingly learnt skills that would be required later in life. Mandela writes, 'I spent most of my free time in the veld (field) playing and fighting with other boys of the village .... It was in the fields that I learned how to knock birds out of the sky with a slingshot, ... to swim in the clear, cold streams, and to catch fish .... I learned to stick-fight – essential knowledge to any rural African boy .... As boys, we were mostly left to our own devices. We played with toys we made ourselves. We moulded animals and birds out of clay .... Nature was our playground.'[21]

Taking the case of the San Bushmen in South Africa Grobler writes, they 'survived by gathering food from the *veld,* including wild fruit, roots, locusts and wild honey and by hunting antelopes and small animals with their bows and poison arrows. They are especially famous for their rock art, in which hunting scenes as well as religious and dancing rituals were often portrayed.'[22] Till today this art is appreciated and forms an important leisure activity for the modern African and non-African visitors and tourists.

The San, according to Grobler, were also 'the most musical people of South Africa, both in the variety of tunes for dances and in the variety of their musical instruments. There were dances in which only women participated, and dances such as war dances and hunt dances, which were for the men. Some dances were seasonal, celebrating events like the first thunder storm of the summer.'[23] The same kind of statement can be made of Africans with reference to other parts of the Continent.

Colonial Period

With the onset of colonialism the leisure space came to be redefined both conceptually and physically. Colonial capitalism and missionary activity had a transformative impact on African rural and urban lives. Introduction of roads and railways caused greater mobility and interaction between the rural and urban populations. Migrant workers needed to create new social networks to 'cushion' the sense of alienation caused by wage labour and town life.[24]

Leisure spaces now became sites for negotiating transition to urban life and also 'spheres of reflection, where workers pondered the nature and dynamics of wage labour, the structures of colonial and capitalist authority, and engaged in activities they found pleasurable.'[25] The leisure of migrant workers even became a cause of worry for the capitalist colonial authorities.

Colonial employers, especially in mining companies used leisure activities like soccer as a means of social control, to keep the workers engaged and occupied and prevent them from pondering over their situation. Citing the example of one mining company in the North Rhodesian Copperbelt, Akyeampong and Ambler state that the employers found 'few enthusiastic African supporters'. This was because everything organized by the employers was seen as 'work' and the workers wanted to be paid for it.[26] It is, thus, not the activity but the perception that goes with it that makes for leisure. Being a social and cultural construct the perception differs sharply 'along the boundaries of race, ethnicity, gender, class, and age,'[27] and, as seen in the above example, it also depends on who initiates it.

Besides, there is the question of moral judgement and how social networking is viewed in a particular group. Thaddeus Metz illustrates this from a survey of two groups of nuns – one German and the other African (in a South African convent). After the obligatory prayers, etc. the German nuns engaged themselves in work like knitting and sewing. The Africans spent time in conversation. Each group 'deemed the other morally lacking; the Germans judged the Africans insufficiently diligent, while the Africans considered the Germans to objectionably care more about practical matters than about people.'[28]

In settler colonies like Kenya and South Africa new forms of leisure, specific to the African colonies, arose among the settlers. In South Africa, for example,

> Visitors to the Cape in the early days recorded that well-to-do farmers had wine on their tables with every meal and evenings were spent drinking a few glasses,

pipe-smoking and playing cards. White South Africans enjoyed entertaining guests at their homesteads or at a picnic. Reading was a leisure time activity indulged in by some colonists, even though there were no newspapers nor libraries for the first 150 years of white settlement in South Africa. The consumption of vast amounts of alcohol was a popular leisure time activity amongst both the white settlers and sailors from visiting ships. There were numerous canteens in the Cape where alcoholic drinks could be bought. Dancing was also a popular pastime, even in the sparsely populated farming areas.[29]

There was a major difference between the leisure activities of the settlers and those of the Africans. The activities of settlers 'were usually practiced in small groups or individually, rather than communally as most of the leisure activities of the precolonial South African societies were.'[30]

Grobler with reference to South Africa continues to write that most newcomers to the cities and towns, that came into being during the colonial period, found that they had less time for leisure than they earlier had in the rural areas. They also found that there was less public space for leisure in the cities. For this reason many traditional activities, like hunting, etc. became entirely inappropriate in the cities. Often the only public places in the cities would be crowded places, such as the narrow streets, the courtyards of buildings and beer halls. Drinking alcohol, thus, became a popular leisure time activity.[31]

Traditionally sorghum beer was the only alcoholic beverage in South Africa (as was palm wine in western Africa), but when the white man settled there the blacks developed a taste for wine and spirits brought in by him. 'Many workers spent their money on heavy drink or *dagga*, to forget where they were'. A compound worker remarked, 'If one is not drunk one is homesick'.[32] 'Leisure' activity thus became the victim of a particular situation and need. Alcoholic drinks in South Africa and other colonies were sold cheap, even given to Africans as payment for their work.

Funerals are among the most important social events on which Africans right across the Continent spend huge resources and free time. In traditional society the dead were usually buried soon after their death and with little ceremony.[33] But now, in the cities particularly, funerals have become a major happening and are an important place for the display of economic and social prestige. Funerals all over Africa are the most expensive event that a person would organise and it becomes a social occasion for the extended family and friends to come together. In South Africa, during the Apartheid regime, it was funerals that provided a space for people to come together in large numbers and covertly plan strategies for political action.

Other than this the pragmatic and adaptive nature of Africans has given rise to new forms of recreation and artistic expression such as particular forms of music that resulted from a blending of Western and African forms. Western musical instruments, techniques and forms were mastered and co-opted into African forms. European church music was quickly adopted by black Christians. The well known Highlife music of Ghana is a result of blending of music played by Western troops in the Cape Coast area with indigenous Ghanaian music. Singing in groups for the Church, particularly, is seen to be a favoured activity among the youth and even older persons in Ghana. In South Africa, blacks took to music that came from the New World, especially jazz, and adapted it to their needs. Western music was, thus, seamlessly blended into the unique rhythms and harmonies of the rural music of Africa. This new black urban music was, by the 1940s, recognized to differ from American jazz, and came to be called African or township jazz, or, in one of the vernaculars, *marabi* played by *marabi*-bands.[34]

Dancing, an important leisure-time activity in traditional Africa, continued to be popular but its forms changed in townships and cities. Though tribal forms of dance gave way to modern western dance forms yet the traditional forms have not disappeared and often the two have come to be blended giving rise to new forms. This hybrid form of dancing can be seen all over – in cities and in the countryside, especially when funeral ceremonies are held, mostly on weekends so that more people may be able to attend. In Ghana it is a common site in open spaces especially on weekends.

Postcolonial

New trends in the area of leisure began to be seen after the gaining of independence and with African countries being drawn into global economies. Urbanization, western education and changing forms of consumption made their impact on people's leisure preferences – both by choice and due to force of circumstances. Change of residence from rural or township areas and to localities earlier occupied by whites only, the opening up of countries to global tourism, the inroads made by varied forms of media, new types of sporting activities – all have had an impact on leisure.

Some interesting phenomena have emerged in many parts. In post apartheid South Africa, with the abolition of the Group Areas Act, people of different races can live anywhere. Though politically the situation has changed yet socially the dividing lines remain. Makhanya and Maree quote the example of Vusi, who moved to an area that under apartheid was restricted to Whites only, where people tended to keep to themselves. Yet Vusi says, 'If there is a party next door, I can't go if I'm not invited.' Had he lived in the township he would party with his neighbours. The writers found that 'where one lives is not where one may be truly at home.' Where one lives, and where one perceives one's real home to be may be two different things. Vusi has shifted from his home in the township. 'But now he waits to be invited. And the invitation doesn't always come.'[35]

A major change has taken place in the tourism sector in which the locals have become actively 'involved in their own transformation, with the entrepreneurial sector leading the way.' It is the cultural tourism organisers who take the lead in this 'transformation'.[36] Claudia Bell highlights the fact that tourism like other forms of 'extractive' industries, can have both a positive and negative potential for the people concerned. It 'extracts' local cultural and historical experiences without regard or sensitivity to how it impacts the self image of the people involved. 'Cultural survival contributes to economic success and economic success contributes to economic survival (even revival)'.[37] Superficially, this convergence of interests appears mutually beneficial but its cost to the culture and to the self image of the people may be shattering.

During the apartheid era in South Africa precolonial monuments were hardly given any place. Now, Makhanya and Maree show that 'in the dramatically altered political climate, ethnic identity, certainly for tourist consumption, has found new life … ethnic entrepreneurs are bringing ethnicity to the market and seldom having to mask their ethnic agendas.'[38] The promoters of this form of tourism are immune to the negative stereotypes they perpetuate.

Bell is similarly aggrieved when she writes: 'Many tourism enterprises feature local peoples as an attraction in themselves. In South Africa this includes Shakaland, a contrived 'living village' where actors perform roles of inhabiting a traditional African village. The actual buildings are leftovers from the film set of the 1987 movie, *Shaka Zulu*. Versions of traditional clothing are worn. A 'chief' in impressive garb and carrying a long spear greets the guests as they arrive. Bare breasted young women demonstrate the preparation of food and drinks to serve the tourist audience.

'Overlooking the Valley of a Thousand Hills near Durban, Phezulu perform dance and drama that locals disparagingly refer to as 'Zulu Shakespeare': dramatic, contrived and unrelated to normal everyday life. These are examples of 'performing ethnicity' for the tourist gaze. Most Africans do not live in such a manner. Ironically, performing a theatrical version of their own past enables them to make a living in the present.'[39]

Bell's incisive essay takes the reader into Namibia where tourism is being developed in order 'to participate in global capitalism' but 'one of the costs (of this exercise) is that as a process, tourism implicitly restates both global and local inequalities.' Highlighting the insensitivity of the global tourist Bell goes on to state, 'The tourists' right to service and satisfaction often means reinforcement of such local inequities as gender dominance, or exploitation of children, families or the local labour force in general. Third World child prostitutes serving western tourists are one of the most chilling examples of this. That delivery of such services reinforces inequalities in the host culture is not a focal concern to those emancipated by their dollars or Euros.'[40] A subordinate position continues to be held by the locals in their eagerness to please and appease the tourists' hunger for seeing what they *wish* to see as local culture. Huge amounts of money are paid by western tourists for a perpetuation of the colonial experience, an ironically the money earned by the host country is spent mainly on developing infrastructure for the tourists only. Bell writes, 'In their search for exotic experiences, tourists to Namibia depend on compliant local people. Inherently, the 'need' is for the ongoing performance of global inequities.'[41]

In South Africa remains of Dutch homesteads built during the early part of their occupation are being projected as South African heritage. Black women dressed in colonial apparel take the visitor around to show how the whites lived with the blacks serving their daily needs.

Eventually it is for the people themselves to decide what they want to draw from the 'leisure experience'. In the sphere of cultural tourism, for example, one could ask the foreign tourist, is it enhancement and expansion of oneself through the experience of another culture or is it perpetuation of stereotypes and a reliving of some kind of nostalgia of an era that is best forgotten, that is sought?

Africans have to decide what they seek through tourism. Again is it a perpetuation of stereotypes created by the coloniser or is it an enhancing alternative vision of Africa and African world view that is sought to be projected through leisure activities and experiences. The questions 'whose leisure?' and 'leisure for what?' could help to make suitable choices.

Notes

1. Akyeampong and Ambler, p. 3.
2. Ibid., pp. 5,6.
3. Ibid., p. 6.
4. Mazrui, 2002, p. 37.
5. Nkrumah, p. 132.
6. Mazrui, 2002, p. 38–9.
7. Davidson, pp. 12–13.
8. Ibid., p. 13.
9. Gyekye, pp. 187–212.
10. Akeampong, p. 5.
11. Nkrumah, p. 9.
12. Ibid.
13. Ibid., pp. 39–40.
14. Soyinka, pp. 39–41.
15. Ibid., 39.
16. Ibid., p. 40.
17. Soyinka, p. 37.
18. Achebe.
19. Sharma, p. 17.
20. Mandela, p. 12.
21. Ibid., p. 11.
22. Grobler, p. 180.
23. Ibid.
24. Akeampong and Ambler, p. 8.
25. Ibid., p. 9.
26. Akyeampong and Ambler, p. 5.
27. Akyeampong and Ambler, p. 5.
28. Metz, p. 327.
29. Grobler, p.183.
30. Grobler, p. 184.
31. Grobler, 189, writes this with regard to South Africa but this applies to colonized Africa in general.
32. Grobler, 190–1, quoting Callinicos.
33. Grobler, 192.
34. Grobler, p.194.
35. Makhanya and Maree, pp. 171–2.
36. Bell, p.105.
37. Bell, p. 97.
38. Makhanya, p. 163.
39. Bell, p. 97.
40. Bell, p.107.
41. Bell, p.105.

References

Achebe, Chinua (1969). *Arrow of God*, Doubleday, N.Y.

Akyeampong, Emmanuel and Ambler, Charles (2002). 'Leisure in African History: An Introduction,' *The International Journal of African Historical Studies*, Vol. 35, No. 1. Special Issue: Leisure in African History.

Bell, Claudia (2012). 'Cultural Tourism and Tourism Culture Safari Lodges in Namibia,' in Dodd, John and Sharma, Veena, ed., *Leisure and Tourism: Cultural Paradigms*, Rawat Publications, Jaipur.

Davidson, Basil (1964). *The African Past: Chronicles from Antiquity to Modern Times*, Longmans, London, p.11.

Godbey (1989). Anti-leisure and public recreation policy: a view from the USA (1975), in Freedom and Constraint: The Paradox of Leisure, Ten Years of the Leisure Studies Association, ed. Fred Coalter, Routledge, N.Y.

Grobler, Jackie (2012). 'From the Communal to the Individual: A Short History of Leisure in South Africa,' in Dodd, John and Sharma, Veena, ed., *Leisure and Tourism: Cultural Paradigms*, Rawat Publication, Jaipur.

Gyekye, Kwame (1995). 'On the Idea of African Philosophy', in *An Essay on African Philosophical Thought: The Akan Conceptual Scheme* (Cambridge University Press, N.Y., 1987), revised ed. Temple, University Press, Philadelphia.

Haworth, John T. (1997). 'Leisure and Health', in *Work, Leisure and Well being*, Routledge, N.Y.

Henderson, Karla A., M. Deborah Bialeschki, Susan M. Shaw, Valeria J. Freysinger (1989). *A Leisure of One's Own: A Feminist Perspective on Women's Leisure*, by Venture Publishing Inc., State College PA, p. 47.

Linder, Staffan Burensteam (1970). *The Harried Leisure Class*, Columbia University Press, N.Y.

Makhanya, Thoko and Maree, Lynn (2012). 'Leisure Among the Majority Population of KwaZulu-Natal, in the First Decade of the 21st Century' in Dodd, John and Sharma, Veena, ed., *Leisure and Tourism: Cultural Paradigms*, Rawat Publication, Jaipur.

Mandela, Nelson (1995). *A Long March to Freedom*, Back Bay Books.

Mazrui, Ali (1987). 'Reflections of the Gender Gap', in *Sport in Africa: Essays in Social History*, Ed. William J. Baker and James A. Morgan, Africana Publishing Co., N.Y.

Mazrui, Ali (2002). *Africainity Redefined,* Africa World Press, Trenton, NJ.

Metz, Thaddeus (2007). 'Toward an African Moral Theory,' *The Journal of Political Philosophy*, Vol. 15, No. 3.

Nkrumah, Kwame (1964). *Africa Must Unite*, Frederick A. Praeger, reprint.

Pieper, Joseph (1963). *'Leisure the Basis of Culture', Leisure : The Basis of Culture*, Randon House, New York.

Sharma, Veena (1994). 'African Arts' in *Arts of Leisure: Multi-cultural Perspectives*, ed. Karin Blair, Giordano Bruno, Netherlands.

Soyinka, Wole (1990). *Myth, Literature and the African World*, Cambridge University Press, Canto Ed.

13

Evolution of Leisure Patterns in Morocco

From Traditional Spiritual Pilgrimers to Contemporary Mall Wanderers

THIBAULT DANTEUR

Contemporary Morocco, which can be observed by socio-anthropologists, results from thousands of years of a tempestuous and rich history. Its social structures and its cultural characteristics as well come from a long-term sedimentation of Berber, Arabic, African and European influences (Abitbol, 2009), from the first roman and Phoenician intrusions during antiquity to the first dynasties after the rise of Islam and from the Andalusian expansion to the French and Spanish protectorate (Allali, 2008). Still today, the Moroccan kingdom follows an economic strategy which struggles, in one hand, to handle its traditions in a globalized post-colonial context, which we would not consider as westernized (Latouche, 1989), and in the other hand, tries to carefully open itself to individualistic and democratic aspirations suggested by its European partners (Vermeren, 2002).

Originally, Morocco was populated by Berber tribes, descending from 'vague 'protomediterranean' groups coming from the East who appeared in the Maghreb during the 8th century before our era and then spread slowly in the Algerian Tell and around the Moroccan Atlas to reach the South of Sahara'[1] (Camps, 2007 in Abitbol, 2009: 14). The Maghreb will then know many colonization waves of deep influences on the social and cultural structures of its autochthonous populations. Coveted by the Phoenicians for its various resources and its strategic position in the matter of Mediterranean trade, it is then the Romans who will extend their African empire to the Berber land where 'corn, grapevines, fig-trees and olive trees were grown for a long time by the local population, which exploits as well the many copper, lead, iron and silver mines at the South of Atlas' (Abitbol, 2009: 17). Until the 7th century, the Berber country knew a continuous series of invasions and political or religious influences, before the beginning, at the end of the century, of the Muslim conquest and the rise of Islam[2], which took more than fifty years, 'three times longer than Arabic armies needed to conquest Syria, Egypt, Iran and Spain all together' (Abitbol, 2009: 33). It is only a hundred years later that Idris Ben Abdallah, born in Medine and direct descendant from Ali, the Prophet's cousin and son-in-law, would rise as the first Moroccan Sultan with the help of a cluster of Berber tribes and founded the first Moroccan cherifian[3] dynasty, therefore opening the long history of the Moroccan sultanate.

Now that we have briefly overseen the Moroccan historical context, we can start to precise the practical details of our contribution. Our point here is to analyse the evolution of leisure patterns in Morocco, and especially to focus on the contemporary example of the particular way in which Moroccan people are using the modern consumption and leisure industries which are accessing its market. We would, in this matter, focus on the retail store industry and its commercial centres and modern malls.

We have followed, in order to do so, a comprehensive and socio-anthropological approach, based on a hundred hours of observations between April and June 2009 and then between October 2009 and June 2010 in many retail stores and shopping centres at Rabat, Marrakesh, and Casablanca. These sessions have allowed many photographs, a hundred of which has been exploited as a precious complement to observation in an aspiration for anthropological field 'dense description' (Geertz, 1973). Another hundred photographs came from anonymous sources having a more direct access to supermarket's environment.[4] The pictures which have been filed and detailed about their contexts, caring for the inevitable off screen's 'invisible presence' (Piette, 1996), have allowed, with direct observations, to keep an ethnographical journal. 'Informal interviews' with many actors, employees, consumers, sellers (Pétonnet, 1982; Olivier de Sardan, 1995; Dujarier, 2008), on the innocent conversation model have completed our data. We also used a technique that could be qualified as 'harnessing of verbal exchange' between visitors, allowing us to collect many results which would have been very difficult to obtain through classical interviews directly on site.[5] This association of 'floating observations' (Pétonnet, 1982) and photography, in an ethnographical approach has allowed a qualitative study of the experiential marketing process at work within modern shopping centres and malls (Holbrook et Hirchman, 1982) and appeared to us as a powerful mean to seize at the best the particularities of our studied fields.

During this two year period of observation in the purpose of our research about food distribution channels[6], we have been led to get interested in the leisure practices of the Moroccan population and in their evolution during history, especially through their interaction with the new industrial firms which are setting up in the kingdom. As a matter of fact, the Moroccan kingdom is opening to foreign investments, companies and visitors in order to support its economical growth and its development, particularly since the realm of Mohammed the 6th, who was crowned in 1999.

In this text, we would analyse the Moroccan mall industry, which is growing for the last ten years and applying at various levels the principles of retailtainment (Ritzer, 1999), focusing especially on the specific and original uses of this environment by the Moroccans.

Therefore, we would first describe some of the main structuring phenomena which have shaped the traditional Moroccan leisure patterns as well as the social mutations which have transformed those during history. In a second part, we would develop the contemporary example of the many malls which are appearing in the country's major urban areas for a few years, advocating for the efficiency of complexity theories' terms and concepts to analyse the alternative uses of such commercial equipments by the Moroccans. And among those conceptual tools, we would mainly consider the morinian hologrammatical principle (Morin, 1990).

Evolution of Social Structures and Traditional Moroccan Leisure Patterns

Structuring Phenomena of the Moroccan Traditional Culture

In order to properly seize the main evolutions of the Moroccan leisure patterns and way of life, it seems necessary to first present some of the structuring phenomena which took a significant part in the shaping process of 'earlier Morocco' (Vatin, 1982) and its traditional society. We would consider three of them as they appear to us to be of a major and decisive importance in the socio-historical evolution process of the cultural and social institutions which rule over the Moroccan kingdom, and therefore directly affect the Moroccan leisure patterns. Thus, we would specify the role of Arabic and Berber tribalism, of some unorthodox and maraboutic Muslim practices and finally the impact of transsaharan trade. Those three features, as we would see, articulate around the figure of the Sultan, who appears to be the keystone of Moroccan society 'from which He is the law and guarantor' (Jamous, 1981: 241).

Tribalism in Traditional North African Societies

Tribalism is surely to be considered as one of the main structures of North African traditional societies and besides is, even in different cultural contexts, one of the major objects studied by the ethnographical and anthropological traditions. In the Maghreb case, the first studies led upon tribal groups were often part of the colonization's ideology (Hanoteau et Letourneux, 1872), and did not 'make any mystery about their destination: to prepare the French conquest' (Nicolas, 1961: 528) and in particular the establishment of the Moroccan protectorate (Michaux-Bellaire et Salmon, 1927). The observation and description of tribalism was, indeed, seen as necessary to help the pacification of the country which was taking advantage from an analysis of tribal society and its power mechanisms. Most of the time, they focused on Berber tribes[7], which was described as founded on dissension and lack of state structures (Montagne, 1930).[8] At the notable exception of the work by Jacques Berque, most French sociologists and anthropologists have sinned through an excess of ethnocentrism which forbid them to go past their western conception of state and political structures. Thus, they were seeing in the Berber tribalism, sometimes a 'primitive republican regime', sometimes 'simple and anarchic manners' (Montagne, 1930), from which they were deducing the need for the French protectorate.

From the 1960s, Anglo-Saxon sociology and anthropology started to get interested as well in the matter of North African and particularly Moroccan tribes, and showed the ambition to articulate the many units which are making it up through the segmentation theory. This notion, for which Durkheim (1893) needs to be credited, was really modeled by Evans-Pritchard (1937) who described, on the basis of his study of the Nuers from Sudan, the main characteristics of a segment society.[9] Such a society is constituted by 'stacks of equal and juxtaposed segments, built from jumbles of family groups and their geographical implantation' (Vatin, 1982: 17). Then, the work of such authors as Gellner (1969) have operated the 'shift' (Vatin, 1982) of this model, in order to apply it to Moroccan tribes, partly taking into account the contributions from French colonization sociologists (Hanoteau et Letourneux, 1872; Montagne, 1930), to describe the Berber 'structural democracy' and 'the balanced opposition of groups which act as specialized political institutions' (Vatin, 1982: 16).[10] Reformulated (Hart, 1965; Favret, 1966) or borrowed (Valensi, 1977; Waterbury, 1970), the segment model and its principles would be very successful among European researchers who study the North-African tribes. However, the critics addressed to Evans-Pritchard's theory (1937), and above all to its excessive application to Atlas tribes by Gellner (1969) started to rise and point its lack of empirical validity. Indeed, the segmentarist theories were to be blamed for the lack of consideration toward economic questions, and in particular the forms of production and the domination relation which they drive (Gallissot, 1978). Moreover, the culturalist analysis (Geertz, 1973) criticized the 'lineage generalization' (Vatin, 1982) of Gellner's theories which underestimated such factors as friendship association, relational alliances or the dependency relationship that occur within the tribe.[11] In the end, in addition to its exaggerated formalism, which tends to fail to fit the empirical observations, and its structuralist tendency to generalize outside of the specific contexts of observation[12], segmentarist theory is mostly criticized for its insistence on strict opposition between makhzen and siba. Such an antagonism is, indeed, from many perspectives, very oversimplifying (Vatin, 1982) and is even presented by some authors as 'a fiction which is supported by the chiefs of lineages' who transmitted it to anthropologists who were questioning them about their autonomy from the makhzen (Pascon, 1977).

With the end of colonization, the works about North-African society and the role of tribalism in its constitution and history are multiplying.[13] Following the studies of Berque (1953) or Pascon (1977), the 'caïdization' phenomenon is underlined to contradict the theory of balance which founds the segmentarist model (Hammoudi, 1980), and to insist on the relationships between tribalism and central power. Besides, such links are proven to exist by many historical episodes which show, beyond any doubt, the political continuity between tribes and makhzen, whether it is about cooperation or political lobbying.[14] In a general perspective and for a long time, Moroccan tribes have simultaneously been one of the most powerful resources of the different dynasties, through their political or military support, as well as they have been one of the greatest factors of political destabilization within the kingdom, sometimes rising 'entire regions ... against the makhzen and its representatives' (Abitbol, 2009: 286). Nevertheless, since the realm of the Alaouites, and among them Moulay Sliman, those rebellions, as vast and violent as they could get, did not really question the Sultan's authority anymore, but rather his vassals'. Indeed, since this period, the monarch's person took a sacred and inviolable aspect for the Moroccan people and tribes (Abitbol, 2009: 286), which could oppose themselves to him but kept a deep respect toward his cherifian ancestries and his religious status which makes him the commander of the faithful.

Islam, Cult of Saints and Maraboutism

The place and role of Islam in the evolution of the Moroccan tribes and society political and cultural structures seems to have been underestimated by the analysis from the colonial science, and by some of the segmentarists as well. Thus, a major part of the literature about Maghreb and Morocco mainly insisted to look after what was left of influences prior to the rising of Islam within the Berber tribal practices, in an obsessional quest for Romanism (Masqueray, 1886). Such authors were captivated by a particularity of North-African Islam labeled as maraboutism.[15] Indeed, even though Morocco has for official religion a sunni Islam of malekite rite, it has known since the 15th century (Abitbol, 2009) the cult of a many saints or marabous and the appearance of numerous brotherhoods.[16] If, from an orthodox point of view, 'Islam considers such a cult as shirk, which is a form of heresy, ... (and) the brotherhoods ... as religious innovators which it is needed to fight' (Allali, 2008: 10), such practices of anthropolatry are still a part of the Moroccan Muslim culture. Thus, during its history, Morocco has known several waves of 'spiritual and intellectual renewal ... marked by the multiplication of zaouia-s and the proliferation of mystic brotherhoods across the whole country' (Abitbol, 2009: 158). Those 'innovators' are adored for many reasons and virtues such as thaumaturgy (Rhani, 2009) or devotional and spiritual exception (Hammoudi, 1980). They are famous for their baraka, which the believers come to seek, even after the marabou's death, around their white mausoleum, and whose powers favour health, luck or land's fertility.[17] Some of those saints federated followers and founded brotherhoods within zaouia-s, taking advantage of several 'assets' such as their geographical situation in a rural area which lacks the State's presence, their ability to alienate one or many powerful tribes and sometimes a cherifian ancestry (Hammoudi, 1980: 622).[18] Sometimes analysed as 'pagan survival' of an era previous to Islam (Bel, 1938), sometimes understood as arbitration tools to control the oppositions between tribal segments (Gellner, 1969), the cult of saints has intrigued the researchers from the time of protectorate (Montagne, 1930), until more recent times (Jamous, 1981; Boubrik, 1999).

The practices of Moroccan Islam, objectively observed, have thus progressively come back at the heart of contemporary researchers' concern, allowing them to take a fresh look on tribalism and its structuralist modeling. Indeed, the paradigm of segment society, such as Evans-Pritchard (1937) defined it, were based on a 'lineage generalization' (Vatin, 1982) and on the primacy of kinship relations. This assertion, adopted by Gellner as well, stands on the reading of Ibn Khaldun, a Muslim historian of the 14th century, and his emphasis on the role of kinship within tribal organization, in link to the Muslim law.[19] However, several authors put into perspective this understanding of the 'North-African genius' (Goumeziane, 2006), since this genealogical relationship 'is not mechanically determined, it passes through imagination. A group of descendants constitutes itself upon an ideological basis which takes 'natural' appearances' (Hamès,

1987: 109).[20] Moreover, if the author of Saints Of The Atlas was as well linking Moroccan tribalism and maraboutic Islam practices, he restricted saints and brotherhoods to a role of arbitration, using their sacred lineage and its pacifist status to temper and solve violent oppositions between segments (Gellner, 1969). This perspective, however, shrugs any kind of intervention from central State off of the equation and presents saints as agents of a fiercely preserved autonomy of tribes. And yet, it appears that this model greatly eludes the relationship linking zaouia and makhzen, which 'both are main poles of mobilization, competitors as well as congruents since the tension between saints and Sultan is resolving in a same religious reference: maraboutism' (Hammoudi, 1980: 617). Therefore, it appears that the study of maraboutism and its political and religious implications, allows to get out of a simplistic formalism which by many aspects does not translate the many complexities of traditional North-African society. Indeed, contemporary works which make 'room for important factors, such as Islamic ideology, perceptions of the religious, expressions of sacred, forces of faith, manipulation of beliefs by actors: princes, doctors, marabous and imams' (Vatin, 1983: 183) allows to link, instead of oppose, tribalism and central power. In doing so, they moderate many of the segmentarist analysis to the benefit of the description of a 'composite society' (Pascon, 1977), way more capable to match the empirical reality of Moroccan society and the complex nature of its social structures.[21] Thus, for Hammoudi, Gellner's observations are not to be generalized to every tribal group, since, by example at Tamgrout, 'the zaouia does not exercise many arbitrations ..., and its geographical implication, as well as those of its subsidiary branches, are way more determined by the relation to central State than by the opening of 'saintliness posts' needed by segmentary violence' (Hammoudi, 1980: 629).[22]

Finally, this complexity of North-African society, this composite characteristic, echoes the very complexity of Islam in general, and of Moroccan Islam in particular, which composes 'a system including religion and way of life, explicit laws and moral prescriptions, personal norms and collective code, individual protection and instrument of a caste or a despot's legitimization' (Vatin, 1983: 187).[23]

Transsaharan Trade as a Structuring Phenomenon

As we have described it, tribalism and practices of maraboutic Islam are linked and both shaped the traditional social structures of North-African culture. In addition to both these structuring phenomena, we would add the transsaharan trade which provided merchandises for the souqs of the whole North-African area trough the international exchanges it drove. The products from the medieval Sudanese area, where stand the actual Mali, Niger or Tshad, and especially gold and slaves, were traded for salt and silver coming from North-Africa (Malowist, 1970; Miege, 1981), using prehistoric roads (Mauny, 1947). This trade is obviously to be linked to both the islamization process and tribalism which took part as well as they took advantage of its development. As a matter of fact, even though archeology has demonstrated the existence of caravan convoys through Sahara which were way anteriors to Muslim conquest or even roman occupation (Brachet, 2004: 117), still the islamization process reinforced this trade (Grégoire et Labazée, 1993). Indeed, many authors insist on the role of Islam in its permanence since 'by bringing closer regions and populations ... it created a vast exchange field spreading through the whole North-African and Eastern area, to the southern edges of Sahara' (Abitbol, 2009: 48).[24] Besides, and reciprocally, the transsaharan trade took a huge part in the diffusion of Islam in sub-saharan Africa, in the Sahel or in Sudan (Brachet, 2004: 118), through the North-African merchants who settled in these areas and sometimes made there considerable fortunes (Bonte, 2000). Finally, this trade was not only a vector of diffusion for goods and merchandises, 'it promoted ideas, values, a civilization' (Abitbol, 1980: 15).

The relation between tribalism and transsaharan trade is of crucial importance in the analysis of the development of this exchange field. Indeed, the crossing of such a vast territory with a relatively hostile topography, including the risks of extreme climatic conditions as well as those of raids (razzias) aiming to capture the merchandises, induced the need to protect the caravans and to seek guidance. To do so, itineraries were determined considering the many stops to be made, the position of water supplies, but moreover also of the tribal compositions of those areas as well as the existence of zaouia-s ruled by powerful marabous (Abitbol, 1980: 6). Therefore, 'the benefit of a saint, the protection of a road are up to negotiation' (Berque, 1953: 292) which are often concluded with a few gifts to the local tribal chief who offers protection or to the zaouia to which he is affiliated[25], in addition to a tax which is received by the tribe whose territory was to be crossed. Indeed, Bourgeot precises that it is necessary to distinguish 'this protection tax ... from the crossing fees to be paid to the chiefs who therefore concretize territorially their political influence and underline a ground preeminence' (Bourgeot, 1978: 161). The Tuareg tribes who control the transsaharan roads, make a substantial income out of the crossing and protection fees or the looting of the caravans. The transsaharan exchanges then take a part that can not be ignored into the group life, its hierarchy's reproduction and the expansion of its territory, to the point that from an exchange system, the transsaharan trade become a real 'societal structure' (Brachet, 2004).[26] It appears that, through this manna which benefits certain nomad desert or more generally southern tribal group, this trade, until its decline with the first European incursions in the 19th century, took a large part in the structuration process of Moroccan society. Indeed, several dynasties which reigned over Morocco are coming from such tribes, and the makhzen, clearly understanding the profit it could make from this trade, has often struggle to increase its control over the caravan roads or the countries they were crossing as it is shown, by example, by the Almoravide's invasion of Ghana in the 11th century (Malowist, 1970: 1632).[27]

Traditional Leisure Patterns in Morocco

The necessity to describe those three phenomena, which have largely participated to structure Moroccan society, is justified by the fact that tribalism, maraboutic Islam and transsaharan trade are almost inevitably crossed when one studies Moroccan traditional leisure patterns. Against certain theories, it turns out that such leisure practices are previous to European colonization.[28] Indeed, many authors, among which Jean-François Troin or Mohammed Berriane, have demonstrated the existence of ludic and recreative activities several centuries before the start of European influences. Those are almost constantly interlocked with events of the religious kind, linked to tribalism and transsaharan trade, such as the case of moussems, by example.

The Example of the Traditional Moussem: Leisure as a Part of the Religious Whole

Among the illustrations of traditional recreative practices presented by Berriane (1989), one finds the example of the moussem, which we would develop here, since it shows brilliantly this embedment of leisure within the structuring phenomena of Moroccan traditional culture as we have described them previously.[29] The moussem, a 'social phenomenon which is deeply rooted into the Moroccan society and culture ..., is a gathering of pilgrims who encounter collectively and periodically around a saint's sanctuary' (Berriane, 1989: 116). It is, then, an event of the religious kind[30], taking place for most of them during the summer and coinciding with the end of harvests. Organized by a zaouia or the tribe which is hosting it, this kind of reunion attracts many populations from rural and urban areas as well[31], who are seeking the saint's baraka and the perspective of break in the 'daily routine' as well as the inversion of the symbolic codes which rule it[32] (Reysso, 1988 in Berriane, 1989: 133). Indeed, if the moussem is an opportunity to consult the marabous, it is in the same time the scene of many leisure activities and often represents a unique occasion of entertainment for many categories of population.[33] It is characterized by the association of religion through the pilgrimage around a saint's tomb, of commercial aspect with the souq which always takes place, and finally of ludic and popular aspect through the diverse shows and activities which captivate its visitors at the fall of the night.[34] These events, true 'polymorphous phenomena' (Chiffoleau et Madœuf, 2005), find their origins in the past of pre-Islamic Arabia, where moussems corresponded to the great markets organized along the caravan roads and where 'exchange operations were accompanied by celebrations with contests during which poets from the main tribes were confronting' (Berriane, 1989: 117).[35] Thanks to Berriane's analysis, we can perceive that if the religious aspect of traditional moussems still was the main attraction – the author speaks about 'the pilgrimage necessity' – leisure activities took part to the attractivity of such events on Moroccan populations, as a recreative 'part' within the sacred and religious 'whole'.

Moroccan Traditional Recreative Activities and Leisure

Thus, the traditional moussems are characterized by their religious and ludic aspect. They appear to be closely linked to tribalism, which takes part in their organization, as well as they are related to maraboutic Islam, which justifies their existence or as they are connected to transsaharan trade, since it allows to provide goods to be sold on the souqs and because it influences the location of certain zaouia-s. It is needed now to precise this ludic 'part' of the 'religious' whole.

During daytime, moussem's activities are relatively restricted and are mainly directed toward religious practices. However, leisure and other recreative occupations are not completely absent. As a matter of fact, souqs are taking place and offer caravan products such as ostrich feathers, salt, spices and many other merchandises which are bought as gifts which would carry part of the saint's baraka. Among those diurnal ludic practices, it is mainly the fantasias that attract the audience which is fond of the horsemen's performances whose different tribes are confronting.[36]

But this is mostly at night that the moussem takes its whole dimension of leisure space, when 'rings the hour of shows, or fraja, upbeat of the event' (Berriane, 1989: 132).[37] Pilgrims then invade the area where the equestrian battles were taking place at daytime which have been replaced by the harkas, gathering of crowds which circle around the diverse artists who entertain the evening. One finds there jugglers, animal trainers, musicians and dancers, storytellers and acrobats, as well as sellers of medicines or mind-readers. The shows and animations go on along the night and even into the tents which have been put up by pilgrims.

All of these activities, from fantasias to harkas, if they are gathered in one place for definite time during moussem, are not, however, restricted to such events. Indeed, most of these activities can be observed at many occasions such as religious holydays as the mwouloud[38] (Pâques, 1971), by example, or along the stops of caravan roads. Thus, harkas are taking place, for many centuries, on the Jemaa El Fna square of Marrakesh, where storytellers and artists occupy the ground, perpetuating the tradition of Moroccan public leisure and shows (Goytisolo, 1999; Arrif, 2006). Moreover, music and dance are fundamental activities of the age-long Moroccan culture (Chiacchiero et Karlsson, 2009), which are sometimes associated to rites mixing dances, chants, and gnawing rhythms. Practiced by some brotherhoods such as the Gnawas (Kapchan, 2007) or the Suffis, those dances are sometimes leading to trance states (Andézian, 2000), which demonstrate the deep cultural link that connects religious and mystic phenomena, tribalism and brotherhoods with spectacular practices, with aspects of what could be considered, at a certain level and from the point of view of the audience, as recreative activities.[39]

Social Changes and Structural Transformations in Contemporary Morocco

Progressive Decline of Structuring Phenomena and External Influences

Morocco, even before the establishment of its sultanate regime, was, as we have seen it, influenced by several attempts of conquest from many civilizations, and never stopped to arouse the covetous glances from the different European kingdoms.[40] Even though, the relations with Europe were not only conflictual, trade between both banks of the Mediterranean was even thriving for years. However, the European influence was to impact the main structuring phenomena which we have described before. And first of all, it touched the transsaharan trade, which stayed 'various and uninterrupted, ... as long as the country stayed faithful to its continental vocation, meaning until the second half of the 19th century which would see North-Africa swing over to its Atlantic side, after its opening to Europe' (Abitbol, 1980: 15). Already, since the discovery of America, and then with the growth of shipping trade, especially from the port of

Mogador (Abitbol, 2009), transsaharan trade started to struggle. Its decline would really begin with the progressive colonization of Africa, which strongly curbed the slave trade which was mainly feeding the caravan trade, therefore drying Saharan merchants and tribes main source of income up[41] (Brachet, 2004: 121).

With the establishment of French and Spanish protectorate over Morocco, at the beginning of the 20th century, European influence became a territorial occupation and the domination of western ideals, in terms of urbanism and economy, imposed deep structural modifications to Morocco. The construction of European quarters – the nouvelles-villes – extending the traditional medinas of Moroccan cities and the development of an industrial economy drove to a massive rural exodus and a progressive settlement of populations. Those social mutations favoured the fall of the tribal structure's influence in the Moroccan society, which began during the 20th century and would reinforce after its second half.[42]

Finally, with the appearance of modern communication means and favoured contacts with international Muslim references, the religious practices were to be individuated and maraboutic and mystic beliefs to decline as well.[43] Indeed, the possibility to access foreign preaches has favoured the diffusion of a religious rigorism, already present within the malekite rite which is nowadays coming up against fierce competition from wahabites incursions coming from Arabia as well as from a temptation for political Islam (Vermeren, 2004). More than ever, there is a situation of religious pluralism within Moroccan Islam, which drives the makhzen to a 'desire for religious truth monopoly likely to strengthen the monarchistic domination' (Tozy, 1998 in Elahmadi, 2001: 3). Then, if the thaumaturge saints or the superstitions are still part of Moroccan Islam, their attraction is not, however, as strong as it used to be.[44]

Modern Social Mutations in Morocco

The combined action of massive migration of rural populations toward urban centres[45], with the commercial and cultural opening to European influences, especially since the massive waves of emigration to France and Spain after decolonization, and with the individuation of religious practices has driven, during the last decades, deep social mutations. Thus, Moroccan society, as well as Berber society, dearly cherished by colonization's anthropologists, is transforming: 'The monetization of economy is qualitatively modifying the personal relations, the demographic pressure is favouring the traditional balances' disintegration, emigration is introducing new cultural models' (Boukous, 1987: 65). Under the pressure of all these factors, Moroccan society's institutions and values are evolving according to a dynamic which is often close to cultural syncretism, through practices which 'are coming close to tradition as well as modernism' (Lazzarotti, 1993: 183).[46] Among those values which found Moroccan identity, Allali (2004) underlines what he calls 'familism', a notion which insists on the fundamental aspect that takes the family cell in Moroccan society.[47] And yet, this central institution, which is family, turns out to be a significant indicator of the mutations that Moroccan society knows, indeed, the constraints exercised by the group upon individuals are progressively loosening and families tend more and more to be nuclear[48] (El Harras, 2006).

Moreover, in addition to economic opening which allows the arrival in Morocco of many foreign companies, the kingdom has made a strategic choice to go in for an economy focused on tourism. In doing so, the entrance of a growing number of foreigners in the national territory brings new cultural influences and diversified ways of life which favour social mutations, especially among the youth (Bennani-Chraïbi, 1997). To these foreign touristic crowds, come in addition the diasporic visitors, who import differentiated consumption habits (Wagner, 2008), as well as a strong immigration of foreign residents, attracted by a cheap cost of life and the exotic charm of a renewed orientalism. This last category settle within the medinas of the imperial cities, where the 'hunt for ryads' is opened to their superior financial means, forcing the locals to a more or less accepted cohabitation (Kurzac-Souali, 2007). Moreover, this touristic turn of Moroccan economy, since the end of the 1990's, drives to patrimonialization process of the geographical and cultural resources of the country (Di Méo, 2007), which favours, through the promotion of authenticity sought by tourists[49] (Bonard et Felli, 2008), a commodification of traditional cultural activities which then turns into touristic folklore (Giraud, 2002; Staszak, 2006).

Evolution of Leisure Patterns in Contemporary Morocco

City Centres and Public Spaces

Because of all these socio-cultural mutations and demographical modifications, traditional leisure activities have necessarily evolved, transformed rather than being replaced by new practices.[50] Indeed, with urbanization and the rise of nuclear families, individuals are both more autonomous and anonymous, in this sense that it is easier for them to escape from others' gaze, through the alternative use they could have of the urban environment. Therefore, Moroccan city centres have progressively become attractions for medinas inhabitants, and, as a matter of fact, 'since several decades, promenade has exercised a massive attraction upon every social classes, including the more underprivileged urban populations' (Gillot, 2002: 268). The nouvelles-villes, thus, slowly became more than simple administrative and merchant areas, but are nowadays diverted into leisure and relaxation spaces through wandering, even outside of stores' opening hours (Berriane, 1988). Grassy areas and public gardens are today more and more appreciated by urban populations, and moreover it is very common to observe, when the heat drops, bystanders settling on any given square of green, occupying traffic circles, median strips or flower beds, even though such spaces could be in immediate proximity with polluted or loud areas (Gillot, 2002). Furthermore, urban populations have for a long time practiced picnics and other moments of rest within 'wild' spaces, located in cities' surroundings, such as Marrakesh's palm grove, by example, which 'has always been a space for leisure, recreation and relaxation for the Marrakesh population' (Boujrouf, 1996: 27). Nevertheless, contemporary uses of such spaces are sometimes diverted allowing particularly women, to take advantage of urban anonymity and of the public aspect of these gardens, in order to have intimate rendezvous without contravening to cultural taboos. Indeed, 'even if it is a place for encounter, the presence of other users allows to think that the moral code of good behaviour, commonly adopted and acknowledged by users, would never be questioned; and thus, virtue and family honour would be preserved'[51] (Gillot, 2002: 272).

Contemporary Moussem's Desecration: The Religious 'Whole' within the Leisure 'Part'

It is necessary, in the light of social mutations that we have underlined, to consider the example of traditional moussem and to observe how such religious events have evolved under the pressure of those socio-cultural transformation factors. It appears that, in its contemporary form, the moussem, as a purely religious event of pilgrimage toward a maraboutic saint, is a declining tradition (Nabti, 2010). Indeed, as well as El Ayadi, Rachik and Tozy (2007) have demonstrated it in the concern of the ziyara, the religious aspect of moussems does not appear anymore as the major attracting element of such events. Authors notice a real desecration of these pilgrimages which, more and more, take the form of vast festivals, where, even if the religious and sacred part still exists, it is progressively embedded in the festive aspect of the gathering. Thus, these events are from now on largely under State's control: 'The organization of the moussem for a long time has whether been ... the saint's descendants prerogative or the responsibility of the tribes hosting his tomb, (and yet) today this organization, including the choice of dates, is within Homeland Department's province, through the local authorities'[52] (Berriane, 1989: 142). However, this decline, described as well by Nabti (2010), is touching especially the religious aspect of those pilgrimage, since moussems have seen their popularity increase, particularly among urban population which tend to consider it as a genuine touristic vacation (Berriane, 1989: 172). Therefore, we clearly observe a shift from a type of traditional event where the leisure 'part' used to be embedded into the religious 'whole', toward a contemporary situation where it is indeed this religious 'whole' which interlocks within the recreative 'part'.[53] Such a shift is demonstrated by the new predominance of leisure activities, which sees traditional practices, previously described, being next to more modern attractions, organized within a real fun house: one could find there dexterity games, merry-go-rounds, stuntmen's display or even outdoor movie theatres sponsored by private companies which use the opportunity to promote their products (Berriane, 1989). With the development of the area allocated to these leisure, which sometimes require important equipments, it is clear that, from now on, 'the marabous and zaouias are no longer the main structuring elements of the moussem's space organization' (Berriane, 1989: 147).

Such a leisuring movement of religious event is identified by Berriane in the concern of Moroccan hydrotherapy as well. Indeed, this Moroccan tradition, which originates back to the roman occupation, was also, from its beginning, associated to religious practices[54], but its modern development has known the same phenomenon of desecration and commodification as moussems did. Indeed, 'hydrotherapy, nowadays, is not limited to a simple gestion of waters, this matter has been used as an excuse to offer, around the source a whole range of services and entertainments where sportive, cultural and artistic animation occupy a large space' (Berriane, 1989: 156). Once again, and through

Berriane's second example, we can see an evolution of traditional leisure activities which make them shift from a leisure embedment, as a part, into a tradition of the religious kind, toward a reversed situation where it is the religious attraction which tends to imbricate within leisure offer. This dynamic, however, does not seem to be totally completed, and kind of a coexistence of both these logic, within a complex and combinatorial system, could be noticed (Vatin, 1983). Especially, if we consider the perception of population, part of whose is affirming a certain rejection for this multiplication of leisure offer (Nabti, 2010). And this is precisely this coexistence of contrary logics that is allowing us to refer to the hologrammatical principle, which states the simultaneous presence of the part within the whole as well as the existence of the whole within the part[55] (Morin, 1990).

All of these social, cultural and economic evolutions take part to the entrance within Moroccan market of new consumption industries, such as the retail store companies, but also of 'new outdoor leisure areas ... on the model of American fun parks' (Colin, 2006: 431), as well as modern malls, which also are mostly of western inspiration. However, in the light of Berriane's analysis, it seems necessary to question the importation of such models and their specific use by Moroccan populations. It is, in particular, very important to focus on the question of whether those modern consumption and leisure activities are resulting from a simple imitation of western practices, or if it is possible to demonstrate a logic of reciprocal borrowing and of re-appropriation, in a dynamic which would come close to the cultural permanence (Sahlins, 1993) and to syncretic hybridation through specific alternative uses that one could analyse through the hologrammatical principle (Morin, 1990).

Globalized Leisure Patterns: The Example of Moroccan Retail Stores and Malls

Leisure as Appeal Products in Diversified Retail Stores: The Part within the Whole

Toward a New Model of Consumption

Gilles Lipovetsky analysed modern developments of capitalism and the rise of consumption society as 'a cultural and social construction which has required consumers education as well as a visionary spirit from creative businessmen'[56] (Lipovetsky, 2006: 29). After a first phase of industrial revolution, scientific organization of work and the rise of primary goods mass consumption, then comes a consumption which is based on standardization and diffusion of equipment goods among larger parts of the public. At that time occurs the shift to retail stores chain which could be considered as a 'commercial avatar of fordism' (Moati, 2001), through industrialization and rationalization of trade activities and work. Various services are more and more offered to consumers and it tends to encourage an individuation of shopping behaviours. This process is part of the hedonism described by Lipovetsky and that Gadrey outlines saying that 'services society starts to assert itself through the growing demand of personal services linked to leisure, culture and entertainment' (Gadrey, 2003: 25). Nowadays, consumers, who are up on their individuation, are freeing themselves of the constraints which were defining their choices and needs, thus 'from a consumer pressured by social constraints of status and standing, we went to an hyperconsumer who is looking for emotional experiences and well-being, for quality of life and health, for brands and authenticity, immediacy and communication' (Lipovetsky, 2006: 12).[57] Such an evolution could be compared to the contemporary understanding of moussem and hydrotherapy in Morocco, indeed the visitors of such activities are nowadays freeing themselves of the 'necessity of pilgrimage' to favour events including a large range of services based on such logic as well-being and comfort. From a constraint of religious context, they tend to go to moussems or sources looking for more routine breaking and expecting proper touristic journey.

This is precisely this pursuit of 'emotions' and 'extraordinary' that are founding the rise of leisure and the appearance of destination malls (Andrieu and Al, 2004). Thus, retail store industry and mall industry are related and partners in Morocco, in France and in the US as well, since retail store firms assume a leading and attracting role within large shopping centres. Following this logic of a consumption defined by demand, purchase locations are 're-enchanted' (Ritzer, 1983), through the 'monumental style of stores, the luxurious interior designs, the radiant domes, the enlighted showcases, everything is done to dazzle, to transform the store in a permanent fest, to amaze the shoppers and create a compulsive and sensual climate conducive to purchase' (Lipovetsky, 2006: 33). The retail store industry and the universalistic shopping centres have applied this strategy founded on pleasure, individualistic happiness and seek for personal leisure. With their appearance within new cultural areas such as Morocco, they drive their customers towards a new model of consumption which detaches itself from social or cultural constraints and where hedonistic ideals and personal pleasure are prevailing. This evolution goes along with a switch from services industry to self-service industry (Gadrey, 2003; Gershuny, 1978), where the customer is 'by himself, independent and free to choose, to take his time, to look closely at products, to buy without suffering storekeeper's pressure. Nobody is selling to him, he is now buying by himself' (Lipovetky, 2006: 112).[58] *Customers are also more and more driven to take a growing part of the shopping process, seeking for individualistic emotions, looking for service customization.*[59]

Attract a Walker, Capture a Consumer

With the advent of consumption society, urban landscapes have been deeply modified, 'everywhere cafés and restaurants, fashion stores, handcraft stores, exhibition galleries, multiplex movie theatres are changing urban space into a recreational city ready for merchant and cultural consumption' (Lipovetsky, 2006: 237). In a symmetrical movement, one could say that commercial spaces such as retail stores, commercial galleries or malls urbanized themselves, imitating the size and form of small towns with streets and squares[60] (Andrieu and al, 2004). Urban space is being commodified while commercial space is being urbanized. It creates a concoction which changes the consumer into a walker, the walker into a consumer in a logic of commodification of public space's 'non-locations' (Augé, 1992). Retail stores industry and gigantic malls which host it take a large part to the creation of this idealized reality by offering to the public what Ferreira Freitas (1996) called 'urban islands' where 'is progressively forged a culture of the ideal city's simulacrum' (Andrieu and Al, 2004: 42). Closed and secured spaces of shopping malls allow to attract walkers who find there an opportunity of an urban activity without cities inconveniences which are insecurity, traffic, cold or heat.[61] This bubble of security allows to easily turn walkers into customers since it is indeed true that 'where insecurity rules, consumption is strongly antagonized' (Chesnau, 2001: 98). This will to capture the passerby makes necessary to adapt shopping centres 'at the level of their offer, playing on the mass effect and diversification to enforce their attractiveness' (Desse, 2002: 6). This diversification has been largely based on leisure activities which became appealing goods aiming to renew the interest of customers bored with classical commercial spaces.[62] Peripheral commercial activities organize its whole space in order to attract and capture the walker/customer, whether it is in terms of its environment layout or of its products staging. In the concern of store's formal organization, many technical devices are at work to satisfy this ambition.[63] The products staging also takes part in many ways to lead customers to believe that they are just taking a walk. Thus, inside supermarkets everything drives to feel like visiting kind of a cockaigne country, where everything is within reach and in profusion, where seasonal constraints are abolished, an abundance horn where life is sweet just as firms names and slogans are clearly expressing it[64] (Danteur, 2009). Bucolic stagings[65] recall Cochoy's analysis which develops the garden metaphor to characterize the supermarket's environment. But technical devices or product staging, if they make easier to capture walkers, are not enough in front of a consumer who became 'unfaithful' and 'easily bored' (Lipovetsky, 2006). Indeed, with the advent of service and leisure industry, customers are looking for a new kind of commercial space where leisure commodification acts as the new decoy.

From Leisure Merchandization to Professional 'Leisuration' of Consumption

In order to diversify itself and capture new customers, department stores industry has decided to develop its commercial layout: huge warehouses which used to host 'selling factories' are not enough anymore. In a first time, it has been necessary to surround, to back up and to accompany supermarkets with different kind of small shops which have to 'fixate' customers on site. Those are classical commercial galleries which have to attract the passerby who feels like he is going to save time by doing all his purchases in the same place. In these very common spaces today[66], leisure is already there through many specialized shops: sports items, cultural products stores, interior design or gardening firms. In a second time, commercial spaces ambiance started to be worked on so that visitors is plunged into an atmosphere of relaxation and pleasure as soon as they get in (Grandclément, 2004). This observation is valid for many firms where one can touch or try products, drink a coffee or just hang out[67], everywhere stores try to develop their playful aspect. Going forward with this logic, and 'in order to follow consumers expectations, ... shopping centers try to develop a concept of shopping center-meeting places' (Desse, 2002: 10), which is, in Morocco, in clear adequation with the seek for public spaces proper to favour intimate encounters such as Moroccan alternative use of public gardens shows it. They also multiply activities which would not be properly understood as having pecuniary aims, such as relaxation areas, nurseries, free wireless internet, cafés. The bottom line is to keep customers from leaving, to offer them more and more services and reasons to come at the shopping centre. However, it is not yet following the American model of 'retailtainment' and its generalization of leisure model to the whole commercial space 'looking for bringing new life experiences to its visitors/buyers' (Andrieu and Al, 2004: 27).

In this matter, it clearly appears that Morocco is a bit forward on Europe which seems to be unsure about this model of offer development. With the Al Mazar mall and moreover with the coming Casablanca's 'Mall of Morocco', investors are claiming this connection with the American model. More and more, in the USA, in Europe and in Morocco as well, experiential marketing (Holbrook et Hirchman, 1982; Grandclément, 2004) is a tool to organize a hedonistic staging of contemporary commercial locations, in order to change yesterday's duty into leisure time. Finally, through the advent of retailtainment, market professionals are going past the sole ambition of leisure consumption to aim at 'leisuring' the consumption.

Retail Stores and Malls as a Proper Leisure Activity: The Whole Within the Part

Personal 'Leisuration' and Non-utilitarian Consumption

So it appears that with the evolution of consumption during the 20th century, one can observe the movement 'from an offer based economy to a demand based economy' (Lipovetsky, 2006: 10) and that because of consumer's new individualized and hedonistic desires, retail industries entered a phase of 'leisuration' of consumption in order to 're-enchant' purchases (Ritzer, 1999). We have qualified it as a 'professional leisuration' of shopping locations. Indeed progressive openings of several destination malls in Morocco seems to show that this tendency does not only concern western countries. Through this 'leisuration' phenomenon – which is symetrical to the aim of diversification through leisure activities followed by department stores industry – appears Morin's hollogramatical principle (1990). Indeed, if leisure become part of shopping centres and retail stores offers, those industries appear in the same time to become proper leisure activities, and as Lipovetsky is outlining it, if 'economists notice the development of leisure consumption, actually there are massive parts of consumption which are functioning as leisure' (2006: 75).

However, beyond the retailtainment model, it appeared during our observations that individuals themselves tend to consider consumption locations such as supermarkets or malls in a playful way, which is consistent with what Berriane explains when he emphasizes on the Moroccan perception of souqs during moussems as a proper moment of leisure. Therefore, we will talk of a 'personal leisuration' phenomenon. Thus, as Cochoy noticed it, 'the attendance at commercial spaces could from now on have other justifications than the only re-supplying, such as perambulation, contemplation or walk' (2005: 92). Such leisure understanding of commercial environment could be compared to the growing use of Moroccan administrative and merchant city-centres for promenade, as described by Berriane (1988).

'Personal Leisuration' and Attraction for an Exogenous Model

In Morocco, the 'leisuration' is not only generated by shopping centres promoters, it is not only professional but also resulting from consumers' representations. Indeed, retail store environment itself is understood as a proper leisure activity by its customers. Thus, we observed that Moroccan supermarkets users are not only using those places for consumption aims, and are often visiting them without any intention of purchase but in order to hang out with their family or simply to have a walk. Indeed, Moroccan visitors claimed their perception of supermarket as a place where one can 'just hang out', where one does 'not buy anything' or 'not much'. It is very interesting to notice the almost systematic use of the sight lexical field with such terms as 'to look at', 'many things here that you can't see at souqs'. It shows a perception of modern commercial environment related to entertainment and show. The take-away-icecream shops which one can find in many 'Marjane' stores reminds us of same shops on beaches and inner-cities and demonstrate that the industry itself has taken in account this non-utilitarian perception of some users. This phenomenon of non-utilitarian consumption could be linked to an attraction for a new commercial model which is associated to western opulence and is to be related to 'reversed exotism' (Gauthier, 2008) as it is demonstrated by the symmetry of tourist behaviour on souqs compare to Moroccans behaviour in malls and supermarkets (Danteur, 2011). However, in the concern of Morocco 'this attraction for novelty is also to resemble to a form of local tourism since there are, in the departments of supermarkets, way more walkers than actual customers' (Abis and Al, 2007: 72). Retail stores industries and commercial models such as malls are seen as 'showcases of the West' (Bennani Chraïbi, 1997), and take part to what we called the second illusion of abundance[68]/pard plain (Danteur, 2009) which is based on the economical, technological and cultural 'development's ideology' (Latouche, 1989). And yet, as Bennani Chraïbi describes it, 'the natural prolongation of this stereotype cultivates a representation of Europe and North America as land of opulence, as consumer's paradise' (1997: 120) which would soon be at reach for Moroccans who see western firms coming with their new consumption model. Yet, the necessary standard of living and ability to pay to access this commercial model such as malls and supermarkets and pure consumption exclude a large part of Moroccan population and turn those people into simple spectators who can only afford to 'hang out, to look'[69] in a logic that could be, once again, considered as reversed exotism (Gauthier, 2008).

The 'Personal Leisuration' as an Appropriation of an Exogenous Model

In her article about young Moroccans and Egyptians facing western cultural influence, Bennani Chraïbi suggests an analysis of the West's representations in Maghreb which she links to three main mechanisms: 'appropriation, attraction and repulsion'. She describes how 'alteration underlines dynamics of fascination and demonization. But it could also happen that what comes from the outside would eventually be appropriated in terms of practices and representations' (Bennani Chraïbi, 1997: 117). This perspective seems to us to be pertinent and allows us to find out more about the 'personal leisuration' of the exogenous commercial environment (Danteur, 2009). Indeed, we can observe that some Moroccans feel a certain attraction because of the 'new' aspect of this commercial model where there is a lot to 'find out about'. And yet, others 'don't really like it', showing kind of a repulsion facing this foreign model which is far from the traditional Moroccan distribution channels. In their minds, 'everything's too expensive', products are 'not fresh' and 'we don't know where they are coming from'. Thus, we have noticed during our observations that some groundless representations about products freshness were the basis of the purchase location choice, especially in the concern of food products (Danteur, 2010). But beyond both those opposed phenomena of fascination and demonization, we notice following Bennani Chraïbi's analysis, a certain tendency to appropriation of this new commercial model by Moroccan consumers through the 'personal leisuration' of retail firms and shopping centres as well. Many customers, indeed, come 'mostly to walk around, to look and listen to discs'. The shopping mall or the supermarket have been turned by users into a leisure activity, a place used to hang out, 'to go out' but 'there is almost nobody who buys anything'. Check-out employees are strangely unoccupied even though the attendance is important. During our observations on the opening day at Al Mazar, the crowd was so compact that we had to wait 15 minutes in order to get in. However, most of the customers would eventually get out with empty hands. Looking at the basket's pile and the amount of carts available at the entrance and comparing it with the number of cars in the parking lot is a good way to get an idea about the repartition between actual customers and passersbys. And yet, at many occasions, we observed in Morocco, whether it was in shopping malls or in supermarkets, that although attendance was important, most of the carts and baskets were available.

As our observations have shown it at the Al Mazar mall in Marrakesh, the attendance is quite important and a massive crowd comes even though the mall's installation was not yet totally finished. However, most of those people were obviously not there with a purchasing purpose. This tendency to non-utilitarian attendance is a permanent feature of our observations within the Moroccan retail industry whether it was at Rabat, at Casablanca or at Marrakesh. Many customers appeared to be more passersby than actual consumers. Therefore we can think that a large part of them are practicing kind of a 'local tourism' (Abis and Al, 2007) which is clearly to be related to what we called the 'personal leisuration' of the commercial environment. It seems to mean that they are re-appropriating this environment and creating a 'consumption (which) has become a space of cultural production' (Warnier, 1999: 91). This kind of 'tourism', generated by the attraction toward the abundance staged by the retail industry (Danteur, 2009) is a clear example of the re-appropriation of the western model of retail into local practices. In this matter, it clearly is to be linked to what Berriane is underlining when he points toward the complex nature of leisure activities in Morocco, which are both 'Moroccanization of imported practices and modernization of old practices' (Berriane, 1989: 368). Such complex phenomena are to be considered as appropriation and acculturation which could be conceptualized through the notion of syncretism. It appears to us that there is of similarity in the use by Moroccans of globalized leisure and of traditional activities as well, which we would qualify as a kind of hybridation within cultural permanence.

Finally, the study of both evolutions of traditional leisure as well as contemporary globalized recreative activity patterns in Morocco seems to us to advocate for the complexity theory interest. Indeed, such complex hybrid situation as the Moroccan leisure patterns has a lot to gain to be described and formalized through the terms of complexity thought, and in this case, especially through the hologrammatical principle. As a matter of fact, such conceptual tools allow us to describe and understand a complex reality without a common tendency in social science to oversimplify and therefore loose sight of the empiric reality. The theories of complexity have in such matters the great quality to favour a unbiased regard and allow to analyse without schematize combinatory situations and composite society such as the Moroccan significant example.

Notes

1. All quotes are freely translated from french by the author.
2. From this succession of cultural influences, with which came along religious beliefs, especially Judaism and Christianity before Islam, Berbers has received a reputation of easy apostasy. It is, without a doubt, to be linked to the writings of Muslim historian such as Ibn Khaldun who described Berbers who 'committed apostasy dozens of times' (Ibn Khaldoun, 1925) and wrote: 'Coming back to their ancient beliefs after each Arabic defeat or with every political crisis ..., it is only after the conquest of Spain ... that Berbers have lost their old habit to commit apostasy' (Ibn Khaldoun, 1925 in Abitbol, 2009: 36).
3. The term 'cherifian' signifies a filiation to the Prophet.
4. Our difficulty to run ourselves photography sessions within Moroccan stores – although we launched many official approaches – justifies this indirect access to such a material through anonymous sources who gave us all the details about these pictures context.
5. In the concern of the 'harnessing of verbal exchange', since the conversations were not easy to transcribe immediately and hardly recordable, they were memorized and copied on session's book as soon and as close as possible. On this technique, see Cochoy, 2008.
6. We have received a grant for mobility from EU's AVERROES programme which allowed us to conduct field observations from April 2009 to April 2011, within the Mohammed V-Agdal University, in Rabat. Our main work is about Moroccan retail store industry, but our interest in the field of leisure was imposed by our observations which showed the necessity to consider such factors as leisure and tourism in the study of Moroccan society.
7. The interest of colonization's sociologists and anthropologists (Nicolas, 1961), has been indeed mostly focused on Moroccan Berber populations (Michaux-Bellaire et Salmon, 1905; Montagne, 1930) or Algerian kabyles (Hanoteau et Letourneux, 1872; Masqueray, 1886). They were considered as marginalized and hostiles

toward the central power (*makzen*). This insistence of the opposition between fiercely autonomous and anarchic tribes (*siba*) and sultanate's institutions without real mastering of its territory, puts those authors into the category of colonial politics. Such a dualistic consideration of North-African social structures was largely exploited as a political weapon by the French colonial State to impose its authority and pacify the populations. Alliances signed with certain tribes or the episode of the Berber *dahir* which aimed to give them a specific status (Abitbol, 2009) testify of this instrumentalization of a overrated opposition between *makhzen* and *siba*.

8. Thus, the most famous analysis, such as those of Montagne, describe a Berber society where tribe is composed by cantons (*taqbilt-s*) allied by a common genealogy, real or fictional. Small patriarchal groups (*ikh-s*) are confronting for the chief position through struggles and alliances (*coff-s*), from which arises a charismatic personality (*amghar*). Oppositions are balanced between equal forces of the different units which join at the jemaa, tribal assembly 'which work to enforce, in their primitive States, democratic or oligarchic institutions' (Montagne, 1930: 7 in Nicolas, 1961: 533) which acknowledge a chief who is able to federate a cluster of *taqbilt-s* within a *leff*. Those are groups of two *taqbilt-s* according to Montagne, who developed a theorie of the chest board to characterize *leff*'s struggles within a given territory (Montagne, 1930). This theory, as well as Montagne's others, was to be criticized for its lack of empirical foundations and its excessive generalization (Nicolas, 1961). Finally, Montagne and the other authors of colonial social science (Hanoteau et Letourneux, 1872; Masqueray, 1886), who attempted to describe the many units composing tribal societies turn out to be 'unable to think North-African societies in terms of political collectivities, ... (and) reduced them to a situation of parcels impossible to put together' (Vatin, 1982: 8).
9. The main characteristics of the model are the patrilinear kinship system, the coincidences between kinship relations and geographical repartition, a principle of fusion/fission at every level of the units which compose a group, a system of chief election and the arbitration role of marabous (Ben Salem, 1982: 122). The work of Evans-Pritchard borrows pieces to Radcliffe-Brown's theory of kinship through filiation (1969) who had taken a specific gaze upon Durkheim's concept of structure (1893). On the origins of segmentation theory and the ramifications of the Anglo-Saxon segmentarist school, see Ben Salem, 1982 or Vatin, 1982.
10. Vatin describes what could be ironically qualified of segmentarist filiation and notices that Hanoteau and Letourneux (1872) already 'present the Berber society as harmonic, in a balance founded on mechanic solidarity, cohesion in similarity as in binar faction' (1982: 16). Montagne describes a tribe standing on a dialectic balance/unbalance which is founded upon 'intern tensions and discussions' (ibid.). The like with Gellner's work is obvious, even if he improves his description and models, based on Evans-Pritchard, these notions in order to extract his segmentarist generalization. His model takes the form of an concentric interlocking of different units, with 'for every circle its function, for every level segmentary structures, its social order, its cohesion, its link to a single lineage, real or mystic' (Vatin, 1982: 17).
11. Hart's work (1965) would suffer the same critics, since authors regret that it does not consider the relation between individuals in the concern of land conflicts, which, rather than to be described as a lineage segmentary system, would be better analysed if understood in terms of network (Munson, 1989).
12. Waterbury's book (1970) is, in this matter, very significant. Indeed, the author proceeds of a double shift by applying the segmentarist model, already imported

from Sudan (Evans-Pritchard, 1937) to Moroccan Atlas mountain tribes (Gellner, 1969), to paste it up to contemporary Moroccan political elites. This generalization of a model without taking in account its context of elaboration is justified by the author through a principle of imitation which drive to a conversion of traditional tribal structures into political organizations. If this pasting of a theoretical model outside of its original context is already subject to critics by itself, it is however the author's method, from our point of view, which is the most problematic aspect. Indeed, Waterbury's hypothesis to apply segmentarism to contemporary political groups is given a priori, and it is only afterward that the author starts to look for empirical confirmation. If this methodological approach is not to be condemned, and fits a vision of the scientific procedure which we would qualify of Popperian (Popper, 1955), it drives him to multiply what Lahire (2005) calls the 'perfect examples', selecting verbatism or historical episodes which confirm his hypothesis and put systematically away every which contradicts his model. Such critics could be addressed to several authors who claim the link to Anglo-Saxon segmentarism, for whom formalism and the seek for unchanging anthropological structures proper to modeling, drive to lose sight of the empirical reality. For a critique of segmentarist theories, see Ben Salem, 1982; Munson, 1989 or Roberts, 2002. On Waterbury's book (1970), see Clément, 1975.

13. These researches seem to be led, in all the social sciences, with more epistemological vigilance in the concern of local specificities which go past the un-precise and general notion of tribal system (Laroui, 1978: 155). Numerous works thus take a part to this renewal of Moroccan society's study, especially through a focus on links between tribal groups and central power of the *makhzen* (Bourquia, 1991; El Harras, 1998).
14. The links between *makhzen* and tribes appear way more complex than the simple opposition in which segmentarists have them locked up. When most Moroccan dynasties were brought to power thanks to the submission (*bay'a*) of powerful tribes, such as the Idrissides, examples could also be found of the inverse influence with situations of rebellion, such as during the Rif war when the caïd Abdelkrim El Khattabi had united the tribes of the Rif area in order to fight the Spanish, the French and even the Moroccan armies of the Sultan, who was feeling threatened by this insurrection (Courcelle-Labrousse et Marmié, 2008). The *bay'a* is at the foundation of the relationship between the Sultan and tribes. It is an act of faith through which the different religious and social authorities are expressing their submission and acknowledge him the royal status (Abitbol, 2009). On the political and religious functions of this bay'a, Allali notices: 'In Morocco, these links of allegiance have been reinforced by the monarchist regime since the rise of Idrissides, less than a couple of centuries after the beginning of the Islamic era. Being for most of them descendants of te Prophet, Moroccan kings have always impersonated the image of Commander of the faithful, making the allegiance not only a formal act of volunteer submission, but also and above all a consecration of the religious rule' (Allali, 2004: 15).
15. Many contemporary authors who have been interested in the practices of unorthodox Islam, regret the fact that 'maraboutism has become, in French, a confused expression which covers all kinds of activities associated with the adoration of saints' (Crapanzano, 1973: 1 in Allali, 2008: 9).
16. Jacques Berque also insisted on this particularity of the omnipresence of sacred in North-African Islam, physically underlined by the multitude of mausoleum scattered across Moroccan territory in particular: 'This signalization of sacred is punctuating the most characteristics spaces of the North-African landscape. And

this is there a difference with the East which does not know such a proliferation of sacred' (Berque, 1957: 3).

17. The cult of saints and their *baraka* could be linked to beliefs which still exist today. In their book about values and religious daily practices in Morocco, Mohammed El Ayadi, Hassan Rachik et Mohamed Tozy distinguish five main superstitions in which a vast majority of Moroccan says it believes: belief in bad spirits (*jinns*), the bad eye, the black magic, the sexual bad spell (*tqaf*) and mind-reading (El Ayadi et al., 2007: 71–73). Berque sees in the diffusion of this cult of saints, since the 13th century, a reaction to the urban and educated Muslim culture inherited from the Andalous: 'The culture which was transmitted to Morocco by Muslim Spain was mainly a culture of jurists. But the preeminence of this kind has been compensated and often fought by the development of rural types, especially mystics' (Berque, 1957: 11).
18. The cherifian ancestry gives huge prestige and respect: 'In all countries of Islam, the greatest respect is given to the descendants of the Prophet. But nowhere else than in Morocco, this Muslim nobility of blood arouses such a veneration. The Moroccan cherif is indeed a kind of 'super marabout' with a peaceful *baraka* whose only presence is enough to ensure the prosperity of a country' (Abitbol, 2009: 159). Therefore, it is not surprising that several dynasties which reigned over Morocco were claiming their cherifian lineage.
19. Hamès summarizes the importance of kinship in the Islamic law: 'The Islamic law (*fiqh*) turns in a large part around questions of marriage and inheritance, … . Everywhere where there is islamization, yesterday and today, marriage and inheritance, according to the Arabic model of the *fiqh* introduce structural transformations in social and political relations driven by kinship relations' (Hamès, 1987: 100).
20. Berque notices this complexity of kinship in Arabic culture as well: 'But, of course, Arabic genealogies do not always correspond to parental reality. They then purely and simply stand on convention' (Berque, 1961: 57). On this 'elective kinship', see also Conte, 1987.
21. Vatin, about the complex nature of relations between these different institutions of Moroccan and North-African society as well, precises: 'We are here getting in touch with one of the crucial points of contemporary studies about 'Earlier North-Africa', which is a 'contradictory symbiosis'. One could notice about it the presence of contrary aspects, the existence of combinatory complexes within separated autonomous ethnic and political entities. The systems of loyalty, the symbolic exchanges, the violence reduction modes, as well as the networks between central institutions and local communities are part of structures and relations, of situations and exchanges which are of a notably specific diversity' (Vatin, 1983: 192).
22. The author goes further in his analysis of complex links between *makhzen* and *zaouia* of Tamgrout of which he describes 'the role of go-between played - with a relative success - between members of central power, or between them and the population' (Hammoudi, 1980: 629). For him, their relations are part of a 'permanent dialectic … even though (central power) has known absences. But this dialectic is made of tension and conflicts and their collaboration happened lately. No more than segmentarist principle is preeminent, the omnipresence of a State which would be manipulating the *zaouia* could be considered as a satisfying interpretation' (Hammoudi, 1980: 636). Triaud goes in this same direction as well when he affirms: 'The brotherhood, in Islam, has no vocation to State power, or only under very exceptional and extraordinary circumstances, in case of vacancy and carency of Islamic institutions … . It is way more willingly looking for the protection which it would receive from central power than for the overtaking of such power. Only exceptional circumstances, linked to

geopolitics and to the personality of its charismatic leader, could drive the brotherhood beyond its boundaries' (Triaud, 1994: 279).

23. Vatin describes further what we have referred to as Islam complexity: 'There is not only one revealed Islam but several interpreted Islam, sometimes contradictory, even opposed: the one of central power manipulating religious ideology to reinforce its own legitimacy, such as the one of local groups using the Muslim vocabulary to contest the regimes or the imposed order, to claim for a greater respect of the rules transmitted in the Prophet's message to promote counter-califs, … . But, … behind these divergences-differences, there are mobilizing elements, powerful integrative capacities' (Vatin, 1983: 187).
24. For the author, the role of Islam in the transsaharan trade reinforcement is based on several factors: 'The establishment of common laws, the adhesion to values and behaviour codes coming from a single faith, the existence of a common language understood by various individuals of different origins and races, the presence of a central political authority insuring people's and goods' security along the caravan roads, … gave a push to transsaharan trade which importance was clear to the Arabs from the start of Muslim conquest' (Abitbol, 2009: 48). Brachet emphasizes on this same point, underlining: 'The Muslim religion, as a moral and cultural order, offered to merchants from diverse regions some common ideological grounds, which has made easier and organized such exchanges' (Brachet, 2004: 118). On the role of Islam in the development of transsaharan trade, see as well Grégoire et Labazée, 1993.
25. Triaud notices, about a saharan brotherhood (*Sanusiyya*), which he studied and which takes a part in the caravan trade organization: 'The brotherhood thus became a protector of transsaharan trade … (but) did not, however, become a commercial firm, it gave its protection to the main economic actors in exchange for regular gifts' (Triaud, 1994: 275). Such an intervention of saints toward tribes, using their *baraka* to pacify them, and therefore access to the transsaharan trade's manna (Triaud, 1994), is close to the role of arbitration defined by segmentarist theories which described a 'peacemaker marabou, from whose arbitration one refers in case of conflict and whose moral protection is sought to cross unsecured region' (Abitbol, 1980: 7). However, this arbitration role is not limited to the reduction of tensions between equal segments, but establishes 'dependency links between protector saints/entrepreneurs and protected clients, … (and) applies as well to collectivities and to individuals (simple travelers, by example)' (ibid.).
26. There is, in our eyes, the main argument of Brachet's article, which presents the structuring aspect of such a trade for Tuareg tribal system through this group's social reproduction as well as the influence's and territory's expansion of this group. Brachet indicates: 'Thus, it appears that inter-individual and intergroup relations which were tied through such a trade, took part to the general political organization of Tuaregs' (Brachet, 2004: 120). Bonte describes especially how the tribe of Laghlâl from Shingitti involvement in transsaharan trade took a part to transform the 'foundations' of their social organization, through 'the development of dates production, which was mostly commercialized in addition to the most traditional salt transportation, the growing use of slave work or the change of organization of pastoral activities to have at their disposal the necessary caravan's animals' (Bonte, 2000: 50). On this influence of transsaharan trade on tribal organization, see Bonte, 1998 as well.
27. The control of exchange channels is then on of the major points of competition between *makhzen*, *zaouia-s* and tribes, as Hammoudi is underlining it: 'The question of resources control is therefore of the strategic kind. And yet, … *zaouia*

and the nomad groups is threatening to deprive the State from it: roads, markets and peasant groups protection are the crucial objects of the competition' (1980: 637). Such a competition has sometimes been resolved through political deals, especially through the nomination of *caids* and the acknowledgment by central power of tribal chiefs political authority (Pascon, 1977), but it sometimes led to repression from some Sultans, who with religious rigorism, imposed their authority and domination on transsaharan trade resources: 'The great combat of Moulay Sliman was the one he led restlessly against brotherhoods. Indeed, he did not stop to publically condemn the cult of saints, even forbidding the *moussems*' organization which gathered every year across the country thousands of people around the many *zaouia-s* in the kingdom' (Abitbol, 2009: 282).

28. Allant à l'encontre de bien des écrits traitant du tourisme et du loisir dans les pays en développement, Mohammed Berriane propose une analyse innovante dès son travail de thèse en 1989, ainsi qu'au long de nombreux articles traitant du 'tourisme national' (1988; 1993; 2001) au Maroc: 'L'intérêt du Marocain pour les activités récréatives ne serait qu'une reproduction mimétique des modèles de comportements que véhicule le touriste étranger; ... . Adopter ce raisonnement sans nuance, c'est oublier que la société marocaine connaissait jadis des activités de récréation et que ses membres effectuaient des déplacements s'apparentant à la définition qu'on donne aujourd'hui aux loisirs et au tourisme' (Berriane, 1989: 111).
29. Berriane develops as second example of traditional recreative practices, the hydrotherapy water sources frequentation, which goes back at least to the roman occupation of the country. This frequentation could be linked as well to the phenomena we have described here since it often includes a visit to the saints within the *zaouia-s*, which very commonly built close to the sources. Such activities therefore includes a very strong religious aspect, linked to the cult of saints and the seek for the goodness of their *baraka* (Berriane, 1989).
30. This religious aspect does not correspond to the orthodox Muslim precepts but to the practices linked to the cult of saints, which is a particularity of Moroccan maraboutic Islam.
31. Berriane, in his Ph.D. dissertation, provides a very detailed mar of the 753 Moroccan *moussems* and their implantation across the country in 1982. He therefore demonstrates the actual contemporary reality of such events. Such festivities, if they are often rooted in rural territoriality, take more and more importance around the urban centres which developed during the 20th century (Berriane, 1989).
32. Reysso (1988) describes how *moussem* is a temporary opportunity to escape from many daily life constraints, in terms of food habits as well as gender relations. Women especially find there an occasion to get out of the domestic sphere and mix with masculine population.
33. Berriane summarizes: '(The *moussem*) offers the first example in Moroccan socio-cultural life of an event which gives an consequent place to recreation and to entertainment, even though its sacred aspect. It goes along with a migration of population which converge to the same point, attracted by the necessity of pilgrimage but also by the need of leisure as well. Most of the time ending the agricultural year, *moussem* is, finally the place for entertainment, sometimes the only one for rural population' (Berriane, 1989: 118).
34. The study of religious phenomena, such as the different pilgrimages in Islam countries, is, since the end of 1980s, a renewed field for social sciences which are interested in religion and analyse their polymorphous aspect, associating religion, trade or leisure. On this thematic, see Chiffoleau et Madœuf, 2005; Aubin Boltanski,

2005 or Nabti, 2010. For an ethnographic study of a Judaic pilgrimage in Morocco, which shares many characteristics with these previous examples, see as well Dakhama, 2005.

35. Finally, the author defines such events' origins in the association of Arabic religious feast tradition and North-African maraboutic cult and souqs (Berriane, 1989). He emphasizes in this matter on Troin's works about souqs implantation in Morocco which already have shown a congruence between souqs organization, religious phenomena linked to cult of saints and festivities organization (Troin, 1971). This associations of different problematic, commercial, religious, historical, recreative, cultural and social as well drive Chiffoleau et Madœuf to speak of the polymorphous aspect of pilgrimage (2005).
36. Berriane notices: 'Heavy summer heats during daytime are slightly reducing the audience and amount of shows. Those are limited to the *fantasia*. The traditional equestrian games attract a large crowd which hang there for hours watching and commenting the horsemen's performance from different tribes, defending its team against other *douar*'s supporters' (Berriane, 1989: 131). Fantasias are ritualized equestrian contests which consist of rival tribes confrontations in ridding or gunning battles.
37. The author precises: 'The exact sense of this word is very significant about the recreative aspect of *moussem*: the terms of *fraja*, *farraja* and *tafarraja* mean respectively show, make a show and watch a show, but the substantive form, 'al fourja', means the relief going with a time of relaxation which comes after a time of constraints' (Berriane, 1989: 132).
38. The mwouloud is an Islamic holy day which celebrates the birth of the Prophet.
39. If the trances which occur during the practices of brotherhoods such as the *Gnawas* could not really, a priori, be qualified as ludic or recreative, those brotherhoods are sometimes showing their rituals during festivals or religious feast, and the population which watch those shows is often associating it with an aspect of leisure and entertainment, as our interviews about Jemaa El Fna's touristic activities have shown it (Danteur, 2011, to be printed).
40. Those imperialist ambitions during History were translated by many European incursion attempts from the Portuguese, the Spanish, the Dutch, the British and the French which had more or less happy endings, as it is shown by the occupations of cities along the Mediterranean and Atlantic coasts since the 15th century. Those European possessions have risen revolts from vast tribal confederations, united by the call for *jihad*, and generated the cessations and betrayals from members of royal families willing to overcome the Sultan. It drove to famous war and battles such as the 'Battle of the Three Kings', in 1578 at Ksar-El-Kebir where three kings died - two rival saadian Sultans and the King Sebastian of Portugal - during en epic combat which ended by a Moroccan victory and the rise of Sultan Ahmed Al Mansour (Nekrouf, 1984).
41. The French military penetration and the Tuareg's rebellion repression put an end to those hundred years old commercial exchanges, especially because of the almost complete extermination of camels during the many combats which opposed tribes and French armies. Brachet underlines, however, the responsibility of certain tribes which committed many razzias and developed insecurity of roads, as well as the role of the drop of interest for Sudanese products or the appearance of new commercial roads, which competed the traditional Saharan circuits, in the progressive decline of transsaharan trade (Brachet, 2004). We will add, furthermore, that those exchanges, if they do not have their past importance, are still persisting outside of

Saharan States' control (Grégoire et Schmitz, 2000), most of the time in a clandestine or informal way, thus 'Sahara is today knowing important transnational migration flux ... (and) therefore takes back its secular function, momentary and partially restricted, of transit and exchange land' (Bensaâd, 2003: 7).

42. Today, if tribes are still doing their *bay'a* to do allegiance to the King, their influence in the Moroccan social structure is largely weakened even if they still are present in the rural population.
43. We furthermore notice that these practices were repressed more or less violently in the whole North-African area by the various regimes willing to monopolize the religious legitimacy, such as in the Moroccan case the Department of religious matters, or by Islamists in Algeria during the 1990s (Andézian, 2000).
44. The statistic inquiry about daily religious practices in Morocco, directed by El Ayadi, Rachik and Tozy (2007) seems to confirm this drop of interest for individual religious pilgrimage linked cult of saints (*ziyara*), in the different social categories.
45. Casablanca's example is in this matter very significant. The city, which had only 1500 inhabitants in the beginning of the 20th century, is today the largest urban area of the country counting more than 3 millions inhabitants (Garret, 2005: 28).
46. If the author, commenting Berriane's work, applies this formula to Moroccan touristic practices, it seems to us, however, that this analysis could be applied as well to numerous fields of Moroccan social life such as religion (El Ayadi, Rachik et Tozy, 2007), food habits (La Vie Eco, 2008), leisure and consumption habits (Bennani-Chraïbi, 1997).
47. We will link here this idea with the tribal spirit notion, and more particularly with the Khaldunian concept of *asabîya*, which designs the cohesion and religious force of a group through the clan spirit (Goumeziane, 2006: 42). Hamès emphasizes this link saying: 'Family spirit is the support of the sentiment that seizes groups which are feeling *asabîya*' (Hamès, 1987: 111).
48. The author advances that 'nuclear family is now the most common structure among Moroccan population. It represents 60.3 per cent of all the families' (El Harras, 2006: 110). It is a determinant change in comparison with the traditional family model, in which many generations were living under the same roof. It strongly impacts the autonomy of young married couple who then access to a new intimacy as well as a more important independence regarding the domestic decisions, where the old authority relation between mother-in-law and daughter-in-law used to be prevailing. The author adds: 'Domestic family cells are already showing signs of individuation and autonomy in regard to kinship. Indeed, the will to affirm a lineage filiation, which used to drive parents to give to their children their grand-parents' first name, tends to weaken' (ibid.: 117).
49. Developed by MacCannel in his book 'The Tourist. A new theory of the leisure class' (1989), the paradigm of the authenticity quest is, using Goffman's theatre metaphor (1973), describing the vain search of exotism which drives touristic behaviour across the world. They cannot, however, access to the 'backstage' areas of the scene which is created for their benefit. In the case of Morocco, the example of Jemaa El Fna square in Marrakesh and its patrimonialization process is of the most significant. On this see Gatin, 2008; Choplin et Gatin, 2010 et Gauthier, 2010. It is this tendency, to try to give to the tourists what they are looking for, which is driving authorities to stage a fake authenticity: 'To keep attracting tourists .... Arabic world cities must adapt and match the evolution of a changing trade and offer to their visitors a different world, in some ways enchanted, which fits their expectations and the promises of East made by travel agencies and magazines' (Colin, 2006: 432).

And to satisfy this quest, touristic promoters do not hesitate to create from scratch patrimonial reinterpretations: 'A certain image of medinas, coming from an orientalist tradition, is today dominating, to the point that it drove to the recent construction of a completely artificial medina in the city of Yasmine Hammamet. Celebrating the Arabic and lousian city, this commercial medina, offered to touristic consumption, aims to enchant tourist' (Barthel, 2004: 1).

50. As Berriane rightly affirms: 'The success of tourism and leisure among Moroccans is not a simple imitation of imported practices' (1989: 171).
51. The author summarizes: '(Public gardens) allow a to take a distance from social norms ... (and) offer to lovers anonymous places allowing intimacy through their configuration, but offering as well a moral cover if the couple is discovered because of their public aspect' (Gillot, 2002: 272).
52. The points of such a systematic take over of *moussems* are diverse for Berriane: 'In addition of an obvious ideological manipulation aiming to enforce central power's spiritual legitimicy, this take over tends to diffuse the image of a national State taking advantage of such mass events to deploy all its symbols: flags, law enforcement, government representatives, local representatives, etc. ... . We must add to this, finally, the moussem take over by the Department of Tourism to enrich and diversify its product' (Berriane, 1989: 142).
53. Berriane provides in his dissertation the reproduction of a journal article which gives the programme of a *moussem*, and which is very significant of this second movement of hologrammatical movement (Morin, 1990): its title, indeed, claims 'May the party start!'. The event, if it still officially is centred on a saint adoration, shows a programme mostly axed around leisure and cultural patrimony promotion (1989: 143).
54. The author precises this similarity between *moussem* and hydrotherapy in the association of maraboutim and leisure activities: 'From the beginning, the religious aspect was dominant in such traditional practices of hydrotherapy. All sources which had healing powers were associated to a saint's tomb. Many legends ... testify of this mysticism which ruled over those practices ... . But the leisure justifications were not absent of such traditional frequentations which often drove families looking for rest and relaxation' (Berriane, 1989: 155).
55. Considered by Morin as the third pillar of his paradigm, the hologrammatical principle, as well as both the others principles of his complex thought - dialogical association of opposed but complementary terms and retroaction which states that products are in the same time cause and consequence of what is producing them - are originally coming from combined aspects of Pascalian thought, chaos theories (Gleick, 2008) and cybernetics (Wiener, 1952; Foerster, 2003).
56. On the intervention of market's professionals in consumption and capitalism evolution, see Chandler, 1988 and Cochoy, 1999.
57. In this matter, there is a clear opposition between Lipovetsky's analysis and those from authors such as Bauman (1990) or Maffesoli (1989) who consider this new consumption's habits as a proof of an end of individualism through what they called neo-tribalism, considering consumption as a pursuit of identity. On this perception see also Dunn, 2010. However if Lipovetsky's perspective differs on the matter of individualism, it joins those authors by underlining the importance of immediacy.
58. Actually if nobody is selling anymore to him, consumer's choices are not to be considered as totally independent and free. Indeed, to avoid 'embarrassment of choice', choices have been 'equipped' by market professionals thanks to devices and techniques such as packaging, marketing and merchandizing. Thus, consumers are led by those devices to choose a product rather than another allowing them to realize

a 'saving of choices'. (On this analysis of choices and their equipment within retail stores, see Cochoy, 1999–2002).

59. Once again here we can see the same logic applied to traditional leisure in Morocco, such as hydrotherapy, and their contemporary evolution. Moroccan users of those activities are nowadays looking for more services and leisure offer.
60. Thus, in Marrakesh, Al Mazar Mall's alleys have been named after local plants, so one walks 'bougainvillea street' towards the Virgin Magastore, one crosses 'jasmine alley' to go to Carrefour.
61. During our observations several situations have illustrated this phenomenon, when Moroccan customers explained that they chose to come to the Mall of Marrakesh, Al Mazar, to avoid the heat of the summer. In another perspective, we could link such alternatives use with the example of public garden developed by Gillot, indeed, in the malls as well, young Moroccans are finding a public and anonymous setting which allow them to have intimate encounters and escape the moral code without being suspected.
62. As Desse outlines it, the appearance of leisure activities within peripheral commercial areas when they used to be traditionally based downtown (movie theatres, restaurants, cultural areas) 'illustrates the growing competition between both those poles of the city' (Desse, 2002: 7), each one empersonning the other, cities are becoming commercial centres, commercial facilities are taking form of cities.
63. Supermarkets and shopping centres as well are open spaces where it must be easy to get in but difficult to get out without consuming. The use of 'magic doors' or turnstiles which 'participates to convert a visitor into a buyer' as Cochoy describes them (2008: 38) is a very meaningful example. Only allowing the entrance, 'they aim less to close a door ... than to lock customers up, in order to force them to get out by a different location ... so that they are driven to travel all over the store passing by products islands or sale shelves and thus to prompt them to make ... a few stops and purchases' (Cochoy, 2008: 38).
64. For example, 'The Auchan's life, the true life', 'The easier life' for French firms such as Auchan and Champion or 'Label' Vie' which is one of the main Moroccan firms name and which could be translated as 'Label Life' (it is a wordplay meaning 'the beautiful life' in French).
65. By example, the fruits and vegetables self-service section in the French firm 'Monoprix' is labeled as the 'picking spot'. Customers will 'collect' and 'pick' their products before weigh them up. Cochoy outlines the pastoral analogy which he expresses as following: 'as a garden, the supermarket has alleys (departments), its squares (lanes), its botanic (price tickets), its gardeners (demonstrators, warehousemen, merchandisers) and its walkers (visitors, customers)' (Cochoy, 2005: 81). In Morocco's case, this garden metaphor is even more accurate since supermarkets or malls are used in diverted ways, by the youth especially, as places of encounter as they are using public garden (Gillot, 2002). The Moroccan industry adopted a strategy emphasizing on the souq mimetism, it developed a product staging which reproduces the traditional markets of the medina, in a logic of hybridation (Danteur, 2009). On such 'traditionalizations' of modernism, see Babadzan, 2009.
66. Whether it is in France, in the USA or in Morocco, the commercial gallery model is largely diffused. It has to be distinguished from the destination mall concept which includes a far more developed leisure offer.
67. The 'Virgin Café' which covers 1000 m^2 inside the cultural item store at Al Mazar in Marrakesh is very significant example.

68. The first illusion of abundance in retail stores industry is working within western societies and is the result of a marketing strategy which aims to create through products staging a world of opulence, without seasonal constraints and preserving humans from comfort anxiety. The second illusion of abundance is external and participates to give a false perception of western societies which appear as cockaigne countries where life is easy and luxurious. For a more detailed analysis of those phenomena, see Danteur, 2009.
69. The Moroccan rate of bankarization is estimated by Al Maghrib Bank to 40 per cent of the population (taking the postal bank network in account) in 2009 and should be around 60 per cent in 2013. To compare, this rate is around 98 per cent of French population. Les dossiers de L'économiste (2009), *Bancarisation: la bataille d'occupation de terrain fait rage*, Janvier, Casablanca. Unemployment is estimated to be 15 per cent of Moroccan active population and average income to 3000 dirham/month (300 euros). La Vie Eco (2008), *Le capital continue de détenir 60* per cent *de la richesse produite au Maroc*, 28 November, Casablanca.

References

Abis, S., Padilla, M. (2007). 'La grande distribution au Maghreb', in, *Afkar= idées: revue trimestrielle pour le dialogue entre le Maghreb, l'Espagne et l'Europe*, nE 13, p. 70–73.

Abitbol, M. (2009). *Histoire du Maroc*, Perrin, Paris.

Abitbol M. (1980). 'Le Maroc et le commerce transsaharien du XVIIe au début du XIXe siècle', in, *Revue de l'Occident musulman et de la Méditerranée*, NE30, pp. 5–19.

Allali, B. (2008), 'Culture et gestion au Maroc: une osmose atypique', in E. Davel, J.P. Dupuis et J.-F. Chanlat (dir.), *Gestion en contexte interculturel: approches, problématiques, pratiques et plongées*, Québec, Presses de l'Université Laval et Télé-université (UQAM), 2008.

Andézian, S. (2000). 'Dire la transe en islam mystique', *Archives de sciences sociales des religions*, 111 | Juillet–Septembre.

Andrieu F., Badot O., Macé S. (2004). 'Hypermodernité et distribution: le cas du West Edmonton Mall', in, *Revue Management et Avenir*, Vol. 2, nE 2, pp. 27–50.

Arrif, A. (2006). 'Place publique pour une parole publique: Jama' Lafna, ou le territoire du malentendu', *La pensée de midi* 1/2006 (NE 17), pp. 144–149.

Aubin Boltanski, E. (2005). 'Le mawsim de Nabî Mûsâ: processions, espace en miettes et mémoire blessée. Territoires Palestiniens (1998–2000).', in Sylvia Chiffoleau et Anna Madœuf (dir.), *Les pèlerinages au Maghreb et au Moyen-Orient*, Damas, Presses de l'Ifpo, 'Études contemporaines', 2005, pp. 59–80.

Augé, M. (1992). *Non-lieux*, Editions du Seuil, Paris.

Babadzan A. (2009), 'L''indigénisation de la modernité'. La permanence culturelle selon Marshall Sahlins', *L'Homme*/2, NE 190, pp. 105–128.

Barrey, S., Cochoy, F., Dubuisson-Quellier, S. (2000). 'Designer, packager et merchandiser: trois professionnels pour une même scène marchande', in, *Sociologie du travail*, vol. 42, nE 3, pp. 457–482.

Barrey, S. (2004). 'Fidéliser les clients dans le secteur de la grande distribution: agir entre dispositifs et dispositions', in, Cochoy, F. (Dir.) (2004), *La captation des publics. C'est pour mieux te séduire mon client …*, Presses Universitaires du Mirail, Toulouse.

Barthel, P.A. (2004). 'Enchanter les touristes en médina: mises en scène et construction de lieux 'orientalisants'. Les cas de Tunis et de Yas- mine Hammamet (Tunisie)', atelier 'Enchantement, réenchantement des territoires?' (sous la direction de F. Bruyas et G. Gillot), Afemam 2004.

Bel, A. (1938). *La religion musulmane en Berbérie: esquisse d'histoire et de sociologie religieuses*, Librarie orientaliste Paul Geuthner.

Benmansour, S. (2008). 'Enquête Style de vie des cadres', in, *La Vie éco*.

Bennani Chraïbi, M. (1997). 'Jeunes égyptiens et jeunes marocains face à l'Occident. Appropriation, attrait, répulsion', in, *Egypte/Monde arabe*, nE30–31, pp. 115–144.

Bensaâd, A. (2003). 'Agadez, carrefour migratoire sahélo-maghrébin', *Revue européenne des migrations internationales*, vol. 19 - nE1 | 2003

Ben Salem L. (1982). 'Intérêt des analyses en termes de segmentarité pour l'étude des sociétés du Maghreb', In, *Revue de l'Occident musulman et de la Méditerranée*, NE33, 1982. pp. 113–135.

Berriane, M. (1988). 'Une nouvelle fonction du centre-ville moderne marocain: loisir et convivialité', in *Éléments sur les centres-villes dans le Monde arabe*, URBAMA, nE19, pp. 205–215.

Berriane, M. (1989). *Tourisme national et migrations de loisirs au Maroc*, thèse de doctorat de géographie.

Berriane M. (1993). 'Le tourisme des nationaux au Maroc (une nouvelle approche du tourisme dans les pays en développement)', In, *Annales de Géographie*, t. 102, nE570. pp. 131–161.

Berriane, M. (2001). 'Les nouvelles tendances du développement du tourisme au Maroc', 13ème Festival International du Géographie de St Dié.

Berque J. (1953), 'Notes sur l'histoire des échanges dans le Haut-Atlas occidental', In, *Annales. Économies, Sociétés, Civilisations*, 8e année, N. 3, pp. 289–314.

Berque J. (1957). 'Quelques problèmes de l'Islam Maghrébin', In, *Archives des sciences sociales des religions*. N. 3, pp. 3– 20.

Berque, J. (1974). 'Qu'est-ce qu'une tribu nord-africaine?', in, *Maghreb, Histoire et société*, Alger, SNED, pp. 23–24.

Bonard Y., Felli, R. (2008). 'Patrimoine et tourisme urbain. La valorisation de l'authenticité à Lyon et Pékin', *Articulo - Journal of Urban Research*, 4 | 2008.

Bonte, P. (1998). 'Fortunes commerciales à Shingitti (Adrâr mauritanien) au XIXe siècle', *Journal of African History*, 39: 1–13.

Boubrik, R. (1999). *Saints et société en Islam. La confrérie ouest-saharienne Fâdiliyya*, CNRS, 203 p.

Boujrouf, S. (1996). 'Nouvelles formes d'occupation de l'espace touristique de la ville de Marrakech: l'exploitation de la Palmeraie', In, *Méditerranée*, Tome 84, 3–1996. Tourisme et loisirs. pp. 27–32.

Boukous, A. (1987). 'Identité et mutations culturelles (Maroc)', In, *Revue de l'Occident musulman et de la Méditerranée*, NE44, 1987. pp. 64–68.

Bourgeot, A. (1978). 'Les échanges transsahariens, la Senusiya et les révoltes twareg de 1916–17', In, *Cahiers d'études africaines*, Vol. 18 NE 69–70. 1978. pp. 159–185.

Bourquia, R. (1991). *Etat, Pouvoir, Société: Zemmours*, Dar Attalia, Beyrout.

Brachet, J. (2004). 'Le négoce caravanier au Sahara central: histoire, évolution des pratiques et enjeux chez les Touaregs Kel Aïr (Niger)', *Les Cahiers d'Outre-Mer*, pp. 226–227 | Avril–Septembre.

Camps, G. (2007). *Les Berbères, Mémoires et Identité,* Arles, Actes Sud.

Chandler, A.D. (1988). *La main visible des managers*, Economica, Paris.

Chesneau V. (2001). 'Les supermarchés du loisir', in, *Cités*, vol. 3, nE 7, p. 93–107.

Chiacchiero, J. and Karlsson, L. (2009). *Conditions of Dance in Morocco: Interviews and observations of Adults and Children Involved in Dance Activities in Marrakech*, University of Stockholm.

Chiffoleau S., Madœuf, A. (dir.) (2005). *Les pèlerinages au Maghreb et au Moyen-Orient*, Damas, Presses de l'Ifpo ('Études contemporaines').

Choplin, M.A., Gatin, V. (2010). 'L'espace public comme vitrine de la ville marocaine: conceptions et appropriations des places Jemaa El Fna à Marrakech, Boujloud à Fès et Al Mouahidine à Ouarzazate', *Norois*, 214/1.

Cochoy, F. (1999). *Une histoire du marketing. Discipliner l'économie de marché*, La Découverte, Paris.

Cochoy, F. (1999–2). 'De l'embarras du choix au conditionnement du marché. Vers une socio-économie de la décision', *Cahiers Internationaux de Sociologie*, vol. 106, juillet, pp. 145–173.

Cochoy, F. (Dir.) (2004). *La captation des publics: c'est pour mieux te séduire mon client* ..., Presses Universitaires du Mirail, Toulouse.

Cochoy, F. (2005). 'L'hypermarché: jardin d'un autre type aux portes des villes', in, *Ethnologie française*, vol. 35, nE 1, pp. 81–91.

Cochoy, F. (2008). 'Progressive Grocer, ou la 'petite distribution' en mouvement. États-Unis (1929–1959)', *Espaces et Sociétés*, nE135/4, pp. 25–44.

Cochoy, F. (2008–2). 'Calculation, qualculation, calqulation: shopping cart arithmetic, equipped cognition and the clustered consumer', *Marketing Theory*, 8; 15.

Colin, A. (2006). 'Du paradis à Dream Park: les jardins dans le monde arabe', in, *Annales de géographie*, 2006/4, nE650.

Conte E. (1987). 'Alliance et parenté élective en Arabie ancienne. Éléments d'une problématique', In, *L'Homme*, 1987, tome 27 nE102. pp. 119–138.

Courcelle-Labrousse, V. et Marmié, N. (2008), *La Guerre du Rif*, Points, Paris.

Crapanzano, V. (1980). *Tuhami: Portrait of a Moroccan*, Chicago, University of Chicago Press.

Dakhama, H. (2005). 'La présentation de soi au pèlerinage de Rabbi Yahya Lakhdar (Maroc)', in Sylvia Chiffoleau et Anna Madœuf (dir.), *Les pèlerinages au Maghreb et au Moyen-Orient*, Damas, Presses de l'Ifpo ('Études contemporaines'), pp. 39–58.

Danteur, T. (2009). 'La nouvelle corne d'abondance ou la double illusion de la grande distribution dans les imaginaires collectifs', in Danteur, T. (Dir.), Vel Zoladz R. (Dir.), Xiberras, M. (Dir.), (2009), *Rusca. Imaginaire et multiculturalisme*, janvier, MSH, Montpellier.

Danteur, T. (2010). 'Actor's rationality and irrationality within the moroccan supermarket industry: Toward a complex approach of food choices', ISA Congress, Research Comity nE45, Rational Choice, 16 July, Götenburg, Sweden.

Danteur, T. (2011). 'L'authenticité par la mise en scène. Analyse dialogique des activités touristiques et culturelles de la place Jemaa El Fna et de leurs représentations', *Tourism imaginaries*, Berkeley, February, (To be printed).

Di Méo, G. (2007). 'Processus de patrimonialisation et construction des territoires', in, *Colloque Patrimoine et industrie en Poitou-Charentes: connaître pour valoriser*, Poitiers-Châtellerault: France

Desse, R.P., (2002). 'Les centres commerciaux français, futurs pôles de loisirs?', *Flux,* nE50, Octobrer–Décembre, pp. 6–19.

Dumazedier, J. (1962). *Vers une civilisation du loisir?,* Editions du Seuil, Paris.

Durkheim, E. (1893). *De la division du travail social,* P.U.F., Paris.

Elahmadi, M. (2001). 'TOZY (Mohammed), Monarchie et islam au Maroc', *Archives de sciences sociales des religions,* 114 | avril-juin 2001, document 114.44.

El Ayadi, M., Rachik, H, Tozy, M. (2007). *L'Islam au quotidien. Enquête sur les valeurs et les pratiques religieuses au Maroc,* Casablanca, Prologues, coll: Religion et société.

El Harras, M. (1988). *Tribus et pouvoir: évolution des structures sociales au nord du Maroc,* CNCPRST, Rabat.

El Harras, M. (2006). *Les mutations de la famille au Maroc.*

Evans-Pritchard, E. (1937). *The Nuer*; trad. Les Nuer, Pans, Gallimard, 1968.

Favret-Saada, J. (1966). 'La segmentarité au Maghreb', In, *L'Homme,* tome 6 nE2. pp. 105–111.

Ferreira Freitas, R. (1996). *Centres commerciaux: îles urbaines de la post-modernité,* L'Harmattan, Paris.

Foerster (von), H. (2003). *Understanding, Understanding. Essays in Cybernetic and Cognition,* Springer-Verlag, New-York.

Gadrey, J. (2003). *Socio-économie des services,* La Découverte, Paris.

Gallissot, R. (1978). 'Sociétés segmentaires et violence politique au Maghreb, critique des interprétations par la segmentarité: rapports d'exploitation et reproduction sociale', in, *Cahiers de la Méditerranée,* 1er semestre, pp. 33–50.

Garret, P. (2005). 'Casablanca confrontée à l'Etat colonisateur, aux colons et aux élites locales: essai de micro histoire de la construction d'une ville moderne', in, *La ville coloniale au XXe siècle: d'un sujet d'action à un objet d'histoire,* sous la direction d'Hélène Vacher, Paris, Maisonneuve et Larose, pp. 27–39.

Gatin, V. (2008). 'L'art populaire et le développement local sous le prisme de l'idéologie: au sujet de la place Jemaa el Fna à Marrakech', in, *Actes du colloque: Art et territoires: Vers une nouvelle économie culturelle?,* 76e Congrès de l'ACFAS, Québec, 6 et 7 mai 2008.

Gauthier, L. (2008). 'L'Occident peut-il être exotique? De la possibilité d'un exotisme inversé', in, *Le Globe.*

Gauthier, L. (2010), 'Jemaa El Fna ou l'exotisme durable', *Géographie et Cultures,* nE 72, pp. 117–136.

Gellner, E. (1969). *Saints of the Atlas,* Londres, Weidenfeld and Nicolson, London.

Gershuny, J. (1978). *After Industrial Society? The Emerging of Self Service Economy,* Macmillan, Londres.

Geertz, C. (1973). *The Interpretation of Cultures,* Basic Books, New York.

Geertz C., Geertz H., Rosen L. (1979). *Meaning and Order in Moroccan Society: Three Essays in Cultural Analysis,* Cambridge, Cambridge University Press, pp. 123–313.

Gillot G. (2002). 'Espaces populaires, pratiques intimes: les jardins publics au Caire, à Rabat et à Damas', In, *Géocarrefour,* Vol. 77 nE3, pp. 267 274.

Giraud, M.O. (2002). 'Esthétiques de l'authenticité. Tourisme et touristes chez les Hmong de Guyane française', *Ethnologie française,* XXXII, 3, pp. 447–459.

Gleick, J. (2008). *La théorie du chaos,* Flammarion, Paris.

Goumeziane, S. (2007). *Ibn Khaldoun. Un génie maghrébin,* Maârif El Jadida, Rabat.

Goytisolo, J. (1999). 'Jamâa El Fna: l'univers des diseurs d'histoires', in, *Sources*, juin, nE113, p. 15.

Grandclément, C. (2004). 'Climatiser le marché. Les contributions des marketings de l'ambiance et de l'atmosphère', *Ethnographiques*, Numéro 6, Novembre.

Grégoire, E. and Labazée, P. (1993). *Grands commerçants d'Afrique de l'Ouest.Logiques et pratiques d'un groupe d'hommes d'affaires contemporains*, Paris, Karthala.

Grégoire, E. et Schmitz, J. (2000). 'Afrique noire et monde arabe: continuités et ruptures', *Autrepart, Cahiers des sciences humaines,* Nouvelle série numéro 16, Éditions de l'Aube, IRD.

Hamès, C. (1987). 'La Filiation généalogique (nasab) dans la société d'Ibn Khaldun', In, *L'Homme,* 1987, tome 27 nE102. pp. 99– 118.

Hammoudi, A. (1974). 'Segmentarité, stratification sociale, pouvoir politique et sainteté.Reflexions sur les thèses de Gellner', *Hesperis-Tamuda,* Vol XV, Rabat, pp. 147–180.

Hammoudi, A. (1980). 'Sainteté, pouvoir et société: Tamgrout aux XVIIe et XVIIIe siècles', In, *Annales. Économies, Sociétés, Civilisations*. 35e année, N. 3–4. pp. 615–641.

Hanoteau, A. et Letourneux, A. (1872). *La Kabylie et les coutumes kabyles*, Pans, Imprimerie Nationale.

Hart, D.M. (1965). 'Clan, lignage et communauté locale dans une tribu rifaine', *Revue de Géographiedu Maroc*, nE8, pp. 25–33.

Herpin, N. (2004). *Sociologie de la consommation*, La découverte, Paris.

Jamous, R. (1981). Honneur et Baraka, les structures sociales traditionnelles dans le Rif, Cambridge University Press et Maison des Sciences de l'Homme, Paris.

Kapchan, D. (2007). *Traveling spirit masters. Moroccan Gnawa trance and music in the global marketplace*, Wesleyan University Press, Middletown.

Kurzac-Souali, A.C. (2007). 'Rumeurs et cohabitation en médina de Marrakech: l'étranger où on ne l'attendait pas', in *Hérodote*, nE127, La Découverte, nE4

Lahire, B. (2005). *L'esprit sociologique*, La Découverte, Paris.

Laroui (A.) (1977). *Les origines sociales et culturelles du nationalisme marocain (1830–1912)*, Maspéro, Paris.

Latouche, S. (1989). *L'occidentalisation du monde*, La Découverte, Paris.

Lazzarotti O. (1993). 'Tourisme et Tiers Monde: de la connaissance au savoir géographique', In, *Annales de Géographie*, t. 102, nE570. pp. 181–187.

Lipovetsky, G. (2006). *Le bonheur paradoxal*, Editions Gallimard, Paris.

MacCannell, D. (1989). *The Tourist, A New Theory of the Leisure Class* (2e édition), Shocken Books, New-York.

Malowist, M. (1970). 'Quelques observations sur le commerce de l'or dans le Soudan occidental au Moyen Âge', In, *Annales. Économies, Sociétés, Civilisations*. 25e année, N. 6, pp. 1630–1636.

Mauny, R. (1947). 'Une route préhistorique à travers le Sahara occidental', Bulletin de l'IFAN.

Masqueray, M. (1886). *Formation des cités chez les sédentaires d'Algérie*, Paris,.

Michaux-Bellaire, P. (1927), *Conférences faites au cours préparatoire du Service des Affaires indigènes*, vol. XXVII, Paris,

Miege, J.-L. (1981), 'Le commerce transsaharien au XIXe siècle', In, *Revue de l'Occident musulman et de la Méditerranée*, NE32, pp. 93–119.

Moati, P. (2001), *L'avenir de la grande distribution*, Éditions Odile Jacob, Paris.

Montagne, R. (1930), *Les Berbères et le Makhzen dans le Sud du Maroc*, Alcan, Paris.

Morin, E. (1962), *L'esprit du temps*, Grasset, Paris.

Morin, E. (1990), *Introduction à la pensée complexe*, ESF éditeur, Paris.

Munson, H. Jr. (1989), 'On the Irrelevance of the Segmentary Lineage Model in the Moroccan Rif', *American Anthropologist*, New Series, vol. 91, no. 2, pp. 386–400.

Nabti, M. (2010), 'Le mussem de Meknès. Le déclin d'une tradition spirituelle', *L'Homme*, 1 (nE 193) | pp. 137–165.

Nekrouf, Y. (1984), *La Bataille des Trois Rois*, Albin Michel, Paris.

Nicolas, G. (1961), 'La sociologie rurale au Maroc pendant les cinquante dernières années: évolution des thèmes de recherche', In, *Tiers-Monde*, tome 2 nE8. pp. 527–543.

Pâques, V. (1971), 'Les fêtes du mwulud dans la région de Marrakech', In, *Journal de la Société des Africanistes*, tome 41 fascicule 1. pp. 133–143.

Pascon, P. (1977), *Le Haouz de Marrakech*, C.N.R.S., Paris – Rabat.

Pélegrin-Genel, E. (2010), *Des souris dans un labyrinthe. Décrypter les ruses et les manipulations de nos espaces quotidiens*, La Découverte, Paris.

Popper, K. (1955), *Misère de l'historicisme*, Paris, Éditions Plon, collection Agora.

Radcliffe Brown, A.R. (1969), *Structure et Fonction dans la Société Primitive*, Pans, éd. de Minuit.

Reysoo, F. (1988), *Des moussems au Maroc. Une approche anthropologique*, Schneldruck, Enschede.

Rhani, Z. (2009), 'Le saint et l'ethnologue: sur les voies de l'ethno-ascèse', *Altérités*, vol. 6, no 2, 2009: pp. 115–128.

Ritzer, G. (1999), *Enchanting a disenchanted world: Revolutionizing the means of consumption*, Pine Forge Press, New York.

Roberts, H. (2002), 'From segmentarity to opacity: on Gellner and Bourdieu, or why Algerian politics have eluded theoretical analysis and vice versa', *Crisis States Research Centre*, working papers series 1, 19. Crisis States Research Centre, London School of Economics and Political Science, London, UK.

Sahlins, M. (1993) 'Goodbye to Tristes Tropes: Ethnography in the Context of Modern World History', *Journal of Modern History* 65 (1): pp. 1–25.

Staszak, J.F. (2006), 'Voyage et circulation des images ...', *S. and R.*, nE 21, Avril, pp. 79–99.

Tozy, M. (1988), *Monarchie et islam au Maroc*, Presses de Sciences Politiques, Paris.

Triaud, J.L. (1994), 'Le métamorphoses d'une confrérie: le cas de la sanusiyya', *Annuaire de l'Afrique du Nord*. tome XXXIII. 1994.

Troin, J.F. (1971), 'Essai méthodologique pour une étude des petites villes en milieu sous-développé. Les structures commerciales urbaines du Nord marocain', In, *Annales de Géographie*, t. 80, nE441. pp. 513–533.

Valensi, L. (1977), *Fellahs Tunisiens. L'Economie rurale et la vie des campagnes aux 18ème et 19ème siècles*, Paris, La Haye, éd. Mouton.

Vatin, J.C. (1982), 'Introduction générale. Appréhensions et compréhension du Maghreb précolonial (et colonial)', in, *Revue de l'Occident musulman et de la Méditerranée*, NE33, pp. 7–32.

Vatin, J.C. (1983). 'Les examens contradictoires. Esquisse de bilan des recherches sur les formations étatiques et identités nationales au Maghreb (XIXe début XXe siècle)', in, *Revue de l'Occident musulman et de la Méditerranée*, NE36, pp. 177–200.

Veblen, T. (1970). *Théorie de la classe de loisir,* Gallimard, Paris.

Vermeren, P. (2002). *Histoire du Maroc depuis l'indépendance,* La Découverte, Paris.

Vermeren, P. (2004). 'Les sociétés maghrébines entre néo-réformisme d'État et pression de l'Islam politique', *Mouvements,*/6 no 36, pp. 61–71.

Wagner, L. (2008). 'Diasporic visitor, diasporic tourist', *Civilisations,* 57.

Warnier, J.P. (1999). *La mondialisation de la culture,* Éditions La découverte, Paris.

Waterbury, J. (1970). *The Commander of the faithful. The Moroccan Elite. A study of segmented politics,* Weidenfeld and Nicolson, London.

Wiener, N. (1952). *Cybernétique et société,* Union Générale d'Éditions.

14

On the Possibilities of Leisure Studies in Mozambique

Historical and Sociological Considerations

PATRÍCIO V. LANGA

In a book edited in 2005, *Negotiating Modernity: Africa's Ambivalent Experience,* Mozambican sociologist, Elísio Macamo makes an argument for Africa as a modern construct (Macamo, 2005). He suggests that 'the awareness of an African cultural identity that can lay claims to a single political and economic destiny was the result of a discursive and practical confrontation with existential conditions brought to the continent by its forced integration into European historicity' (Macamo, 2005: 6). This means that in 'the process of coming to terms with slavery and colonialism ... a specific kind of African identity was constituted' (p. 6). Macamo (2005) further contends that the African experience of modernity is ambivalent. This form of ambivalence takes up the predicament of promise and denial. He draws attention to the central contradiction of colonialism and how, paradoxically, it opened up new possibilities for individual Africans.

Macamo (2005) draws his argument from the regulation of native labour in colonial Mozambique, which was, he argues, the privileged way the Portuguese colonial policy makers of that period chose to erect and establish their domination over African societies. The regulation of native labour was premised on the twin ideas that, on the one hand, the proper fulfilment of the European civilising mission depended upon a *vigorous policy of making Africans work* and, on the other, that *Africans needed firm Portuguese guidance* into the *world of wage labour*. Macamo (2005) argues, however, that Portuguese tutelage claims over *Africans effectively prevented Africans from fully integrating into the world of wage labour and amounted*, therefore, to a denial of the modernity promised by such a policy.

It is against the background of Macamo's argument on the African experience of modernity as a continuing link between promise and denial that I would like to situate my engagement with leisure as a social construct in Mozambique. For this contradiction is also present in the historical and sociological nature of leisure in Mozambique. In order to understand the genealogy of the present, it seems important to historicise the social construct of leisure with regard to three periods: the colonial period, post-independence, and the present. The initial preconditions of leisure can be situated within the context of the colonial regulation of native labour. In other words, there is a sense in which it could be argued that leisure was the hidden side-effect of the regulation of native labour by Portuguese colonial authorities in Mozambique. The possibility of leisure emerged from its denial. The period immediately after independence in the mid 1970s was characterized by the attempt to build a socialist society with strict moral regulation of social life. With the collapse of the socialist experiment ten years later and the adoption of neo-liberal and market-driven economic principles, leisure finally became a commodity – certainly another working hypothesis.

My thesis, therefore, is that leisure has been enduringly present in the social fabric of modern Mozambique. Paradoxically, leisure studies have been absent from social inquiry in contemporary Mozambican society. Would it be fair to assume that social scientists have turned a blind eye to one of the dimensions of social life that could offer a privileged account of political, economic and cultural phenomena in Africa?

This paper is organized in four sections. It begins with a brief historical account addressing the absence of a sociology of leisure or leisure studies in Mozambique. This absence occurs despite the abundance of leisure as an experience of social life. The second section looks at some theoretical approaches to leisure studies in order to position the argument. The third section provides some evidence of the social construct of leisure in three historical and sociological phases in Mozambique, and the fourth section presents final considerations on the possibility of a field of leisure studies in Mozambique.

The History of an Absent Presence

The Portuguese sociologist, Boaventura de Sousa Santos, proposes the notion of a sociology of absences to account for non-hegemonic or even counter-hegemonic social experiences. For Santos (2003: 238) 'the sociology of absences consists of an inquiry that aims to explain that what does not exist is, in fact, actively produced as non-existent, that is, as a non-credible alternative to what exists. The objective of the sociology of absences is to transform impossible into possible objects, absent into present objects'. In this sense, this paper is also about the sociology of absence: the absence of leisure studies in Mozambique. How can we turn the non-existence of leisure studies into an existing practice? How has leisure been produced as a non-existent reality in Mozambique?

I presume that it is more appropriate to talk about the study rather than the sociology of leisure in Mozambique. There have been no deliberate and systematic leisure studies in Mozambique. However, Mozambican social life is filled with experiences of (popular) leisure activities such as games, i.e. tchuva[1], songs, and amusement activities (Ismael, ca.1997; Guerreiro, 1962). Some of these leisure activities would take place even in conditions highly adverse to leisure. For instance, in the repressive context of forced labour during colonialism, singing resistance songs was a recurrent way for the workers to express their feelings. As argued by Ambler (2003), the various manifestations of colonialism and capitalism inspired new ideas about leisure and new kinds of leisure, and in the process realigned relations of power and redrew their boundaries. Why then have Mozambicans not shown any interest in leisure studies? My supposition is that there are at least two main reasons for this.

These reasons would perhaps be what Santos (2003) calls the logics and processes through which hegemonic criteria of rationality and efficiency produce non-existence. For Santos (2003) non-existence is produced whenever a certain entity is disqualified and rendered invisible, unintelligible, or irreversibly disposable. On the one hand, the general under-development of social science research in colonial Mozambique, as well as immediately after Mozambique's independence, might well have contributed to the lack of leisure studies. On the other, and more recently, the crisis of the '*sociological imagination*[2]' (Mills, 1959) due to the growth of consultancy and applied research on subjects such as HIV and AIDS has dominated the research agenda. These two hegemonic forces, I suggest, have prevented the emergence of creativity in social research.

Underdevelopment of Social Sciences

The field of social sciences and the humanities was consistently under-developed by the colonial authorities. Prior to Mozambique's independence in 1975 the social sciences were not taught at the country's only higher education institution, the University of Lourenço Marques (ULM), which has existed since 1962 (Mário et al., 2003; Cruz and Silva, 2005). The General University Studies of Mozambique, the first designation for ULM, started with courses in education, medicine, agronomy, forestry, veterinary sciences and civil, mining, electrical and chemical engineering. By 1968, when it became ULM, it had acquired departments of theoretical and applied mathematics, physics, chemistry, biology and geology. As we can see, no social science discipline was taught.

As the war for independence, and international criticism of Portuguese colonial rule progressed, the university expanded to include courses in Romance philology, history, geography, economics and metallurgical engineering. Soon after independence, following the attempt to introduce a socialist regime in the country, courses in Marxism and Leninism were taught at the Eduardo Mondlane University, formerly ULM, renamed in honour of Eduardo Mondlane, the founder and first president of Mozambique's ruling party Liberation Front of Mozambique (FRELIMO).

As Mário et al., 2003 puts it:

> the Faculty of Marxism-Leninism came into being to provide instruction to all university students, and the Faculty for Combatants and Vanguard Workers was inaugurated to enable party cadres to acquire higher education. The university also acquired the Museum of Natural History, the Historical Archive and the Mozambican Institute for Scientific Research, which later became the Centre for African Studies. Scientists from the Soviet bloc and sympathizers (expatriates) from all over the world filled the shortage of trained teaching staff.

A bachelor's degree in Social Sciences was only introduced in the mid 1990s with the establishment of the Unit for Training and Research in Social Sciences (UTRSS). Prior to that, isolated courses and programmes would include some sociological content and literature, but not on a steady basis to train sociologists. Until the year 2000 all Mozambican sociologists were trained abroad, since there was no institutionalized sociology programme or course in any faculty.

In higher education, a new law was enacted in 1993 liberalizing the system and allowing private suppliers to enter the field. The number of higher education suppliers expanded exponentially, leading to the constitution of a differentiated and diversified field (Beverwijk, 2005, Langa, 2006). Sociology was then introduced as an institutionalized discipline in various higher education institutions. Notwithstanding the latest developments in the social sciences, particularly the establishment of sociology as an institutionalized discipline, the positions and concerns of Mozambican sociologists have not been marked clearly, especially with regard to research. Most sociologists, or those who regard themselves as such, have rarely earned advanced postgraduate qualifications in the field or discipline. There is no journal of sociology[3] or any other specialized area of sociology.

Pervasive Consultancy Culture

Much of the social research in southern Africa, and in Mozambique in particular, is dominated by the defiant academic culture of consultancy. According to Mouton et al.,

> Consultancy is widely prevalent across the Southern African region – whether people see it as a positive form of academic work (to enrich themselves, to increase their networks, to transfer knowledge to industry) or as a necessity born out of poor academic salaries and working conditions. The challenge for universities in the region is to ensure that such activities do not further undermine and weaken the already fragile base of many scientific institutions. (Mouton et al., 2008: 206)

How and to what extent consultancy has usurped the space of creativity in the social sciences in Mozambique still needs to be examined carefully. The sentiment amongst most academics is that they are facing TINA: There Is No Alternative to survive as scholars on such meagre salaries. They are forced to engage in consultancy research, most of it on the subject of HIV and AIDS or other related subjects determined by those who demand their intellectual labour. This situation might have exacerbated the neglect of leisure and other interesting areas where social scientists could have used their expertise.

I propose to undertake a brief historical and sociological examination of the preconditions of leisure as a social construct in 'modern' Mozambican society. By modern society I mean the kind of society that emerged from the colonial encounter and its aftermath. As already mentioned, for Macamo (2005) the African experience of modernity is ambivalent precisely because of the nature of that encounter. 'Colonialism was the historical form through which modernity became a real social project on the African continent. Colonialism, however, was premised on the denial of that same modernity to Africans' (p. 8). My claim is that leisure in modern Mozambique inherently reflects that ambivalence. This paper may serve as a modest starting point towards the establishment of a systematic inquiry into leisure in Mozambique. In this sense, I focus my argument in proposing tentative lines of inquiry from which leisure studies might be undertaken in Mozambique in the future.

Leisure Studies in its Different Formulations

The systematic study of leisure is quite a recent phenomenon, dating back only to the period after the Second World War (Zeleza, 2003). This novelty contrasts with leisure as an ancient human experience. In the light of this contrast a number of questions arise: Why is it that leisure was not an object of social inquiry for such a long time? Is it because everyone took it for granted? Leisure is a ubiquitous phenomenon, in developing as well as developed, poor as well as rich countries, and it assumes a multitude of forms. At the same time, in the 1960s, when the sociology of leisure was being institutionalized, universities across North America were creating a subject called 'leisure studies' (Roberts, 2010).

According to Roberts (2010), the undergraduate and postgraduate programs originally prepared students for careers in, and were conducting investigations relevant to, parks and other public recreation services, but the curricula and the research interests of staff spanned the whole field of leisure. Roberts (2010: 1) states that 'from the 1970s onwards, leisure studies departments and courses spread throughout universities in the UK, Australia and New Zealand, and then, albeit far less densely, throughout the rest of Europe, Asia and Latin America'. I did not find significant records on systematic study of leisure in Africa in that time. Then he goes on to argue that sociologists who study leisure have been as likely, probably more likely, to be based in leisure studies rather than squarely in sociology departments, and within leisure studies the boundaries between sociological and other contributions have never been clear.

The notion of leisure as unobligated or discretionary time is historically quite recent, a product of industrialization, which sharpened the separation of the times and spaces of paid work and other activities (Zeleza and Veney, 2003). Zeleza and Veney (2003: xi) rightly remind us that the connections between work and leisure have always been complex, quite contradictory and ever changing. They point out that those who have been interested in and theorized the relationship between work and leisure, mapping its evolution and conducting specific kinds of research, have mostly concentrated on time-budget studies which sought to identify the ways in which people structured their days around such dimensions as domestic duties, subsistence, sleep, employment and leisure (Haywood, et al., 1989: 2 cited in Zeleza and Veney, 2003: xi).

Classical Formulation

Despite its novelty, there are classical formulations of leisure studies whose approaches are still relevant for the contemporary study of leisure. For instance, Sahlins (1972) has argued that agricultural societies usually had a larger fraction of leisure time than modern societies, based on the seasonal nature of agricultural work. Central to this argument is the idea that the amount of leisure time available to members of hunting-gathering societies appears to be far greater than formerly thought. Some scholars also argue that the advancement in agricultural technology and cropping intensity resulted in progressively decreasing leisure for farmers (Just, 1980).

This argument requires a critical re-assessment of that feature of traditional 'surplus theory' which sees adequate leisure for reflection and invention as an indispensable prerequisite for the elaboration of culture. The leisure afforded hunter-gatherers or simple agriculturalists cannot be considered a perfect indicator of 'affluence' when that leisure is the product of marginal value (Just, 1980). For Just (1980: 105) 'leisure time acquires psychological, economic, and social value only when it has become sufficiently scarce to require economising allocation'. In these circumstances leisure – or the lack of it – may still be regarded as a significant dynamic force in cultural development, but in a way opposite to that conceived by traditional surplus theory.

Modern Formulations

A different subject of concern to contemporary scholars of leisure has been the question of whether the competitive demands of the progressively more global economy have eroded leisure time. A range of economic and sociological perspectives on this subject has emerged in recent decades, even though general – and especially international – trends are difficult to establish. For instance, economists have usually defined leisure in opposition to work and more specifically as a residual of the work day – the time left for unoccupied, unremunerated, idle and unproductive activities. In these terms, leisure was in the main regarded as a consumption good – something that could be obtained only by previous income, and therefore something that one effectively bought.

The Nobel laureate Gary Becker published a paper in 1965 in which he developed his theory of the allocation of time (Becker, 1965). His argument was particularly prominent in developing a different approach to leisure studies. He regarded leisure as the time needed to consume the goods and services that individuals purchased with their income. On the same line of analysis, Staffan Linder, a Swedish economist, in his book, *The Harried Leisure Class*, proposes a new way of looking at leisure. His premise is quite easy: for him, labour consists of the time one spends on a job, the expertise that goes into the work, and several other factors. Linder argues that as one's wages and productivity rise, the value of one's time consequently also rises. This leads one to expect more value from all of one's time, including one's free time. The consequence is that people spend their leisure time in more and more intense, hurried, 'efficient' leisure activities. Thus leisure becomes less about relaxing and more about getting relaxing stuff done (Linder, 1970). Both Becker and Linder offered a different interpretation of leisure that emphasized the duration of the act of consumption. The two approaches were consistent in some respects with sociological investigations of modern leisure. These emphasise the historical changes whereby leisure became an increasingly structured activity that no longer existed in clear opposition to the production process.

The other perspective in leisure studies comes from the Frankfurt school. The emergence of mass culture is perhaps the most negative description, seeing modern leisure as totally integrated into and determined by the demands of the capitalist economy. The American sociologist and economist Thorstein Veblen examined in detail the social significance of leisure. He regarded leisure as a form of competitive display among modern social elites. He combined sociology with economics in his classical, *The Theory of the Leisure Class* (1994 [1899]), arguing that there was a basic distinction between the productiveness of 'industry,' run by engineers, which manufactures goods, and the parasitism of 'business,' which exists only to make profits for a leisured class. The principal activity of the leisured class was 'conspicuous consumption', and their economic contribution was 'waste,' an activity that contributes nothing to productivity (Veblen, 1994).

All the approaches briefly discussed here reflect not just the epistemological and methodological differences, but more importantly that leisure – and the study of leisure – has been relevant in the description and analysis of modern European and North American societies. The question that emerges again is: Why has leisure not been an object of social inquiry for long time in Africa? Zeleza and Veney (2003) seem to be signalling a new era in the study of leisure in Africa. That is why I have briefly summarized their approach here. In the next sections, I shall attempt to set the scene for the social inquiry into leisure in Mozambique.

The Invention of Leisure through its Denial

The backdrop against which leisure studies can be undertaken in Mozambique should consider three historical and sociological contexts. The first context covers the colonial period from 1890s to 1974. This is the period in which leisure can be regarded as a product of the encounter between the colonial subjects and the Portuguese settlers. In this period, particularly through the regulation of native labour, we can identify the central lines of the *bio-power* (Foucault, 2004; Lemke, 2001) of the settler over the subjects (see: Mamdani, 1996). In this sense, the colonial state exerted total control over its colonial subjects by using technologies of bodily management and surveillance (Serra, 1997). *Time* including *free time* that could be devoted to leisure was a prerogative of Portuguese citizens, i.e. the colonial authorities. I have called this phase the invention of leisure through the regulation of native labour, and I shall discuss the reasons for this in the next section.

Covering the period from 1974 to 1985/6, the second context is marked by the experiment of the socialist regime that followed the country's independence in 1975. After independence the ideal of public service was subordinated to the political ethic of public service delivering to the people (Macamo, 2003). Not only had public servants to assume an unselfish moral code of conduct, but *time* – including free time that could be dedicated to leisure activities – was subject to the scrutiny of the guardians of the moral authority. Emblematic in this phase is the figure of the '*Xiconhoca*' that was mobilized to caricature the antithesis of the '*Homem Novo*' (New Man).

As Nielsen (2010: 1) puts it,

> In an attempt to leap into a socialist future, the ruling Frelimo party created the Homem Novo (New Man) immediately after Independence in 1975 as a figure devoted to the eternal revolution. As immoral antithesis, a peculiar cartoon figure, Xiconhoca, was created to represent those moral aberrations which impeded the full realisation of the socialist utopia.

In this phase, leisure was *reinvented through moral regulation* in the sense that new codes of conduct, time and work, were established in the context of socialism to orient people's everyday life. I will discuss further the arguments relating to this phase in the next section.

The third context covers the period from 1986 to date. During this period Mozambique experienced a transition from socialism to democracy and a market-driven economy with various implications for everyday social life. My hypothesis here is that in this phase the idea of leisure has become more individualized and fragmented, as – in the absence of explicit state policies to regulate people's daily life including their free-time – it is related directly to the market. Leisure has become a privilege of the few who have jobs and are targeted by the emerging tourist industry.

Invention of Leisure through the Regulation of Native Labour

Portugal needs, needs absolutely, to prosper without any delay from the heritage of Africa, and that prosperity can only come from productivity. Today, the crowning and fundamental problem of management entrusted to the enlightened zeal of Your Excellency is to force the overseas provinces to produce, and perhaps the most difficult aspect of this problem is also the only practical solution of the national crisis … . We need the work of natives, even to improve the conditions of these workers; we need it for the European economy and for Africa's progress. Our tropical Africa cannot be cultivated except by Africans. The capital that lends itself to exploit it, and that is so needed, will demand labour for the farms, abundant, cheap, and resistant; and that labour in such conditions cannot be delivered by the European migrants, who are decimated by malaria. The blacks, only the blacks, can fertilise Africa, and a race whose efforts still today, in the course of countless centuries, has not produced a spontaneous rudiment of civilization, will never draw legions of workers unless progress acts on it with all the incentives and all the compulsions of a trust, all the motives of charity, and all the generosity of vigilant action, of energetic and powerful processes (António Ennes, cited in Serra, 1997: 79, my translation from the original Portuguese).

This long excerpt is taken from one of the hundreds of documents and reports that regulated and justified the regulation of native labour in colonial Mozambique. It exemplifies the privileged way in which Portuguese colonial policymakers chose to erect and establish their domination over African societies. As Macamo (2005: 10) puts it, 'the regulation of native labour was premised on the twin ideas that, on the one hand, the proper fulfilment of the European civilization mission depended upon vigorous policy of making Africans work, and on the other, that Africans needed Portuguese firm guidance into the world of wage labour'. Paradoxically, however, it was precisely that tutelage claim over Africans that effectively prevented them from fully integrating into the world of wage labour, which amounted to a denial of the modernity promised by that very same policy.

From an historical point of view, and with regard to leisure as a social construct, I want to suggest that the period of recurrent use of forced labour also represents the first instance of a clear social division of time. There was time for the settlers and time for the colonial subjects. It was the settlers who established the *time to work*, *time to rest* and time for other vital activities, including perhaps some *free time*. In fact, Africans were frequently characterized as lazy, indolent and idle people who need to be forced to work (Covane, 1996). Forced labour characterized a particular kind of late colonialism practised by Portugal. Anderson (1962) called this (*Chibalo*) '*ultra-colonialism*'. One of the features of ultra-colonialism was to develop technologies of power that would allow Portugal to extract as much as it could in terms of work-force from the natives. Within the territorial space that was under direct tutelage of the Portuguese colonial administration, Serra (1997: 80) identifies four types of power: 'physical-power' (físico-poder), 'body-power' (corpo-poder), bio-power ('bio-poder'), and 'psycho-power' (psico-poder).

In this context (1890s to 1974), colonialism in Mozambique revolved around the question of how to make the Africans produce the raw materials such as *copra, sisal, sugar-cane, tea, cotton and rice* for the colony. It was on that basis that both the companies that had concessions in Mozambique and the Portuguese colonial administration reorganized the use of time by families and established panoptic mechanisms of surveillance (Serra, 1997). The four types of power were geared to: (a) know and follow who should pay the Hut Tax; (b) know and follow who should work; (c) how to plan and effectively collect taxes from the workers; and d) how to save resources from an extremely repressive state to ensure voluntary compliance.

The question here is that everybody had to work. Year after year, the technologies of power to discipline and punish (Foucault, 1991) those who challenged the system became more oppressive. The panopticization of the social life of the natives was very effective. The surveillance was carried out by fellow African customary chiefs (*Regulo*) (O'Laughlin, 2002) through the administrative apparatus put in place by the colonial state.

As O'Laughlin, (2002: 517) states,

> until 1961, under the labour codes of the Indigenato, only 'citizens' (Portuguese or assimilated) enjoyed the right to determine where, how and under what conditions they worked. All able-bodied men defined as 'native' were obliged to work, an obligation considered satisfied only if they had capital sufficient to live off the income, or exercised a profession, or cultivated fields of a size fixed by statute, or produced export crops in specified quantities, or did wage-work for a minimum period fixed at six months per year. Women were initially assumed to have a productive role in agriculture or in the domestic economy. Men over 60 and under fourteen years were exempt, as were the ill, infirm, police and customary officials.

A sociological approach would enable us to examine how this system came into being as well as its efficacy. Following Macamo's (2005: 67) line of inquiry, work and social order are best studied in dialectical relationship. In this sense, I would suggest that leisure and social order also constitute a dialectical relationship. The analytical challenge is then to explain how a specific set of conditions and factors led to a specific set of outcomes, rather than to account for large-scale changes in terms of the transition from tradition to modernity.

In other words, leisure can be conceived as a social relation that is both the substance and the result of social action. The relationship between leisure and social order can thus be best examined as an attempt at ordering social relations on the basis of notions and practices of leisure. My own paper does not follow this approach in detail, however, because my main goal is to signal the ways, possibilities and lines of inquiry for an eventual field of leisure studies in Mozambique. From this perspective, leisure appears to me as a privileged site for making out and describing how particular societies and individuals were constituted.

The historical and the sociological approach can complement each other in providing a practical account of leisure as a social reality. On the one hand, the historical approach can provide the context in which a particular social order was established and the conditions created for certain phenomena – here the panoptic regulation of native labour – to take place. On the other hand, as suggested by Serra (1997), the lines of bio-power and the technologies of surveillance during the colonial period were effective because they rested upon the multi-layer involvement of actors both as managers of the system (*colonislismo de gestão*) and as its enforcers (*colonislismo de execução*).

In other words, the hegemonic forces that, through the regulation of native labour produced the panoptic control over the bodies of the subjects, also created the conditions in which leisure became possible. These conditions still need to be examined further, for instance, through examining various practices of resistance against forced labour. O'Laughlin, (2002: 523–4) suggests that 'the ambivalence of chiefs and the linguistic dualism of the Indigenato meant that it was sometimes possible to express resistance in jeering songs, making the hidden transcript public. As an overseer passed, for example, peasants chanted, 'This monkey is stopping here, why? He is stopping here because he has nothing else to do'.

Invention of Leisure through Moral Regulation: The *Xiconhoca* Caricature

> First we have to do the mental work of decolonization of all Mozambicans at all levels. In place of the colonial mentality, a new mentality, a revolutionary mentality … . (Samora Machel, cited in Serra, 1997: 95)

The period from 1974 to 1985/6, the second phase in my historical typology, is marked by the experiment of the socialist regime that followed the country's independence in 1975. To ensure that the revolutionary and utopian project would not fail, the ruling party FRELIMO set itself to establish the moral standard for the new society and its individual members. The first public speeches by the FRELIMO leadership where characterized by an emphatically ethical tone. In his first triumphal rallies from the Rovuma to Maputo in 1975, the first president of the republic, Samora Machel, was less concerned with capitalist exploitation than with the moral degeneration of his people particularly in the cities (Macamo, 2003).

It was through moral condemnation more than by the physical torture and violence that had characterized the colonial regime that FRELIMO sought to cathartically purify its individuals and produce the 'New Man'. One of the powerful creations of the socialist regime for its revolutionary project in Mozambique was the caricature of '*Xiconhoca*' an antithesis to the 'New Man' (Macamo, 2003; Nielsen, 2010).

> As immoral antithesis, a peculiar cartoon figure, Xiconhoca, was created to represent those moral aberrations which impeded the full realisation of the socialist utopia. Whereas the Homem Novo (and the socialist future) soon succumbed to the forces of neo-liberalism, the Xiconhoca surprisingly

continues to surface as antithesis to shattered but collective imaginaries. (Nielsen, 2010: 1)

The 'Department of Ideological Work' (DTIPF) (*Departamento de Trabalho Ideológico do Partido Frelimo*) published a brochure of Xiconhoca cartoons in 1979 with an additional explanation of its immoral character (DTIPF, 1979):

> Xiconhoca symbolizes the internal enemy; those Mozambicans who, through their ideas and actions, serve the interests of the imperial enemy and thereby compromise the ... revolutionary process in our country. Xiconhoca is the traitor who leads Smith's racist troops in their attacks on our territory; the agitator and rumour-monger who sows confusion among the masses; the racketeer and speculator who consciously makes necessary products disappear in order to make an easy profit; the bureaucrat who complicates the lives of the workers, the marginal alcoholic and criminal; the lazy gangster who boycotts production; the opportunist who focuses only on his own personal ambitions and uses every means possible to satisfy his needs; the racist, the tribalist, the regionalist. Those who defend the interests of capitalism and imperialism are identified with the Xiconhoca figure.

There are many more descriptions of *Xiconhoca* in the press. Back in those days, the *Xiconhoca* cartoon could also be found on panels and walls in major Mozambican cities. According to Frelimo the *Xiconhocas* needed to be subjected to revolutionary vigilance, identified, fought and neutralized. The *Xiconhoca* was associated, above all, with the immoral vices of urban life, which, according to Frelimo's political elite, had spread excessively during colonial rule (Darch, ca., 2011), Hall and Young 1997: 84; cf. Jenkins 2009).

In 1983, FRELIMO established the 'Operação Produção' (Operation Production) programme.

> Operação Produção was a programme introduced by the Mozambican government in mid-1983, after the IV Congress of the Frelimo Party, to relocate unemployed people from the major cities to rural areas where they would grow food. The programme did not emerge suddenly or without warning, but was rather the logical culmination of several identifiable social and political trends. These included Frelimo's strong strain of anti-urban puritanism: towns and cities were seen as corrupt and corrupting, and people were being expelled as early as 1975. In addition, there was a willingness to use social engineering to achieve political ends, which also manifested itself in projects such as the aldeias comunais or communal villages. The uncontrolled and as it turned out uncontrollable influx of rural people to urban centres in search of employment and better living conditions was a major problem for the Frelimo government. It increased the unemployed population in the cities and towns, putting additional strain on health and education services. It probably reduced the capacity of the countryside to produce food. It was also widely believed that marginais or improdutivos, as the unemployed were called, would almost inevitably turn to crime or prostitution to survive, and this was seen as contributing to social instability. In 1982, a residence card was introduced alongside the regular ID card, to show that an individual had the right to live in the city. By the time the Operação Produção proper was launched, individuals

> needed an ID card, a residence card, and a work card or cartão de trabalho to justify their presence in the city. (Darch, ca., 2011)

This characterization of social life in the early days of independence, and the attempt to build a new society cathartically purified from the immoral practices inherited from the colonial era also provides the context in which to question the place of leisure in such a society. The categories of time and work again appear as central. For at a time when a new society was being built, there was no time for free-time: everyone had to be continuously engaged on the revolutionary work-front. A study of leisure in this context must, therefore, re-examine the concepts and above all the preconditions of time, work and leisure. My hypothesis here again, as in the context of the colonial regulation of native labour, is that leisure was inevitably constructed in confrontation with the hegemonic moral forces that aimed to produce its non-existence.

The Marketization of Leisure: The Birth of Contemporary Tourism

The fall of the socialist experiment was due to widespread malfunctioning of the economic, political, and social order, and FRELIMO decided to rethink its ways and search for an external response to the continued crises. This situation opened the door to the institutions of Bretton Woods, namely the World Bank (WB) and the International Monetary Fund (IMF). As a consequence, the structure of social relations, time and work changed considerably. The ethics that accompany the neo-liberal conception of the human replaced what remained of the altruistic revolutionary utopia. Contrary to the ideal of public service that characterized the revolution, the ideal of public service in neo-liberal times is fed by the fundamental belief in human nature as a competitor. That competitor is the 'homo-economicus' (Macamo, 2003), who duly replaced the revolutionary 'New Man'.

A structural adjustment programme was adopted as the remedy for the maladies of the failed revolutionary experiment. Structural adjustment was supposed to pull the economy away from the brink of collapse. It also created the conditions for the emergence of new social categories and actors such as the socially excluded, poor and vulnerable, and different layers of consumers. Amongst other 'industries' – including the aid industry to help the socially excluded, who had particularly suffered from the severity of the policies of structural adjustment that produced dozens of unemployed – this new context also marks the birth of the leisure tourist industry as one of the most promising sources of revenue for the state. Mozambique and its beautiful landscapes were (and are) celebrated and marketed as a tourist destination, with the production of ample tourist leisure imagery. The unanswered sociological question is: who are the (tourist) consumers? The socially excluded will not have the capacity to become consumers. Leisure has become a luxury. Market-driven social regulation excludes those without the means to consume.

A sociological analysis would be appropriate here to examine which categories of individuals can access the privileges of (tourist) leisure. Becker's (1965) *Theory of the Allocation of Time* and Linder's (1970) *The Harried Leisure Class* could be of use here. The two offered an alternative interpretation of leisure that emphasized the duration of the act of consumption. Leisure, in this context, was the time needed to consume the goods and services that individuals purchased with their income. The issue then is to examine who are the individuals in the context of neo-liberalism that have the capacity for consumption. This economic approach is consistent in some respects with sociological investigations of modern leisure. These have emphasized the historical changes whereby leisure has become an increasingly structured activity that no longer exists in clear opposition to the production process (see also: Hirschman, 1973).

Final Considerations

In a sense, one may argue that leisure studies are indispensable to understanding the social fabric of modern Mozambique. Yet particular circumstances have prevented leisure studies from being established as an object of inquiry in the country. There are many reasons for this. I have briefly pointed out what I consider the main reasons. One has certainly to do with the underdevelopment of the field of social sciences and humanities since colonial times. As a matter of fact, social sciences are a very recent phenomenon in Mozambican higher education. Perhaps due to its late establishment, scholars in this field in particular are vulnerable to the pervasive culture of consultancy which erodes creativity and sociological imagination. It is generally accepted that the pervasive consultancy culture is undermining the development of critical thinking that could inject more imagination into the study of society. At any rate, leisure phenomena in Africa have become so multiform and present that we can no longer afford to ignore them if we seriously want to get a grasp of our social life.

I have proposed three angles from which leisure studies could be approached in the Mozambican context. The three hypotheses are informed by an historical and sociological perspective. The first is to look at leisure in colonial Mozambique. In doing so, I propose that leisure should be examined as a side-effect of the oppressive regulation of native labour which used its panoptic and bio-power to control colonial subjects. In acts of resistance, but not only these, certain forms of leisure were produced. Secondly, I propose that we look at leisure as a result of the cathartic moral purification introduced by FRELIMO in its attempt to build a socialist society. While the regulation of native labour intended to produce docile individuals who could work, FRELIMO's moral purification was aimed at producing the 'New Man', a perfectly decolonized citizen. However, the outcome was dissidence. Finally, leisure could also be studied as a commodity in the context of the new market-driven economy. In this sense, I have looked briefly at the suggestion that this might be the time for leisure tourism to be born in Mozambique. These three scenarios represent different ways of establishing a field of inquiry into leisure in contemporary Mozambique.

Notes

1. Txuva, Ncuva or N'tchuva varies in its orthography and is also referred to as the African Chest.
2. The term *sociological imagination* was coined by the American sociologist C. Wright Mills in 1959, to describe the type of insight offered by the discipline of sociology.

3. The newly (2010) established Mozambican Sociological Association is currently launching what will be the first Mozambican Sociology Journal.

References

Ambler, C. (2003). Writing African Leisure History. In P.T. Zeleza and C.R. Veney (eds), *Leisure in Urban Africa.* (pp. 3–18). Trenton: African World Press.

Anderson, P. (1962). Portugal and the End of Ultra-colonialism 2, *New Left Review* (16). pp. 88–123.

Becker, G. (1965). A Theory of the Allocation of Time. *The Economic Journal*, Vol. 75, No. 299, pp. 493–517.

Beverwijk, J. (2005). *The Genesis of a System: Coalition Formation in Mozambican Higher Education, 1993–2005*. Czech Republic: CHEPS/UT.

Covane, L.A. (1996). *Migrant Labour and Agriculture in the Lower Limpopo Valley.* 1920–1992. Unpublished Ph.D. thesis, Institute of Commonwealth Studies, University of London.

Cruz e Silva, T. (2005). Instituições de ensino superior e investigação em ciências sociais: a herança colonial, a construção de um sistema socialista e os desafios do século XXI, o caso de Moçambique. In T. Cruz e Silva, M.G. Mendes de Araújo and C. Cardoso (eds). *Lusofonia em África – história, democracia e integração Africana*. Dakar: CODESRIA. pp. 33–44.

Darch, C. (ca. 2011). *Mozambique History Net. Operação Produção, May 1983 – May 1988.* (Online). Available: http://www.mozambiquehistory.net/op_producao.html. Retrived, 27 August 2011.

DTIPF (1979). Xiconhoca - o inimigo. Maputo, Departamento do Trabalho Ideológico do Partido Frelimo.

Foucault, M. (1991). Governmentality. In G. Burchel, C. Gordon, and P. Miller (eds), *The Foucault Effect: Studies in Governmentality* (pp. 87–104). London: Harvester Wheatsheaf.

Foucault, M. (2004). Naissance de la biopolitique: cours au Collège de France, 1978–1979. *Edited by F. Ewald, A. Fontana and M. Senellart.* Paris: Gallimard.

Guerreiro, M.V. (1962). Jogos, brinquedos e outras diversões do povo maconde/M. Viegas Guerreiro. In: Garcia de Orta: Revista da Junta das Missões Geográficas e de Investigações do Ultramar/Junta das Missões Geográficas e de Investigações do Ultramar. Vol. 10, no. 2 (1962), pp. 283–303.

Hall, M. and T. Young (1997). *Confronting Leviathan. Mozambique since Independence.* London: Hurst and Company.

Hirschman, A.O. (1973). 'An Alternative Explanation of Contemporary Harriedness,' *Quarterly Journal of Economics*. November. pp. 634–637.

Ismael, A. (ca. 1997). A study on n'tchuva-game: an ethnomathematical aproach In: *Educação, Empresas e desenvolvimento em Moçambique.* Feliciano de Mira (et al.). Évora: Pendor, pp. 87–103.

Jenkins, P. (2006). Image of the City in Mozambique: Civilization, Parasite, Engine of Growth or Place of Opportunity? in D.F. Bryceson and D. Potts, (eds): *African Urban Economies. Viability, Vitality or Vitiation?* Basingstoke: Palgrave Macmillan, pp. 107–130.

Just, P. (1980). Time and Leisure in the Elaboration of Culture. *Journal of Anthropological Research.* 36 (1). pp. 105–115.

Langa, P. (2006). The *Constitution of the Field of Higher Education Institutions in Mozambique*. (Unpublished Master's Thesis). Cape Town: University of Cape Town.

Lemke, T. (2001). 'The Birth of Bio-politics': Michel Foucault's lecture at the Collège de France on neo-liberal governmentality. *Economy and Society 20 (2) pp. 190–207.*

Linder, S.B. (1970) 'The Acceleration of Consumption,' The Harried Leisure Class. New York: Columbia University Press.

Macamo, E.S. (2003). Da Disciplinarização de Moçambique: Ajustamento Estrutural e as Estratégias Neo-Liberais de Risco. *Revista Internacional de Estudos Africanos. (6)*, pp. 231–255.

Macamo, E.S. (2005). *Negotiating Modernity: Africa's Ambivalent Experience*. Dakar: Codesria.

Mamdani, M. (1996). *Citizen and Subject: Contemporary Africa and the Legacy of the Late Colonialism*. Princeton: Princeton University Press.

Mills, C.W. (1959) *The Sociological Imagination*, London: Oxford University Press.

Mouton, J., Boshoff, N., de Waal, L., Esau, S., Imbayarwo, B., Ritter, M., and van Niekerk, D. (2008). The State of Public Science in the SADC Region. In P. Kotecha (ed.), Towards a Common Future: Higher Education in the SADC Region: Research Findings from Four SARUA Studies (pp. 197–302). SARUA: South Africa.

Nielsen, M. (2010). Antithesis without thesis. Virtuality and its negation in Maputo, Mozambique. Paper to be delivered at the EASA Conference, 24–27 August 2010. (Online). Available: http://pure.au.dk/portal/files/34321825/Morten_Nielsen_Antithesis_without_Thesis.pdf. Retrived 27 August 2011.

O'Laughlin, B. (2002). Proletarianisation, Agency and Changing Rural Livelihoods: Forced Labour and Resistance in Colonial Mozambique. *Journal of Southern African Studies,* 28 (3) pp. 511–530.

Roberts, K. (2010). Sociology of Leisure. *Sociopedia.isa*

Sahlins, M. (1972). Stone *Age Economics*. Chicago: Aldine.

Santos, Boaventura de Sousa (2003). *The World Social Forum: Toward a Counter-Hegemonic Globalisation (part I)*. Paper presented at the XXIV International Congress of the Latin American Studies Association, Dallas, USA, 27–29 March 2003.

Veblen, T. (1994) (1899). *The Theory of the Leisure Class*. Penguin Twentieth-century Classics. Introduction by Robert Lekachman. New York, N.Y., USA: Penguin Books.

Zeleza, P. (2003) Introduction: The Creation and Consumption of Leisure: Theoretical and Methodological Considerations. In P.T. Zeleza and C.R. Veney (eds), *Leisure in Urban Africa*. (pp. 3–18). Trenton: African World Press.

15

Transformation of Leisure in Nigeria

ARETHA OLUWAKEMI ASAKITIKPI

Theories of Leisure

The concept of leisure in African societies is a phenomenon hardly spoken about in history books or in present literature. This is not the case with Western scholars who have over the years interrogated the word as it affects and is perceived in Western societies. Within such discourse, leisure is interrogated within the confines of labour and finance, as a reward for physical or mental work, or as an aspect of socio-cultural development.

A number of Western scholars have come to view leisure as a contrasting verb for work. This foundational thought means that in the discourse of leisure words such as enjoyment, celebration, pleasurable, freedom are used in analysing leisure while in the case of work, words such as toil, strenuous, exertion, duties are used. Based on this, a fundamental notion is that leisure becomes a reality only when some element of work has been done by members of a given society. In other words, without work, leisure cannot exist nor can it be given meaning within a given culture. At this point a distinction is made between the quality and quantity of work as against the quantity and quality of leisure activities. Thus manual labour in some societies may determine or attract a certain quality of leisure while a mental form may attract another.

Within this line of thought are the assumptions that work whether physical or mental is exertion. Exertion in this context is distinguished from physical and mental exertion whereby the later demands mental skills and concentration while the former demands physical skill and body fitness. Both forms of skills are believed to be essential for the development of a society. While physical power and skills are needed for a society's physical development, mental skills are essential for the planning and supervision of these physical activities. Leisure on its part is also believed to involve exertion with the major difference being that the exertion expended to work is compulsory (but not always unpleasant) while exertion in relation to leisure is voluntary and optional and always pleasant (Kuic, 1981). Within this concept is the ideology that work is compulsory as a foundation for survival at the individual and social levels. It is this criterion that qualifies physical activities such as house and road construction activities as work when compared to equally physically intensive sport activities such as football or handball. Such sport activities though defined as leisure can be just as exerting as physical work but this exertion is qualified as leisure basically because it is voluntary and optional. This principle can also be applied to mental exertion which classifies business and human management, planning, supervision and research into a variety of subjects like science and technology as work while engaging in activities such as in-door games of chess or monopoly as leisure. In both cases of leisure, continuous exertion whether physical or mental, leads to better understanding of the activity (professionalism), psychological gratification, confidence, creativity, improvements, continuity and appreciation. These in turn brings out a higher quality leisure experience relaxing both the mind and the body.

Leisure has also been defined in relation to the economics of surplus and social stratification. Just (1980) brings forth the various western traditional theories of leisure and work which believes that members of a society need adequate leisure time to reflect on abstract concepts which ultimately will lead to inventions and innovations that will improve the society and elaborate their material culture thus allowing for cultural evolution and development. For this to occur, the society must have a surplus food production culture which in turn will encourage an increase in population. A society that has food security and adequate population strength will encourage division of labour and specialization in varying aspects of development not directly related to the development of human life needs such as food, shelter, clothing and protection. At this level of development, members of the society can concentrate on other aspects of the society's development and this includes abstract creations such as music, art and leisure. Thus, the social/individual display of leisure is as a result of the psychological freedom obtainable when the tasking problem of ensuring daily needs are met for human survival is removed and this can only occur when the society has achieved a high level of surplus food production and food security. On the other hand, societies that have not been able to achieve this level of surplus will entail the members of the society having less time for leisure and more time expended on labourious activities for survival.

Leisure is also defined within the confines of time and money. Kuic (1981) defines leisure as free time in which to do fun things, buy things and especially avoid thinking (of survival?). This is in line with the traditional theories analysed by Just (1980) which believes that when a society achieves the stage of development where less time is spent on food production more time can be made for the creation of new wants and gratifications for work in the form of leisure. In line with this Hatcher (1988) considered the thoughts of 15th century English scholars who observed that the longer hours the majority members of a society spent on working with low wages, the less time they would have for leisure time but the more money the few but privileged would have to enjoy the fruits of the land sown by the majority. It was thus essential that the majority be encouraged whether by force or cohesion to work because it was their long hours at work that maintained and sustained the economy of the society as well as the elites that dwelled in it. When wages were increased as compensation for the long hours spent at work, it was observed that the majority spent less time at work and more time in search for leisurely pleasures, the purchase of material goods and the consumption of food. This action led to the development of social vices such as drinking, slothfulness, immorality and disorderliness. This was not good for the society as such actions by the majority led to underdevelopment. The economic development slowed down considerably with little being produced by members within the society but a lot being imported from external societies to cater for the acquired foreign tastes of the majority who no longer worked. This would ultimately lead to material and technological dependency and a weak society. To avoid this, the minority had to continuously ensure that the majority worked long hours and spent fewer hours on controlled forms of leisure which would not harm the society as a whole and the social structure in particular. It is along this thought that Kuic (1981: 461) states that:

> Leisure is not toil but enjoyment ... it is not freedom from work but rather the development of a work based culture that makes meaningful leisure possible.

From the various theories considered, Western scholars are of the belief that leisure has a number of attributes and these are: leisure is time bound, there is a time for leisure and a time for work, valued in relation to money and materialism, culture determined and controlled to ensure the development of a society and its people. Such definitions suggest that firstly for optimum leisure (in relation to amount and quality) to be achieved, the individual in particular and society in extension needs dominance and economic strength (this demands a prior high food and monetary surplus level). On the other hand the less the economic strength and dominance a society/individual has (and this suggests a prior lower food and monetary surplus level), the lower the quality and amount of leisure that can be achieved. Secondly, the more freedom members of the society have from economic production the more time members of the society will have for the developing and partaking of more gratifying, rewarding, abstract and complex forms of leisure. Thus, more energy will be exerted on voluntary leisurely activities. In contrast, the more time spent on production and development the less time the society and majority of its members will have for leisure. Thus the members will exert more energy on compulsory labourious activities. Thirdly work is an activity done by individuals for economic development and ultimately for the sustenance of the society while leisure is its reward. Both are created and controlled by minorities within the society. This creates a complex situation whereby some members of the society work long hours to ensure that a minority enjoy longer and more quality leisure hours.

Nigerian Leisure Analysed from Prehistoric to Pre-Colonial

Archaeological studies of early occupation of what is today known as Nigeria show a constant migration of large population from the Sahara by pastoralists into savannah regions. Major items predominant in all the sites found in present day Nigeria were pottery and animal remains. The pottery remains may be an indication of a form of a culture dominated by labour that involved the preservation, cooking, moving and storage of surplus food. While the animal remains suggest major hunting expeditions which must have been labour exerting and compulsory being an activity meant for survival.

A major archeological finding that gives an insight into the socio-cultural setting and possibly of the leisure pattern of ancient Nigerian people is rock art. Adepegba (1995) who has done some work on this art form was able to identify three major sites where rock paintings were found in Nigeria. One of such sites is at Igbeti (in present day Oyo State), where engravings on a rock shelter were discovered and this is believed to have been associated with a goddess of women's occupation. Wescot and Williams (1958) make a brief reference in their end notes (as a suggestion for future academic research) of the complex relationship between the wall paintings at Igbeti and the *Iya Mapo* festival which is a celebration of sacrificial rites in honour of the gods of the hills who are believed to symbolize to the people strength and longevity. The paintings depict abstract shapes that resemble fish like forms accompanied with other geometric shapes that look like triangles. Though the ethnographic accounts of Wescot and Williams do not directly mention the rock paintings two of the photos accompanying the article are of the walls of shrines and a building decorated with a number of abstract images. The festival itself involves a lot of singing, dancing, eating and entertainment.

The second major site was found at Birnin Kudu which is a village between present day Kano and Bauchi States in Nigeria, where paintings which represent cattle were found. Some were in the form of sketches while others were painted in red and white. Close to this site is Geji which is about 24 kilometres south of Bauchi town where a rock shelter consisting of figures painted mainly in red was found. Though some of the objects depicted could not be placed those that could be placed include antelopes, full cows, cows merely represented by their horns, clothed men as well as monkeys and horses. These hunting scenes also indicate a form of work culture which buttresses the presence of animal remains found through Archaeological excavations.

The last major site identified by Adepegba was found amongst the present day Marghi people who live at the edge of Mandara hills in northeastern Nigeria. Their paintings are made as parts of an initiation rite, betrothal or a preliminary marriage. The rite which is called *mba* takes place during an annual religious ceremony. It involves every male of the society that has reached the age of 17. The initiates and would be husbands retire to the rocks outside the village, each followed by a younger boy to make paintings which remains as the records of the individuals fulfillment of the initiation rites. The paintings are stick representations of different subjects ranging from the actual written names of the individual (this shows the influence of western formal training) to picture representations.

Scholars who have studied a number of the art works found in Africa conclude that the artists produced the rock art as expressions representing symbolic and literal meanings of social and ritual performances (Mitchell, 2003). What is not certain is if the artists produced these paintings as part of an individual prompting or as part of the necessary prerequisites of social ritual performances. There are tempting notions that would seem to suggest that the artists were priests who can be likened to modern day journalists who are trained to document, capture and store information of events happening within and outside their societies for an audience seeking for information and entertainment. In this case the information is not just for the living in the society but more importantly, for the supernatural as well as the unborn. On the other hand, the artist may represent the creative members of the society who need to express themselves and their notion of the society they lived in. If likened to the first option, the rock artists would seem to be producing the representations not as leisure but as work. If on the other hand, the paintings represent personal efforts the activity of painting would seem be more closely related to a leisurely act with the aim of gaining psychological, social and religious gratification from the living the supernatural and the unborn who will respond either through admiration or blessings as is the case with the Marghi people.

The economic and social structure of such ancient societies has been likened to present day hunter gatherers who believe that the rock paintings are a direct reflection of their reality. For them, a hunting scene drawn before the hunt ensures success while for others the paintings are done after the hunt as a symbol of thanksgiving. Here two scenarios can be considered with the first being that the artist paints the figures on behalf of the people. This connotes a stage of division of labour which suggests that the artist knows the process of the hunt enough to represent it through art and may or may not be a part of the hunting process. For the artist, representing the scenes of a hunt that are too dangerous for human comprehension is work in itself and not necessarily leisure. Ability to represent a visual forecast or account of a hunt may be considered from either the communal or individual levels. At the communal level, the priest presents the paintings as his contribution towards the success of the hunt being the spiritual representative of his people while at the individual level paintings are presented as either supplications or representations of personal success. This suggests that the priest is a commissioned member of the society trained or set aside to capture the society's supplication or thanksgiving to unknown forces believed to have powers to shape and determine the people and their destiny through abstract art forms. The second scenario suggests individual artists who actually participated or will participate in the hunts and feels compelled to capture their fears or prowess through visual representations as a prerequisite for a successful hunt now or in the future, or as part of a ritual or initiation process. For them, the paintings are representations of their personal identity as defined within their social setting (as with the case of the modern day Marghi people). It forms a social statement that unites the artist with the society and the gods. Just as with the previous case, the artist produces the rock art as a prerequisite for success now or in the future in relation to an important activity bordering on survival and social acceptance. This is evident in the fact that the rock arts do not represent visualized symbols of production activities such as stone tool production, plant gathering or other daily activities. Rather the symbols represented reflect aspects of their physical and spiritual survival such as their gods, fishes, cows, antelopes, water and trees.

To the ancient artists, the rock arts were not meant to be decorations of habitual locations nor symbols of individual glorification as is the case with many rock paintings that adorn present day Abuja (the capital of Nigeria) depicting political aspirants who need public recognition to achieve political positions (Kunde, 2011).

Whether the art represents individual or communal identities or supplications, it is apparent that the act of leisure is not in the art itself but in the actions that occur after the art has been made. Consequently, within this context leisure is centred on the rituals of thanksgiving, done communally in reverence of the spiritual forces behind the success. For such ancient societies, communal leisure must have been an essential ingredient in ensuring unity within small bands. Unity in itself was strength against the forces of nature. To ensure the continuation and sustenance of this unity, rituals were fundamental. Such rituals were spiritual in nature, being a major method through which the people united and communed with supernatural forces believed to be able to determine and influence their destiny as a people. Within the rituals were social celebration which symbolized and sealed actions believed to have brought the people closer to their gods while enabling them to successfully move from one physical and spiritual level (as a people) to another.

Ancient occupants of present day Nigeria began to depend less on rocks and natural enclosures and started to settle down and become more sedentary. This period was characterized by farming and fishing which became a major preoccupation of the people as against pastoralist which demanded migration. A major feature of this stage was pottery making (Alabi, 2005; Breunig, 2005). Pottery was essential as a storage and utility item. Archaeological evidence shows a strong relationship between pottery making and metallurgy in Nigeria as with many other parts of Africa. It is upon this relationship that an old Sudanese saying that the potter is the wife of the blacksmith is hinged (Aremu, 2005: 135). These factors encouraged an even more settled life for the ancient occupants of present day Nigeria. Improvement in technology meant more advanced methods of farming and storage leading to more food being produced, ability to hunt bigger game, build stronger houses for protection against animals and human enemies and conquer more lands and people. These activities encouraged an increase in population as well as religious, social and political activities.

The changing phases of technology also affected the culture of work as well culturally defined divisions of labour and gender relations. Some scholars theorize that in the early societies, men were associated with hunting as a full occupation while the women gathered, planted and preserved. As pastoralists, the men tended the animals while the women tended the soil. As agriculture became the occupation of settled societies, the need to hunt and gather greatly reduced and so also the need to migrate. Various levels of division of labour were developed. For example, crops and animals were classified along gender lines with crops such as yam, oil palm and palm wine being that of the men and vegetables and cassava being female crops. In relation to animal protein, it was the duty of the man to hunt for large game in the forest while the woman kept smaller animals like goats, chickens and ducks.

Fadipe (1970) in his analysis of the pre-colonial Yoruba setting states that farmlands were far from residential areas. Such farm areas were places of work and temporary residence while annual festivals were done in the towns or residential areas. Women had gardens in the towns and were not expected to take part in the tilling of the ground in the farm lands located some distance from the town. Their involvement with the farmlands outside town was mainly to assist their men with the weeding and eventual harvesting of the crops. Scholars have attempted to quantify the amount of work done in the agricultural process based on gender. For example, in carrying out the tasks for agriculture, the men prepare the field, a short but strenuous task while the women were expected to aid their men with the weeding along with their children, a task that was more lengthy and strenuous. Harvesting was a male occupation though again done with the assistance of their wives and children while food processing, cooking, storage, preservation and selling the food items in its various forms was the occupation of the women (Fadipe, 1970; Ogbomo, 1997). This analysis paints a picture of men encouraging female members of their society to work harder and longer to ensure that they (the men) have more leisure time at their disposal. The import of the culture of work in many pre-colonial Nigerian societies cannot be understood if analysed using western theories of work and leisure.

Division of labour was not limited to gender alone but also based on age and social status. There were the elders whose position was determined by age and past achievements, leaders and priests who were either appointed by the gods, men or by birth, there were the free born and the slaves, and age grade associations. According to Ogbomo (1997), male elders of pre-colonial Owan exploited the labour of young members of male age grades or kinship associations because traditionally the members of the council of elders were not to engage in any form of communal labour. Those outside the council of elders such as male heads of lineages as well as individuals mobilized children, relatives, friends and members of the extended family to assist in farm work. In some societies, such male work force associations meant that women did less strenuous work on their husband's farms (Ojo, 1966) The success of such an arrangement depended on the individual's social and kinship network. In return, the contractors were expected to entertain the workers with food and drinks as well as to share his harvest with the needy in his kinship network. Thus the more successful his harvest, the more he had to share his products in order to attract a larger labour force for the next agricultural production cycle. Such work force arrangements organized through the age grade system was a major bonding element for men in many pre-colonial Nigerian societies. It was within such communal bonding that leisure activities also occurred.

Women were not a part of these age grade work force. Their duties revolved mainly around converting the plant and animal products into edible forms either for home consumption or for sale. In some cases they help their husbands to market the farm products with an agreement as to how the profit will be shared. Fadipe (1970) points out that the process of converting raw plant and animal products into consumable stages is a specialization undertaken by various women at commercial levels. Thus while one group of women convert one form of raw product into a consumable form for sale another group converts another also for sale. This specialization was important in the social development of women in various ways. First, it helped to ensure that the women in totality were relatively free from individually going through the tiresome process of food processing at the household level while ensuring a variety of food items were available to feed her family. Secondly, such female occupational specialization economically empowered women to enable them further develop themselves and their families. Thirdly, the ability to quickly purchase processed food items to prepare a variety of dishes for family consumption left the women with enough time to go into specializations outside food production such as salt production, pottery making, soap making, basket weaving, cloth production etc. These products were sold at local markets dominated by the women of the society.

Ogbomo (1997) interrogates the theory that the advancement in agriculture left the men with more time for leisure and women more burdened with the responsibility of feeding and caring for the family. Ogbomo (1997) puts forward an argument which considers the notion of work, leisure and social stratification within the delicate balance of male leisure and female dominance/power in many pre-colonial Nigerian societies. He considers the fact that because women are the ones responsible for the processing, cooking and storage of food, women had the power to determine more than her Western counterparts of the time. Secondly, women's involvement in religious affairs further empowered them especially in making decisive decisions in the society. Thirdly, most Nigerian societies were made up of various female associations which were strengthened by number and theme.

Ogbomo is of the opinion that these factors seemed to create a complex social structure that compensated women who worked harder than their men with more social power in unity through associations than their male counterparts. Within these associations, women created leisure. Sometimes these activities demanded the exclusion of the male gender in any form (even as babies). One of such Nigerian customs is that performed amongst the Owo women who over the years have built a leisure culture around the production of a prestigious cloth which demands that their men be banned from partaking in the activities yet must wear the cloth for social identification during major social ceremonies (Asakitikpi, 2005).

Leisure activities in Nigeria are typically marked by traditional cultural practices; festivals, and entertainment in the form of musical performances with singing and drumming, dancing, and exhibitions. Falola (2001) described Nigerians as people who value celebrations. The celebrations are designed to mark certain milestones in the lives of the people such as birth and death. The process usually involves food and drinks in abundance while festivals are hinged on religious practices and beliefs. Within these celebrations, leisure activities can be viewed from within two categories namely the entertained and the performer. In many western cultures, a clear demarcation is made between these two groups of people. Thus there is the entertainer and the entertained, the performer and the audience. This clear cut demarcation is not always so clear cut during many pre-colonial Nigerian leisure activities. For example, in story telling, a major tactic used by the story teller is to involve the listeners in the story telling process. Part of the story involves the listeners singing and responding at various levels of the story. Likewise, in the presentation of drama, the audience is made to be a part of the story through active participation. This trait transcends into communal leisure aspects of festivals and initiation ceremonies. Ethnographic accounts of such leisure activities like the performance of a pre-colonial Urhobo practice called the *Udje* (Ojaide, 2001) which reached its peak at the beginning of the 19th century (1920s to 1930s) gives an idea of this concept. The origin of the Udje was war and fights which led to disputes and the accompanying judgment led to the victorious groups singing songs of about the defeated group and their points of weakness while boasting of their own prowess and skills. The defeated groups in retaliation composed songs about their opponents and ultimately it became a contest to see who could compose the most unique and original satiric songs against the opposing team. The audience was an active part of the event as they reechoed the poems while singing and dancing to support their teams. Teams won based their ability to respond to the various satiric attacks of their opponents. Within this atmosphere the *Udje* performance did not only involve a series of public poetry renditions but also a lot of dancing, singing and eating.

Leisure and the Colonial Experience

In many pre-colonial Nigerian societies, celebration marked the major avenue through which the people engaged in leisure activities. Such occasions of celebration were marked by life, death and rituals which emphasized spiritual obligations that would lead to either spiritual metamorphism or transition. During the pre-colonial era, such events stopped work in its track irrespective of the task or day of the week. The number of days set aside for such celebrations depended on the person involved and type of event. If the event is based on the birth of a baby, the people and time allocated to the celebration may not be as lengthy or as elaborate when compared to the death of an elderly and important member of the society and this may involve the whole society celebrating for between ten days to two weeks (Guyer, 1992). Part of the celebration activities would include eating, dancing, singing and drumming at the communal level while sitting down to talk and share experiences are activities done at interpersonal and group levels. Similarly, during occasions for rituals, initiations or festivals, celebration activities may go on for days and even weeks. The major difference being that rituals and other similar events are done within a calculated phenomenally determined time frame (for example the first harvest, the first rains, etc.) while events such as death and birth are not predicted and occur more frequently.

The relationship between space leisure and work is a complex one that is highly dependent on cultural norms and values. Certain public spaces were set aside for both work and leisure activities, especially if the space is physically large and central in the geography of the settlement. Large public spaces were designed to serve both as space for inter-communal markets while also serving as intra-communal venues for festivals, social gatherings and meetings. It is based on this ideology that in some Nigerian pre-colonial societies, a central and large public space in the day time serves as market square, an avenue for trade and commerce and at night the same space transforms into the venue for moonlight dances and festivities. This again is different from central production sites where specialized items such as dye production, cloth weaving or dying or carvings were produced by either members of specialized guilds or family production units. In such public spaces, leisure has limited presence. This again is different in relation to public spaces set aside for farming activities which were usually located miles away from the residential areas thus discouraging leisure activities. Leisure activities took place within the residential areas, in open spaces such as communal meeting areas or buildings, market places and religious sites. Such areas are usually in the form of large spaces big enough to accommodate a large number of people at the same time. This again suggests that leisure was not a practice or done alone but within a communal setting.

The coming of first the missionaries and later the colonialists introduced new definitions of work, leisure space and time. A major redefining of space was creation of urban cities which witnessed rapid trade and commerce, government investment in infrastructural facilities, colonial government administration and massive population migration from the rural to the urban. The urban cities represented public spaces that were not controlled by Nigerians from indigenous societies, reflecting very little of the social and physical structures of their areas and ultimately disempowering and segregating them. Colonial division and authority over urban space was enacted through the Township Ordinance of 1917 which classified Nigerian cities into first second and third class towns. According to Fabiyi (2006), first class towns usually represented the seat of government while second and third class towns were mainly trade centres where European depots were established. A second major policy of the British that redefined space was the Segregation Policy which based segregation on a variety of factors such as health, security, religion and cultural differences (Rasheed, 2006). Based on these policies, Europeans were resident in well laid out areas while the natives were allocated to smaller plots of land upon which to build. While the British reserved areas were well laid out, spacious and equipped with modern infrastructures the smaller plots allocated to the indigenes were smaller, the houses more crowded and the infrastructures overstretched.

The contrast in space made the hundreds of indigenes that came from the villages to redefine their conceptualization of luxury and leisure. Economic empowerment was the basic reason for many urban migrants, though the first set were literally forced to come to the cities based on the introduction of the head tax by the colonial government (a system designed to ensure cheap labour based on European capitalist ethics of work and leisure). The contrast in the aims of the various periodic sets of Nigerian urban migrants who eventually found their ways to colonial cities is interesting. While the earlier set would have preferred to stay within the confines of spaces they were familiar with, the people they knew and the customs they developed, following sets were eager to leave a system they defined as barbaric and old, too slow to catch up with modernity. For such people, the cities promised things the villages could not. Financial empowerment for the foundational migrants was essential in fulfilling the obligations of the head tax which could not be met in the villages as the economic system and valuation were localized within the rural areas and such obligations could only find relevance within the urban context. For consequent sets of migrants, working for the colonial government in a colonial city was an essential tool in acquiring a wealth measured and valued based on colonial criteria which overshadowed that of the rural. Thus a man who was once culturally defined as wealthy because he had many wives, children and cattle was reduced to poverty when measured against the urban worker who earned the colonial 'money' with which foreign material goods (which were considered of superior quality to the indigenous) could be obtained. Ability to acquire European goods meant having access to the more valued material wealth which connected the indigenous to the international. It was within this definition of wealth that the colonized urban Nigerian dweller redefined leisure.

The supervisory work of colonial administrators and contractors introduced another form of work which involved talking and commanding as against manual labour which many if the Nigerian urban migrants did. For the urban Nigerian migrant who worked in colonial offices, sites and homes, the contrast between manual work and supervisory work created a culture which connotes hierarchy. The less manual work done, the higher the social class, the more people placed under an individual during a work process the more control and the more power. For the urban migrant, getting people to work for you (just as the colonial government officials enforced) meant that those at the top of the work hierarchy did less work and had more time for leisure activities. During the colonial era, Europeans represented this ideal class. They owned cars and had to be chauffer driven, they owned spacious houses built within well laid out areas and had maids and servants to clean and cook, they worked in offices and had messengers and assistants whom they sent on errands and always available to fulfill every command of their masters. Material wealth, a high social class and high hierarchical job positions were major criteria upon which wealth and leisure were defined. Doing little work and having access to large amounts of material wealth, engaging in activities that demanded little mental exertion with enough time to organize social get-togethers and displays of wealth were essential for leisure to have a high value. The Nigerian urban migrant desired these leisure apillages.

The only set of Nigerians that came close to achieving this euphoric lifestyle was the Nationalists, educators and business men or contractors. Such people became even more powerful when the colonial government handed over power.

The colonial government introduced and encouraged the use of technology as a means of information transfer and leisure. Though the mass media had some limitations, for example, the newspaper limited information transfer to only those that were western educated by the missionaries. Secondary beneficiaries needed the missionary educated to read, translate and explain the meaning of the information. These limitations were reduced in the case of the radio which demanded merely a listening ear. The first form of the radio was presented as loud speakers erected on the wall of public buildings such as the public library, post offices and other prominent places. The words and music coming out of these speakers were radio broadcasts mainly from England. Radio in Nigeria began as a public technology whereby people gathered together at certain times in the day to hear what the radio had to say. Even those who had receivers in their houses had to accommodate not only their family members but also extended family members and neighbours. Despite the herculean task of listening to a box that spoke none of the local languages, speaking a more advanced form of the English language in the midst of static and interference, the radio caught on with the Nigerian populace as a major form of leisure.

The radio set as an instrument could not be tuned to other stations and the programs were restricted to BBC programmes. Individual subscribers were limited to expatriates and the highly educated. While the common man rallied around the public loudspeakers. The very wealthy could purchase their own wireless sets and tune to any of the stations they could capture. These wireless sets were characterized by distortions and interference which could ultimately frustrate the listener. Generally, the colonial government felt that the redistribution project was a waste of time as most of the colonized indigenes did not understand the English language well enough to decipher the messages but more importantly, the colonial government could not use the radio as a mass media propaganda tool to establish their cultural dominance, authority and right to govern. It was based on this that the BBC's General Overseas Programme introduced local news broadcasts as well as local music. Even this was not too useful as majority of the audience were not conversant with the three major languages used in broadcasting local programmes namely Yoruba, Igbo and Hausa.

By the early 1950s there was a high demand for private radio sets with Africans outnumbering the Europeans and this called for more locally produced programmes. The British government took advantage of this call to introduce listeners to colonial works and achievements. The Public Relations department organized this and talks on subjects such as water supply and electricity provision given by the provincial engineer. Other major talks include 'How Trains Are Moved on the Railways' given by the traffic superintendant and 'On Infectious Diseases and their Prevention' given by the health officer. The aim of these talks was to publicize the administration's infrastructural achievements. The radio became an invisible friend to the Nigerian populace. Though a friend that spoke but could not listen but served as a major method of leisure and relaxation.

The mass media effort of entertainment and information was supported with films by the colonial government. The beginning of colonial film can be linked to the introduction of various technological as well as infrastructural achievements of the colonial government. During the World War II the British government established the Colonial Film Unit which consisted of mobile cinemas that travelled to urban and rural areas screening short films, documentaries and newsreels. According to Larkin (2008), the unit was headed by William Sellers, a health officer in the Nigerian government who had used magic lanterns and film screenings as early as 1920s to instruct colonial audiences about the dangers of plagues. The organization established its own magazine called *Colonial Cinema* which was a quarterly print out distributed to professionals and enthusiasts all over the British Empire. Sellers made some of the first films shot in Africa and had been campaigning for more funds which he got because of the need to inspire the war efforts amongst Africans.

According to Larkin (1997, 2008) there were two distinctive film forms in Nigeria. One was the commercial cinema which focused on entertainment films from the Asia (India and China) as well as more Western forms from the USA and UK for urban viewers who paid for the privilege to watch. Then there was the mobile film unit which were educational films created by the government to show a mixture of documentaries, newsreels and dramas aimed to instruct the audience about the achievements of the state as well as to educate them on modes of health, farming and civic participation. These mobile units travelled all over the country in both urban and rural areas. Such films were usually accompanied by short lectures. According to Falola, the themes of the early films were dominated by cultural issues, the impact of the British rule on Nigerians and the criticism of the assimilation of Western habits.

From Independence to Now

The criteria that made up the Nigerian colonized definition of wealth and leisure were the same criteria that encouraged corruption in the independent Nigeria. The need to control people and resources with the aim of securing personal forms of wealth and leisure as against national development led to series of military coups and countercoups, mismanagement of resources and funds, unaccountability and greed.

Today with the proliferation of the mass media, private television and radio stations bring to the urban as well as the rural Nigerian populace music and drama while the film industry has grown into the internationally appreciated Nollywood. The mass media being one of the major avenues for leisure in Nigeria encourages individual leisure as against communal. Entertainment is done in a sedentary manner as against the active participant role played in pre-colonial Nigeria. This transformation is not only in relation to the media and the way and manner in which it is consumed but also in relation to the content and what that content is representing in the Nigerian society.

True leisure should be an activity aimed at relaxation of both the body and the mind. Transformations in Nigerian definition of leisure have seen a change in value in relation to material, time and space. This is essential in understanding the full history of Nigeria.

References

Adepegba, C.O. (1995). *Nigerian Art: Its Traditions and Modern Tendencies.* Jodad Publishers, Ibadan, Nigera.

Alabi, Raphael (2005). 'Early Agricultural Societies; Innovations in Technology and Economy Before AD 100' in *Pre-colonial Nigeria: Essays in Honor of Toyin Falola,* ed. Ogundiran Akinwumi, Africa World Press, Inc. pp. 87–104.

Aremu, David (2005). 'Metallurgical Traditions: Origins, Technology and Social implications' in *Pre-colonial Nigeria: Essays in Honor of Toyin Falola,* ed. Ogundiran Akinwumi Africa World Press, Inc. pp. 106–133.

Asakitikpi, Aretha (2005). 'Owo Women's Religious Textiles'. In *Yoruba Religious Textiles: Essays in Honour of Cornelius Adepegba.* Renne, Elisha and Agbaje-Williams, B. (eds) Bookbuilders, Ibadan. pp. 71–88.

Ayandele (1966). *The Missionary Impact on Modern Nigeria 1842–1914.*

Breunig, Peter (2005). 'Groundwork of Human Occupation in the Chad Basin, Northeast Nigeria, 2000 BC-1000 AD' in *Pre-colonial Nigeria: Essays in Honor of Toyin Falola*, ed. Ogundiran Akinwumi Africa World Press, Inc. pp. 105–132.

Fadipe, Nathaniel (1970). *The Sociology of the Yoruba.* Ibadan University Press, Ibadan, Nigeria.

Falola, Toyin (2001). *Culture and Customs of Nigeria*. Greenwood Press, Westport Connecticut, London.

Guyer, Jane (1992). 'Small Change: Individual Farm Work and Collective Life in a Western Nigerian Savannah Town, 1969–1988' in *Africa* pp. 465–489.

Hakeem, Haruna (2003). *A Cultural History of the Uneme: From the Earliest Times to 1962.*

Hatcher, John (1988). 'Labour, Leisure and Economic Thought before the 19th Century', *Past and Present,* No. 160 pp. 64–115.

Just, Peter (1980). 'Time and Leisure in the Elaboration of Culture', *Journal of Anthropological Research,* Vol. 36, No. 1 pp. 105–115.

Kuic, Vuken (1981). 'Work, Leisure and Culture' *Review of Politics,* Vol. 43 No. 3 pp. 436–465.

Kunde, Matthew (2011). 'New Form of Rock Painting in Nigeria' http://ezinearticles.com/?New-Form-of-Rock-Painting-in-Nigeria&id=6069696.

Larkin, Brian (1997). 'Indian Films and Nigerian Lovers: Media and the Creation of Parallel Modernity Africa', *Journal of the International African Institute,* Vol. 67 No. 3.

Larkin, Brian (2008). *Signal and Noise: Media Infrastructure and Urban Culture in Nigeria*. Duke University Press, Durham London.

McCall, John (2000). *Dancing Histories: Heuristic Ethnography with the Ohafia Igbo*. The University of Michigan Press.

Mitchell, Laura (2003). 'Material Culture and Cadastral Data: Documenting the Cedarberg Frontier, South Africa, 1725–1740' in *Sources and Methods in African History: Spoken, Written and Unearthed* ed. Falola Toyin and Jennings Christian University of Rocher Press, pp. 15–32.

Ogbomo, Onaiwu (1997). *When Men and Women mattered: A History of Gender Relations Among the Owan of Nigeria*, University of Rochester Press.

Ojaide, Tanure (2001). 'Poetry, Performance and Art: *Adje* Dance Songs of Nigeria's Urhobo People' in *Research in African Literatures* Vol. 32 No. 2 pp. 44–75.

Ojo, Afolabi (1966). *Yoruba Culture: a Geographical Analysis*. University of Ife and University of London Press, London.

Olaniyi, Rasheed (2006). 'Transformation of the Sabon Gari' in *Nigeria's Urban History: Past and Present,* Hakeem Tijani (editors). University Press of America, pp. 133–144.

Wescot, Joan and Williams Peter (1958). 'The Festival of *Iya Mapo*' in *Nigeria* Num. 58 pp. 212–224.

16

Leisure in Historical Perspective

The Case of South Africa – Past and Present

MOKONG SIMON MAPADIMENG

Leisure is a feature of every human society, whether traditional or modern, industrial or non-industrial, and developed or non-developed. The form it takes is largely determined by its specific context. Notwithstanding this, and what seem to be recognisable leisure studies, it has been observed that leisure has not been adequately and satisfactorily studied, theorized and analysed. As Paul Tiyambe Zeleza (2003) noted, despite leisure being as old as human society, its systematic study is only recent. Highlighting this lack of theorization and analysis of leisure as a social phenomenon, Moorhouse (1989) remarked that leisure studies tradition as it currently exists, is nothing more than an analytical and conceptual morass that serves as an obstacle to its further growth and development. Hence criticism of leisure studies' underdevelopment. This paper provides a brief but critical approach of leisure studies, noting some of the theoretical clarifications in the conceptualization of leisure. The review is done with the view to clarifying and laying out the theoretical framework that would ground the subsequent analysis in the form that leisure assumed in South Africa, both during the apartheid and post-apartheid periods.

Leisure Conceptualized

Too often in leisure studies, attempts to explain and define leisure and leisure time make reference to leisure's relationship to paid work. This, Zelesa (2003) attributes to industrialists' consideration of leisure as comprised of discretionary, unobligated, residual time and activities that are separate and free from paid work and other obligations. Parker (1976) thus defined leisure as '… time free of work and other obligations, it also encompasses activities which are characterized by feeling of comparative freedom' (in Moorhouse, 2003: 20). These theorists believe that industrialization has created a clear divisions between paid work and leisure. This view is however refuted by post-modernists, according to whom technological revolution as marked by the new Information and Communication Technologies (ICT), has dissolved the spatial and temporary divisions that existed between work and leisure, making it possible for people to access both work and leisure activities at the same time and in the same place. Moorhouse (1989), for instance, argues that the boundaries between leisure and work have become rather fluid with leisure popping up all the time and in all places. It is nevertheless emphasized that while this fluidity is real, the links between work and leisure cannot be ignored. Hence Moorehouse's assertion, while still acknowledging that leisure is autonomous sphere not only influenced by work but also by other institutions, 'you can't keep work out of leisure and leisure out of work'.

Leisure activities are thus considered as having both production and consumption component to them. This is demonstrated in Moorehouse (1989: 20–21)'s argument that leisure activities such as sport and arts, like psychologically and mentally demanding work, are not idle and carefree. A sport activity, for instance, involves active production by players as well as active consumption by spectators. Similarly, Zeleza notes that leisure activities such as sport, spawn and are supported by a whole range of other leisure activities such as gambling, shopping, reading and tourism, all of which 'have own infrastructure and interests, conditions and constraints, content and contexts, practices and pleasures' (2003: xvii). Perhaps a recent key example is that of the 2010 FIFA world cup tournament held in South Africa which has witnessed the booming in business as marked by production and consumption of merchandise associated with the event such as the SA-unique noisy plastic horn and fans' favourite, *vuvuzela*; T-shirts, flags, and soccer balls.

This points out to the complexity of leisure as a concept which has subsequently led to the recognition that it is not easy to define, highlighting the need to acknowledge its diverse and complex nature. Hence it is seen as better defined and understood from the perspective of participants, as it would mean different things to different people.

This brings up yet another crucial point in leisure literature i.e. the contesting of the view that leisure is free as implied in Parker's definition above. Contrary to this notion, it is argued that leisure and leisure time activities are shaped and influenced by an array of other factors. Zeleza (2003) points out to four main factors which he calls the four Ps i.e. *Participation*, by which he refers to the extent to which participants in leisure activities are involved in their production and consumption (be them passive or active); *Place* i.e. where leisure activities are taking place i.e. produced and consumed such as at home and outside home; *Provision* (i.e. who provides leisure activities – a public provider, private or voluntary sector; and *Politics.* Zelesa's four Ps necessitate the need to investigate questions such: who are participants in the production and consumption of leisure activities?, what are the costs involved and/or what resources are needed to access and enjoy leisure activities?, which leisure activities?, where do leisure activities happen?, is it in a highly accessible place?, are leisure activities provided by a public entity to the wider public at no cost to members of the public or is it by private profit making entity at some cost to members of the public?, and what are implications for ability to participate either as a producer or consumer? As he observes, various schools of thought on leisure, such as Marxist, feminist and pluralist, provide competing explanations of factors that influence the choice and consumption of leisure as well as meanings attached to leisure. Such factors as identified in these competing accounts include social inequalities along the lines of class, gender, race, and age and the attendant's differential access to, choices and experiences of leisure activities. Further to these rather overt factors, which Zeleza refers to as acknowledged conditions, he argues that there are also unacknowledged conditions that influence leisure such as attitudes, perceptions and values. Hence for him, diversity of leisure conditions for different people account for the diversity of leisure activities.

These conditions, for Zeleza, constitute the contextual framework within which leisure is produced and consumed. To illustrate this rather crucial point by Zeleza, which would underlays my historical analysis of leisure in South Africa, it is necessary to quote him at length: '... the provision of leisure is tied to broader transformation in a country's or region's political economy ... the economic and historical contexts of leisure cannot be overemphasized. The development of the overall economy, its ebbs and flows, simultaneously sets and reflects the broad contours of class formation, social relations, and ideological values, which, also simultaneously, are reproduced by, and refracted from, the dominant leisure activities. Similarly, the nature of leisure activities, their organization, meanings, and participants change over time. It is critical, therefore, to place leisure activities in their concrete economic and historical contexts, rather than see them as manifestations of some abstract and timeless ideals of freedom and well-being ...' (Zeleza, 2003: xxii).

Leisure in Apartheid South Africa

As noted above, Zeleza made a crucial point about the significance of a country's political economy and hence its economic and historical context in shaping and determining leisure dynamics. Under apartheid South Africa, the context was defined by racially exclusive policies which separated and divided the population on racial basis in all spheres of life including leisure. The country had an economic and political system referred to as apartheid capitalism under which economic and political rights were racially distributed, with whites enjoying greater rights over all black races i.e. Indians, Africans and Coloureds.

The legislation that had direct impact on leisure in SA under apartheid is the Separate Amenities Act of 1953, which was supported by other discriminatory laws such as the Group Areas Act of 1950, the Population Registration Act of 1950, Prohibition of Mixed Marriages Act of 1949, and the Immorality Act of 1950. The Group Areas Act of 1950 introduced racial zoning and gave the government the power to racially allocate specific residential and business areas to various race groups, while the Population Registration Act of 1950 defined and classified people through population register into racial categories. The Prohibition of Mixed Marriages Act of 1949 prohibited marriage between persons of different races while the Immorality Act declared as illegal interracial sexual relations.

As part of this wider context of racial discrimination and segregation, the Separate Amenities Act of 1953 prohibited inter-racial contacts and use of recreational spaces and facilities. It legalized the racial segregation of public premises, vehicles and services, declaring facilities for different races as unequal. In effect, the Act racially excluded black people, considered as inferior to whites, from public premises, vehicles or services as the facilities were reserved for whites. As Alf Stadler (1987: 118) observed, the spatial zoning effected through apartheid laws '... conferred a certain degree of rationality on the separation of amenities and services for different racial groups: transport services, hospitals, schools, recreation, and so on. Signboards bearing 'Whites Only', 'Nie Blankes/Non-Whites,' or 'Blankes/Whites' were a common sight in racially segregated areas such as sport fields, recreational parks, and beaches, under apartheid South Africa.

The resultant effect of these laws was that not only were black South Africans segregated against but were also economically disempowered, making it difficult if not impossible for them to afford access to certain leisure facilities, services and activities, as well as other privileges reserved for whites. As Stadler (1987: 116) pointed out 'South African segregation involved the overt and explicit use of state power to dictate social, political and economic relations between racial groups through the control and allocation of the spatial environment.' Further, he argues, racial zoning proletarianized the members of black bourgeois or black aspirant bourgeois, limiting and depriving them 'entirely of access to opportunities to exploit the advantages they might have stood to gain by virtue of their ownership of property' (Stadler, 1987: 117). Further, both blacks and whites enjoyed and spent their leisure time is segregated places, as blacks were not allowed to enter better equipped facilities reserved for whites.

By the same token, further residential segregations and divisions amongst black communities, i.e. Indians, coloureds and Africans, implied that they too could not spend leisure time and engage in leisure activities in common spaces. Thus, while the apartheid racial system oppressed and marginalized all blacks, i.e. Africans, coloureds and Indians; it however also thrived on division created amongst blacks through a further racial hierarchy of privileges whereby both coloureds and Indians were given more privileges and rights than Africans, but still remaining below whites. This racial hierarchy of privileges, rights and opportunities was mirrored in what came to be known as the tri-cameral parliament of South Africa introduced in the early 1980s to provide representation for both the coloureds and Indians. The tricameral Parliament was comprised of three houses, i.e. the House of Assembly for whites with larger representation, the House of Representatives for coloureds with the second largest representation and the House of Delegates for Indians with smaller representation. This arrangement left out black Africans who remained confined to the bantustans and homelands as well as townships.

These racially determined privileges and deprivations had influence on who can access, afford, and enjoy which leisure facilities, activities, and opportunities. Under residential segregation, whites had what are popularly known as suburbs reserved for them and characterized by well-built homes with top class facilities, services and infrastructure such as tennis courts, swimming pools, etc. Indians and Coloured lived in relatively better homes and residential areas while black Africans were severely deprived and confined to rural villages with poor infrastructure (e.g. gravel roads, inadequate telecommunication lines, bridges and schools as well as hospitals), and poor services. They also were confined to urban centres' peripheries in townships and informal settlements.

In sport, whites were able to populate sporting codes such as rugby, tennis and golf, all of which require not only early exposure at younger age but are also pricey to join. Townships and rural villages had no sporting facilities such as stadiums, tennis courts, and golf courses. While whites had access to financial support and sporting facilities as well as training, their black counterparts had to make content with playing and training on dusty, hard grounds. They also had to resort to forms of entertainment in games that required no monetary expenditure such as the indigenous games like morabaraba, mmela, diketo, bolopi/indize/xitumbelelani (hide and seek in English), taleta/openi, mpa/gqaphu, magava, moriba. All these were and remain largely freely available and involve no much cost in terms of special facilities, equipments, uniform, etc.

Leisure in Post-apartheid South Africa

The collapse of the apartheid system and the establishment of the new democratic majority led state in South Africa following the first ever democratic election in 1994, ushered in what one could call a new context. This new context, as would be noted below, has not however marked a complete break with the apartheid past as the past legacy still lingers on and continues to bedevil the new order. Under the post-apartheid democratic regime, great efforts were made by the new democratic regime to bring about societal transformation through both redress of past injustices and a different development and growth path.

Central to these efforts was the scrapping of the apartheid policies and laws and the promulgation of the new constitution as underlying foundation of democratic order, within which progressive legislations, policies and programmes were introduced to effect in various spheres of life. These include the Affirmative Action Programme, the Employment Equity Act, the Skills Development Act, the Black Economic Empowerment Programme, the Gender Equity Commission, and the Human Rights Commission. These were all meant to steer transformation in the workplace and other socio-economic spheres of life, in a way that the historically excluded groups are represented and actively involved in the mainstream economic, political, cultural, education and other activities of the of the country.

Under the new dispensation and policies, gradual changes have become increasingly becoming evident. This can be noticed from the increase in the size of the black middle class as a result of the new economic and educational opportunities. The Black Economic Empowerment (BEE) programme, has seen government giving priority to black entrepreneurs in the procurement of most of its businesses for delivery of public services such as building of schools, construction of roads, clean water provision, and other infrastructural development projects. Similarly, the Employment Equity Act as well as the Skills Development Act have enabled a growing number of blacks to take up senior positions within workplaces, contributing to improved income earning and the attendant living standards. The management structures have thus changed to reflect the country's demographics. It is now common to find historically white dominated management structures now featuring representation of blacks and women, and in some rare cases, people with disabilities.

The historical residential divisions are slowly melting away as black middle classes are moving into the historically reserved white privileged areas, with their children too penetrating the historically white schools. The historically racially segregated leisure spaces and public amenities such as beaches, recreational parks, and entertainment centres have since 1994 been integrated.

Notwithstanding these remarkable changes, there are however still some huge challenges to transformation marked by persistence of old racial inequalities accompanied by new forms of socio-economic inequalities, mainly class-based. The majority of the people, and mainly black Africans, are still trapped in poverty and thus unable to access and afford the newly opened leisure opportunities as the economy has been growing but without creating jobs. Hence the SA economic growth is dubbed jobless growth marked by costs cutting strategies and profit maximization, as opposed to job creation. The public service continues to struggle to deliver descent basic services such as electricity, roads, primary health care, education and clean water to ordinary South Africans.

This state of affairs has triggered service delivery protests across the country. Shannon Walsh, for instance, remarks as follows in her study of one of the informal settlements in Durban's Kennedy Road: 'In a place like Kennedy Road, where 7000 people live with only five stand taps, where children die when shacks go up in flames, where people are forced to relieve themselves in the bushes because there are so few toilets, an where children must play in refuse, in a place with all these harsh, daunting realities, it is with urgency that people demand a better life. Even under such dire circumstances, people continue to stand up with dignity and honour and say 'enough is enough' and to demand their rights to ask for the basic necessities of life which many of us take for granted. The demand for land and housing reflects with outmost clarity what people need. This is what they want, and if transformation of this country is really going to take place, this is what they must have' (Walsh, 2007: 165).

Also writing on informal settlement residents' struggles for better life and basic services, was Fazel Khan, who covered the story of the shack dwellers in Durban's Foreman Road, quoted one the of the dwellers' leaders during the protest in demand for decent housing:

> We the shack dwellers of Durban, democrats and loyal citizens ... cannot and will not continue to suffer the way we do. Our voices cannot be stifled ... we braved heat, hunger, thirst, exhaustion and police repression ... we had our day in court ... we won recognition of our right to speak. Today we march on the city because today we stand up for our right not only to speak, but to live, to breathe, to eat, to sleep and to work in dignity and safety (Khan, 2007: 179–180). The implication of these is that, for the majority of South Africans, access to the historically reserved but now open public leisure spaces and activities, remains constrained not due to racial factors but economic factors.

Along with the dismantling of historical segregation, and largely due to inefficient management of service delivery programmes partly as reflected in quotes above, has seen the degradation of public amenities, especially in the inner cities. Recreational parks that historically used to be well kept, maintained and reserved for whites, are today generally neglected. They have instead become homes to the urban unemployed and the underclass. Services to these facilities by municipalities have witnessed steady decline.

Further, the scrapping of the racially exclusive laws and the collapse of the apartheid state, have not necessarily resulted in a situation whereby South Africans enjoy leisure time and engage in leisure activities together. This is attributed largely to the apartheid separate development legacy whereby the historically segregated spaces and activities continue to shape and reinforce collective racialized identities of those occupying them (see Zegeye, 2001: 9–10, and Misgun and Oakes, 2007: 120). Arts festivals are the case in point. They remain largely racially divided and less integrated as is evidenced by festivals around the country such as the predominantly white Afrikaans festivals known as Aardklop, Klein Karoo National Arts Festival and Opie Koppie; the predominantly black African festivals e.g. Mapungubwe and Macufe, and Moretele Park music concert. Racially integrated festivals, from the point of view of diversity of participants, would be the annual National Arts Festival held in Grahamstown, the annual Cape Town International Jazz Festival, and the annual Cape Town Book Fair, amongst others.

Also less integrated despite the scrapped racially segregating policies is night life in South African cities with exception of only few night entertainment areas. Through her observational study in Durban, Shabashni Moodley (2007), found continued discrimination in one popular night club, which she refers by a pseudonym, Café' de La Rouge, situated in Florida Road. Moodley (2007) provides an account of how the owner-manager of this night club exercised systematic exclusion of blacks, especially black males, from the club. She also observed that out of 100 patrons in this club, only 25 were Indians, 8 black Africans and 2 coloureds, mainly females while the rest were white males and females. Even interactions within the club, such as dancing and conversations, she observed, occurred on racial lines (Moodley, 2007: 128). Moodley however found that this racialism was absent at the Tyger Tyger night club in Cape Town.

A similar observation and discovery was made by both Misgun and Oakes during their study at the Durban beachfront. They discovered that the scrapping of the racially discriminatory policies and laws which historically divided the beach front into racial categories, has not helped to eliminate divisive racial practices and attitudes amongst beach goers. They observed, amongst others, that the South part of the beach front is perceived by mainly white and Indian beach goers as unsafe, crime, dirty, disorganized, crowded, chaotic, and less developed. Yet, this is a beach front which was historically well maintained and equipped with amenities' infrastructure and facilities, and is nearest to the public transport route. The latter aspect of it explains why the majority of the black African's poor would go there in larger numbers. Interestingly, Misgun and Oakes found that even some middle class black Africans tended to perceive south beach as unsafe and occupied by criminals. However, they also noticed that notwithstanding what appears to be a common concern amongst middle class Indians, whites and black Africans; there was still little, or no, interaction and mixing amongst them as reflected in the following statement: 'There were hardly any 'racially' mixed group activities. Activities such as fishing, beach soccer, the surfing shows, and picture taking on the piers of the North Beach are were always performed by members of the same 'race'. Such activities did not even trigger casual conversations between people of different 'races.' Even visits to the changing and toilet facilities were very different according to 'race' on North Beach' (Misgun and Oakes, 2007: 123).

Conclusion

During his inauguration as the SA's first democratically elected state president, Nelson Mandela articulated in his speech the vision for a new democratic society in which all would enjoy human dignity, freedom, justice and a sense of common belonging. A society, as he proclaimed, of which all humanity will be proud. Thus concluding his speech with the statement 'Never, never and never again shall it be that this beautiful land will again experience the oppression of one by another and suffer the indignity of being the skunk of the world.' Nelson Mandela was however not naïve in his articulation of what the new SA society should be but instead acknowledged that its realization would not come easy unless all South Africans bond together and embrace this common vision. Hence his assertion: 'We understand it still that there is no easy road to freedom' (See http://www.famousquotes.me.uk/speeches/Nelson_Mandela/, accessed 10 August 2010).

The present paper presents evidence that suggests that while some major strides have been made through progressive, transformatory policies towards the realization of the vision articulated in Nelson Mandela's speech in 1994, i.e. that of overcoming the past racial injustices and inequities; there is however still a long way to go as the road is not easy. While the new policies have seen the growth in the black middle class with incomes that enable them to afford and access the leisure activities, opportunities, and facilities which were historically reserved for whites, the lingering legacy of apartheid past however continues to influence and shape racial attitudes and identity formations amongst South Africans. This, together with racist practices as evidenced by how historically segregated spaces such as beaches and night clubs are utilized, undermines interracial mixing and the building of a united, non-racial nation. Thus, while the new context in SA has created new economic opportunities for blacks, it has however not done so in a way that empowers largest numbers of the population. Rather, there are deepened race and class-based inequalities with large masses blacks are still trapped in poverty and unemployed. This suggests a much rather complex and perplexing situation in SA today of both, on one hand, limited interracial mixing in spite of the common shared class identity amongst races due to persisting racial perceptions and stereotypes towards black Africans, and on the other, the challenges presented by new forms of class inequalities whereby the majority of black people remain marginalized. This is further complicated by a general neglect of public recreational amenities such as inner-city parks due to poor maintenance which has seen these parks becoming permanent, unpleasant homes for the urban unemployed and urban poor instead of serving as recreational leisure time spaces. This does not only imply challenges to broadening access to leisure facilities, activities and opportunities, but also broadly to efforts at realizing the vision of a new democratic free, non-racial society in which all South Africans enjoy equal opportunities as articulated by Nelson Mandela during his 1994 inaugural speech.

References

Misgun, B. and Oakes, W. (2007). 'The White and Black Sands of the Durban Beachfront'. Pattman, R. and Khan, S. (eds) *Undressing Durban*. Durban: Madiba Publishers.

Moodley, S. (2007). 'Nightlife in Durban and 'Racial' Divisions'. Pattman, R. and Khan, S. (eds) *Undressing Durban*. Durban: Madiba Publishers.

Moorhouse, H.F. (1989). 'Models of Work, Models of Leisure'. In Rojek, C. (ed.) *Leisure for Leisure*. MacMillan Press.

Khan, F. (2007). 'Struggles and Triumphs of Shack Dwellers'. Pattman, R. and Khan, S. (eds) *Undressing Durban*. Durban: Madiba Publishers.

Stadler, A. (1987). *The Political Economy of Modern South Africa*. London and Sydney: Croom Helm.

Walsh, S. (2007). 'If You Don't Die First': Fire, Water and Women in the Shack Settlements in Durban. In Pattman, R. and Khan, S. (eds) *Undressing Durban*. Durban: Madiba Publishers.

Zeleza, P.T. (2003). 'The Creation and Consumption of Leisure: Theoretical and Methodological Considerations. In Zeleza, P.T. and Veney, C.R. (eds), *Leisure in Urban Africa*. Trenton and Eritrea: Africa World Press, Inc.

Contributors

Francis Lobo, Honorary Professor, School of Business, Edith Cowan University, Perth, Australia and Former President of the Research Committee on the Sociology of Leisure, International Sociological Association.

Michael Toohey, Lecturer in English Language and Western Culture with the Zhuhai College of Beijing Institute of Technology, Beijing, China. His major research interest is the history of leisure in nineteenth and twentieth century settler and post-settler societies.

Grant Cushman, Emeritus Professor of Parks, Recreation and Tourism, Lincoln University, and Honorary Professor of Sport and Leisure Studies, Waikato University, New Zealand.

Bob Gidlow, Adjunct Associate Professor in Sociology at Lincoln University, New Zealand, specializing in the area of leisure theory and social theory. Grant Cushman and Bob Gidlow were also the Co-Editors-Chief of the *World Leisure Journal* (the Official Journal of the World Leisure Organization), 2010–2012.

Ma Huidi, Director, Center of Leisure Studies, Chinese Nation Academy of Arts, Beijing, China.

Ishwar Modi, President, Research Committee on Sociology of Leisure, International Sociological Association; President, Indian Sociological Society, and Director, India International Institute of Social Sciences, Jaipur.

Iwan Gardono Sudjatmiko, Member of Research Group on Social Transformation, Department of Sociology, University of Indonesia, Depok, West Java, Indonesia.

Irsyad Zamjani, Member of Research Group on Social Transformation, Department of Sociology, University of Indonesia, Depok, West Java, Indonesia.

Adrianus Jebatu, Member of Research Group on Social Transformation, Department of Sociology, University of Indonesia, Depok, West Java, Indonesia.

Gholamreza Ghaffary, Associate Professor, Department of Social Planning, University of Tehran, Iran.

Atara Sivan, Professor, Department of Education Studies and Associate Dean, Faculty of Social Sciences, Hong Kong Baptist University, Hong Kong. She is also the Editor-in-Chief of the *World Leisure Journal* (Official Journal of the World Leisure Organization).

Elie Cohen-Gewerc, Senior Lecturer, Faculty of Education, Department of Research, Beit Berl College, Israel.

Scott North, Professor of Sociology, Graduate School of Human Sciences, Osaka University, Japan.

Erwei Dong, Assistant Professor, Department of Health, Physical Education and Leisure Studies, University of South Alabama, USA.

Manuel Enverga, Instructor, European Studies Program, and Lecturer, Department of Anthropology and Sociology, Ateneo de Manila University, Philippines.

Zerrin Arslan, Assistant Professor, Head of Department of Sociology/Faculty of Science and Literature, Antakya, Hatay, Turkey.

Veena Sharma, Former Fellow, Indian Institute of Advanced Study, Shimla and Former Secretary, ISA Research Committee on Sociology of Leisure.

Thibault Danteur, Research Engeneer, CETU-ETIcS, University François Rabelais, Tours, France.

Patrício V. Langa, Faculty of Education, University of the Western Cape, South Africa and Faculty of Education, Eduardo Mondlane University, Mozambique.

Aretha Oluwakemi Asakitikpi, Ph.D., Sessional Staff, Department of Comparative Literature and African Studies, Monash South Africa, and Executive Member, International Sociological Association Research Committee on Sociology of Leisure (RC 13).

Mokong Simon Mapadimeng, Associate Professor, Department of Sociology, Northwest University, South Africa, Member of Executive Committee of the International Sociological Association (ISA), and Past President of the South African Sociological Association (SASA).